Whispered Dreams

Book Two
A Whisper of a Mystery
Trilogy

M.A. APPLEBY

Copyright©2017 ~ M.A. Appleby

Whispered Dreams
By M.A. Appleby
Printed in U.S.A.

ISBN: 978-0692921333

2nd Edition 2017

All rights reserved solely by the author. The author guarantees all contents are original and do not infringe upon the legal rights of any other person or work. No part of this book may be reproduced in any form without the permission of the author. The views expressed in this book are not necessarily those of the publisher.

Information regarding permission, contact: info@maappleby.com
Visit Author website: www.maappleby.com

Cover, graphics, layout design, and all inserts by M.A. Appleby
Photo by V. M. Little

Fictional Novels by Author: *A Whisper of a Mystery Trilogy*:
The Ancient Whisper, Book One ~ ISBN: 978-0-6929-2129-6
Whispered Dreams, Book Two ~ ISBN: 978-0-6929-2133-3
Journey of a Thousand Steps, Book Three ~ ISBN: 978-0-6929-2134-0
Award Winning Non-Fiction: ~ ISBN: 978-1-4984-9873-9
    RAISING DAVID AGAIN
    A Guide To Understanding The Uniqueness of Brain Injury And How Our Faith Sustains Us

Dedication and Acknowledgement

To all of you who went on this journey
of writing with me,
From the first hand-written notebook,
And then on to the finished project, I thank you.
You were patient and listened
when I needed a sounding board,
You were calm when I got on my soapbox to rant,
and present when I needed a hug.
Then there is my mentor, Sylvia Richter,
whose support has always been positive and encouraging.
Her input was just as invaluable as her friendship.
Thank you, all of you!

Table of Contents

Chapter One	The Carriage House	1
Chapter Two	Success and Laughter	29
Chapter Three	Testing Theories	49
Chapter Four	The Royal Visit	71
Chapter Five	Decisions and Consequences	87
Chapter Six	A Trip To Remember	108
Chapter Seven	Anticipated Turmoil	130
Chapter Eight	Choices; Some Good, Some Bad	154
Chapter Nine	A Deserved Recognition	176
Chapter Ten	Cheer Up	199
Chapter Eleven	The Heir is Missing	236
Chapter Twelve	A Family Mourns	253
Chapter Thirteen	The Blue and Silver	279
Chapter Fourteen	Whispered Dreams	297
Chapter Fifteen	The Republic of Vanuatu	311
Epilogue		350
Books and Resources		363

"You've gotta dance like there's nobody watching,
Love like you'll never be hurt,
Sing like there's nobody listening,
And live like it's heaven on earth."
~ William W. Purkey

Chapter One

The Carriage House

The view from the top of the rickety landing of the Carriage House looks out across the horizon and peacefulness embraces me. Puffy cumulus clouds move slowly past in an otherwise perfectly blue sky. Everything seems right in our little corner of the world. From this distance, a billow-like haze of dust follows a procession of specks which appears to be heading in our direction. Watching the dust trail, it reminds me of the day I came here and the events that led to our new life in Virginia.

My family and I are so ingrained in the little community of Jasper that it feels as if we've been here much longer than we have! No one knows our real last name or that we moved here under the guise of deception. They have no knowledge we are in the Federal Witness Protection Program or that my husband Ravi met with an untimely death. We hold that kind of information to ourselves. So far, no one has questioned that the Thompson Family is anything other than everyday people.

It's still amazing how the always-in-control Ellen D. Thompson (the former Ellen P. Andress) can turn our family tragedy from a horrible situation into a triumph. We've always prided ourselves on our individuality and ability to go with the flow if something untoward happens. We try to make the right decisions when faced with odd occurrences, and I consider each member of my family to be sturdy individuals who are capable of almost any achievement.

How we came to be here and why is only half of the story; the other half could fill a volume. If our circumstances were known, it's a sure bet that our neighbors might not be so friendly. The reality of it is that my world turned upside down one day and I've been trying to cope with the circumstances ever since.

It doesn't help to dwell on what we endured, nor does anyone need to know how we purchased this piece of property. To the outside world, we are merely trying to give Ashwood back its former prestige as a working horse farm and stables. The dairy and milking cows, abandoned during the last millennium, were never part of the equation. Nevertheless, the structures stand as a testament to those who persevered during a long-forgotten era.

We have done a marvelous job of taking charge of this old place. Since we came, the Manor House transformed from a dilapidated and crumbling dwelling I saw nearly three years ago, to the magnificent masterpiece it is today. The mere fact that we reside in such a residence is at times overwhelming to me, and I thank God for his wisdom in seeing the bigger picture because, at that time, it was truly overwhelming.

For the most part, my life was going according to my life plan. Almost a month before graduating from college, I met my husband Ravi (short for Ravenalt) who was tall, dark, and handsome. He was a gentle soul with an easy smile, courteous and polite, and I loved him the moment we met.

We married after a short courtship and moved into a little house in the suburbs of Chicago. Before the children arrived, I began to develop my interior design business as my husband traveled for his job. After our first child was born, we quickly outgrew that house and moved to a large two-story brick home, a short distance from Mother and Daddy.

Each of my children are vastly different; however, they had the common interests of soccer, softball, and music lessons. We enjoyed our life with our three children and often traveled around the country to visit national parks or museums.

Although our household was hectic, we always had time to spend with my family, as Ravi said most of his were gone. Sadly, Daddy passed away six years ago, but we included Mother and my sister's family as often as we could, celebrating birthdays, anniversaries, and naturally all of the holidays!

On a rare vacation, my widowed Mother stayed with our three children while we flew to the sweet-scented Island of Kauai. From the moment we stepped off the plane, we felt the *aloha welcome* when presented with fresh flower leis.

It was a glorious week of sunbathing, eating, and traveling around the island in a blue convertible, where we stopped to enjoy the scenery to absorb the Hawaiian culture. At an outdoor stand near our hotel, we joined a group making kukui nut leis, which we sent home to our children. I don't recall now whether they made it to our home.

Ravi and I were returning from this glorious week of consuming exotic foods, and it was at the Kauai Airport when things became fuzzy. Asking Ravi to wait for me, I ran to the restroom before the boarding started, taking my carryon case with me. My purpose was to dig through the case to find the antacid tablets.

A woman who was dressed exactly like me was waiting inside the restroom. Before I could react, I believe it was she who pushed me into a stall to administer a distasteful drug. I felt a prick at my neck then became helpless in a matter of seconds. I don't remember anything after that until well-meaning Samaritans took me out of the restroom.

If I concentrate hard enough, I can conjure the smell and taste of that drug which makes me gag thinking about it! Somehow, there was an explosion, where I witnessed the destruction of the jet that Ravi had boarded without me.

When the drug-induced stupor wore off, I was no longer at the Kauai airport but sequestered inside a fortress. I can distinctly remember how angry I was because my captors kept insisting that their *people* only meant to keep me from harm. Their intention was not to make me feel like a prisoner, however, the longer they kept me there, the longer the feeling persisted. And the absolute worst part was being locked inside!

In the time it takes to blink, my life changed!

Thoughts of that time often cartwheel me back at unexpected moments. It could be anything as small as the jingle of a tiny bell, a single word, a phrase, or the scent of lemon.

After nearly twenty years of marriage, I thought I knew my husband; however, he was harboring many secrets. One was the fact that he had a brother. As it turned out, my captor is Ravi's brother. The shockwaves from this revelation continued long after the menacing person named Captain Jam-ale took me back to the Kauai Airport in their attempt to right their wrong.

What sticks in my craw is the fact that my brother-in-law, King Akdemir of Saudi Arabia (the former Crown Prince I called Abdul) kept the mystery of how and why my husband died a closely guarded secret. It was his people who took me out of Kauai in the first place!

After they took me back, an airport worker found me in the restroom, sick from the drugs Jam-ale gave me. Airport Security turned me over to Homeland Security where I tried to explain my situation. They didn't believe my ridiculous story, but why would they without proof? I had painstakingly written my notes on pilfered blank pages from books I took from Abdul's library. They were hidden at the bottom of my case, but they were not there when I searched for them!

Homeland Security called in a Special Unit of the FBI, as a team was on the island to investigate the wreckage of the airliner. It is when I first encountered the supposedly Special FBI Agent Andrea Simmons. As I tried to explain my circumstances to her, she kept insisting that Ellen Andress was dead and I could not be who I claimed to be. Hours later, her deceiving partners in crime (Lenard and Gene) showed up.

It has been nearly three years now, but what happened is as fresh in my memory today, as if it happened yesterday. Everyone thought that Ravi and I perished in that airplane explosion, he unfortunately did, and it has taken a while to get over that particularly frightening period.

Unresolved events pop in and out of my mind. Why didn't Ravi share the fact that he was a crown prince and had family in Saudi Arabia? Why didn't he share his real name of Basim Obagur? Another memory starts to tumble back of that first day Lenard and Gene brought me here. They deceived me into thinking my husband was a criminal.

Maybe I'm still upset with those two idiots that passed themselves off as special FBI agents. They cooked up that ridiculous plan and duped me into thinking we were all safe. They made me crazy and pounded at me relentlessly for hours, making sure I understood their preposterous rules and protocols. They misled me, and I was stupid enough to go along with it!

Why didn't I trust my gut and go to the authorities sooner?

It's the stuff of nightmares, and that's how it comes out sometimes. They are nightly forays into a chilling, incongruous void that makes my skin crawl. I still don't understand how these dishonest people were able to confiscate all my possessions (along with Mother's) to purchase half of Ashwood. Nor would those nefarious numbskulls ever reveal who bought the other half, except for a man named Mr. C.

Before the not so real agents left me, Lenard made me promise that I would keep my mouth shut and follow their list of protocols. Phony baloney Gene then handed me a packet of papers, an oddly shaped key, and a wad of money. I remember being so irate that all I could do was shake from rage and very nearly spontaneously combusted on the spot!

It was a day later that I learned about the debt that had accumulated. Lenard refused to contact the silent partners, and we required immediate funds to exist in the here and now. The local banker refused to lend us money, and the vendors wouldn't extend further credit. Out of desperation, Glen and I went to the local racetrack, doing something that would guarantee instant income. I still laugh at his facial expression when we won all that money; it was priceless!

Lenard and Gene were nothing special except Andrea's hired thugs. Those three people had me so mixed up that I began to believe what they told me. I learned later that their dramatics was all part of their elaborate plan to deceive me. These phony people are the ones responsible for placing my family here at Ashwood, which we are still trying to sort out.

Once we paid off the vendors, we could start our phases of renovation, but it was with unique challenges. In a house of this size, with two wings per side that have five bedrooms and three bathrooms each, it was a daunting task.

I must keep my anger in check.

Watching the dust-trail from the vehicles, it reminds me of the shiny black limousine that brought me to the Ashwood Estate that first day. It drove down the same road, but there was no inkling of what would transpire or the bizarre events that followed, except for a persistent feeling that something odd was about to happen.

The last of the original descendants of Ashwood was Miss Abigail. She was the one who applied for and received the Century Home plaque from the National Register of Historic Homes. When we did our extensive renovations, we could as quickly have lost that plaque at the front door if we didn't follow their stringent guidelines.

It was a mystery as to why the Ashwood heirs abandoned this place, but perhaps it was the enormous property tax bill and the millions needed to fix it up that deterred them. Both the local banker and the Ashwood estate executor warned Miss Abigail to keep the house in good order. What she didn't know was that the banker and the executor invested unwisely, leaving her virtually penniless.

Why can't I concentrate on anything today?

Each room had layers of wallpaper that we carefully and painstakingly removed. On one occasion, a worker came across several drawings that were sandwiched between layers in one of the children's bedrooms. Although several are crudely drawn by a child, the name is unmistakably that of AJ Ashwood Jr., dating from 1898. All seven are framed and hang in the upstairs hallway.

I glance across at the Manor House. Our new windows sparkle in the sunlight as a shadow passes slowly across the middle windows on the second level. I then think of the original owner, Mrs. Sarah Ashwood and how she stood her ground, incorporating ingenuous features into the architecture that caused quite a stir at the time. There are a few secrets that even her husband knew nothing about, and we are ever so grateful for those!

My thoughts wander back to the most unsettling aspect of starting a new life here. Although we gained a fantastic pair of caregivers, we also inherited a mountain of unpaid bills. It took a little time, but we conquered the problem systematically and succinctly by selling the bulk of the antiques and collectible objects that remained with the house.

Glancing up to see where the trucks are now, the dust is starting to dissipate as they turn down the two-way road that leads to our driveway. It reminds me of the limo again and the horse named *Lightning* that we later renamed *Didgeridoo*.

If I close my eyes, I can still see that beautiful bay munching grass out in the pasture as he raised his head when he heard the crunch of the gravel in the driveway. It was also the day that I sat on the fence, overwhelmed by about everything that had happened. He came to nuzzle the top of my head, which made me weep.

The day our horse *Didgeridoo* died, we met the local veterinarian, Dr. Jessica. She is a sassy, no-nonsense woman, who weighed in with her findings of how he died. She concluded that *Didge* received a lethal combination of illegal drugs and an experimental drug with no name.

It could be the same drug administered to me during my abduction, but no one can prove this without a sample. The local sheriff's department conducted a brief, but thorough investigation. Sheriff Rockford (Rocky for short) wrote it off as a fluke and filed the paperwork, as no solid leads turned up.

We had hired a new man, Reed, who questioned whether we were running away from the MOB or something more sinister. Reed sure turned out to be a great asset.

Inexplicable events began to happen around the property. I tried to contact Lenard and Gene several times, then nearly panicked when his cellphone went straight to voicemail after only one ring. When a message announced the number was no longer in service, it was time to contact the FBI.

Because it was between Christmas and New Year's, I had to leave a message. A few days later, a Mr. Hopkins called to ask how the FBI could help me. He told me to hold while he checked on the names I gave him, then came back to say that there was no record of Andrea, Lenard, or Gene. He then suggested that I call the CIA. That's when Adrian Sellers came into our lives.

After documenting all of our information, I made an appointment and went to CIA Headquarters where I met with the Office of Intelligence and Analysis. It is where I first met Adrian Sellers and Mr. Levi Johnson. I realize now that facts would have come out eventually about Basim/Ravi and Daddy working for the CIA. But it took Daddy's letter of explanation, hidden away for so long in the vault at CIA Headquarters, to clear things up.

What saddens me, is that both Daddy and Ravi were not honest with Mother and me about their double lives. It would have spared us untold grief had we known! Mother and I are still stunned to think that we were in the dark about their connection to the CIA.

As our discovery unfolded, we learned that the valuable antiques and collectibles were supposed to stay with the house to get me to use ancient (and stolen) currency. It would have exposed the fact that my Daddy had this treasure hidden. The people who masterminded the charade reasoned that I would use it to bail myself out of a sticky situation. However, I outsmarted the culprits by selling the antiques without their knowledge, which we felt the repercussions from, for years.

We have reasoned that there were most probably two private investors that had to have been working on an elaborate plot for a long time. They had their sights set on this property, so they didn't suddenly show up as we were led to believe. Somehow, they began to manipulate events and *caused* the opportunity to present itself, using my family as pawns in their offensive scheme.

Although most of the issues have worked themselves out over the years, perhaps I'm still harboring a deep-seated resentment for these unsavory people and their acrimonious misdeeds. Mother quietly says to let this go, because it doesn't help to dwell on what we had no control over. It's quite harmful to keep such wrath inside. We should be grateful for what we have now. Mother is correct, of course.

And in spite of everything, we are grateful.

At first, I thought Adrian was full of himself, a bit too confident, but in all actuality, he's quick to smile, focused and dedicated, and a consummate professional, albeit with an unusual sense of humor. His loyalty leaves me a little breathless to this day. He has all but given up his career to live with us, remaining to protect us from the peculiar things that continue to happen around Ashwood, and we are grateful he is here.

Sometimes I try to imagine what we could have done instead of what we did. Would CIA Agent Adrian Sellers be involved with my family in due course anyway?

We can't go back nor can we rewind time or have a do-over. In all fairness, Mr. Adrian B. Sellers, CIA Agent extraordinaire, could not have spared any of us from anything. A little voice inside my head is saying to let it go. The absurdity that *was* my life and what it is now has developed into our new routine, and I **must** learn to accept it, and not fixate on the what if's for everyone's sake.

Adrian thinks that Prince Dimmy holds more mysteries to himself, now that he has taken his place as King. I'm convinced that Uncle Dimmy has a hidden agenda and it has everything to do with my son, who will have to make a life-altering decision when he turns twenty-one. We dance around this, but it's subtly alluded to upon occasion. Since we aren't privy to the inner workings of the Saudi government, Adrian also thinks that one day we'll know the entire truth, especially if Jason agrees to live there.

We had a lot going on with the renovations in the Manor House in full swing--righting a portion of the precariously leaning horse barn, installing sophisticated surveillance equipment, and waiting for the other shoe to drop. Now, we are in the throes of chaos that surrounds the garages, as we restore the top portion to livable quarters again. It is where jockeys, servants, and people gainfully employed by the Ashwood Clan lived until the early 1950s.

Our caretakers, Glen and Mona Murdock, took care of Ashwood and remained when the funds ran dry from the estate. The crooked banker and the mysterious investors needed them to stay on until they had their plan in place. It was a difficult time for them as they existed on their meager savings, ate vegetables from the garden behind the house, and sold Mona's baked goods in town.

Mona looks and talks like a doting grandmother. Any day will find her in the kitchen with her hair pulled back and wearing a stained apron. The first day I came here, she quickly admitted she used the kitchen to bake bread and pastries for the local bakery when they needed money. Under the circumstances, how could we penalize her for that? Hadn't she and her husband been punished enough?

Glen is a different story. He reminds me of a craggy old western character, complete with overalls, dusty boots, and calloused hands. Glen also has an endearing quality about him much as my father had. His remarks are forthright, if not brutally honest, and he alone took charge of the horse barn along with the boarder's horses, to keep the wolves at bay before a buyer was found for Ashwood.

The house feels happy to us. Who wouldn't love it here? As the modifications and renovations took place, we added unique touches. We left Miss Abigail's little elevator, but the contractor removed the dumbwaiter, as it was a constant reminder of how things can go wrong when small children play hide and seek.

This enormous house has people to occupy some of the empty rooms, and the nursery has the laughter and chatter of children once again. Noise is always tumbling back and forth from the center of the house as Jason's music joins Curlie's piano cords that filter up from the living room. The endless rumble of feet as they transverse the main and back staircases only adds to this joyful sound.

My thoughts suddenly veer toward the significant life-altering decision my son will make in a few years. I try to squelch it as it's too painful to think that Jason would want to live so far from his family. At seventeen, he's a young version of his father and nearly as tall, dark and mysterious, but also as loving and polite. Jason will graduate from high school this summer but has no firm plans for college yet. Mother and I have tried to steer him toward something mechanical, but so far, he has not shifted in that direction.

Our extended family dines together most evenings in the formal dining room where we talk about the day's events, often going in tangents that have absolutely nothing to do with the topic. During one of those times, Glen questioned why wine and water were the only beverages served to the adults with dinner. Mother and I both said that it's what we've always done.

Glen bluntly said, "I don't like wine, and prefer Tennessee sippin whiskey, Missy. Can't I drink that?" We all stared at him in disbelief as he thought he was supposed to like whatever we served; it was there, so he drank it. Mother started to laugh and recalled never allowing Daddy to put his beer glass on the table. We realized that new house, new rules apply here, so we complied.

Our farm dog, Rosie, woofs and I look down at her from the landing. She won't climb the unstable stairs and heads off to the pasture when I don't come down.

The architect made changes to the Carriage House plans for the umpteenth time, and it will be a comfortable place for Dr. Jessica and Reed to live once they're married. Good grief, Married! Their wedding is three months away, and there's a myriad of duties to assign, preparations to finalize, and lists to prepare!

Adrian startles me. "Hey, Ellie…" Gingerly navigating the rickety stairs, he holds two cups of coffee while trying to maneuver with a roll of drawings under his arm. "You have an odd expression on your face. Are you making your lists in your head again?"

"Yes, as a matter of fact, I am."

Handing me a steaming cup, he says, "I thought you might need these. It'll be great, sweetheart, you need to stop worrying. You always manage to get it done on time."

"But it never stays on budget, Adrian. Besides, that's not what I'm worried about now. I didn't tell you that the architect said the floor joists are so rotted, they can't support the second floor. We're fortunate they didn't fall onto our vehicles. I'm sure you wouldn't want a hole in your convertible top. It's no wonder they left it empty. How could anyone live here the way it is?"

"I've only been up here once and didn't see a bathroom. Maybe the residents had an outhouse," Adrian chuckles.

"There is a bathroom, and a shower room, but they aren't huge. The plumbing is atrocious, and it's the Manor House mess all over again, and so is the electrical. We were lucky it didn't catch fire and burn the whole thing down to the ground. She also has bad news about the garage doors."

"What's wrong with the garage doors? They look okay to me." Adrian leans over the side to check them out. "They could use a coat of paint."

I lean over the rail to look at the six pair of old doors that are barely fastened by their unique hinges. Dark green mold slowly moves up from the bottom giving it an odd looking shadow. "Paint isn't all they need. See that green stuff? It means mold will be an issue and the termites had a party for so long that they destroyed them to the point that no amount of wood filler will help. I hope we can find replacements that won't cost an arm and a leg, like every other thing we've done here."

Adrian laughs, and says, "Ah, the money pit again. Are you thinking of going to the racetrack for some fast cash, Mrs. Thompson? I still need lessons in that department. You could teach me how to win, you know. I'm a great student--and I learn quick."

"Even Daddy wondered how I did it." Absently running my hand along the split wood on the top railing, I'm crunching imaginary numbers in my head. "If we don't have the funds to cover the renovations here, yes, we'll go to the track, but quite honestly, Adrian, giving you lessons in betting isn't something that I can teach you."

"Come on, Ellie. Can't we give it a try?"

"No, Adrian. I don't want to burst your bubble, but I don't think you'll get it. And being a quick learner has nothing to do with it."

"Okay. Didn't you say the workers were starting today? Is that Grayson coming down the road with his crew?"

I'm stirring the foam on top of the cup with my finger. "Yeah, the architect permitted him to proceed. I hope he gets it done before Reed and Dr. Jess come back from their honeymoon. They could stay in the house with us if it isn't."

"Are you concerned that the garages won't have the same status as the Manor House?" Adrian asks candidly, "Do you care if it doesn't have that Century plaque?"

"No, I merely want to preserve as much of the original Mrs. Ashwood's pride and joy as we can. I imagine how happy she is when we restore it and make it all pretty. The main thing is that it has to be safe and habitable."

Adrian moves to shield his eyes, then rolls them in a comical gesture to the right and left. "Maybe Mrs. Ashwood's ghost is smiling at us right now." He gives a little salute in the direction of the middle window, but there is no shadow now. "You don't suppose she'll come after me for mentioning her, do you?"

"That's funny, Adrian, have any of our resident ghosts come after you, ever? They've never come after any of us. They're friendly, and we cohabitate quietly."

Adrian reaches to touch my face tenderly. "Mrs. Ashwood would be proud of what you've done here because it's spectacular. By the way, Levi called a little while ago and asked if I would go to Langley next week."

Levi is Adrian's direct supervisor at the CIA. We have learned over time that Levi is a wonderful friend and mentor, devoted to his job and coworkers. He calls me occasionally to see if I'll coerce Adrian into going back to the CIA full time. I know he's kidding and calls to check up on us.

"I need to meet Grayson downstairs."

"You better let me go first, so you have something soft to land on," he says.

Sticking my finger into the foam on top of my coffee mug, I bring it to my mouth for a taste. "What's going on in Langley Land? What did you put in my coffee, Adrian; it tastes good in a coffeehouse kind of way."

"Levi said there might be a small job for me and would I tear myself away to come there for a few days. It's nothing too exciting. I'm not going out of the country or anything. I added something, do you like it?" Adrian grins.

"There's the usual stuff going on here, Adrian, nothing we all can't handle. You should go. Oh, I know what you put in the coffee; thanks, I like it, sweetie."

At the bottom of the steps, Adrian turns to say, "I'll leave you to take care of your stuff. I told Levi nothing is pressing here, and I can leave in a day or two, maybe three or four depending on what's going on here."

"Adrian, you don't have to say anything more about it. You should go, we can handle things here without you. May I ask you a question first? Aside from the training, you conduct here, do you regret giving up your job with the CIA to stay with us?"

Adrian reaches for my hand and brings it to his lips, and then he begins to nibble comically. "I have no regrets, my sweet Ellie. I love you and would do it all over again if I had the choice. You know, we need to plan our wedding. Soon, don't you think? Not that I'm getting anxious or anything, but you know, I do have urges."

"Ha Adrian! Let's get Reed and Dr. Jess's wedding out of the way first, shall we? We have a bazillion things to do before that happens! Be patient, and I promise you that our time will come."

Adrian leans to peck my cheek as three trucks clear the front gate. "I will let you get to work then. See you at lunch."

Mr. Grayson, our general contractor, jumps out of his truck, reaches for his hard hat and a handful of drawings, while the other vehicles line up along the garage doors.

When the first truck stops, a familiar voice calls, "Mornin, Ms. Thompson, it's a great day for a demolition. We could raze this whole thing and start from scratch. It might be easier and less costly if we do that."

"Hello, Mr. Grayson. That isn't in my budget." I'm hoping he stops, so I don't have to be rude to him. He rubs me the wrong way, and I can't put my finger on it, but it's something odd at the way he looks at me, or how he talks.

"You can still change your mind, you know," he says with a wink.

"I won't change my mind, not after paying the architect for all the changes and getting the permits for this."

Where does he think I get money, a money tree?

"The big rig with the beam will be here about ten." Pulling up a garage door, he says, "Looks like you got everything out so we can get started." Grayson then asks, "After all this time, please call me Tom; you don't have to be so formal with me."

"Would you try to preserve as much as you can? We'd appreciate it if you could save the interior doors and as many baseboards and woodwork as possible. That is if they're in good shape and the termites didn't eat them."

"Sure, you can count on us." Grayson waves to the men in the trucks. "Got the latest drawings?" Taking the roll Adrian handed me, Grayson spreads it out on an improvised table inside the first garage.

"Here you are. It's the latest and greatest and hopefully the last one you'll need," I sigh.

"Do you have the original drawings of the garages, Ms. Thompson? Mind if I borrow them?" Grayson asks.

"No, these are copies from the architect for only what you're doing. Why would you need the original plans?"

"Oh, thought there might be something we need to address is all," Grayson says smiling.

"These are what she sent over for you. I think you have all you need right here."

Why do I feel as if I have to play hardball with him?

At that, Grayson retreats up the rickety stairs as Rosie runs toward me. Stooping to pat her head, I spill most of my coffee on the ground. Walking into the kitchen, Mona is busy whipping something up in her state-of-the-art mixer. She gazes up at me distractedly, smiles, and gives a slight nod of her head in greeting.

"Ellie, dear," Mother calls from the Morning Room. "Can you come in here and look at these? The girls and I need your opinion on something."

Several items are spread out on the table where my Mother, Francesca, is standing with one hand on her hip and the other on her mouth, chewing.

"I see you've been busy, Mother. Can't you wait for Dr. Jess to get here? Shouldn't she be making the decisions, not me?"

"We need your opinion on this if the whole thing is going to work out properly. You know I love Dr. Jessica, dear, but she isn't the best judge of wedding preparations. She's coming by today, and we need to steer her toward the right color. Mona and I also thought she might like these for the reception, besides the wedding cake. What do you think? Here, take one."

"They're beautiful. Tell me again how we got roped into this reception thing again?"

The pretty pastel little morsels remind me of the delicate pastries Dimmy's chef made while I was held captive. *Déjà vu* suddenly flashes wildly in front of my eyes and Mother becomes alarmed at my expression, touching my arm gently.

"Ellie? What on earth is wrong with you? You haven't even tasted them, and you're making quite a face. Why are you questioning the reception now? It's a bit late for that, dear. All the plans are in place, apart from the items on this table."

"Sorry, Mother, what did you say?"

Mother picks up the plate and sticks it in my face. "You consented to have the wedding reception here. You wanted to show off the new patio.

Ellie, they are pastries. Take one and see if you like it first. They taste like delicate little flowers." Cooing, she pops one into her mouth.

As I put one into mine, a distant memory surfaces. Dimmy and Jamale are sitting at an impossibly large dining table, in an enormous room, in a faraway place I don't wish to remember! "Where did you get the recipe for these, Mother? They taste like the ones Uncle Dimmy's chef made!"

Mother seems startled and doesn't react for a moment. "He can't be here for the wedding, so he offered to send them for the reception."

She then proceeds to stuff another tiny piece into her mouth and then rolls her eyes upward. Did I do that same thing? Did Dimmy and Jamale laugh, as I am now doing at Mother?

"I don't remember asking him to do anything for the wedding."

Mother pops another piece into her mouth, moaning happily. "Ellie, if you don't want to serve them, we won't. But honey, they are delightful."

"I thought after all this time that the things that affected me there would have stopped haunting me by now," I whisper.

Mother immediately understands that I'm referring to Saudi Arabia and the time I spent there in captivity for close to two and a half months. It was a terrifying time for all of us as my family had buried Ravi and me, or so they thought.

"I didn't know about the pastries, Ellie. I am so thoughtless. We won't serve them if you feel at all uncomfortable. I'll tell Akdemir thanks, but no thanks."

"I have to get over the shock of seeing them, that's all. The delectable morsels will be wonderful, and Dr. Jessica will love them for her wedding reception. Please don't mind me; it's only a little flashback."

Mother is alarmed, asking, "Do you have those often, Ellie?"

"Please don't worry about it; they come and go quickly, mostly."

Tears start to form in Mother's eyes. "That must have been a truly awful time for you, sweetheart. It was no picnic for us either."

I reach to hug her. "I never know when it'll hit. It's odd things that trigger it. Do you need help with something else?"

I know what's coming.

"Maybe you should talk to someone about this." Mother has mentioned this many times.

"We've talked about this before, Mother. I told you that I feel too self-conscious to spill my guts to a total stranger."

Mother puts her hands on her hips. "Ellie, it might help to get through your unresolved feelings. Something that awful and deeply embedded can be so negative."

"I don't have time right now to spend lying on someone's couch. Sorry for snapping at you, what else is there to discuss?"

Moving on to the next item on the table, we decide to steer Dr. Jess toward light blue tablecloths, midnight blue napkins, and springtime flowers for the centerpiece arrangements.

"Mother, there is an impossible mound of paperwork I need to get to before the end of the day. I'm a little on edge with all the stuff going on here and at the garages. I love you. Please carry on without me."

Mother smiles sweetly. "Okay Ellie, but you should seriously think about seeing someone, I know it would help you."

"I'll think about it. It's not a priority on my list this week."

Things have been too quiet around here.

It's times like these when people are complacent, and odd things start to happen. Is this one of my warnings of something to come, or am I worried about nothing as Adrian thinks I am?

Could he be right and I'm worrying needlessly? Mother has said on numerous occasions that we haven't worried enough, and Glen says we should all be apprehensive due to the peculiar things that happen here. He thinks we don't worry enough!

Oh, for heaven's sake, am I driving myself nuts for no reason?

Stopping at the library table to look over the original drawings for this house, I silently thank Sarah Ashwood for her brilliant ideas that do not appear on the original drawings. Why did Grayson inquire about the garage drawings this morning? Am I allowing little things to affect me now?

I am usually so in control and focused.

The ancient documents suddenly chomp through my thoughts, and my mind starts to wander again. Carried inside old books, they traveled the world with Ravi and Daddy, most likely on clandestine meetings, or wherever agents of the CIA went on missions.

It might be time to let His Most Royal Highness King Dimmy (pain-in-the-ass) know that we are in possession of them. As I'm thinking this, the house phone rings.

Since I can't bring myself to address him as King anything, I trip over my tongue to say, "Ak-dim-er, it's so nice to hear from you."

The line is silent for a moment, followed by a faint click. Adrian declared two days ago that our entire system of electronics was bug-free. Thinking that it must be on his end, Dimmy doesn't seem to notice.

Akdemir's cheerful voice says, "Hello, my dearest Ellen, your family is well, I trust?"

"They are well, thank you. And your family as well?"

I've come to detest this tedious back and forth, but apparently, it's something Dimmy feels is necessary. He asks the same questions every time we talk, and for lack of anything better, I give him the same answers in return.

"They are all well, Ellen; and Jason, he is doing good in school and eager about his graduation soon?"

"Yes, he can't wait for that day to come. He keeps hinting about a grandiose present, but don't get any ideas about a car, because I already told him that if you send one, it will go right back to you!"

"Dearest Ellen, I understand how you feel about gifts, and I will not send Jason a car."

"Let's make sure you understand what that means, shall we? That means no vehicle of any kind. I mean no motorcycle, no off-road vehicle, nada. Do you understand nothing with two, four, or six wheels? Am I making myself clear on this?"

"Yes, Ellen," he says with a chuckle. "I will honor your wishes. Now, I want to know if the little pastries made it to your home without damage. Has the bride sampled them yet? What is her opinion of them?"

"Oh, they have indeed arrived. I ate a few, and they are as delicious as I remember. Your pastry chef never disappoints, Dimmy! Dr. Jessica hasn't been here yet, but I'm sure she'll love them for her wedding day."

Akdemir laughs again, and I imagine his self-satisfied smile. "Good, good, I will inform my chef that this is 'a go,' as you would say. How many of the pastries should he make to send over for this momentous occasion?"

"How many is he willing to make?"

"I will see to it that he makes enough for all of you to enjoy. It is unfortunate that I cannot be there at the time of the wedding. I want to send an additional item; however, I want it to remain a surprise for the bride and groom."

"You can tell me, Dimmy, I'm good at keeping secrets."

"No, no, no. It will be a secret for all of you. Again, my sincerest regret for not being able to join you for this occasion. We have pressing matters to attend to here."

I don't give a rat's patutti about his pressing matters, but perhaps it's time to tell him about the documents and put the responsibility back onto him. "I thought you should know that we have the rest of the missing ancient documents."

After a slight lag in his response, he says, "That is wonderful news! I was under the impression that Fariq had them. He is pressuring me to submit to, you do not need to know about that. Has your Mr. Levi authenticated them and does he think they are what I seek?"

"Yes, we are sure they are the right ones. They were with my father's papers. They were found recently in one of their vaults when they did an audit." I'm not about to tell him that I've had them for a while. Perhaps it's because I want to stick it to him a little bit. I'm still having trouble keeping my feelings in check, as I'd much rather not have any communication with him whatsoever.

"Excellent, my dear Ellen. Have they been deciphered?"

"Mr. Levi is sure they are what you need to keep you in your chair at the Royal Palace. His teams are always thorough, and the notes attached explain that part exactly."

Levi informed us of the pressure Dimmy's half-brother, Fariq, is putting on him to vacate the Royal Palace. He asked last week whether I had decided on how I was going to handle the transfer of the documents. He also astutely pointed out that the Ministers who comprise the Royal Allegiance Council might be in a quandary without them. Could I please move things along for the sanity of his office?

Adrian thinks the latest 'buzz' about the rightful heir and unrest in that part of the world means that all the ancient documents must be united with the ones Dimmy already has to complete the rightful heir succession thing.

"What does the note say, Ellen?" he asks anxiously. "Have you read it? I must know right away if they are the missing documents!" Akdemir says quickly.

"If you will hold a moment, I'll go get them." Turning to the undetectable sliding panel in the bookcase behind my desk, I carefully retrieve the delicate bundle, unravelling the ribbon on the top one. "Are you still there, Dimmy?"

Akdemir seems uncharacteristically impatient today. "Yes, I am here, Ellen. What do the notes say about the documents?"

One of Levi's crackerjack people deciphered each bundle of fragile papers. Unfolding the note on top, I slowly read as Dimmy expresses his excitement. He interrupts when I get to the part about how his family should conduct themselves in their households, how they will divide the deeds and warranties (worth a small fortune) among the family, as well as the right of succession.

Without reading any of the other notes, he interrupts me, saying, "Yes, yes! You hold the very documents that I need. I am so pleased that you are in possession of them. It will indeed convince the Royal Ministers that I am the rightful heir. It will ensure our line of succession that we need to preserve. You have no idea how grateful this makes me, Ellen."

"There's more, Dimmy. Don't you want me to keep reading?"

"That is sufficient for now, Ellen. Maybe one more."

"Here's a newer document that names both you and your brother, Basim, and any heirs you might have."

"Excellent, Ellen. That is all I need to know."

"That's all you need to hear? There's a lot more, Dimmy." The interesting thing here is that this newer document doesn't name anyone else, not Fariq, nor any of his many half-brothers, sisters, or his ridiculous number of cousins.

No one knew that half of the ancient documents were not even at the Royal Palace. It was after Ravi left his homeland that they traveled back and forth. They were to stay with the rightful heir to the throne, which was Basim/Ravi.

"With this information, I will continue to preside over our households and implement significant decisions on our behalf. When may I have them, Ellen?"

"I don't suppose we should send them by regular mail."

"No, we cannot take the slightest chance they will be intercepted. You could send Jason with them…" Akdemir says candidly.

"That will not be an option. There has to be another way."

Akdemir says softly, "I will see that Jason comes to no harm. Do you not trust me by now, Ellen? You could send Mr. Adrian with them."

What is this man thinking?

"It has nothing to do with trust, Dimmy. Here's a better idea, why not send one of Jam-ale's men to get the documents? Or better yet, why don't you send him?"

"I cannot allow Jamaile to be away from the Royal Palace for any length of time without me unless it is of extreme importance. Moreover, I cannot spare him right now."

"I thought your precious documents would fall under extreme importance."

"We will think more about this, and both you and I will come to an equitable solution, my dear Ellen. Perhaps they should stay with Jason for now. Knowing you have them may be enough. I must go now. Do give my best regards to your family."

I know when he says this that the conversation is coming to a swift close. "Let me know if you come up with a plan."

As I say goodbye, Ak-dim-er is hanging up on me, but not before there is a rather loud CLICK in my ear, and another that is barely audible. Nevertheless, this triggers the memory of that damn door when Jam-ale locked me into that room!

How could something that insignificant still affect me?

Attacking the stack of mail strewn across my desk, I begin to open and separate the contents into piles. Then wonder if Dimmy was recording our conversation. Or have his enemies, who are now my enemies, infiltrated the palace and he is unaware of this?

Switching to focus on something else, I open a letter from the Virginia Racing Commission that states they have finally resolved my formal complaint against the driver who undermined the rules during that harrowing race last season. Three previous letters were non-committal because it came down to not being able to find the driver in question. They couldn't prosecute anyone without more information, but I countered with a threat from Levi and his CIA connection (with Adrian's blessing) and they somehow miraculously found the driver. They gave him, the owner, and his trainer a stern warning and a hefty fine.

We'll keep our eyes open for any further monkey business at the racetrack. I suspect that the people responsible for the offense are also involved with the demise of our horse *Didgeridoo,* but we can't prove it, yet.

After lunch, I stroll through the library on my way to my office. Stopping to unroll the delicate old blueprints, thoughts swirl in my head about Sarah Ashwood and her architect. She must have endured interesting discussions to get him to incorporate her unusual oddities into this house. How did she get around the secrecy issues with the contractors?

The unusual staircase that's hidden on the first floor in-between the library and billiard room is a wonder. It goes up through the levels to the attic, then crosses over, dropping down to the back of the closet in my master bedroom. So far, this has remained a closely guarded secret that no one else except my immediate family knows about, not even Adrian.

I wonder if there was any time in the house's history where the family needed it as we did? What was Sarah Ashwood's purpose for placing it there? The only reason I'm able to come up with is that it was designed to help runaway slaves, but the house was built nearly thirty years after the Civil War was over. Either way, we are grateful for its presence.

The basement of this house was a scary place back when we first moved in. It was where Mona did the laundry, stringing clothes in the winter when it was too cold outside to dry clothes on the line. The laundry was then relocated to where the laundry accumulates, near the bedrooms on the second level.

The basement was a musty and damp place that had a fair number of spiders and cobwebs. Sometime in the Twentieth Century, an unwieldy coal-fired furnace was added, along with a separate room for coal. During our extensive renovations there, the old coal chute was removed along with leftover chunks of coal where it was chucked out along with the furnace. The new air handler and replacement takes up half the space and is a state-of-the-art cooling and heating system that is controlled by an equally smart programmable controller.

The National Register of Historic Homes members had a hard time with the HVAC installation, as it didn't fit in with their stringent rules governing their requirements, but they reluctantly agreed to leave the century plaque at our front door as we weren't about to tear it all out.

Also in the basement, we found the large safe that Gerald Tillman (the local antique dealer) insisted was in the house, and it did contain some of Mrs. Ashwood's valuable jewelry, which we sold for a tidy sum. The real surprise was the wine cellar and an old bunker, leftover from an Ashwood descendent, installed during the Cold War of the 1960s, which we made into a shelter and surveillance monitoring room. It's where Adrian's teams come to train on occasion.

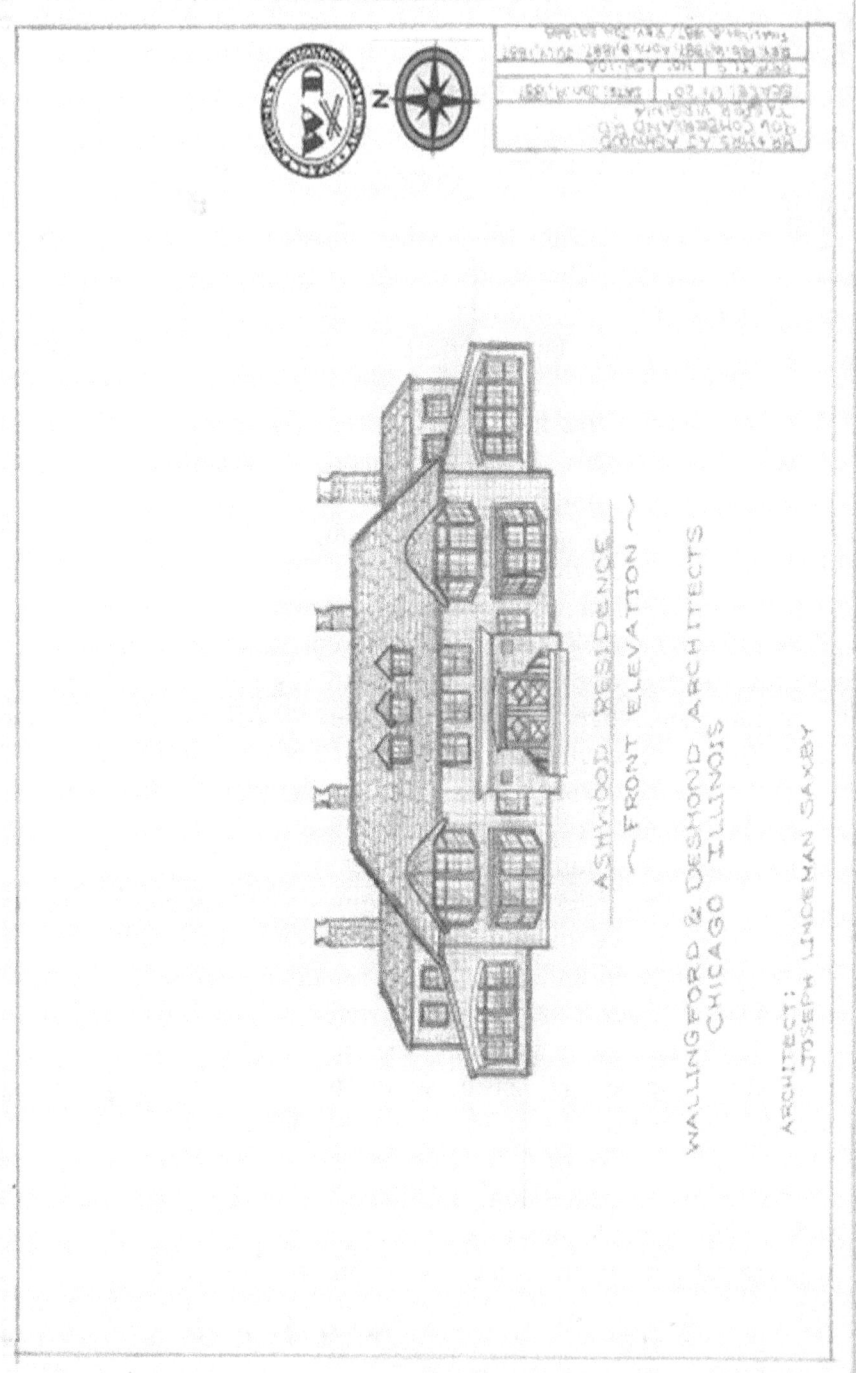

Whispered Dreams

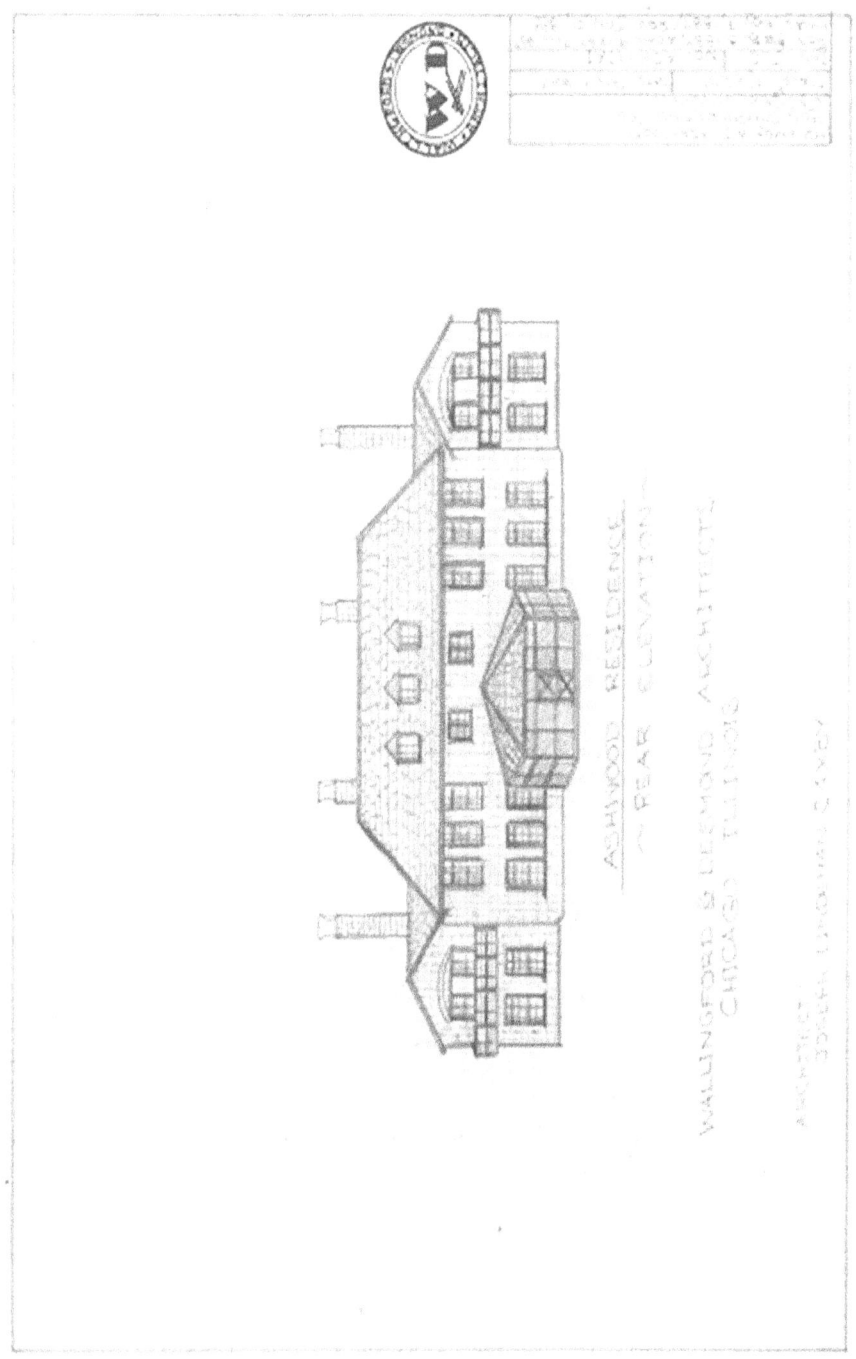

Whispered Dreams

The library is where the family usually gathers most evenings after dinner, but tonight, everyone has scattered, most likely because they think I'll come up with another job for them to do before Reed and Dr. Jess's wedding.

"Adrian, can we talk?"

Cocking his head to the side, sipping lazily at a glass of wine, he says, "What's on your wonderful mind, Ellie May?"

"I spoke with His Most Royal pain today. I finally told him we have the missing documents. After I read him one of the deciphered notes that Levi gave me, he said he didn't need to hear any more. I found that a bit odd because he squawked so much about them. We ruled out using regular mail and couldn't decide on how he would get them."

Adrian seems thoughtful. "I don't suppose we can send them Fed Ex or something. What about a special messenger?"

"We thought about doing it that way, but neither one of us could come up with the right person to *play* courier. Do you have any suggestions?"

Adrian closes his eyes, and then opens them, saying, "Why don't we fax them directly to his office?"

"Do people still use faxes? We didn't consider that."

Raising his eyebrows, he says, "Why doesn't he send his big man guy over to get them?"

"He said there was turmoil over there and he couldn't spare Jam-ale right now. He suggested that I send Jason and I told him that would never happen. Then he suggested that you take them."

Adrian laughs, taking a sip of wine, he says, "I could do that. All I have to do is clear it with Levi. I do possess special qualifications for extraordinary assignments, you know."

"I do agree that you are an extraordinary and special person, sweetheart, however, if there is turmoil as Dimmy says there is, no one from this family should go there. I do consider you family, you know. I suppose we shouldn't trust that Fariq person. He might be lurking in some hidden passageway waiting to pounce on one of us. Could Levi send someone he trusts? Why not do that, okay? Don't you think it makes more sense to do it that way?"

"Tell you what, Ellie, let me run this by Levi to see what he thinks. You know, Mr. Wonderful will be coming for Jason's graduation this summer, so why don't we wait until then to give him the real documents? Then everyone can stay where they are, and no one has to worry," Adrian concludes.

Rubbing my temples, from a slight headache that has been plaguing me most of the day, I agree that it's okay. "That sounds like a plan, Mr. CIA man. Maybe Dimmy doesn't have to have the originals in his hot little hands. He did mention they should be with Jason."

"What else is going on, Ellie? What else is bothering you? Did he say something to upset you?"

"It isn't what he said, Adrian, it's what happened when I answered the phone and when he hung up."

Adrian leans forward, and his expression changes from amusement to a serious one. "You have my attention, like what?"

"There was a faint click when we first started to talk, then a louder one when he hung up, followed by another one that was barely audible. I don't remember ever hearing those types of sounds when he and I talked before."

"I checked every device personally that we have here and there was nothing unusual with any of it. The sound you heard could have been on his side, you know. It sounds like there were too many clicks," Adrian mumbles.

"I'm a little jittery today. There's so much going on here. It must be all the wedding stuff and the last of the renovations. Was someone listening in on our conversation, do you think?"

"Are you losing your edge there, Mrs. Thompson?" Adrian puts his arms around me, drawing me closer, whispering endearments into my ear.

"Didn't think so, Mr. CIA man, and maybe I'm tired. On a good note, the Virginia Racing Commission finally responded to my complaint."

Adrian pulls away to drain his glass, setting it down on the coffee table. "I know you've been waiting to hear from them. Didn't they already send you three letters?"

"Yes, but this one says that they've levied a hefty fine on the driver and reprimanded the owner, and the trainer, giving them a warning. I know it's that blowhard, Jenkins, who wanted to ban us from racing at Billingsworth. If they do it again, they're out of racing. It doesn't say they're out of racing altogether, but they certainly won't be welcome to race at our local establishment again."

Adrian looks surprised. "Did they mention Jenkins by name in the letter? May I see it?"

"You can see the letter if you promise not to get upset. They didn't give any names, but I know it's Jenkins."

Adrian follows me into my office, and I hand him the letter. His head bobs back and forth, then he stares at me, and I know, what his facial expression means.

"No, it doesn't name Jenkins, but he'll figure out that it was you who filed the formal complaint. They'll be gunnin for you, Miss Ellie."

"Gunnin for me, Adrian?"

Adrian throws the letter on the desk and puts his head against mine. "I wish you would hang up your spurs and let those bullies pick on someone else for a change."

"You think I wear spurs, Adrian?"

Even though he tries to be funny, there's an underlying concern that is present, and he's suddenly serious. "You better start practicing and carrying your little Glock. If you don't trust Dimmy and his people, then you sure as shootin better not trust the ole boys down at the track, either."

"Adrian! I can't hide from these people. At some point, we'll have to confront them, either on the race track or somewhere else! Here, I'll practice on you." Using my right hand as a make-believe gun, I pull my thumb and aim it at Adrian.

"Ellie, you never point a loaded gun at anyone unless you intend to do them harm!" Adrian pantomimes that he's been shot in the heart and falls backward onto the sofa as if he's dying.

"Oh Adrian, you are overreacting."

Adrian raises his eyebrows. "Am I, Ellie?" he says haughtily.

"What you are is overacting! If you're interested, there's a nice local community theater you can join."

"There is little success where there is little laughter."

~ Andrew Carnegie

Chapter Two

Success and Laughter

We are in the Morning Room having breakfast when I suddenly recall that I wanted to discuss a particular phrase with Adrian. He's reading the newspaper when I interrupt him.

"I've been trying to remember a saying about keeping your enemies close to you. Do you remember something like that, Adrian?"

Laying the newspaper aside, he says, "Do you mean the one about keeping your friends close and your enemy's closer?"

"No, that's not it. I wish my brain could remember it."

"Do you mean the enemy of my enemy is my friend?" he offers.

"That might be it. Would you wait here until I get my laptop?"

"Sure, I'll get another cup of coffee."

After grabbing my computer, I return to do a quick search using the words enemy and friend. "Adrian, it says here that you should forgive your enemies, but you should never forget their names. And the best way to destroy your enemy is to make him your friend. Should you want to make peace with this enemy, you will have to work with your enemy."

"Isn't that the same thing, Ellie?" he asks.

"Not exactly. It's a proverb. The concept is used when two parties have a common enemy. They can work together to advance their common goals."

Adrian screws up his face in concentration. "If you're referring to Dimmy, are you saying that maybe he should employ this tactic in his dealings with his half-brother Fariq? I see the wheels of your mind turning, Ellie. What's going on in there besides this enemy stuff?"

"It's hard to explain, but I've had this weird feeling all day. I can't quite put my finger on it, and my mind keeps wandering. I can't stay focused long enough to get anything done. It happened the other day too. Do you think it's the residual from that drug they gave me?"

"Not being a doctor, I wouldn't know, my dearest. But now that I think about it, we probably shouldn't get involved with Akdim's mess."

"Why not?"

"If you think that this Fariq character is also our enemy, because he's Dimmy's enemy, we should keep our distance. Unless someone puts in a formal request, Levi won't let us get involved. It has everything to do with foreign policy. That could be very tricky, and they might misconstrue our intervention as meddling."

"I wouldn't call what we're doing as meddling, Adrian. I would call it something else. Besides, my love, we're already involved, right up to and including our eyeballs!"

Sighing heavily, he adds, "We can't interfere in that type of thing. Remember what happened to your husband and your father? You don't seriously want to step into the middle of that do you?"

"We can't interfere with their stuff, but they can waltz in here anytime they want to? You act as if we aren't involved, Adrian, and we *so* are."

"Ellie, if you are referring to when Dimmy and Jammy came here unannounced; you forget that he purchased the investor's half of Ashwood. At that time, he had every right to come onto the property. How about we don't worry about all that until there's a clear threat, okay?" Adrian says, pressing his lips together in a thin line.

Does that mean he thinks I will let this go for now?

"Yes, but he did it without our knowledge. That stupid banker sold it to him before we even knew it was up for bids. They came at two o'clock in the morning, as I remember and honestly, Adrian, they were our enemies at that time. Jason is or will be involved with them in the future, so we are already tangled in their web. Besides, you are knee deep in it by being here."

Adrian grins. "You're getting worked up over nothing. I don't see the problem. Can we drop it for the time being, please? Can't we find something else to talk about, sweet cheeks?"

"Why are you brushing me off? What does Dimmy's foreign policy have to do with us?"

He seems frustrated. "Okay, I don't know how it all works. It's highly complicated, and it would take a college course to understand. It's almost as complex as how they choose their king."

"Why is that so complicated? I thought the king thing was right of succession, as in there's the king, then his oldest son, followed by his brother, then his next brother, and then it follows down to other people.

"There is far more to it than that, my little bonbon. Your father knew all about that, remember?"

"Did he? Speaking of which, I don't exactly remember him talking much about anything of substance, especially the part about working for the CIA. Even when we went to the racetrack, we talked mostly about horses. Anyway, what if there's turmoil over there? How long do you think it'll take before it comes over to our neck of the woods? Maybe it's already on its way, darling. I don't see how Jason is considered an heir with all the other brothers there are. I'm genuinely worried that something is wrong there."

Adrian stretches his arms out to me. "Okay, you might be right. Come here you little vixen."

I bat his hands away, saying, "Can't you be serious for one moment?"

"Come on now, who are you mad at, me or Dimmy?" he sniffs.

"Your transparency is showing, Adrian. Be serious, will you? Are you trying to defuse the issue so I won't get bent out of shape? You are worried, I can tell. You're as shook up about this as I am. Maybe even more so. And you are two clicks away from calling Levi, am I correct, Mr. CIA man?"

Adrian has a strange look on his face. "If you have a weird feeling, then we should pay heed to that. I'll call Levi if it makes you feel any better."

"Thanks, Adrian. You know…we all feel safe when you're here with us."

"I should hope so. You had to adjust to far more than I did when I gave up my career and moved to Ashwood, Ellie. I fell in love with you *and* your amazing family."

"Something has been at the edge of my mind all morning. I keep catching myself thinking of all the events that brought us here. It's making me crazy for some reason!"

Adrian starts to walk away, then turns, saying, "Put it out of your mind if you can and try not to think about it. Maybe you're wondering what Jason wants to do with his life after graduation. Could that be weighing down your mind?"

"Maybe that's it, Adrian. Thanks for listening, sweetie."

I don't think Jason knows what he wants to do after graduation. That's not what's bothering me at all. Mother seems distracted, too. She has been very involved with the wedding preparations. Perhaps it is all the wedding plans that are bothering us both.

As Reed and Dr. Jessica's wedding day approaches, the ornamental trees we planted last year are starting to bloom. My daughters, Melanie (almost fifteen) and Curlie (who turned eleven recently) are excited to be part of the wedding. As junior bridesmaids, they practice walking up and down the center staircase in their little high-heeled pumps and midnight blue dresses. The constant clicking sound is echoing in the hallway, and it's slowly driving me to distraction.

Everyone has their jobs to do: Melanie will oversee the butterfly boxes while Curlie takes care of the flower petals she's supposed to pass around after the wedding. Dr. Jess wants people to throw roses at her instead of rice. Adrian has the wedding rings, as he's Reed's Best Man, while Mona and Mother take responsibility for the guest book, gifts, and whatever else might need attention. Jason and his pal from school will park our guest's cars in the pasture for the reception.

Dr. Jess put me in charge of the catering company. She stressed over whether there was ample time to set things up without bumping into the three-piece orchestra as they set up their instruments. Trying to calm her, Mother stepped in to assure her that she has placed her wedding into competent hands and to let it go and let us worry about the details.

A large white canvas tent is set up over our new stone patio, anchored at each end with hefty wires and spikes. Workers strategically hung three small chandeliers over the wood dance floor, stringing lighting along the inside near the top.

The wedding menu sits on an easel at the front entrance near the elaborate wedding cake that the baker in town made for Princess Jessica.

Mother and I never heard of displaying a menu for a wedding, but Jessica insists she starts a new tradition. She thinks it'll catch on and other brides will follow this lead.

We think it's a weird thing to do.

Knowing how sensitive a bride can be before her wedding, we kept this observation to ourselves. A few feet away will be Dimmy's hundreds of tiny pastel pastries, displayed on a multiple-tier tree, which was also Dr. Jess's creation.

Besides the delicate pastries, Uncle Dimmy sent several bolts of blue and silver material. Since the wedding theme was light and midnight blue, this was strung around the party tent and down the bride and groom's table, clouding it near the buffet, the wedding cake, and under the little pastries.

When Dimmy's surprise came, it nearly unhinged Reed. A delivery truck dropped off an elaborate carriage near the barn. Reed laughed so hard he had to walk away. How was he going to get his no-nonsense ungirly-like fiancé into that carriage?

The intention was to transport the wedding couple from the church in town to the party tent after the ceremony. When I called Uncle Dimmy to inform him that his surprise arrived, he suggested that the Arabian Stallions (the ones he gave us the first time he was officially here) to pull the carriage, but Glen knew better and said we'll use our Clydesdales, as they're used to pulling a wagon.

How comfortable is the odd-looking carriage, if it must travel the eight or so miles from town after the ceremony? Glen and Reed did a dry run with the help of Mel and Curlie. They discovered rather quickly that the carriage rolled and rocked in such an awkward motion, that the girls couldn't wait to get out of it!

As predicted, when Dr. Jess saw the carriage, she took one look at it and said she was not Cinderella. Never in a million years would she have dreamt this thing for her wedding day. We all speculated about what Uncle Dimmy had in mind when he sent it. Did he expect this reaction from everyone?

Reed couldn't contain himself and started to laugh. Jessica stared at him and didn't say a word, which made him laugh even more. That was the end of the carriage ride until Dr. Jess relented at the last minute. Could it transport the bride and groom from the Gate House near the end of the driveway to the party tent instead?

When the wedding day finally came, it took place almost on time, and the couple had a brief, but elaborate carriage ride to their reception, which was orchestrated by Master Glen, and pulled by *Frick* and *Frack*.

The wedding photographer took several photos of the carriage, placed the bridal party along the center staircase inside the Manor House, and lined them up next to the fireplace in the living room.

The food was terrific, the wine flowed freely, and the butterflies flew from their little boxes as if by a hidden switch. The wedding came and went in a blur, as most memorable events that are long in planning seem to do.

Reed and Dr. Jessica left yesterday for their much-anticipated three-week honeymoon to the Mexican Riviera. It gives us ample time to complete the inside of their Carriage House. It's been slow going, but after the beam went into the ceiling of the garages to support the floor for living quarters above it, Grayson pronounced it as sound as a new build.

The same manufacturer who provided the new windows for the Manor House returned to install new ones for the Carriage House. A sturdy set of stairs now leads up to an enlarged landing, and the new front door is old looking, yet is new. It will be the first time I've been inside since the painters were here two days ago.

The workers did a great job making these 1,920 square feet of living space comfortable. It's more than adequate for the three bedrooms and two baths, and Dr. Jessica even has a small office.

Mr. Grayson saved the original black hammered hinges from the garage doors, and they are restored to their original beauty. The new garage doors are made of cypress and are worth every penny of the over $30,000 it cost for the twelve pairs of them to be delivered and set into place. It hasn't received even a nod from the members of the National Register. Perhaps the changes are too significant.

The bleep of a truck horn brings me back out to the landing. As I walk down the stairs, a young man from the furniture store throws the door up, then lowers the lift. When I reach him, he hands me a clipboard with papers and yells to his helper inside the truck.

As the items are taken off, I check them off the list, adding sticky notes, hoping that this will help guide them to the proper room once they're inside.

Rosie woofs, running out of the barn with Adrian close behind her. "This never ceases to amaze me," Adrian says when he gets to the truck. "How you do all this, and it comes together like a decorator magazine!"

Hugging him, I say, "Thanks honey, I miss doing this. I've had a lot of practice, you know. I hope they like it."

"You're so creative, Ellie, and I know that Reed and Dr. Jess will love it here. That reminds me, Jason will be so jealous. He thought Jess and Reed would find a place in Jasper closer to her office."

"Let's go up. I think the boys are trying to put the bed frames together. He never said anything to me about that."

"Then he said that he and Mack thought they could use this as a bachelor pad." Adrian pokes his head into a room. "This is a pretty color."

"Mack? Is that his friend that helped move the cars for the wedding? I thought his name was Rolly? Where would he get an idea like that?"

"I thought it was the same kid. Does it matter? Anyway, Jason thought he could talk you into letting him live here, that is after you fixed it up. Since this is off the table now, he's already approached me about vacating the Guest House."

"What did you say to that?"

"Jason might have mentioned something about it. He said that it might be time I moved into the big house with you and let him and Mack learn what it's like to be grownups. After all, they are seniors, or it was something like that."

"I was thinking how wonderfully non-typical my teenagers are. They're trustworthy and responsible, and they haven't given me anything to worry about, until now."

Laughing, Adrian says, "He also mentioned, that because he is a senior, he could use a new car for his graduation present. Or was it a motorcycle?"

"Does he think we'll give him a car? I was thinking more like a good wristwatch and a little lecture about how to pay for college extras."

Adrian jokingly says, "Maybe he knows how to bet at the racetrack like you do and he can buy one himself."

"You're pulling my leg, Adrian. He never said any of that! It's you, who wants a motorcycle. Why don't you go buy one?"

Adrian chuckles. "He did ask about the Guest House."

"And you said?"

"I told him it was none of his business and he gave me a strange look. I guess he wonders what's wrong with us, Ellie."

"Oh, he does not, Adrian!" Taking a swipe at his arm, he's backing up when we hear a loud thump. Running to the farthest bedroom, we find the furniture boys laughing. The king size bed frame is the size of a twin bed.

"This might take a while," he says. "I should ask Reed to help."

"That's a good idea."

Reaching for the walkie-talky, Adrian's cellphone chirps. We know by the ringtone that it's Levi. "I'll be right back." A few moments later, he returns to say, "Levi said there's a disturbing development near the…" he mouths the word 'palace' without saying the word out loud. "You might want to go catch the news."

"Okay. What kind of disturbance did Mr. Levi mention?"

"He said…" Adrian rolls his eyes toward the back room. "Go see what it's about, and I'll come when I can."

Slightly alarmed, but not in a dead-run, I get to my office and turn on the small TV. The all-news-channel has cameras that pan left and right in an area where a bombing scene takes place. People run helter-skelter around what looks like a marketplace in a desert-like setting. As the camera scans the area from left to right again, Jam-ale's unmistakably large body and face fill the screen, then he is gone when the camera scans back and forth a third time.

Why is he out in the middle of that?

Adrian strolls in and plops himself down on the sofa. "Reed was busy so Glen's there to help supervise the boys now that the bed frames are together properly. What's happening over there?"

"The scene that is coming across the screen is awful. It looks like a bombing with explosions, something about an oil field. The reporter mentioned a major disturbance, but he didn't say where it was taking place. What does this mean, Adrian? Should we worry about anything? Is this the turmoil we were all expecting?"

He shrugs his shoulders. "I don't know."

"Jam-ale was in the crowd," I say quietly.

Adrian seems surprised. "Was he? Why don't we try to call Dimmy to see what's going on? Why would Jam-ale be outside?"

"I asked myself that same question. Dimmy always maintained he doesn't get involved with the mundane stuff outside the palace unless it has something directly to do with disputes with certain things. Could this be a dispute with his family? He didn't elaborate much past that."

All circuits are busy, so Adrian calls Levi. He reports that all communications are down in that area right now. We are not to worry, as this sort of thing happens more often than we can count. Give it time for someone to jury-rig something together, an hour or two at most.

"Just when you think it's safe to go back in the water," Adrian says, muttering under his breath.

"What does that have to do with what's going on now, Adrian?"

"Do you remember when that movie *Jaws* came out and everyone thought it was okay to go back in the water, and it wasn't?"

"Oh, the *Jaws* movie, but what does this have to do with sharks? It doesn't have anything to do with sharks, does it? It does have everything to do with safety. Adrian, we are safe here, aren't we?"

"Yes, Mrs. Thompson, as a professional who has pursued your family's safety for many years, not to mention what you've spent on surveillance equipment for this place, I pronounce you extremely secure!"

"How sure are you about that? Someone could sneak onto our property when you aren't looking, Mr. Secure, I-Got-The-Perimeter-Covered man."

"Okay, so they got through our defenses one time, don't you trust what I'm telling you?" Adrian pretends to look wounded.

An uncomfortable feeling starts to develop in the pit of my stomach. "Of course, I trust you, but it doesn't have anything to do with that. Dim man's enemies are our enemies now, aren't they? What's to stop them from coming here to finish the job?"

He chuckles. "Finish what job, Ellie? Does he know you call him that?"

"Could his lunatic brother, Fariq, come here and…? I've said it to his face, and he laughs, so I guess it doesn't bother him. I trip over my tongue every time I try to say his name. It *is* hard to pronounce. You call him different names, too. You know what this reminds me of, Adrian?"

"Is this like a knock-knock joke? Okay, what does this remind you of, Ellie?" Putting his fingers along his temples, he shuts his eyes, saying, "Wait, you were going to say Desert Storm, weren't you?"

"Yes. Where were you during that time, Adrian?"

"I was newly into my training, but yes, I was there. I wanted the organization to send me to Paris, but the muckity-mucks decided to send a group of us in to see how we'd stack up to their regulars. As I recall, it was downright hot there. I never did get used to it."

"Was it a bad experience?"

Adrian shakes his head. "No, it wasn't bad per se, but I can't tell you everything, you know that. And did you know that Desert Storm was Desert Shield before it became Operation Desert Storm?"

"No, I didn't remember that detail. What year was it?"

Adrian looks as if he's lost in thought for several minutes. "I think it all started in 1990. It could have been sooner than that, but we only know part of it. It was all very hush-hush back then."

"Now I remember. It put a damper on our spirits because it was the year my parents were celebrating their thirtieth wedding anniversary. Daddy and Ravi were away a lot that year. They said they were in California or Idaho, but they could have been over there then, isn't that a possibility? Do you think we could ask Levi to go back into the files for us?"

"Ellie, we can't go digging into their files for no reason. Levi wouldn't share that type of information with you, anyway, so put it out of your pretty little mind, honey."

"What if I make a fuss and demand that information? Don't I have the right to know? Could I subpoena them to talk to a judge?"

His face shows concern. "Ellie, please let this go, its water over the aqua duct."

I'm trying to ignore his pun. "You know something, Adrian. I can tell that you know something and you're not sharing it with me. I demand to know what you know. Please don't act like those baboons named Lenard-the-terrible, and his asinine accomplice Gene, and skirt the issue!"

"Do not compare me to those two imbeciles. Besides, how do you know I have anything to tell you?" he grimaces.

"Because you have that strange look in your eyes, the one that means you're holding something back. I'm a good study of character, or I was before I met Leotard and Genocide."

Adrian starts to laugh, then takes in a deep breath, letting it out slowly. "Haven't heard you reference those two clowns like that in a while. Okay, but you must promise me that you won't be alarmed. I can only tell you certain things because you're not an agent."

"Okay, I promise."

"Do you remember that first time we sent you down to the shelter? There was an intruder that broke the perimeter."

"Yes..."

"Remember how I stayed upstairs and wrote you a note to stay there until morning? Those were not Akdim's men who came into the house."

"You let me think that it was his men."

Adrian frowns. "There were reasons why I couldn't tell you, Ellie. I had to withhold that from you."

"But you printed that note that said everything was all clear."

Adrian hangs his head, reaching for my hand, he says, "Ellie, I was doing my job then. We apprehended two men who were subdued and taken into custody immediately. I will go as far as to say that you will never have to worry about them coming back again, ever," he grins sheepishly.

"What did you do with them, shoot them where they stood? Who were they?" I am beyond curious.

"You won't let this go, will you?" he says frowning.

"No, not until you tell me who they were and what you did with them."

Adrian takes another deep breath, exhaling slowly. "Levi identified them as mercenaries. He thought they were part of the Uncle Ruggeri group, but it turns out that they weren't. And they didn't have fingerprints."

"Ah yes, the Uncle Ruggeri debacle. Wasn't that before the proverbial crap hit the fan?"

"That's a good one, Ellie," he says laughing.

Daddy's adoptive family brought him to Argentina after he escaped from France after WWII; however, this uncle was responsible for making his life miserable. After he left to go to college in Canada, he put the nightmarish hell behind him.

"That gives me the creeps, Adrian. Am I to understand that these men don't exist? They do things for large sums of money and don't care who they hurt, you mean?"

Cocking his head to the side, he grins, saying, "See, I told you that you would be a good agent! Your mind is always working, and you come up with nearly the same stuff as I do."

"Flattery will get you nowhere, Mr. CIA man."

"And you're right about that; they don't exist. We live in an intriguing and fascinating world, Ellie May Thompson, soon to be Mrs. Adrian B. Sellers. Some people don't play fair, and some people are plain greedy."

"What happens now, Adrian?"

"We wait," he says solemnly, kissing my fingers.

Reaching around him and kissing his lips, I ask, "What do we wait for?"

"We wait for Uncle Dimmy to ask for our services. Then we do the same thing we do every day, Ellie; we live our lives. You finish the Carriage House, and I'll go back to the barn. Either way, they win if we show them fear. We win if we carry on like nothing ever happened."

"That sounds good in theory, Adrian. What about Dimmy? I can't believe I'm about to say this, but do you think he's safe?"

"I do not doubt that he is. Jam-Jam swore his allegiance to all of us, and he will do everything in his power to keep his word. In the worst-case scenario, Mr. Kingly will show up here to stay with us until the turmoil is over."

"I don't like that scenario. Can you conjure one that doesn't have Uncle Dimmy here at all?"

Adrian hugs me, saying, "Come on Ellie, you're a fighter! You can get past this."

"Yeah, I am a fighter, but you have to admit this is worrisome. Okay, I'll try not to worry so much anymore."

"That's my gal!" Adrian takes my hands, putting them on his face, he starts to squeeze my fingers.

"By the way, that thing about the enemy of my enemy is my friend? You were right; it has to do with foreign policy. I did a little research, and it has everything to do with a person named Kautilya who wrote a book about the *Source of Sovereign States*."

"Who's Ka till e a?"

"He's the author. It seems that if a king is situated anywhere immediately on the circumference of the conqueror's territory, the conqueror is considered the enemy. If the king is somewhere *close* to the enemy but separated from the conqueror only *by* the enemy, then that one is the friend. It pretty much means the same thing about the enemy of my enemy is my friend."

"Or, is it the enemy of my friend is my enemy? Either way, Fariq will never be considered our friend, Ellie. I love how your mind works! Marry me, and we'll have a bunch of brainy and weird children."

"Adrian, don't you think we already have enough brainy and weird children?"

"Yes, we do have enough of those. We can wait for grandchildren."

"Grandchildren!"

Adrian plants a kiss on my forehead and practically runs out of the library. "Gotta go now, see you at dinner!"

Standing near the front windows, I watch Adrian as he approaches the Carriage House. He waves to Glen, as the older man ambles down the stairs. Their heads nearly touch as they both laugh at something.

When did they become so chummy?

Heading back to the Carriage House, my thoughts turn to the news alert. The newscaster alluded to the oil that is burning uncontrollably in a nearby field. What happened during *Desert Storm*? It took a long time to put out those fires if I remember correctly. How long will it take for this chaos in Saudi to settle? Could our people be there right now?

Be safe, Dimmy. Don't let anything happen to him, Jam-ale. I suddenly realize that I'm praying for his safety. It is the same person, who not long ago was my enemy, who is now my friend.

How bizarre is that?

We managed to finish the Carriage House mere days before Reed and Dr. Jess were expected to return from their honeymoon. Once they saw it, they were overjoyed with their new home, settling in to open their wedding gifts.

With our family obligations out of the way for now, and King Dimmy is out of my mind (and out of sight) for the foreseeable future, we're finally able to concentrate on training with the horses again, but at the back of my mind is the issue of new horses.

On a bright spring morning, Jason and I are waiting for Mel and Curlie at our usual place at the picnic table on the back porch.

"Hey Mom," Jason says. "I thought that we should get another Standard or two. *Lester* and *Raindrop* might be too old to run in the championship races."

"I was thinking the same thing, sweetie. Nothing against Glen or Reed, but I'd like to see what's available this time. Would you like to come with me to pick them out?"

Jason must realize that he might not be here when that time comes, hesitating, he looks toward the pasture. "Yeah, I sure would like to do that with you."

We have an unspoken thing where we don't talk about his big decision, yet it hangs in the air like a water balloon waiting to pop. It makes me sad to think he has this weighty decision to make and I can't interfere, no matter how I feel about it. "That's a little premature, Jason. We have plenty of time to look for more horses."

Jason shakes his head in agreement. "Mom, something's come up, and I need to talk about it with you. Mack wants to train with us. You remember him, don't you? He helped me park cars at Reed and Dr. Jess's wedding. I've been thinking that we're going to need another driver down the road. I know how much pain you're in when you sit on the race bike."

"I'm confused. I thought the kid who parked cars was named Rolly. Now you're saying it's Mack? Didn't his parents start a stud farm?"

"He hates the name Rolly. Can we give Mack a try? He comes to help in the barn sometimes, and wants to train with us as a driver."

"Is he eighteen? If he isn't, he's underage, so we'd need his parent's approval."

"He'll be eighteen in a few months. He doesn't get along with his Dad. They fight all the time. He complains that he doesn't take him seriously. He wants him to go off to college, and he flat out doesn't want to."

"This could lead to a confrontation, Jason. Haven't we had enough of those? And it could also cause bad feelings that could affect your friendship with him, sweetie. You know that saying about hiring your friends, or is that about selling them your car?"

"Mom, he doesn't wanna work for his Dad, and he'd be here and trained if I decide to, you know."

"I do know what you mean. Why don't you ask Mack to come home with you after school tomorrow so we can talk about it?"

Jason gives me a peck on the cheek while reaching for his cellphone. "I'll call him right now and tell him the good news. Tell the girls I'll be waiting in the car. Thanks, Mom."

"Don't thank me yet, we've not met his parents, and we don't know how that'll go."

As I walk into the kitchen, Mel and Curlie are coming down the back stairs. They grab their gourmet lunches, kiss me goodbye as they head to the waiting car. Moments later, Adrian walks out of the Guest House near the pool, waving in my direction. He's dressed in combat fatigues, not his usual jeans and a colorful polo shirt. Since his latest trip to Langley, he's in exceptionally good spirits. Levi asked that he train with a new group who are due to arrive at Ashwood shortly. They're supposed to be camping somewhere out in our back forty acres.

"Mornin to you Ms. Ellie." Adrian is using a lazy put-on drawl. "How are ya doin today thar, little lady?"

"Good morning yourself, Adrian. That stuff you've smeared on your face is hilarious." The image of a ridiculous tree stump table pops into my mind. "You look like you could blend in with the trees. Seriously, you remind me of a table I saw once."

"Here, gives me a smooch, sweetie pie." Adrian puckers his lips and grabs my arm. He's a comical sight with smeared green and brown streaks along each of his cheeks and a camouflaged bandana around his head.

Backing away to keep him from getting close to my face, I have to laugh at him. "No way! Don't smear that stuff on me!"

Adrian's white teeth look unnatural when he smiles. "Do you think Miss Mona has time to whip me up an omelet this morning?"

"You're not helpless, Adrian. Make it yourself."

"You're in a fine mood this morning, Missy. What's up with you? Did you sleep on the wrong side of the bed again? Maybe you need a little company at night?" Adrian grins.

"Sorry, Jason mentioned his big decision without saying anything, and it must be bothering me more than I care to admit."

"My dear little buttercup, you shouldn't worry about that stuff before it happens, that's still a few years off."

"You're right. Something else is bothering me. Dimmy sent a telegram! A telegram Adrian! He says it was a little disturbance and we're not to worry as everything is fine and honky dory."

He seems curious. "Did he mention anything about the oil explosions or the fires?"

"No. He didn't mention the oil explosions or the bombings, nothing! He said, everything is okay there, and he'll see us in June for Jason's graduation. That's it, can you believe it?"

He starts to laugh. "What did you expect from him, Ellie?"

"I expected some explanation as to why we couldn't get in touch with him! Or why he didn't think to call us before now to say he was alright."

Adrian looks surprised. "You do care what happens to him! And you think he should've told you all about the little disturbance that rocked that part of the world?"

"Yes, if we're family, he sure as hell should have told me what it's all about!"

He wrinkles up his face, rolling his eyes upward. "Sweetheart, he can't tell you any more about that than I can tell you what the team is going to do in the woods later today."

"Yes, he can! Especially if the little disturbance migrates over here!"

Adrian shakes his head. "No, he can't. It won't migrate over here, Ellie. That's what my team and I are here for."

Putting his hands in the air in a practiced jujitsu maneuver, he comically runs into the picnic table, knocking the screen door open into the kitchen.

"Is everything a joke to you? Can't you be serious for one minute?"

Adrian recovers quickly. "You are worrying about nothing, Mrs. Thompson."

"Jason also wants his friend Mack to train with us. I don't understand. Have you or Glen said anything about me not racing anymore?"

Adrian walks to the breadbox, raises the lid, and reaches in to remove a plate. Grinning, he says, "Thanks, you little sweetheart. You remembered to save me a pastry. Glen and I may have said..." His words become inaudible as he begins to stuff his mouth.

"Funny, Adrian. Now I have a sit-down with a strong-willed teenager who wants to take my place as a driver. His parents probably won't approve of this, you know."

"You worry too much, my little lotus blossom. Are you concerned Mack will be better at it than you are?"

"That never entered the equation. Now there will be more unhappy people in the racing world who don't like me!"

Adrian doesn't offer advice related to children very often, but when he does, I listen. "Have the meeting with this kid and give it to him straight. Tell him that you'll talk to his parents because he's under the age of eighteen. If they agree to let you train him, you could offer him a small salary. If they're starting out, they might welcome the training, because that knowledge can go a long way when you're trying to establish a stud farm."

"We don't have a stud farm, Adrian, and we race here."

"I know that doesn't have anything to do with what they do at their place, but I don't see where it's a competition either. It would still be good training for the kid and would let you off the hook a little bit."

"When did you get so smart, Mr. CIA man? That's excellent advice coming from a person who has no children."

Adrian lifts an eyebrow, stuffing more pastry into his mouth. "I do my homework, Ma'am. I feel like I do have children. I watch you and admire how you handle your kids. You're strict but loving, fair and reasonable, and you don't cave when they need discipline."

"Thanks, that was nicely said. Oh, I almost forgot to tell you. His Royal High and Mighty pain-in-the-ass wired $80,000 into the renovation account to start his wing makeover, so I have some more work to do upstairs. I'm sure he wants it done in time for his visit this summer."

Adrian blows his cheeks up like a balloon. "I'll bet you can't wait for him to get here!"

"Yeah, we all know how you bet, Adrian. You know, he never said anything about his precious ancient documents that he was so eager to get his hands on for so long. Maybe that fighting near the Royal Palace means that the crazy Fariq retracted his men. Maybe Dimmy told him that he has all the documents and he backed off. Maybe Dimmy called his bluff."

"Wow Ellie, you would seriously make a good agent. Unfortunately, I'd like to stay and chit chat, but I gotta go now."

As he says this, a distant whomp, whomp, whomp sound is heard. It must signal to Adrian that the group is arriving. He guzzles the rest of his coffee and stuffs the last of the pastry into his mouth as he points upward, waving as he runs out the back door.

Not a minute later, the old golf cart whizzes by in a blur.

Roland N. McMillan, Jr. is courteous and nearly as tall as Jason. Where Jason is dark, Mack is fair-haired and slightly heavier. After introductions, Jason excuses himself to stand out in the hallway, where I can see his legs through the fireplace screen.

Mack seems mature for his age and his easy smile reminds me of Reed the first time we met. We settle into a pleasant conversation along with lemonade and cookies to break the ice.

"Please call me Mack, Mrs. Thompson. I hate the name Roland," he says nervously. "I hate the name Rolly even more. My Mother is the only one that can call me that. Thanks for letting me come over to talk with you about racing, it means a lot."

"Tell me why you want to train with us, Mack."

"I want to train with Jason because it looks like a good challenge for me. I've been here sometimes when Jason is training with *Raindrop*. I stop by the barn sometimes after school, Mrs. Thompson, so I don't have to go home. Jason told me all about what you have to do, and I'm certain I can do it."

"Harness racing isn't rocket science, Mack, but it does take a certain amount of dexterity and discipline to race."

"I went to the track a few times to see Jason race. After my Dad saw both of you out there, he wouldn't take me again after I told him I wanted to train with Jason."

"Can't you do that type of thing at your place?"

"Dad doesn't want to race. He says there's more money in breeding the horses. I don't wanna do the breeding part."

"I suppose Jason filled your head with all kinds of ideas, the least of which is the amount of hard work it takes to concentrate on staying safe out there on the track."

"I'm a hard worker, Mrs. Thompson, ask any of my teachers. I can clean out the stalls too if you need me to do that." Mack seems sincere. "I don't wanna work with my Dad. Jason says you'd give me a chance. I love horses, but I don't wanna breed them." Mack takes a cookie and a sip of lemonade, then sits back to stare at me.

"What does your Mother say about this? Have you discussed your plans with her?"

Mack's face softens. "She's the one who encouraged me to come and talk to you. She doesn't understand why Dad is so bullheaded. He told me that real men breed the horses that win and I should suck it up and go to college as he did. I haven't done anything for him to mistrust me, but he does. I've never been expelled from school; not even had to stay in detention. Not once!"

"Do you have any brothers or sisters, Mack?" It may have a bearing on why his father might treat him a certain way.

"No, I'm it, the only son. He thinks that what I wanna do is stupid."

"What did your Dad study at college, animal husbandry?"

"Oh, no Ma'am, he studied mechanical engineering. He had his own business and sold it off a year ago for millions. He wanted me to take over the business, but I told him it didn't interest me. He got furious, and that's when he retired early and decided to—oh, I see where you're going with this."

"If he's going into a new field, Mack, how is he supposed to do that without any training? Perhaps he was hoping you would go to school to do that, so you could help run the farm with him."

Mack stares at his hands. "I didn't think about it that way. Why didn't he come right out and say that? Why doesn't he talk to me? Instead, he yells, and then we both get mad."

"Maybe he's worried about your future. There's nothing wrong with a father doing that."

Mack seems sullen. "Mrs. Thompson, he has it in his head that the races are all fixed. If I race like Jason, it'll somehow belittle what he's trying to do at our place. It doesn't make any sense to me."

"There might be some truth to that accusation, Mack."

His face registers surprise. "I didn't mean for it to sound like…he was accusing you of something!"

"I didn't take it that way, Mack. I can tell you with the utmost certainty that Jason and I do not participate in anything illegal and we don't intend to, ever. Some owners follow the rules, and that's what we do here, but there is an equal number that might not be as honest as we are. Those are the ones we have to be careful of."

"So, my Dad was right?" Mack stammers.

"In a way, he's partly correct, but there are ways to get around those people, and we can still win and do it honestly."

If Mack sticks around, he's bound to get an earful.

Mack seems thoughtful, wrinkling his forehead as he digests this information. "I still wanna train with you and Jason." Mack stares me straight in the eyes, and says, "I won't disappoint you or let you down! I can be your second son if you let me."

"Before I agree to this, I'll have to speak with your parents. Right now, you're underage, and we need their signatures on a release form before you can start any training with us. It isn't all fun, Mack. You'll have to help out in the barn, too."

Mack smiles, saying, "If you let me work here, I'll do anything you ask me to do."

"If your parents agree to this, you'll have to put in some hours after school and on weekends. It'll be on a trial basis of three months or so and take another three months after that before you can qualify to race at Billingsworth."

"Thanks, Mrs. Thompson, I won't let you down."

"Don't thank me yet, Mack. I'll teach you everything I know about driving the race bike, but you'll be training under Mr. Glen and Mr. Reed."

Mack looks puzzled. "What if my Dad doesn't agree with the training part, will you still let me work here? And I thought you were the trainer."

"I'm a driver, not a trainer; there's a difference. If your parents don't agree, then you can't train or work here, Mack. That's the way it is. We can't start the relationship on a sour note. Now, if your parents do agree, I can offer you a small salary. After the trial three months are up, we can talk about a raise. Does it still sound like something you want to do?"

"Okay, I think I understand everything you're saying. And yes, it's something I wanna do. I guess the next step would be to get my parents together with you."

"Don't worry, Mack, if your parents don't give their consent when you turn eighteen, I believe that you can decide for yourself. I'd rather it be under good circumstances rather than usurping your father's authority. I don't want to put a wedge between your parents and the Thompson family, as that could never end well."

*"Learn from the past,
set vivid, detailed goals for the future, and live in the only
moment of time over which you have any control; now."*
~ Denis Waitley

Chapter Three

Testing Theories

A few days later, Mack's parents arrange to meet with me to discuss their son's working at Ashwood. We are in the library having a strained, but cordial conversation. It's evident from the start that Meredith McMillan is a gentle, refined woman who cares about her son's welfare. It's equally apparent that Mack gets his charm from her.

Mack's father, Timothy, on the other hand, is a grayish bulldog-looking man who doesn't look pleased to be here. Mack begins to cringe when he opens his mouth to expound on his son's unwillingness to try a semester of college, and it becomes clear whom he blames.

"Mr. McMillan, I understand your trepidation when it comes to your son. Would you allow Mack to leave the room while we discuss why you're here?"

Timothy's demeanor is gruff. "He wants you to call him Mack, does he? Let's get something straight right now, Mrs. Thompson. Roland doesn't belong here. Get on out of here, Roland, so the grownups can talk."

Mack abruptly stands and turns toward his mother, who gives him a knowing nod, and he leaves the library. I chuckle to myself, as there are four legs on the other side of the fireplace screen, as Jason and Mack listen in on our conversation in the hallway.

"I put up with bullies like you all my life, both on and off the track and I can assure you, that I have no intention of taking charge of your son's life…"

"Now that we have that out of the way," Timothy says, rudely interrupting. "I…

"You didn't let me finish, Mr. McMillan. If you came here to spit in my face, then you can leave now. On the other hand, if you want to help your son, you can stick around and give him the benefit of the doubt."

Meredith takes a stance in deference to her husband's rudeness. "Mrs. Thompson, although my husband is discourteous; I will not apologize for him. I would like to see what you do here. Would you show us, please?" Meredith says sweetly.

Timothy has his face in his lemonade, clearly ignoring us.

"I would be happy to show you if you will follow me out to the barn."

Meredith says in a quiet tone, "Timothy doesn't always make the right decisions when it comes to our son. You are right; he is a bully."

"You have my sympathy, Meredith."

Meredith sees the expression on her husband's face. His lips are pressed together into a thin line, reminding me of a muskrat.

"Timothy, Mrs. Thompson is kind enough to allow our son the benefit of training. Are you coming?"

"It's not the training he needs, Meredith," Timothy bellows.

Meredith knows how to handle her husband. "It's what he wants to do! We are going to allow our son to follow a path of his choice whether you agree with it or not. Rolly wishes to train with Mrs. Thompson and her son. You need to let him decide his future. Are you coming outside with us?"

I am waiting near the doorway to escort them to the barn. "Follow me, if you will…" Jason and Mack are already there, getting prepared for our demonstration. As Meredith follows me, a reluctant Timothy drops his glass onto the coffee table, and we go through the kitchen toward the back door.

Meredith hooks her arm through mine, and we chat as if we've been friends for years. She comments on how spacious and beautiful our house is decorated, how clever this is, how extraordinary that is; who is our talented decorator? When I tell her that it was a collaborative effort, with the help of hundreds of construction workers, which took about a bazillion dollars, she laughs.

I cautioned Jason to keep quiet until our demonstration was over. If, after the McMillan's decide right there on the spot not to allow Mack to train and race with us, then we'll discuss further options.

When the McMillan's left, Meredith said that they would make their decision within a week. Whatever that might be, I'm hoping they say yes for his sake. Mack's enthusiasm may dwindle once the heavy training starts, but Jason feels that it'll be a good fit should he decide to quit racing.

About a week later, Meredith calls to say that after a little coercion, they both are giving their blessing for Mack to train with us. She lorded something over Timothy that had been brewing for a long time, and he gave in quickly.

But I know a little secret that swayed the decision in our favor.

Construction crews are at the Manor House once again to reconstruct and renovate Dimmy's part of the house. His must-haves include a suite befitting a person of his noble stature. To accommodate his entourage, our architect divided the attic into two separate spaces for each wing side.

A firewall was added, including bracing the floor and ceiling with additional beams. Both wings now have new staircases into our distinct parts of the attic. Once this work is completed, both wings will have separate HVAC units, thus allowing everyone to be comfortable at any time of the year.

The outside entrance that Akdemir's people insisted we include caused quite the uproar. Our architect, Lenore Berskinski, ALA, emphasized that: 1) the structure would look like a boarding house, 2) would jeopardize the integrity of the outside wall structure, and 3) would most likely render our National Register status null and void!

City officials agreed with her. So, score one for our team and zero for Dimmy! His people were not at all pleased to hear that they were not getting their way but eventually went along with it for the sake of keeping peace within the family. After all, they will have their private areas entirely to themselves, with a door they can bolt from the inside.

When I asked Dimmy for more funds, he replied quickly and efficiently with another wire transfer.

Our architect also reconfigured the front part of that wing to accommodate my sister Terre and her family. The common area at the very front of the house where the large windows overlook the driveway will double as a bedroom should the need arise.

Adrian sneaks up behind me as I put a book on a shelf in my office, and reaches around me where I stumble into his waiting arms. "Ahhhhhh."

"Glen says he needs you in the barn, my little cheese whiz."

"You could have used the walkie-talkie! You scared the crap out of me!"

"I know, but this is so much more fun. I have to accompany my team back to Langley for a few days. The gang here has everything under control, and Mack has picked up the slack in the barn, so you shouldn't miss me."

"Is it a clandestine or covert operation that you can't tell me about?"

In a husky voice, Adrian says, "Right, Ma'am, if I told ya, then I'd have ta kill ya." Changing back to a normal speaking voice, he adds, "You know, I didn't think Mack's father would let him train with us."

"That was sure a wondrous thing."

"What did you do to get him to change his mind, Ellie?" Adrian questions.

No one needs to know how that came about, because it still disgusts me. "What makes you think I had anything to do with it? Besides, can't tell you, then I'd have to kill *you*!"

"Okay, fair enough. Mack's here, and that's all that matters. Glen says he's a hard worker and hasn't given him any grief yet."

"I'm glad his parents gave their consent. We'll see how things go within the next few months. When do you have to leave for Langley?"

"The group is scheduled to leave in the morning. Hey, I have an idea. Why don't you come with me this time? Levi won't mind. We could snuggle."

"How can I leave in the middle of all this mess?"

Adrian nuzzles my neck. "Why don't you leave it with Francesca? She's a tough lady. She can handle it. You can't come to work with me, but we could get a hotel room. How about it?"

"It wouldn't be fair to leave this mess with Mother. The plumbers are coming tomorrow, and you know what that's like. I have to be on-site to negotiate and run interference with all the other trades that will be here. Our time will come, Adrian. I assure you, but not right now, okay?"

Adrian gives me a long kiss on the lips, and I absently put a hand to my mouth, remembering the encounter with Timothy McMillan that suddenly changed his mind about Mack. He cornered me in my office because he kept thinking about what I said that first day about dealing with bullies. Although he did not mean to be so forceful; he merely thought I had given him a signal.

Timothy must have been dreaming because I gave him no such signal!

He was so embarrassed at his inappropriate gesture that he turned it into a total turnaround, allowing Mack to train with Jason, and that was the end of it. I know from experience that it's never how things end, there's always something more. Timothy is sociable with some of the other horse owners around Jasper, and maybe he'll lay in wait for us as they do.

Now that Mack has joined our team, Jason thinks it might be time for me to hang up my racing jacket. He suggests that Mack train with *Lester* this season, but I'm having an internal struggle with my feelings.

I vacillate between what I *should* do and what I *want* to do. It's always difficult to give something up when you haven't entirely completed your goal. In this case, I set out to prove to the racing world that a woman can learn to train, race, and win.

The truth of the matter is that the pain from the old tailbone injury is keeping me from achieving this. Am I ready to segue into being an merely an owner? Perhaps now that Mack is here, he and Jason can bring the dream to life, while I let it go.

Dr. Jessica and Reed joined the family for dinner last week. She casually mentioned a pain management clinic that will inject Reed's knee. He somehow tripped, coming down hard on his bad leg and he has been limping noticeably. It's possible that the injections will help him cope with the pain to avoid standard opioid medications. A few weeks after Reed received his treatments; he can't believe how much they have helped him.

Suddenly, a thought begins to formulate in my mind! Could an injection in the right place help me manage the pain long enough to win a race?

After careful deliberation, I want to give racing another go and contact the same facility to inquire whether they will do this for me. Pain or no pain; I need to win with *Lester*!

Two weeks later, a disgruntled Glen has the jog cart ready on the practice track for me, but he's not looking too happy, grumbling, "Why don't ya give this stuff up? You're plumb loco, Missy." He shakes his head and talks under his breath. "Don't blame me if ya get yourself hurt this time." He's as concerned as any father would be.

"I'll be fine, Mr. Negative Nellie. You do your thing, and I'll do mine. Hey, whatever happened to, I've got your back, Missy?"

"I do got your back, but I don't think ya oughtta do this is all," he mutters.

After getting the first injection, there's little pain when I sit on the bench. "Glen, I'm confident this is going to work."

"Ya shoulda stayed retired and let Mack do the trainin with Jason," he mumbles.

"What a Negative Nancy. Who said I retired, Glen?"

"Maybe you should," he stammers, "stayed retired, I mean."

"Oh, quit your complaining Old Man and drop it, will you? I have to prove something to myself."

"What do ya have ta prove?"

"You'll see." Since the children are at school today, it's an excellent time to try this. Fiddling with the reins and crop, I purposely move about on the bench. If this doesn't work, then I'll hang up my helmet, but if it does work, I'm in it to win!

Glen gives me the signal to get ready. On his mark, *Lester* starts moving at a comfortable pace. So far, so good. As we come around the track, there's a surprised expression on his face.

"Go 'round again," he says. After a second go-around, Glen waves for us to come alongside him.

"How'd we do, Glen?"

"You weren't squirmin on that bench. And you don't have that pained look on your face like ya normally do," he says excitedly. "Look at this time, Missy!"

"Wow! I'm fine Glen; there's no pain! I'll be able to race on Saturday."

Glen wrinkles his forehead, reaching down to touch my shoulder, he says, "Then why are ya cryin?"

"Tears of Joy, my old friend, they are tears of joy!"

Forging ahead with training for Jason, Mack, and me, the exuberance is short-lived when the Racing Commission informs us that Mack's license will not be forthcoming. Even though we know that he has passed the examination, I'm betting five hundred bucks that I know who's behind this little snafu.

Since Adrian has not returned from his latest trip to Langley, I can't ask him to go to bat for us, and it will have to wait until he returns. Mack is understandably disappointed with this news, but we all assure him that it's merely a temporary setback and we'll deal with it.

It will give me the opportunity to prove another one of my theories. To achieve a champion status, *Lester* must move up in class during the next several races. It'll take work, but this gives the racing teams a real sense of purpose.

Our goal has always been to give Ashwood Stables back its long-lost prestige. Old Miss Abigail and the other resident ghosts of the house can rest in peace if we can achieve this. I imagine they're cheering us on as we train. At least it gives me comfort to know that they are here with us.

Are you with us Mrs. Ashwood?
Was it you that sighed?

Reed and Glen will drive the trucks to Billingsworth Racetrack. I'm a little bummed that Adrian isn't here as I have a good feeling that things are going to go our way today. Memories of Daddy flood back and the times we spent together as we felt the thrill that came with the anticipated win of the day.

"It's a beautiful day to win," he'd say. "Don't tell your Mother we've been at the track."

As we reach the grounds at Billingsworth, the aroma of new-mown turf fills the air, which reminds me how quickly something long anticipated can come and go. When I first embarked on my journey into the betting area, I learned that if I didn't take the time to study statistics for the races that day, Daddy and I wouldn't get a piece of the action.

Over the years, the winnings paid for my college education, set up my interior design business, and also paid for a sizeable down payment for our first house. It also helped us here at Ashwood a time or two.

It has to be my day to win!

Jason and I have spent the last few weeks not only training diligently but also studying the entries of the other owners. We want to know which ones are running stakes races and which are in claiming ones. I have included Jason because he has that innate ability to understand my system. Adrian thinks that this is all nonsense, attributing it merely to luck. Like Glen, he doesn't know how it works. They have tried my system a few times, but they haven't won much.

We sometimes go to the track on days we don't race to place simple wagers. It appears easy to others when I put my finger on the name of a horse, but it isn't on the fly, as much time and effort go into it beforehand!

It's imperative to know how the horse you wager on performs, and what the competition is for any given race. I know from experience that if you don't put in the proper sweat equity and the effort to understand the statistics for the horses that race that day, picking a winner or driving the winner to victory will not be easy. It's the prerequisite for a handicapper to win.

It poses an interesting theory about how we as the driver can maneuver our horses into the winner's circle. If you are a skilled driver and your horse is a strong contender, is it possible to avoid the pitfalls of losing by outmaneuvering the other drivers? Is this trickery or is this skill, because it sure isn't luck.

Of course, all the other drivers, trainers, and even the owners want that same outcome. That being, the one that declares their horse the winner. However, our primary objective today is to race and help *Lester* and *Raindrop* move up in class.

Jockey Jerry waves to us when we come into the barn. As usual, our stalls are at the farthest end of the barn, but we don't necessarily care, because we like where we are. We aren't concerned that the arrogant owners haven't accepted us. What does bother us is that we must prove ourselves repeatedly. Today might change all that.

I'm feeling mighty lucky today!

After Jason and I meet with the chief steward and he goes over the rules, asking us the usual questions, he releases us to race for the day. He does caution that there has been some talk (he means gossip) about Ashwood Stables and our ethics, but I'm guessing it's that same old bully tactic to get us not to participate.

Jason complains as we walk away, saying, "What do we have to do to win acceptance around here?"

"It's simple, Jason; we must keep plugging along and do things by the book. You've heard the expression; slow and steady wins the race? We'll take our horses up and through classes slowly and surely. That's how we'll do it because it isn't whether we're accepted or not that's important. What we care about is winning fairly, training hard, and achieving the status we need for Ashwood Stables; the rest will follow naturally."

Shaking his head, he places a hand on my shoulder. "But, why do we have to do that, Mom? Did everyone else here have to do that, too? It seems so ridiculous to me."

"Let it go, for now, sweetheart, okay?"

I'm not nervous until Glen says to keep my eye on the prize. "Please tell me you didn't place a bet on us." When he doesn't answer, I know that he has. "Glen, what did you do?"

"Ya said ya was feelin lucky today. Thought ya might win. It was only twenty bucks, ta place. Thought you'd be happy I was bettin for ya instead of against ya."

"You bet against us? I cannot believe my ears, Mister Glen!"

The expression on his face is priceless. "NO! I never bet against ya b'fore! Taday I put down twenty bucks for ya to place. Is that okay?" He snarls in his adorable old man way, but I know he means to win, place, and show.

"Yes, it's okay. What kind of odds did you wager?"

"Get that stuff outta your head right now, Missy. Ya gotta concentrate on what ya have ta do out there," Glen laughs. "If ya do win, you'll be motioned to keep goin around the track for a victory lap. I'll be waitin for you and *Lester* in the winner's circle."

The bugle sounds the call, and I get goosebumps as my body starts to shake. It used to happen every time I came out to the parade, but it lessens each time, thank God. The shaking only lasts until we're out on the track, then I forget about everything to concentrate on the race.

As the other drivers line up, we start to move toward the track. For once, *Lester* is in a good position behind the mechanical arms, but I know that doesn't always guarantee a spot near the favorite. Once the drivers go halfway around the racetrack, they'll encourage their horses to accelerate to the finish line, and we might be following in their dust.

It is where skill and training come in and where most drivers fail. I need to be ready for all contingencies, whether they're good or bad. *Lester* has moved into favorable spots instinctively in the past, but there are some new horses out here today, and they have as much of a chance at winning as we do.

The injections in the tailbone area have helped enormously, and there is no pain to speak of, so all energy will go into racing today. When the mechanical arm swings forward, horses and drivers begin their usual shifting as *Lester* starts to move at a leisurely pace. Some of the drivers are already moving forward as others close in from the side.

As we near the one-quarter mark, crops start to fly across the air to land on their horses. As I'm thinking how lucky we are to be where we are, *Lester* moves forward in a burst of speed. The interesting thing here is that my crop is still in the same position in my left hand as when we started.

"CONCENTRATE!"

Glen's voice echoes loudly inside my head. "Feel *Lester's* movements – be *Lester*." I always found humor in this when he said it, but it helps as I relax the reins.

The track marshal is leaning forward with a checkered flag near the finish line, pointing at us, motioning for us to keep going. At first, I'm confused, but glancing behind me, all the other horses are about two lengths away and have begun to slow down.

Lester leisurely continues to take us on our victory lap. As we near the winner's circle, Glen and Jason suddenly appear out of the crowd. A proud Glen clicks the lead rope, as Jason walks beside the race bike.

Patting *Lester* on the rump gently, he says, "Oh my God, Mom, you did it! It was you and *Lester* all the way. You were way out in front of everyone! I'm so proud of you!"

"I knew I should put more money on ya Missy!" Glen says smugly. "Good boy, *Lester*, Good Boy!"

Did Glen just do a little jig?

"*Lester* did it; I was merely along to hold the reins."

A photographer begins snapping photos of a blissful Glen who is poised with a flower garland around *Lester's* neck, while I remain seated on the race bike. Since I've never been to the winner's circle before and no one coached me on what to expect, I didn't remove the goggles or take off the helmet. We're going to laugh at this photo for many years to come, because of the unbelievably stupid expression the camera has captured of my face.

Our new barn mates immediately surround us when we return to our barn. It's not a bad showing for the rookies we are. By now, I'm both exuberated and exhausted. If Adrian were here, he'd make me laugh and try to stuff food down my throat.

Texting him that we won, there's no immediate reply. He must be out doing maneuvers, or he's at the gun range practicing. Reaching into the cooler inside *Lester's* stall next to the wall, I sit down on top of it to rest.

Glen is outside rubbing *Lester* down while Reed and Mack wait with *Raindrop* in the parade section, as Jason races in about thirty minutes. Instinct suddenly kicks in as muffled footfalls come into the barn. Pivoting off the cooler and flattening myself against the wall in an attempt to become invisible, moments later, an unfamiliar man's voice starts to whisper, "Did ya see what that bitch did out there today?"

"Yeah, she mighta won today, but she won't win next time," an equally gruff male voice sputters.

Voice one snarls, "We'll have ta tell Jim and do somethin about that real quick."

"You're not thinkin about what I'm thinkin, are ya?" voice two mutters.

Voice one says, "What are ya thinkin, ya idiot?"

"Like what happened the last time?" voice two says.

Voice one snorts, "Are ya just plain stupid, Earl?"

"Guess you're right, but we gotta do somethin afore she gets more wins," voice two mumbles.

I'm fearful that the men might come into *Lester's* stall, as nothing is standing between them and the mesh gate.

"She ain't here. Let's go, Earl. We'll catch up with her later and then we'll..."

"They're a buncha snivelin snitches!" voice two mumbles.

When they move away, I breathe a sigh of relief. Cautiously poking my head around the corner trying to catch a glimpse of the men, I pull off my jacket, exchanging it for a sweatshirt. Glen is coming into the barn when I tell him I'm going to the truck. He mutters an acknowledgment, asking me to check in with him when I get there.

Adrian texts a few minutes later: **How does it feel to be a winner!**

I text him: **Great!**

Adrian texts: **Sorry not there!** Not a minute later, my cellphone vibrates.

"Adrian! You missed the greatest race of my life! I wish you were here."

"I'm sorry for not being there. I'll do better next time. FYI, something's afoot, and I want you to be careful."

"What does that mean, Adrian?"

"Just that, you should be careful. Do you have your Glock with you?"

"No, but I'm on my way to the truck now to get it."

"I can't tell you much yet, but Levi has something on his radar that may be the other mess we were worried about before. Are you alone?" he sounds worried.

"I am right now. Glen's taking care of *Lester*. They came in right after the men left."

Adrian's loud voice blasts, "WHAT MEN? You didn't say anything about any men."

Oops, did I fail to mention this to him?

"Um, the men who were saying what a bitch I am."

"Why are you by yourself, Ellie? Did you forget our rules?"

"Reed and Mack are with Jason and *Raindrop*. Honestly, I didn't see the need to make one of them come with me."

"Get your Glock and get back to the barn as soon as you can! We can't put anything past these people!"

"Do you have names for these people?" I inquire.

"No, just stay safe, do you hear me?" he says, clicking off.

After retrieving my pistol, and sending Glen a text, I'm coming around the corner where I almost bump into Jenkins, who is walking with two men. I surmise they don't recognize me in street clothes and the ball cap I've stuck on my head.

Ducking around the building, I turn to see them moving slowly around our trucks. When the vehicle alarm Adrian installed goes off, they walk away quickly. He set the alarm to beep if anyone so much as sneezes near our vehicles. After ten times, it will shut itself off.

The disturbing part is that the two men are unmistakably the ones who were near our stalls in the barn. Were they scoping out how to undo the hitch, so *Lester* and *Raindrop* have an unexplained accident? Do they plan to medicate one or both with the 'race day med' and put us out of commission again? Why did they wait until now, when Adrian isn't here?

Mack texts: **Jason ready 4 parade, R U coming?**

After I text Mack that I'm on my way, I call Adrian to explain what happened. "I know," he says, "the signal came from the alarm. Oh, Ellie, I can't believe I'm not there for you."

"It's okay; you're here all the other times. I don't understand why they're doing something now. Can't you parachute in?"

"Even if I leave now, I can't be there for another three hours…unless. Hey, you have given me an idea. You'd make a great CIA agent."

When I join Mack and Reed, Jason's race has already begun. Reed mentions there was a little incident and he wants to talk about it later. Jason is doing fine on the track today; he's alert and mindful that the other drivers may have it in for him because I won a race today.

When a driver deliberately tries to invade Jason's 'space,' we collectively suck in our breaths. Then *Raindrop* must sense something, and moves ahead before anyone has time to blink.

"Nicely done, Jason," Reed whispers. "Number Eighteen got himself in some hot water."

"So? No one's going to reprimand him, Reed. If they do, it'll take months before they respond and then we'll be told that they can't do anything about it."

"I can't let this go, Miss Ellen. I'm going to file a formal complaint with the Commission."

"I suggest you hold off on that. We'll have to take our chances and not say anything. They think we're a bunch of sniveling snitches, anyway. They said that about me. No sense in giving them more ammunition."

Reed starts to chuckle. "Where did you hear that, Miss Ellen?"

"I had a little encounter a few minutes ago. I wish Adrian were here."

"Me too, I kinda feel safe when he's around," Reed says, without taking his eyes off Jason and *Raindrop*.

"You do? Do I make you feel unsafe, Reed?"

He turns to see the odd expression on Mack's face. "Oh no, I didn't mean it that way!"

"Hey, Jason moved into second place! He's right behind the favorite," Mack chirps, avoiding eye contact with us. "Are you guys watching this?"

I've figured that Mack doesn't want to know very much. After all, he has family drama to deal with, and ours compounds things.

"Come on Jason!" Mack yells. "Woo hoo! Nice going Jas. Mind if I go get them, Mr. Reed?"

Reed tells Mack to go ahead, hanging back with me. "That kid can't wait to get out on that race track. He's ready, Miss Ellen. He'll ease into it, I suppose. It comes so naturally to him like it does for Jason."

"Okay, Mr. Trainer. If you think it's that easy, then I suggest you try sitting on that bench and take a spin around the track a time or two," I mumble.

Hanging his head, I take a playful swipe at his arm. "Oh geeze, not that you have to work harder at it. Sorry, Miss Ellen, I stuck my foot in my mouth again, didn't I?"

"No, Reed, I appreciate your honesty. Okay, tell me what happened with your encounter."

"Some guys were snooping around the barn near our stalls."

"What's so unusual about that? Some guys were snooping around our trucks, too."

"How do you know that?" he asks.

"Because Adrian sent me to the truck to get my pistol."

"All I know is that they were talking to Jockey Jerry and some others, but he didn't tell them anything. Jerry came looking for you and said we should be careful."

"What should we be careful of, Reed?"

"Some people were not pleased that you won today. They might be out to get you or something like that," he says.

"Could they be the same idiots I saw with Jenkins? I think we already know who sent them, Reed."

"You saw what happened to Jason. I think we should skedaddle out of here and not come to race for a while, Miss Ellen."

"Reed, it's not our first rodeo. They can squawk all they want to, but they can't tell us not to race."

"I sure hope you're right, Miss Ellen. I don't want anything to happen to you, not while Adrian isn't here."

A deep voice behind us booms, "You should take your friend's advice, lady."

We turn to see several men standing behind us. Most of them are unfamiliar, except for the two scruffy ones in the middle.

"Why don't ya leave now? You could drop out of racin altogether and avoid some trouble. Somethin bad could happen to one of your horses, again."

I recognize his voice as the one near our stalls.

"Ya don't b'long here." I peg this man as Earl.

"Drop out now, and we'll guarantee no harm will come to ya or your horses," a fourth man growls.

As I take a step closer to the men, Reed grabs my arms to keep me next to him. "You think you can bully us and get away with it? Not this time fellas, I'm here to win, and you can't stop me."

"We'll see about that," the deep voice booms. "We'll see about that!"

The men move away, and when they're out of sight, Reed starts to hug me so tightly that I can't move. "Are you insane woman? You can't go around calling everyone a bully! They'll do more than that when you get all up in their face like that!" Reed laments.

"Reed, I can't breathe…"

"Sorry, Miss Ellen, but you practically challenged them to a shootout at the OK Corral. They're waiting for you to make a mistake! I swore to Adrian I would keep you safe and out of trouble, but you're trouble waiting to happen. I got scared when those men threatened to harm our horses."

"I was ready for them. I had a feeling something was about to happen, so I snapped the camera on my cellphone a few times and recorded the whole conversation. What could they have done in broad daylight, Reed?"

"For starters, they could have accosted us," he sighs.

"I seriously doubt they would do that with all these people around us. Besides, I sent it to both Adrian and Sheriff Rocky. Come to think of it, they shed some light on one of our mysteries, because up until now, we had no suspects responsible for *Didge's* demise."

"How are we going to prove anything?" Reed seems glum for a second and then adds, "Those guys couldn't have been the ones who killed *Didge*. They're too big and clumsy to have slipped into the barn."

"I don't know, but it's their word against ours. The only piece missing to our puzzle is who put those guys up to it. I have my suspicions about that, too. Come on, let's get back to the barn."

My cellphone vibrates, and Jason's face appears. He has texted a message: **Where R U?**

I text Jason: **on my way.**

When we catch up with him, an excited Jason nearly runs me over as he reaches to hug me. "Mom, did you see the race? I came in second! I almost won!"

As he expresses how his race went, it doesn't sound as if he had any trouble at all. I know what it's like out there on the track and I start to wonder about what he sees versus what the rest of us see, as our perspective must be completely different.

"It was a good race. I had no trouble keeping our position once it opened up for us," Jason adds.

Reed seems curious. "What about keeping clear of the driver who invaded your space?"

"Did you see someone do that?" Jason questions.

None of us thought of this angle of racing. Maybe when we put Mack into the mix, we'll have a better picture of what it's like, both on and off the track. Until then, we're tired and happy about what we did at the racetrack today.

As Glen and Reed lead the horses toward our trailers, several people are milling around them. Adrian's last text said the cavalry was on its way, but it appears as if they have already arrived.

"We got here as quick as we could, Mrs. Thompson." Adrian declares. "All Ashwood's trucks and trailers are clear, and you are free to go whenever you give the word."

"How did you get here so quick, Adrian? Did you fall from the sky?"

His grin gives him away. "We didn't fall from the sky, but we did come *from* the sky. Our helicopter came in handy again."

"Thanks for coming to our rescue." Adrian looks embarrassed when I start batting my eyelashes at him.

"Could you not do that in front of my men?" Then he shakes his head, as there are several women training with him this time. "Teams," he corrects, "not in front of the teams, okay?"

"Did you have a chance to run that photo I sent you?" I ask him.

"Yes, I did. Let's talk when we're in the truck." Adrian then begins to bark orders at his people. "Get one vehicle in front of the first horse trailer, and one behind the last trailer and let's move out."

We're in the last vehicle and pulling out when Adrian turns toward me but doesn't say anything. I'm wondering what he's going to say about the altercation with those men. Does he have an opinion as to what they were doing by our trailers?

"Say it, Adrian, you know about my big girl pants."

"First, I'm very proud of you, and I'm sorry for not being here when you won your race. Today of all days! I wanted to see you win!"

"We're all still in shock over that."

He smiles, saying, "I will make it up to you. How did it feel to win?"

"*Lester* was amazing. I was merely there to hold the reins. It's too bad I didn't know about the injections sooner as it could have spared me so much grief. What were you about to tell me?"

Adrian is quiet for a moment. "I don't know how to say this to you." I'm about to pinch him. "Spill it, Mr. CIA man!"

"It's almost as complicated as that whole thing about the Basim-Ravi, Abdul-Akdemir, Lenard, Gene, and Uncle Ruggeri fiasco all rolled together."

"No, please tell me there isn't anything like that going on. I don't think I can handle any more surprises, Adrian."

"I need to tell you anyway, Ellie. They found Andrea Simmons."

"Is that a good thing, or a bad thing?"

"I'm not sure. Andrea didn't exactly work for Uncle Ruggeri as we thought."

Asking myself if I want to know more, I say, "Where did they find her and who *did* she work for?"

Adrian sighs heavily. "She infiltrated Ruggeri's group many years ago, ingratiating herself with Lenard, but she isn't who she appears to be. She didn't tell Lenard certain things, because he would have given that information to us long before now. The unfortunate part about all this is that she is quite dead."

"I'm not sorry that she's dead, but if she didn't work for Lenard or Ruggeri, who did she work for?"

"Her real name is Solana, and she was either employed by Fariq or his partner."

"Oh crap, now what? Is he going to show up here and do us in, is that it? How worried should we be about this?"

"Tell you what, let's not get too excited about the speculation of things that might not happen, Ellie. Let's concentrate on what could happen instead. It's entirely possible that Fariq could do some real damage. We already know he has a long arm. He might be behind the men who accosted you and Reed today."

"About that, do you think I'm a bitch, Adrian? Sometimes I feel as if I come across as one, but do you think I am?"

Adrian seems startled. "No, Ellie. You sometimes come across as a little intense, but that's who you are. Don't let that get to you. When you get it in your head that you're right about something, you set about to prove it, that's all. You don't complain and whine about stuff, you attack the problem and solve things," he says gently.

"Thanks, that was a nice thing to say."

"We're probably dealing with a madman, or lunatic, Ellie. We can't prove any of it. Right now, it's a theory. Levi's team believes they're bound to turn up other things because we always…"

"…get your man, I know. If he's as sneaky as Dimmy told us he is, then he could be almost anywhere..."

"…doing almost anything," Adrian says, finishing my thought.

"He could even be at our house right now and who would know? What about Mother and the others!" I suddenly stiffen.

"Don't worry; we have that covered. When we landed, we put a team out on the perimeter and went in slow and easy, contacting Francesca and Mona. They're all fine, a little upset they all had to go down to the shelter for a little while. The ladies were in the middle of something, so they weren't happy to leave the kitchen."

"What about the girls? Mel and Curlie were supposed to be out shopping today with Dr. Jess. She's taken an interest in the girls; they might be potential babysitters, and she wants to spend some time getting to know them better."

"That's interesting. Could the announcement of an impending birth be far off?" Adrian inquires.

"No one said anything to me about it."

"We called Dr. Jessica to apprise her of the situation, and she agreed to meet our Agent Sara. The girls didn't mind, because they had the bulk of their shopping done. Sara is entertaining them right now."

"I liked Sara the moment I met her. I'm glad she's here. I thought this was all over except for Jason's big decision. Why can't it be over, Adrian? Why must we be tortured like this?"

"Maybe that's their intention."

"Are you telling me everything, Adrian? You aren't holding anything back?"

"Oh, that information is on a need to know basis, Mrs. Thompson. I can't talk about this anymore."

The *need to know rule* the fake FBI agents Lenard and Gene odiously drummed into my head suddenly flashes before my eyes. "I'll give you need to know! You tell me this instant or I'll throw you out of this truck!"

He must be kidding because two seconds later, he begins to laugh. "You probably would have thrown me out of the truck," Adrian quips.

"Don't make me hurt you, tell me everything."

"I'm serious about Andrea/Solana and Fariq, Ellie. However, as far as we know, the men who threatened you are a bunch of local hooligans.

We don't know yet who paid them to scare you. We have been in contact with Sheriff Rocky, and he's checking the photos and recording you sent."

"Thanks, we appreciate your coming to our rescue again, Adrian."

"We don't know how this will play out and that's why we're here. If we can establish that Fariq has people on his payroll at the track, maybe we can flush him out," he adds.

"What I'd like to know is how this stuff happens here."

"We don't know how or what he intends to do. However, we will find out, and we'll do something about it. That's all I can tell you right now, sweetie."

"I am so tired of this twenty-act-play. What do we do in the meantime, hold our breath?"

"Come on, my little pumpkin! My special teams are ready and able and here for you and your family." Adrian gives a little salute.

"How did Andrea, um Solana die? Do I want to know?"

He screws up his face. "I was hoping you wouldn't ask. Solana died of an overdose of an unidentified experimental drug with no name. But this time it disfigured her face somehow."

"I can conjure up the taste and smell of that drug by closing my eyes. The sick feeling it gave me returns to the pit of my stomach as if someone waved it under my nose. That's a bad way to go, Adrian, even for her. If the drug disfigured her face, how do you know it's her?"

"It's her alright. There's one more thing. There's a downside to having my teams here in Virginia. I have to bivouac with them while they're here, so I have to vacate the Guest House," he says sadly.

"Oh, you poor dear. I will miss our nightly chitchats and our little trek out to the spa."

Adrian sticks out his bottom lip, and with sad puppy-dog eyes, he says, "What I'm gonna miss is Miss Mona's cooking."

"Maybe she'll take pity on you and send you our leftovers," I say laughing.

"That would be very nice if she could spare a crumb or two."

A week later, my confidence slips away when *Lester* and I are boxed in so early, that there's no place to go. We spend the entire length of the race between two race bikes and two disgruntled-looking drivers who pretend we don't exist. Telling myself that it's okay, I'll merely wait and bide my time.

The following week, Jason and I are studying the tote board and the papers on statistics that were stuffed into my bag this morning. Glen will place a wager, doing a little something on the side. What I'm about to do will undoubtedly create a stir, or we'll chalk it up to a learning experience. I also predict that once a certain race is over and we've won our prize, Glen and I will have to speak with the racetrack manager before the end of the day.

Since our horses show real promise, they'll run in non-selling races, because we don't want to put them into claiming ones. We reason that we don't want to lose what money it took to purchase them before we have a chance to see if they can win a sizeable purse.

I know which drivers and owners we'll be up against and the strategy is to be at the head of the pack the whole time. *Lester* has been chomping at the bit to be first again, and that's precisely how we're going to run the race.

Glen knows how serious this is for me. He may not agree with what I'm doing, but he backs me two hundred percent! His only caution is not to push *Lester* too hard. *Lester* has flat-out paced his hooves off in the past. Have I been so careful, that I've held him back? Today he will have my permission to do it his way.

Glen unclips the lead rope, and we move past him as he gives me his best fatherly gaze, and says, "Ya be careful out there taday."

"We'll be alright," I whisper. "It's going to be a winning day today, remember?"

"Ya say that almost every time we come here, Missy. Hope your right." Glen puts his thumb up in his gesture that all things are A-OK.

When the mechanical arm slowly retracts, I loosen the reins and wiggle them to allow *Lester* to move at his own pace. He instantly quickens his speed, moving away from the other drivers and race bikes to take up the favorite's position on the inside rail.

At this point, I can't seem to slow him down and probably shouldn't try, as it feels so right. We all thought *Lester* liked to race side by side with other horses, but maybe he loves being out in front of them more. A slight motion comes into my peripheral vision to our right, but *Lester* takes this as a challenge and accelerates his pace.

As we come to the finish line, the camera catches us with a quick wink as the track marshal signals us with a checkered flag, motioning for us to make our victory lap.

"You're a good boy, *Lester*!" At the sound of my voice, he angles his head back, and I imagine he's having a little chuckle. "You're wonderful. You're going to get a special treat for all you did for us today!"

This time, I'm ready for the photographer by pulling off my helmet with the goggles still attached, and pulling my braid over my shoulder. When we get to the winner's circle, a beaming Glen waves to us. When we get close to him, he leans in to whisper, "I never doubted ya, Missy. But ya do know that some people are gonna have egg on their face after taday."

"It'll be more than that Glen, but I can't say the words in polite company. We need to gather our gear quickly and move out as soon as Jason's race is over."

"Don't push *Lester* so hard next time, because there was some blood in his nostrils."

"It wasn't me, Glen; it was *Lester* all the way. The only thing I had *any* control over was hanging on."

"It was mighty excitin ta watch, Missy. I thought when ya said ya was gonna be up front it meant ya was gonna be honest." Patting his pocket, Glen says laughing. "Thanks for this. I surely do 'preciate it."

I have enough time to get to the fence to see Jason move out to the track. He has a favorable position behind the mechanical arm, but it's disappointing as the shenanigans play out on the track. Despite this, he gets a third place.

While Reed, Jason, and Mack put the horses and gear into the trucks, I hang back to wait while Glen heads toward the betting window to collect our winnings. He'll also negotiate a transfer of ownership, because our little extra thing won, too.

As predicted, Glen and I are asked to meet with the racetrack manager for a little chat. According to some people, we've made a spectacle of racing. They've lodged a formal complaint against Ashwood, although he will not divulge who filed it. That's interesting, as no one complains when the Jenkins or Lassiter's win?

Does he think we don't know who is behind this?

However, that's not the worst part of the racetrack manager's lecture. What was I thinking, claiming a horse owned by Mr. Jenkins? Am I altogether stupid?

We have struck an arrow where it hurts, and apparently in the right pocketbook, too. The manager mentions that there might be some people out to get us, but again, he will not say who it is.

It doesn't matter, as Glen had so much faith that he won the twenty dollars he bet today, several times over. He didn't understand why we put in a claim, but he's certainly glad now that we are the proud owners of a horse named *Truly Yours*!

"Forgive all who have offended you,
not for them, but for yourself."
-Harriet Nelson

Chapter Four

The Royal Visit

In the few weeks that Adrian's special teams are here at Ashwood, they look as if they are guests at our small hotel we call the Manor House. The three women who came this time will stay in Mother's sitting room on cots we brought in, while the four men are in the main floor bedrooms near the mudroom. Adrian is delighted that he can remain in the Guest House and is pleased it turned out this way.

It took some convincing, but it made perfect sense that his teams stay at the house with the rest of the family. Adrian and Levi thought through my reasoning and pronounced it sound. With all the construction winding down and with all the people who continue to troupe in and out, the teams can watch and listen easier than if they were sequestered out in the field. They will save camping outside for another training session.

Their command post was set up down in the shelter, which allows four members of the team to rotate, where they can review the countless videos from all the cameras, except for the one in my office, as this is off-limits to everyone. The logistics for internet and cable access was finally resolved and should we need to spend any length of time in there, at least we'll be able to watch streaming movies.

Adrian doesn't let up on his teams one iota. The objective is to teach them how to go undercover while appearing as natural as possible. They wear street clothes and do menial jobs to keep busy, help in the barn, and also paint and paper while observing the many workers who remain to complete the upstairs renovations.

Adrian and Levi both think that Fariq won't try anything while so many people are on site here at Ashwood, but we've been surprised before. During one of our monthly telephone conversations, Ak-dim-er seems beyond irritated when I casually bring up what continually happens here in Virginia.

"When Fariq and I came face to face, I told him that I was in possession of the ancient documents, Ellen. Many Royal Ministers were present, and although he was visibly upset, he left quietly. The Royal Ministers then put out two proclamations this week. One named me to the Royal Palace as the rightful King, without dispute, which excludes all others. Then the second one that named Jason as the next in line to follow me. I am grateful that Fariq did not ask me to produce the documents."

"Doesn't that seem strange that he left and didn't ask to see them?"

"I told the Ministers that the documents are in a safe place and they concurred that everything was in order. If push comes to shove, we will have to decide to have the documents sent to me. Until that happens, we will wait," Akdemir says.

"Do you think that this madman is responsible for some of the odd things that happen around here?"

"I would not be surprised at that. My dearest Ellen, he will not hesitate to harm you and your family as he is a ruthless individual. He will try anything to take the throne; he still feels that he is entitled to the family fortune. His purpose is to possess all that is mine; however, I believe that he will not stop until he achieves this, or he dies trying."

I am incredibly apprehensive about this news.

I want to put my hands through the phone and wring His-Most-Royal Highness' pain-in-the-ass's neck! Instead, I say, "Thanks for the advice, I'll let Adrian and Mr. Levi know what's going on there."

Whispered Dreams

Odd things have begun to happen. It started about a week after Adrian's team arrived. They are not merely ghostly events, but baffling and mysterious things such as; I'll set a book down in one room, then find it in another. Mel complained she couldn't locate her favorite t-shirt and two days later, she discovered it rolled up and thrown down the basement stairs.

Curlie announced that some of her loose change she kept in a little bowl on her dresser went missing, and Jason grumbled that he couldn't find his guitar picks, but found them the next day in an odd trail leading to his closet. And the list goes on and on. Adrian tells us all not to worry, as the incidents seem harmless. Perhaps someone is having a good laugh.

As renovations begin to wind down, it comes as no surprise when Dr. Jessica announces that she and Reed are expecting. Reed is genuinely overjoyed, doting on his wife any chance he can. She finally admits to her workaholic schedule and is scaling back her responsibilities at her practice, which allows her interns time out in the field. She is also in the process of interviewing prospective veterinarians, who might want to join her practice, and then take over when she's on maternity leave.

As preparations continue for Jason's high school graduation and the completion of my sister's wing accommodations, we're also preparing for Uncle Dimmy's impending visit. It precipitates Curlie's concern about what the impact will be on our existing household once Aunt Terre and Uncle Dennis move in. Mother says she'll work out a plan where everyone has a job, thus making the chores a bit more even. Her chart will hang in the kitchen, along with the menus for the week.

Unexplained incidents continue to happen with increased frequency. We've tried without success to capture the culprit on tape and have surmised that it has to be coming from within the house. Are our ghosts trying to tell us something? We've all but ruled them out as, after all, there haven't been any shadows leading us toward or away from things since we found the old Duesenberg in the dairy barns.

Adrian and I are out in the southern pasture, sitting on the fence with Rosie at our feet. "I'll bet you five hundred bucks that someone is tampering with the tapes."

"Are you saying the footage is missing?" Adrian frowns at the thought of this. "Did you review them and find missing minutes?"

"I reviewed only the ones from my office. Your man, Carl, says he hasn't found anything, but I say there's missing footage!"

Adrian appears stunned. "If you're accusing one of my team members, Ellie, you'll have to do better than that."

"I've reasoned it has to be a member of your teams. It isn't my family or you. I didn't have a good feeling about Carl when he first came, and it hasn't gone away."

"We screened and rescreened these people, Ellie. I'd trust each of my team members with my life because I'm that sure of them!"

"It has to be the only explanation for why we can't catch whoever is doing this. It isn't one of our ghosts because I would know if it were. Why can't I go to the shelter then?"

Adrian tries to keep concern out of his voice. "Carl never said he was keeping you out of the shelter."

"Doesn't that give rise to suspicion? Even Mother and Mona are getting edgy about the stuff that's going missing or moved. Glen said that he found a bottle of liniment on the floor of *Frack's* stall. He swore he locked it up the day before."

"I see what you mean, Ellie. What do you think we should do?"

"Can we set a little trap for the culprit?"

"Sure, let's try that," he says.

Adrian will conduct a full sweep of every building on our property, including the barns and garages, not saying anything to his teams. It will take him about two days, as he has to do it when no one's watching. Putting Special Agent Sara in charge of the entire team (which includes Carl), Adrian has given her orders to reconnoiter out in the field for practice maneuvers.

While Adrian is busy, I review and recheck the footage from the surveillance equipment in my office, and there's nothing unusual on them. Wandering down to the basement to grab a bottle of wine for dinner, I don't turn on the small light, just in case. Out of curiosity, when I pull the shelves away to reveal the steel door, there's something that looks like a spider web over the lock. Stepping gingerly away, I call Adrian, but he doesn't answer his cellphone.

Agent Carl Jacobs told Adrian that while a threat is present, he will keep the door locked at all times and he alone will be responsible for the single key. He doesn't have the only key; I only let him think he does. Wondering if this is booby-trapped, I call Adrian again, and this time he answers.

Adrian understands our potential dilemma. He asks me to stop any further movement. When he gets to the basement, he puts a finger to his lips and moves gingerly into the wine room where he sniffs here and there like a dog.

"Stand back," he whispers. Holding a small device, a string shows up in the darkness. He motions to back away, and we go out to the southern pasture, where we know it's safe to talk. Adrian makes two calls.

He has a strange look on his face. "I'm going to give it to you straight, Ellie. I found some equipment in Reed and Dr. Jess's bedroom that I know you didn't authorize. Do you still have the original invoices from the surveillance company?" Adrian says soberly.

"You don't think they're responsible, do you? Gerald Tillman sent us to them. They're a reputable company. There must be another explanation. I have all the invoices in my office. What was that string thing?"

Adrian seems genuinely perplexed. "I don't know. I've never seen anything like it before."

"It looked like part of a spider web to me. Then how did you know what to do with that thingy you used?"

"Levi's electronic guru, Jewels, gave it to me. He said it could detect ultraviolet light. If there's ever something that I can't see, I'm to point it at it. Whatever it is will show up."

"This is straight out of a James Bond movie, Adrian. We can't go into the shelter. If Carl comes back, he'll know right away we've been there."

"It's kind of clever, Ellie. Something is there alright; it showed up very clearly. Let's see if Sara has anything." Adrian tries to contact Agent Sara, but there's no response. "We'll have to be as sneaky about this as he is. Sara isn't answering. I don't have a good feeling about this."

"We only have three days before Terre gets here! We have to get this under control. Terre won't want to stay here if we don't stop this ridiculous stuff!"

I'm beginning to get a sharp pain in my chest as fear starts to set in. Adrian must see the terror on my face and reaches to reassure me that we must keep a positive attitude. Using the walkie-talkie, he begins to alert Glen and Reed, instructing them to round up the boys, Mona and Mother and meet us on the back porch. Adrian assures them that everything is under control, holding off telling them his plans for fear they might panic.

Levi's instructions are to stay at the Manor House. About an hour later, several U.S. Marshalls, Sheriff Rocky, and their bomb squad unit slowly move up our driveway in silenced vehicles.

As the Marshalls go in search of Sara and the other team members, handlers take search dogs into the house while Adrian continues his sweep, discovering additional equipment in the dining room, the Guest House, and the downstairs hallway.

"The squad gave the all clear sign," Sheriff Rocky announces stoically about an hour later. "The Marshalls are on their way back to the house, but the news is not good. They found the group and thought they were all dead, b'cause none of them were movin. Your Agent Sara was wakin up and told them she studied languages and detected a slight slur when that Carl person said a certain word."

Adrian goes into CIA mode. "What kind of word, Sheriff?"

"Didn't say, but he immediately became defensive and overtook them usin a Police Taser first, then injectin them with somethin. When everyone was unconscious, he took all their weapons, and any communication devices they had, and hightailed it right outta there."

Adrian reaches for my hand, pulling me into his arms. Tears are forming in my eyes. "How on God's green earth can this happen? What do we have to do to get this monkey off our backs? What are we going to do?"

Sheriff Rocky waits patiently. "I don't know what you're mixed up in, Ma'am, but this is outta my league. Your man Adrian and his teams are the best at this, not us. We'll stand by, should you need assistance, Mr. Adrian."

"Thank you, Sheriff, we'll take it from here," Adrian says politely.

We have a right to be upset. Our *secure* world is not very secure right now and those who have sworn to keep us all safe are now the ones that have come into question. Although Levi and Adrian assured us of our family's safety, I'm understandably skeptical.

The surveillance equipment invoices are right where I put them, as they were hidden. All papers for the stables, along with the remaining ancient documents, are safely behind a panel in my office. Checking the invoices against the actual equipment, it becomes apparent that none other than the General Contractor, Mr. Tom Grayson himself, installed the additional pieces Adrian found.

Stopping to question myself, I wonder if I said anything derogatory about Dimmy. None comes to mind although I did refer to the King a few times as his Most Royal pain-in-the-ass, and mispronounced his name several times.

What could be so significant that someone wants to spy on us?

The U.S. Marshalls went to Grayson's address; however, it came as no surprise when they found his house was vacant! A neighbor said that there were no long goodbyes, no garbage cans left at the curb, he went poof!

"Carl's gone, Grayson's gone. What does this mean, Adrian? It's the Leotard and Genocide theatrics all over again! How is this even possible?"

"I know this is disturbing, but you have to stay positive, Ellie. Levi told me they are covering every contingency."

"Again, we have to rely on Levi. Do you think he's as sick of this stuff as we are?"

Adrian mutters, "I would sleep with your Glock and carry it with you to be sure."

Depression slowly begins to seep in because this transcends all reason. "Will everything happen all over again?"

"Ellie, you have to stop thinking like that!"

When the rest of the family weighs in on our situation during our nightly discussion around the dinner table, Jason is the first to voice his opinion.

"Mom, we all need you to be the rock that you are. Don't let them get to you or they'll think they won. United we stand, remember?"

It reminds me that we said that, and it wasn't too long ago either.

Mel chimes in with, "Divided we fall."

Curlie's face shows fear, and she begins to whimper. "I don't know what to say. I'm scared, Mama."

Adrian says, "Don't worry, sweetheart. We won't let anything happen to you. I promised you a while ago that we'd protect you, and we'll find and catch whoever did this."

Mother's unimpeachable wisdom comes shining through as she says, "We must have faith that we'll be alright, everyone. Let's all pray for the men and women who came here today. They risked their lives for us, and we should be grateful."

Even after all we've been through, and after all the training Adrian has had, along with the strong fortitude of each person who dwells within this house, there is the slimmest chance that something awful might still happen.

And that, most of all, is what worries me.

Terre and her family are due to arrive at any minute. We're sitting along the fence at the entrance to Ashwood to welcome them to their new home. They left the greater Chicago area five days ago, taking a detour to give their moving van time to get here. Everything has been set up per her instructions.

After part of Adrian's teams went back to Langley, Agent Sara wanted to stay, but Levi explained that a new team would be coming. This time, the agents are seasoned members that include only those handpicked by Adrian and himself. This team will consist of Jake and Josh, who are traveling with Terre and her family.

A cloud of dust on the distant horizon signals their arrival. When the two-car entourage turns down the two-lane road, Adrian squeezes my hand and whispers, "They're almost here, no worries, Ellie, okay?"

"I'll try…"

By dinner that night, everyone has settled into their rooms. They've been on a tour of the Manor House, the barns, and the property. We then settle in for our first meal together, all fourteen of us. Arriving mere minutes after Terre and her family, Adrian's group will camp outside with Jake and Josh.

About a week later, we are waiting for Uncle Ak-dim-er's visit. We are not outside sitting on the fence, as protocol dictates that we greet his Most Royal Highness (pain-in-the-ass) lined up in the vestibule.

Adrian taps his earpiece, giving the thumbs up sign as the waiting royal limousines are granted access through our gate. One of Adrian's men stands guard at the entrance as another is near the front door. From where I stand, Jake steps toward the rear door of the first limousine as Josh moves toward the second vehicle. As the limo door opens, Jam-ale climbs out, turning to reach in to help Uncle Dimmy and another man.

Once the men are near the front door, Josh helps a young woman, out of the limo along with another woman. Although their faces are partially covered, I know who they are. I recognize the woman who helped me dress that first night I had dinner with the Prince and his Bigness. Trying to stay focused, I put this information into one of the filing drawers in my brain marked CLOSED.

When the Royal Household reaches the vestibule, per pre-set protocols, Akdemir introduces the man as his aide Turlock. He does not look familiar. The women do not receive introductions and stand off to the side until we're finished.

Protocols came for the arrangements of the three men, but not for the women. Deciding that we'll not worry about that, because they can figure it out for themselves!

Their specific protocols also dictate that '*King Akdemir and his entourage are shown their set of suites,*' along with serving them '*refreshments*' upon their arrival. They must be given '*several hours of rest*' before '*providing a meal from the prearranged menu*' to be '*served precisely at 7:00 p.m.* (EST).'

Once we complete the royal formalities and the group is resting, Jam-ale appears in my office doorway. Ducking his head to fit under it, he says, "Ma'dame, His Royal Highness King Akdemir wishes that you come to speak with him in his suite."

"You can tell his Royal Highness that I am head of household here, and I happen to be in the middle of something important. If he wishes to speak with me, he can come down here."

Jam-ale's face registers surprise. I've decided not to treat Uncle Dimmy and his entourage any differently than any other guests (protocols be damned). We did not go out of our way for the private investor, Mr. C and I don't intend to do it for him. A shudder runs up my spine when Lenard's face pops into my mind. He was so adamant about that visit, not to mention his ridiculous protocols!

"As you wish, Ma'dame, I will inform His Royal Highness." Ducking his black mane under the door opening, Jam-ale backs slowly away.

Ten minutes or so later, Ak-dim-er wraps on the doorjamb. "May I have a word with you, dearest Ellen?"

Shoving the stacks of papers to the side of the desk, I motion for him to sit on the sofa, but I don't stand up. "Certainly. Is your suite to your liking? Are you comfortable, Dimmy? You have rested from your long journey?"

"Yes, my dearest Ellen, we are quite comfortable." Akdemir gives my office a good look around, and by the expression on his face, he's probably comparing it to his ginormous library back home.

"Did we perform our duties to the Royal Family when you arrived? Is there anything you require?"

"You followed the guidelines to the letter. My people are most comfortable. Sheyanna has a list of items that she will need to prepare for our meals. Unfortunately, our chef was unable to accompany us on our journey, but Sheyanna will see to everything."

"Your aide Turlock sent a list of the ingredients. We secured most of them already, but if Sheyanna needs additional items, one of the men will be glad to take her into town. She is the older of the two women who came with you today?"

"Yes, after she rests for a while longer, one of your men can accompany her to your shopping place," Dimmy says politely.

I know better than to come right out and ask if the younger one is his mistress. "Of course, Mother will be delighted to accompany her. And the younger one? What is her name?"

"Her name is Tieynza. She is Sheyanna and Turlock's youngest daughter. Turlock is my mother's brother, my uncle, and most trusted adviser. You will remember the women from your stay with us?" Dimmy smiles sheepishly. "She is young; however, she is not my mistress, Ellen, she is my niece. They are part of the Royal Household, you see."

"I never meant to insinuate that she was..."

"I do not have a mistress or a wife since Fariq had them removed some time ago. I felt that the women would be safest with us rather than leave them at the Royal Palace. Turlock has two additional daughters that have been sent to London to study. It is not safe for the rest of them to be at the Royal Palace without us. Fariq has been hiding, but we know he is capable of surprise. May I have the ancient documents, when it is convenient for you, of course."

"I will see that you have them before dinner tonight."

"Thank you. I am delighted to be here again. Jason looks well. He seems more mature than when I last saw him. His resemblance to Basim is uncanny."

"He reminds me a lot of his father. He has some of his better qualities."

"Thank you for making us so welcome, dearest Ellen. I will see you at the designated time for dinner. Excuse me now."

When I don't say anything and don't stand up, he nods his head and leaves my office. It will be a long three weeks, but hopefully a smooth visit without any bombshells. Once I hand over the ancient documents,

I will assume my role in any future schemes he might have will be minimal.

Jason's graduation day has arrived. Each graduate can invite ten guests to attend the ceremony, which means that someone will have to stay behind. To remedy the situation, Levi advised that King Akdemir and his entourage remain at Ashwood.

When the graduation festivities are over, we return to the Manor House to start our party. During dinner, Uncle Dimmy stands to propose an uncharacteristic toast. He wishes Jason health and happiness on his journey, whatever that might be. There is no mention of him going to Saudi Arabia, no comments of taking up his rightful place as his heir, and everyone breathes a collective sigh of relief when he finally stops talking and sits down.

After dinner, Jam-ale asks us to assemble in the living room so that Uncle Dimmy can present gifts to the family. To Jason, he bestows a sum of money for the express purpose of higher education, no mention of a car, motorcycle, or anything with wheels. Moving quickly, I pluck the check from Jason's fingers, at which time he moans that he wanted to hold it for a moment.

Uncle Dimmy gives Mel and Curlie mounds of fabric, several pairs of slipper-shoes dyed to match, and gobs of jewelry. While they drool over that, Mother graciously accepts a small chest that contains loose precious stones. She puts her hand to her mouth to express delight, then asks what she should do with them.

Jam-ale then pushes a large box toward me. When I open the flap, it contains a wooden world globe with a brass ring around the middle. He stands beside the box and leans down to press a small indentation. The top of the first globe opens, and a smaller orb pops up from the middle. No wonder Jam-ale laughed at me that day in the library, he knew the secret and chose not to say anything.

"Oh look, this one's in English. I admired this piece in your library, but Jam-ale never mentioned that it opened. Thank you for your extravagant gifts, Uncle Dimmy."

"You are very welcome, my dear Ellen. I trust that all of you like your gifts?"

As Mother fawns over the precious stones, the girls touch the fabric and the jewelry, saying they feel like princesses. Catching Dimmy's glance as he's about to say something, I silently will him not to, because I'm not ready to deal with that yet. I hope to never deal with it, but Adrian knows my girly girls. It's only a matter of time before they figure it out for themselves.

We settle into a routine of sorts, with my family going on about their business as Dimmy and his people go on with theirs. We get up early, while His Royalness and his group seem to be on a later schedule. We attribute that to the difference in time, but it suits us perfectly because we aren't bumping into each other.

Jason, Mack, and I take turns practicing early in the morning before it gets too hot. It will be the first time all three of us are practicing together. Our trainers are giving Mr. Jenkins' horse, *Truly Yours,* to Mack to see how he'll handle him. Glen still chuckles over how we acquired this horse.

Adrian thinks that by having this horse, we could be waving a red flag at a bull. Glen and Reed are cautious trainers and would only allow him to race if they think he'll do fine in the mix; otherwise, *Truly Yours* will remain a practice horse here at Ashwood.

We had no way to hold our walkie-talkies when we practiced, but once Adrian modified our headsets, we were able to hear our trainers and vice versa. Our headsets work much like the wireless units motorcycle riders use when they're out on the road.

"Missy, get in the chute position," Glen's voice resonates in my ear.

"Let's see what *Raindrop* and *Truly Yours* will do with *Lester* there," Reed adds.

"Did you hear that boys?" I say.

"Yes, Mom," Jason says.

A beat later, Mack says, "Yes, Ma'am."

Lester inches his way up the middle as *Truly Yours* begins to hog the inside. "Why don't I go around the outside," I offer.

Glen tells Mack to nudge *Truly Yours* to the left so I can move into the middle, but he won't budge. Then Reed tells Jason to nudge *Raindrop* to the right as far as he can without going out of bounds. As *Truly Yours* inches his way closer to *Raindrop*, the room between them closes.

"Can you see this? I wonder who taught him that little maneuver." Pulling the left rein slightly to give a signal to *Lester* to move toward the rail, *Truly Yours* begins to veer toward the inside again as if he's trying to block me. "Glen, can you see this?"

"Yeah, Missy, don't understand it. Can ya try getting *Lester* in b'tween 'em again?"

"I'll try, Glen, but he doesn't seem to want me there."

Glen and Reed are near the fence gate as Turlock, Jam-ale, and Jake approach. Suddenly feeling self-conscious, I now wish we'd aborted our training today. The injections are slowly wearing off, and it's increasingly more difficult to sit on the dimpled bench. The doctor warned me that this could happen. It's put up or shut up because there can be no more injections for a while.

"Mack, get *Truly Yours* either ahead of or behind *Raindrop,*" Reed pronounces in my ear.

Mack replies, "He won't budge, sir. It's like he's stuck to him with glue!"

"Jason, can you move behind or forward?" Reed asks.

"It's like there's an invisible rope holding these horses together," Jason grumbles. "Whenever I move *Raindrop*, *Truly Yours* moves in the same direction!"

Glen and Reed begin to wave us off the track. Jam-ale moves to speak with them. They talk for a few minutes as Jason, Mack and I remain on the jog carts. He then approaches *Truly Yours,* where he runs a hand along the outside of each leg, and then checks each hoof.

Jam-ale converses with Glen and Reed again, then goes back to the horse and starts poking into its right ear, then does the same thing to the left one. He then asks me to call Adrian.

Adrian says he'll be with us as soon as he can get away from going over plans for our upcoming trip to the racetrack with his new teams, Alpha and Delta.

Glen saunters over and bends to whisper, "The Big Man thinks there's somethin fishy gonin on with that horse, Missy. Reed's gonna call Dr. Jess ta make sure."

Dr. Jess will send the new doctor she recently hired because she won't come near our animals due to her pregnancy. Dr. Hamilton did not appreciate our snooping into his background, making that abundantly clear the first time he came to Ashwood. Adrian assured us that he is indeed a licensed veterinarian and fully accredited.

We've been fooled before, and more times, than I care to count!

Adrian joins us as Dr. Hamilton arrives. He is a tall, thin man with black-rimmed glasses that enhance his dark brown eyes, but the baseball cap gives him a comical appearance, along with the torn blue jeans and hand tooled boots.

He looks into *Truly Yours'* left ear, then opens his bag to extract a small magnifying glass and slender needle-like tweezers. He asks that someone hold the horse as he swabs the area and Jam-ale takes hold of the halter that keeps the horse from moving his head.

Dr. Hamilton extracts a small black oblong object that reminds me of a beetle. It doesn't move. "What on earth is this?" he mutters.

"I have never seen anything like it," Reed gapes quizzically at the object.

Dr. Hamilton rudely observes, "And surely not in an animal's ear!"

"Welcome to my world," I mumble to myself. At that instant, I wonder if the whole world has gone bonkers.

"May I have that?" Adrian has a small plastic bag open and asks Reed to drop it in. He seals the bag, and puts it into his shirt pocket, then leans toward the doctor to talk. Dr. Hamilton then excuses himself and walks toward his vehicle without saying another word.

"What did you say to him, Adrian? He didn't even say goodbye," I ask.

Adrian bends to whisper, "I told him that he isn't to speak of this to anyone because the IRS is auditing you. He seemed worried about something of his own and said he had to go take care of another patient."

"You are such a clever devil. Is that thing what I think it is? Why didn't we notice it before?"

Adrian sighs. "I don't know, but the Big Guy thinks the horse will respond now that it's out."

"I don't get it. *Truly Yours* never acted that way before today."

"Maybe that thing was just activated, Ellie."

"How could a little thing in his ear be responsible for that horse not letting me into the middle? Horses don't respond that way unless they're trained to do that."

Adrian does his imitation of the Twilight Zone tune, rolling his eyes and clutching his chest. "Maybe it's some high-tech stuff from the future. Have to get back to work," he says patting his pocket. "I'll let Levi's team have a go at this. Maybe Jewels can come up with something."

Jam-ale stands close to *Truly Yours* whispering to him. He understands these animals perhaps in ways we'll never know. It reminds me of his gentleness, and it also reminds me of how ruthless he can be. Is he responsible for taking my notes out of the bottom of my red case when he took me back to Kauai? Perhaps I'm still a tad angry with him, but Adrian made me swear never to bring it up. He and Mother both remind me that our minister's sermon last week was all about forgiveness. I should forgive and forget the incident.

By now, we're milling around the horses and carts. "How did you know it was something foreign in his ear? It looked like a big scab to me, like an old injury, or something," I say near Jam-ale's shoulder.

"I have seen this," Jam-ale says looking down at me. "Horse goes in a straight line, will not turn. It makes horse crazy. Fariq has many friends, in many places."

"Fariq has many enemies, too, Jam-ale."

The smile that replaces the scowl on his face shows those beautiful white teeth I saw the day I threw the cup and saucer at his head. He lets out a little chuckle as if he remembers that little scene too.

"I wish *not* to be your enemy, Ma'dame. You have the temper," he says under his breath.

Knowing he can squash me like a bug, I say, "I wish not to be *your* enemy, either, Jam-ale. I know people who have worse tempers, mine's not so bad."

"Then we have the agreement between us. We are not enemies. We will fight alongside each other to protect our friends."

"For once, Big Guy, we agree. But it's not only our friends; it's our family, too."

Jam-ale shakes his big mane. "Yes, we will fight alongside each other to protect our family and friends," he says, moving lithely away.

Glen whistles to get our attention and motions for us to get back on the jog carts to see if *Truly Yours* will respond now that the unidentified object (which Mack and Jason dub the UFO) is out. After several go-rounds on the practice track, he and Reed are satisfied that the horse will now respond to Mack's commands.

It'll be interesting to hear the explanation we're going to get about this one! I don't care who put that beetle thing in *Truly Yours* ear, what matters is that it *was* there! Could Mr. Jenkins be responsible for this? He had a whole night before he brought the horse to us after we won him. Could Fariq's long arm fit into this?

Are we back at square one? Will our lives replay events as they did in the movie Groundhog Day?

A few days later, *Lester* and I are on the practice track following the boys doing a leisurely pace when the bench gives way beneath me. It happened so fast, there wasn't time to react, and I came down so hard that my tailbone is either bruised or broken again.

The fall knocked the wind out of my sails, and as I lay on the track, I can see *Lester* struggling with the drag the broken cart bench creates as it slices into the compacted limestone.

"Ellie, can you hear me?" Adrian's voice brings me to the surface.

"Yes, I can hear you. I have a terrible headache and an equally bad pain in my butt."

Adrian picks me up and gingerly carries me to the Guest House. The only relief from the excruciating pain will be hydrating water and cold compresses. He'll tell me later that he went back to the practice track to investigate. He concludes that the modification to the bench might have compromised its structure. Perhaps it was only a matter of time before it broke on its own. He saw no indication of tampering.

It's time to hang up my helmet and concentrate on Jason and Mack. I might be more helpful to them by instructing them from the owner's standpoint. Although I can no longer race, it's not the end of our racing.

A few days later, most of the men are loading up the trucks as Uncle Dimmy, Turlock, and Jam-ale get into a limousine. They're all going to the racetrack. Mel is taking my place as gopher while Curlie and the girls are at a birthday party. Everyone else is with Terre, Mother, and Mona.

I'm lounging on a chair near the pool. Terre has brought out glasses of lemonade and snacks. Sitting down on the opposite chair, she asks, "Can I get anything for you?"

"There isn't a whole lot you can do to fix this, Terre. It will take up to six weeks before the pain completely abates. I'll have to sit on a donut cushion to avoid pain. When I can sit, that is."

"I wish I could do something more for you. We're not used to seeing you lying around."

"Adrian left the walkie-talkie. He's in the Guest House doing some paperwork. How are you getting along? Things have been so hectic that I haven't had time to ask if you like it here."

"I absolutely love it, Ellie, we all do. The girls love their room, we love ours, and the family space is perfect, but then I knew it would be."

Terre and her family fit in so well here that it's hard to imagine what it was like before they came. At least we did something right. I have missed her so much, and Mother is happy to have them all here with us and doesn't hesitate to tell us at every opportunity.

"The risk of a wrong decision

is preferable

to the terror of indecision."

~ Maimonides

Chapter Five

Decisions and Consequences

The pain slowly subsides, but I'm still unable to sit on any chair without the donut cushion. Mother and Adrian insisted I consult with a doctor, who confirmed there's nothing to be done except take pain medication and stay away from doing what aggravates it, such as sitting on the race bike seat.

It's a flexible appendage that will eventually snap back into place unless I want to undergo surgery to remove the coccyx altogether. But it doesn't sound like something I want to pursue.

I also know when to quit.

The family is aware that Melanie is more moody than usual, fussing more about her appearance, taking to wearing long skirts. It's quite a departure from her usual attire of torn jeans, colorful T-shirts, and sneakers. She no longer pulls her dark raven hair back in a casual ponytail, instead, she leaves it to trail down her back instead.

She must be stewing about something when she confronts me one night. Tieynza came to her one day to say how pretty she is, like the princess she is. That could explain her strange behavior.

"I thought she couldn't speak English, Mel."

Mel's face contorts. "I'm teaching her, Mother!"

"What exactly did she say, sweetheart?"

"That if Jason is the heir to the throne, then Curlie and I are Princesses; Curlie and me, PRINCESSES! That's why they gave us all that stuff. They want us to have it for Jason's Great Ceremony!"

I try to remain calm, as I know what's coming. "What great ceremony are you talking about, Mel?"

"The one where they crown him prince of something, that GREAT CEREMONY." Mel is unusually loud and sullen.

I need to say something witty, not sound condescending, or she'll go off on me again. "Mel, that's a long way off, honey. We don't have to worry about that until Jason turns twenty-one. And as far as you and Curlie are concerned, we don't live over there, sweetie."

"But we are *princesses,* Mom. And that is my cousin and Uncle and Auntie that are here right now! Why didn't you tell us about this? Geeze Louise! Why didn't Daddy tell us this stuff? Now he's not here, and we may never know anything about that side of the family!"

"I made a decision not to say anything, sweetheart. Think about what you said. Who is going to see you be a princess if you live over there? How many of your friends do you think will come to visit you? Would you want to leave everything you love? You would have to give all that up to live there. You would be by yourself, without us, as we sure won't give up what we have, Mel."

Mel seems unusually defiant. "How will I know if we don't go there? How about I go back with Uncle Dimmy and find out? Didn't you ever want to be a princess when you were little? Didn't you dress up and act like a princess, ever?"

"No. You're describing Aunt Terre. I have always been fascinated with horses. I'm the one who wanted to be a jockey, remember? There was no time to play dress up back then. I was too busy with my horse."

Melanie says in a quieter tone, "Curlie and I think you should let us go anyway. Just because you aren't going to be one doesn't mean Curlie, and I can't be a princess!"

"Mel, you might have something here. Maybe we can come up with a solution. Maybe Uncle Dimmy would host a wedding."

Mel's face softens, and she reaches out to hug me. "I thought you would say something like over your dead body like you always say and that would be the end of it."

"I would never have said that, Mel. Maybe I would have, but we can find a solution, can't we?"

"I never thought you'd want to go back there after all…could we ask Uncle Dimmy before he leaves? We all think it's time you and Adrian made it legal anyway. I know it's silly, but I want to see what it's like over there. I don't really want to live there, Mom. I couldn't be away from you and Grandma and the rest of the family," Mel sighs. "Until I go away to college, that is."

Thoughts swirl in my mind. Would Adrian agree to this? Could we lose Jason somewhere in the mix, if we were to do this? Can we take the chance that Fariq will pop up out of nowhere and do us harm? OH CRAP! Do I want to put my family through that? Can I stand to subject myself to being in the Royal Palace again?

"I'll talk to him, Mel, but Adrian and I need to discuss it. If everyone agrees, we'll see if it's feasible. But the possibility exists that no one else wants to do this. Are you ready for that answer?"

"That's all I'm asking. Talk with Uncle Dimmy and Adrian." Mel looks pleased with herself, saying, "Thanks, Mom."

Oh boy, what have I done?

Once I'm able to sit down without cringing, Akdemir asked if we might have tea together a few days before he and his entourage departed. I'm tempted to say no, but then remember that he isn't my enemy, his enemy is *my* enemy.

We are in the library sitting across from each other talking about the weather, our horses, what's on the menu for this evening, and we skirt any real issues until he brings up the ancient documents.

"Thank you for taking good care of them, Ellen. They are very old and very valuable to my people. I would like to speak to Jason about them, perhaps let him know how critical his role will be to the Royal Palace in the future. Are you in agreement about this?"

"I don't think that's such a good idea right now. Please wait for another time."

Blowing lightly on his hot tea, he says, "You seem rather preoccupied. Have we brought you stress by being here? Or is it the pain you are feeling?"

"No. You've been ideal guests, and we've enjoyed it. I know Mother has liked her time with Sheyanna and Mel and Curlie had a great time with Tieynza. They like the gifts you brought. And thank you for including my sister's family. Everyone is talking about the jewelry."

Dimmy eyes me warily. "Has the pain subsided from your fall from the racing seat, Ellen?"

"For as long as I live, my dear Dimmy, there will be a pain in my derrière." He seems confused until I point to the donut cushion I'm sitting on, then he laughs in understanding. "May I ask you something?"

"Of course, my dear Ellen, you may ask anything."

"Can this crazy Fariq drop from the sky at any time and come in here like that madman who was after my Daddy and Basim/Ravi?"

Akdemir studies me for a moment. "That is an interesting question. I suppose that he is capable of doing any bad deed, however, dropping from the sky is not his style," he says candidly.

"It may not be his style, for all we know this might have been a conspiracy he concocted with the people who put us at Ashwood. Do you think Fariq knew my father?"

Akdemir shakes his head. "That is highly unlikely. Fariq would have been a small boy when Basim and my father came up with their plan to take him out of Saudi. Perhaps Fariq's mother might have been instrumental in some of the goings on after that."

"He is younger than you, which makes sense, but why would his mother have anything to do with anything?"

"Some women can be wrathful," Akdemir says, sipping his tea. "especially when they feel their son is better than another. Jealousy is often the culprit."

"You could have said don't worry, Ellen, we have everything under control and we'll get the bad guys."

Akdemir smiles weakly, as lines form on his forehead, which speaks volumes about his awareness of the volatile situation in his country. "I would be misleading you if this were said. There will always be enemies of the state; that comes with the territory, as you would say. Along with our enemies are allies. These allies are the ones we count on to help us in our quest to apprehend the evil people and remove them from our society."

Dimmy says this in such a comical way that the theme from the spaghetti western, *The Good, The Bad, and The Ugly* starts to float around in my head.

"You're not exactly making me feel better. Are you saying that Fariq's mother is responsible for his behavior now? I'd like to know you have this situation under control, Dimmy. I don't mind telling you that this is stressful for us."

"We are prepared for most anything, my dear Ellen. Fariq cannot penetrate our defenses. If he does, I hold the one thing he cannot dispute."

"Are you referring back to the documents? Is this what you are lording over him?"

"My father included a special document that bars Fariq or anyone else from using a force of any kind to achieve ascension to the throne. Even if he murders me and takes Jason, the ancient documents are written in such a way that he will be bypassed."

I am speechless.

It does not happen often, and when I don't respond, Akdemir rises to stand in front of me. Waving his hand near my face to get my attention, he says, "Ellen, are you all right?"

"No, I'm not alright. What do you mean if Fariq kills you and takes Jason? You want my son to come over there in a few years with this lunatic on the loose? How can you guarantee his safety?"

"You have my word on this, Ellen. The Royal Ministers will also make sure of his safety. Jamaile and his army will guard him closely. He will have a personal bodyguard."

I take in a lungful of air. "That doesn't make me feel any better. What kind of assurance can you give that Jason will be safe?"

"I am very sure we will keep Jason safe, once he is in the Royal Palace. He will have a trained guard that will remain with him for life. You need to trust me on this," Akdemir states with conviction.

"What you aren't saying is that you can't guarantee his safety until he is *in* the Royal Palace? Jason has to get around the crazy people who seem to surround you? I want to trust you, but I have a funny feeling that things are not safe there."

Akdemir is quiet. "I do not know what I can say that will make you understand that we will do our best to make sure Jason is safe."

"Let's talk about this another time, shall we? I'm a little overwhelmed right now."

We change the subject, talking on for a few more minutes until Jamaile comes to the door to escort him upstairs. For the rest of Dimmy's visit, we avoid any mention of Jason's decision, sticking to the dangers of racing instead.

He doesn't hesitate to mention how hazardous it is; look what happened to me. I argue that Jason is young, healthy, and physically fit. He hasn't given any of us the slightest worry he'll jeopardize his safety.

Adrian pops his head into my office to ask if I'm okay. He can tell by looking at me that something's wrong. Informing him of my conversation with Mel, I ask if he has any thoughts on this subject. Is he open to the idea of a wedding in Saudi? He surprises me by saying we should ask Uncle Dimmy, as he's all for it.

"It would be wonderful for all of us, Ellie, and for our family. I'll even bet my Mother, my brother Samuel, and his wife would come with us. I'd go for it if you want to do this, most definitely."

"You might win this bet, Adrian. How much of a security challenge will it be?"

He cheerfully says, "It would be a nightmare, but we can get through anything, can't we?"

I'm surprised by the ease with which Adrian has accepted this as a way to start our new lives together. What will Mother say? When we mention it to her later, she is hesitant for a moment, but will undoubtedly go along with whatever we want to do as she feels that it will bring closure to my ordeal.

When I approach Dimmy about our proposal, his reaction is that of joy at the prospect of hosting our wedding. Then mentions that he'll take it upon himself to arrange a traditional ceremony for us. Now, all we have to do is choose a date.

A night after Dimmy and our esteemed guests leave, we announce that our wedding will take place in Saudi Arabia in November. We also inform everyone that our last names will hyphenate, becoming Thompson-Sellers. Questions abound as to how my children will handle their last names, and it rapidly turns into a name-slinging game.

Melanie thinks Obagur should be included while we leave off Andress as it's a made-up name. "My name would be Melanie Louise Obagur slash Thompson slash Sellers."

Curlie thinks that Andress should be a part of it, mostly because she's known that name since birth, placing it right after her middle name with Sellers at the end, because that's the order of things. "My name would be Cuthbertina Angela Andress dash Obagur dash Thompson dash Sellers."

Adrian chimes in with, "Maybe we should make it Sellers dash Thompson because S comes before T in the alphabet.

Mother laughs, saying, "If I kept all my names, including the ones given to me when I came to Virginia, it would be, Francesca Germaine D'Usseault Acuna Peters Dillon."

We break into laughter when Jason says, "You're all wrong, it should be: Jason Leigh Peters dash Dillon dash Andress. Wait, scratch Andress, dash Obagur dash Thompson dash Sellers. That's the right order."

"Can you repeat that?" Mack asks.

"Where do you figure Peters fits into this, Jason?" Terre questions, "That was your mother's and my last name before we married."

"How did Dillon make it in there?" Dennis asks.

"Okay, let's drop it, shall we? You can all keep your names the way they are. Adrian and I will hyphenate ours. That will settle any conflict."

"Have you thought about how we'll make this trip to Saudi, Ellen?" Terre asks. "We'll have to take the girls out of school."

"No, we haven't thought beyond that."

"We'll figure it out," Adrian says.

The consequences of taking this trip to Saudi will present itself soon enough. It's a chance of a lifetime, or at least it will help us to expand our geographical knowledge.

Throughout the summer, Jason and Mack help their horses move up in class, mindful of what all of us are telling them, inching their way to the upper levels of racing. It's also during this time when I try to teach Adrian the subtle points of handicapping.

Adrian is an intelligent man, who can't seem to wrap his head around my system. He gets frustrated when I encourage him to pick a winner without my help. He wins small amounts, but not the big bucks he thought he would.

Starting from the beginning, we go over the information I printed out for him, again. Unfortunately, this doesn't convince him that it's essential. As long as he thinks this, he will fail to win.

We are at Billingsworth Racetrack with *Truly Yours* and *Lester*, as Reed decided to scrub *Raindrop* from the lineup today because he has developed a sore spot under his hopples.

After the horses are in their stalls, Jockey Jerry spots me outside the rear of our barn, and we stop to chat for a moment. All the others, except for Glen and me have gone toward the grandstands. Suddenly, there's a loud pop sound followed by a small white flash. For a split second, the hairs on the back of my neck tingle, but I can't quite wrap my brain around the word to describe it. A cloud of white smoke billows out from the rear of the barn near our stalls.

Jerry turns to me with a terrified expression, saying, "What was that, Ms. T?"

"I'm not sure Jerry, but get your horses out of here – NOW! Hurry, tell the others to do the same. Cover your mouth and nose and take them out the front entrance!"

"Don't go in there, Missy!" Glen cautions.

I pull out my cellphone to press a prearranged number that will broadcast a text: **SOS-GET HELP!** "Stay out here, okay? I'm going in." Moving cautiously toward our stalls, I cover my nose and mouth with my shirt as apprehension grows into dread.

The closer I get to our stalls, the more the stench of something familiar permeates the air. By now, sounds of panic abound as horses and people begin to react as mass confusion ensues in our barn.

At *Lester's* stall, I clip a lead rope onto his halter, as Jason calls from behind me. Handing him the rope, I tell him to go outside. Then I wait for the cloud to dissipate, glancing into *Truly Yours'* stall. He's down and not moving.

Adrian is behind me, gently pulling me away, leading me out of the barn to where Glen and Reed are standing with the boys. He tries to reassure me that help is on the way.

"I don't get this! I thought this nonsense was going to stop!" I'm shaking.

Glen thinks this is absurd. "I'd like ta know who's b'hind this. What are you gonna do about this, Adrian?"

"I don't have any answers yet, but I'll get to the bottom of it, I assure you." Adrian lets out his breath. "It'll be interesting to hear what the racetrack people are going to do about it."

To stem the flow of unwanted gossip that their track is hosting horse killers, Billingsworth is shutting down the racetrack. People are shouting from the grandstands when the announcer says to vacate the premises as soon as possible and do come back soon. All of us are being asked to leave. Until the authorities have a chance to investigate, the racetrack will keep the lid on things, because they don't want the negative publicity.

When Sheriff Rocky shows up, he says we'll do this by the book. The word is that nothing had ever happened like this before we came along. NOTHING!

I'm pacing around the area, kicking stones with the toe of my boot. "Adrian, let's send the men and boys home with *Lester* and the gear. I'm not going anywhere until I get some answers."

"I figured as much. I'll tell the boys to saddle up and go home."

Our teams are understandably disappointed racing will be curtailed for the time being, but we also tell Jason and Mack that it's a little setback. We've had them before, and we'll most likely have them in the future.

"We can make up for this another day. It means more practice for you," I say, trying to smooth over a tough situation.

There's a battle raging in my head over this.

Adrian adds, "This is beyond comprehension. Levi will never believe this one!"

"What manner of madness is this, Adrian? Again, we have another dead horse? I refuse to quit. I won't let people bully me into quitting! How could this happen to us twice, TWICE! If Jenkins didn't want us to race *Truly Yours*, why in the hell didn't he shoot him, instead of what he did to him?"

"I don't think he's involved, Ellie. It's excessively sophisticated for the likes of him. Why don't we wait until the Sheriff does a little investigating before we point accusing fingers at anyone? Wonder what the Medical Examiner has to say about this."

An hour later, the ME has seen our downed horse, commenting about how *Truly Yours* died. He'll conduct a postmortem, then mentions that he's genuinely appalled at the insensitivity and waste of this senseless killing.

In all his thirty-eight years of traversing the barns, nothing remotely like this has ever happened at Billingsworth, or in the county for that matter. The usual culprit in the demise of a racehorse is, of course, overmedication--not an ugly gaping hole in its neck!

I would like to point the finger at Mr. Jenkins or one of his cronies, but in actuality, there's no real evidence to lead us in the direction of *any one* person in particular, because there are so many who *could* have done this.

Hours later, we are back at Ashwood, and I'm soaking in the spa trying to rid my body of the tenseness of the day. Adrian steps in to sit with me.

"I'm sorry, Ellie. That was a terrible way for the horse to go. I was hoping you would be in the mood for something special tonight, but instead, this overshadows things."

"I'm sorry too, Adrian. Dr. Jess said he didn't suffer if he died that quickly as it went straight to his heart. She has Dr. Hamilton checking with the medical people to see if there's anything that can identify that object shot into his neck. What kind of surprise are you talking about, sweetie?"

Adrian grins. "You have to guess. I bought you something recently. It's small, and it fits on a finger on your, um, left hand."

"Oh, Adrian; no one would guess what that is! Could it be a ring perhaps? A diamond ring, my dearest?"

Sitting up in the water, he says, "How did you guess? Can I give it to you now so you can feel better?"

"I welcome anything to help make up for the awful day we've had."

Adrian jumps out of the spa. "I'll be right back." Dashing into the Guest House, when he returns, he slips into the water with a rose between his teeth. Holding out a small box tied with a tiny red ribbon, he says, "For you, my little cumquat, will you marry me?"

"Adrian, what a romantic person you are." Unravelling the bow, the diamond ring nestled in blue velvet is stunning. "It's beautiful," I sigh, blinking back unexpected tears. "I'd say this trumps the day we've had!"

Taking the ring out of the box, he pushes it onto my outstretched hand. "Francesca came with me. I figured she would know what you like and she was right. I can tell you like it."

"It's fabulous! Thank you, darling," trying to talk as I choke up again. "This means we are now officially engaged!"

Sinking into the water up to his neck, Adrian says, "Yes, I think it does. I've had it since before Jason's graduation, but it was never the right time to give it to you."

"This does make me feel better, Adrian."

"Honestly, Ellie, I'm not sure that the crazy things that happen to this family are isolated incidents."

"There has to be some code of reasoning out there that states that several things have to float around in the atmosphere until they attach themselves to someone or something."

Adrian laughs, then snorts like a pig. "Where on earth did you hear that one, Ellie?"

"I think it has something to do with the law of the universe. Maybe it's written somewhere in some philosophy book."

Adrian smiles sweetly. "Philosophy. You mean like, *I say if your knees aren't green by the end of the day, you ought to seriously re-examine your life?*"

"Doesn't that pertain to gardening? Where did that come from, a comic strip?"

"Yes," he says, "How did you know that? It's from Bill Watterson, Calvin & Hobbes, does that fit?"

"Sort of, try this one; *Forgive, O Lord, my little jokes on Thee, and I'll forgive Thy great big one on me.* Robert Frost, English Literature, grade ten or eleven, I think."

"Hum," Adrian says. "Wait, I have one, *Life is the hyphen between matter and spirit*. It's Guesses at Truth, by Two Brothers."

"You are waxing philosophical tonight, sweetheart. I see a whole new side of you."

Sipping his wine, Adrian doesn't say anything for a while, and then he suddenly sits up in the swirling water to say, "*I hope life isn't a big joke, because I don't' get it,* by Jack Handley."

"Hang on; I remembered another clever saying. '*To live is so startling, it leaves little time for anything else*,' by Emily Dickinson. I can't believe these are still in my head after all these years. I remember another one. *The mass of men lead lives of quiet desperation. What is called resignation is confirmed desperation. From the desperate city, you go into the desperate country, and have to console yourself with the bravery of minks and muskrats...*"

Adrian interrupts to ask, "What's a minks?"

"It's an animal; it's part of the quote. Where was I?"

"You mean you weren't finished?" he says, tapping my head with the rose stem.

"No, there's more. Don't you think it's poignant? It's by Henry David Thoreau."

He doesn't seem amused. "You memorized a lot of stuff. You know Ellie, you don't have to show me up every ten minutes."

Spraying Adrian with foam, I say, "Come on Adrian, don't take it like that. *Life is not always fair. Sometimes you get a splinter even sliding down a rainbow,* by Terri Guillemets. Don't you get it?"

"No, please enlighten me!" Adrian is unusually sarcastic.

"It isn't what is thrown at you; it's how you play the game."

Adrian bolts straight up in the water, making a splash. "Are you saying that we've been coming at this...?"

"... all wrong. Maybe we should take a step back at this whole thing from where I first met Prince Dim-Dim and found out my dead husband was his brother. I'm quite serious about getting a whiteboard and putting all the main players on it with lines to where they lead."

"That might be the best thing, Ellie; maybe we should concentrate on that. We might come up with the whole enchilada and who done it before Levi and his team does."

"I do love a good mystery, and this is surely one for the books!"

"Okay you two, quit hogging the spa and move over," Terre says, as she and Dennis slip into the warm water. "I'm sorry about what happened at the track today, so let's talk wedding plans instead."

"You knew Adrian was going to give me a ring tonight?"

"Yup, let's see it, sister dear," Terre says, reaching for my hand.

"I don't feel like talking about that right now. Can we do that another time?"

"It'll sneak up on you before you know it, Ellie. Besides, it might help take your mind off everything. Oh, my God, this is gorgeous," she shrieks.

Dennis slowly shakes his head. "Don't listen to her, Ellie. She's excited to leave the United States for parts unknown. Did you tell her you bought your dress already, Terre?"

"Sister dear, why did you do that? We haven't discussed bridal colors yet."

Terre laughs and splashes Dennis. "A woman doesn't have to have a reason to buy a new dress. I should have purchased that matching bag and pumps when I had the chance."

"You do know there is a traditional dress that we have to wear, don't you? If I have to dress like them, then you do, too."

Terre seems skeptical. "What kind of traditional dress?"

"I'm sure that miles and miles of material will be involved," I say laughing into my wine glass.

"It's like a sack," Adrian volunteers. "And you have to ride a camel into town wearing it. We all have to wear them, men included." He can't keep a straight face and starts to snigger, snorting into the water.

"No, you don't! Don't listen to him, Terre. Adrian, don't tell her stuff like that, she'll have nightmares!"

"Camels are involved?" Dennis asks in surprise.

Adrian hoots. "Do you honestly want to ride a camel, Dennis? And you're not at all fazed about wearing a robe?"

"It's more like a caftan, and we aren't doing the camel thing, Adrian. I already told Dimmy that camels would not be involved."

Adrian sticks out his lower lip as if to pout. "But sweetheart, I was so looking forward to the spitting camels. I was…"

"You need to stop this. They do a traditional ceremony much the way we do it here, complete with wedding cake…" I am sorry the moment the words leave my mouth as a memory surfaces.

Dennis starts to laugh uproariously. "And shoving it in your partner's face…" He then sees the dubious look on Terre's face.

"I remember Dennis." Terre is solemnly staring at him with a deadly gaze. "And it was *not* funny."

Trying to steer the conversation away from that unpleasant scene, I say, "No, they seriously don't do that there. The bride and groom carefully place the cake into each other's mouths. None of that smashing in your face is going to go on, right Adrian?"

"Sure, sweetheart, anything you say," Adrian says, laughing.

"I believe it's an insult to the families if you so much as smear it into the bride's face," I add.

"What about the honeymoon?" Dennis asks, trying to change the subject. "Are you two planning on one of those?"

"Now that you mention that, Dennis, I've been planning that from day one," Adrian says.

"You are going to love this, Ellie. Akdemir is sending you and Adrian to Paris for a week," Terre smiles sheepishly.

"Terre, how do you know this? He never said anything to me about it. When did he say that? I would have remembered that part."

"Are you kidding?" Adrian is beaming. "Because I've never been to Paris. I've wanted to go but never had the chance. It'd be really cool to do that."

Smiling sweetly at Adrian, "You mean romantic, don't you darling?"

Adrian pretends to swoon, ducking his head under the water to blow bubbles with his nose.

"The rest of us will stay at the Royal Palace so we can get to know each other better," Terre adds.

"We have plenty of time, Terre, its months away. Can we stop talking about it now? I'm sad at what happened today, but happy about my new ring!"

When Terre tries to bring the conversation back to the wedding, I ask that she give it a rest for now. We'll worry about it tomorrow because we've had some wine and nothing is making sense to us right now anyway.

Especially, after the day we've had!

Sheriff Rocky and Deputy Slim have no news about our second dead horse, *Truly Yours*, but they vow to track down the culprits. Until our arrival in Jasper, nothing has ever happened in their sleepy little community in such rapid succession. The odd things that are happening to our family is a complete mystery to them.

Deputy Slim says there's no rational reason for these bizarre events. While they continue, Agents Josh or Jake will be with the children when they go to town or their activities. It gives us peace of mind knowing they're here with us.

Two beautiful horses are dead. I don't seek revenge as much as answers. Aren't most of our enemies incarcerated, or otherwise dead? Terre and Dennis have expressed their concern and have begun to question us about how the ex-Andress family came to be in Virginia in the first place. Adrian took them aside to tell them that they'll have to wait until we have a moment of peace to delve into that.

When is the right time to tell them of our misadventures? How am I going to explain what happened to Ravi? How much does Terre know about Daddy? Did Mother clarify that he was not who we all thought he was?

Suddenly remembering the police whiteboard that Adrian and I talked about starting a while ago, I'm more determined than ever to find out why my family has been on this strange journey.

Taking a large sheet of crosshatch and starting at the top of the page, I begin to label the heading FAMILY TREE. Centering on Daddy and Mother's real names of PASCAL L. PERRENAULT and FRANCESCA G. D'USSEAULT, I use the right side of the paper for their information. I print their adoptive parent's names, the towns in Argentina where they went to live after the war and divide it out with known adoptive relatives.

On the left side of the paper, I add Lautaro Ruggeri, the infamous uncle that made my Daddy's life insufferable, King Basim and so on. It is going to be a mishmash of people until we can connect the dots.

Adding myself and Terre to the right side below Mother and Daddy, I start printing our information, our marriages and children, until I get to Adrian who is near the bottom.

On the left side, across from my name, is Basim/Ravi, which is under his father, King Basim, who is a line across from my Daddy. Under Basim is his brother, Akdemir. Since Dimmy said he has fourteen half-siblings besides Fariq, I leave space for them but don't list any of their names.

It sickens me to write Lenard, Gene, and Andrea/Solana's names, but they are involved, so their names go along the extreme left side while Mr. C and the silent partners go under them.

What I need are photos, but then I abandon that idea as there are none of most of the people. Once I'm satisfied, I start drawing lines to connect the players. Some lines intersect while others flow to each other.

Somehow, we're all connected, but the common denominator seems to be missing. I also believe the men we have encountered at the racetrack have something to do with all this, but the troubling thing is, that they don't fit in anywhere. It's beginning to look a lot like a jigsaw puzzle. When the lines lead to no one person, I flatten it, placing it under my other large drawings.

I am not ready to show anyone, especially Adrian.

As if we needed more stuff to do, we added wedding plans. Terre has received endless lists of procedures that the Royal Palace requires us to study before our trip to Saudi Arabia. It is imperative that we understand their customs and abide by their rituals before we set foot in the Royal Palace. Terre cheerfully informs me that she has named our wedding trip *Desert Bliss*.

Melanie expresses her opinion (very loudly) that these rules seem cruel and unusual punishment. Adrian, in turn, stresses the importance that everyone needs to understand that the country we are visiting has social practices and customs that are conservative and based on Islamic Law. The men are not as affected as the women (and children), because there are fewer rules for them.

Levi came to Ashwood to discuss these protocols. He has a code file system in which he names all of his team events and has named this one *Desert Caper* (ignoring Terre and her Desert Bliss). We'll abide by these rules because we must respect their customs and wishes, no matter how much we might not like them.

> PROTOCOLS FOR WOMEN:
> <u>Royal Palace of His Most Royal Highness,</u>
> <u>King Akdemir Halim Abdul Obagur</u>
>
> - Women will travel in separate vehicles.
> - Women are not permitted to attend public events with men outside the palace walls.
> - Women must dress conservatively, ankle-length dress/skirt with sleeves and absolutely no pants or jeans are acceptable.
> - Women must wear head covering, across the lower part of face if in public.
> - Women must not display affection in public.

Levi didn't hesitate to say that this trip is presenting a nightmare for security not only for the family but for the other teams traveling with us. He keeps suggesting that we reconsider our venue. Can't we get married on the Canadian side of Niagara Falls, as it's so lovely the month of November? When we ask the family, everyone, including Mother, was so disappointed, that we forged ahead with our plans for the trip, discarding Levi's nutty suggestions.

The logistics for security is a mindboggling task in itself, and as Levi and the other's pointed out, other factions we have no control over might come into play. Part of the equation is the added security for our honeymoon to Paris.

The good news is that Levi isn't worried about Ashwood Stables, as most of the Alpha and Delta teams will remain with the rest of the household, but he is concerned about all the other things that could go wrong.

Could Murphy's Law come into play here?

Levi's latest idea is that we cancel the trip altogether. Can't we have a lovely quiet garden wedding in our backyard, as Reed and Dr. Jess had?

"If it's that complicated, we won't go, Adrian."

"We'll figure it out, Ellie. Levi thinks we might have to go to Canada for a few days before we fly to Germany. We would stay there a day or two, then proceed on to the Royal Palace. It's a diversion."

Am I overly sensitive about all this? "I don't understand. Why would we do that when Dimmy can send his private jet to our local airport? We could fly straight there like he does when he comes here."

"Levi discovered that we couldn't do that. It has something to do with Homeland Security. If Dimmy isn't aboard the jet, it won't be allowed to land here in Virginia," he explains. "It has to land at an international airport."

"That sound like a bunch of hooey. When did that restriction come about?"

"My little pumpkin, security is at level orange. There's some international rule now that says his jet has to go to New York first if he's not on it, and we can board it there."

"That sounds like mumbo jumbo to me, Mr. CIA man."

"That's good Ellie. The jumbo jet has mumbo jumbo, or is it gumbo limbo? Maybe it's chicken gumbo. I don't understand it either, and it's hard to explain, or Levi is doing it this way to confuse the enemy. He said that we have to do it this way or we don't go."

Adrian sees my expression.

"Confuse the enemy? If you don't think it's safe or you have a bad feeling about this, then we won't go. It's your call. I'm only doing this because my family begged me. And I feel like I owe it to my children to see what their father's life was before he left. Jason especially needs to see what he might be in for if he decides to live there. It may help him with his big decision down the road."

Adrian hugs me and tries to dance with me around the room. "And all this time I thought you wanted an exotic wedding, my lovely flower petal. I want to go, Ellie. We merely have to figure out how we'll do it, that's all. If we have to go to Canada and Germany or Timbuktu, we will! It will be the most exciting wedding in the world, you'll see."

TIMBUKTU?

The word Timbuktu reminds me of how I felt when the malicious FBI agents, Lenard and Gene, first brought me to Virginia. I questioned where we were going as the landscape looked like any other state from the air. I tried to guess that it might be Maryland, Washington D.C., or even Timbuktu! Then Gene said it was the great state of the Thoroughbreds.

Why are those two despicable people still haunting my thoughts?

"You know Adrian, in the last few years, I took chances on many things and probably went blindly into some of them, but I took them nonetheless. I took a huge chance when I went along with those idiots Retard and Goofy, taking the road less traveled by uprooting my family to bring them to Virginia. Things turned out all right. I don't have bad vibes going into this *Desert Caper* thing as Levi calls it, so we should do it."

"I know you took a lot of chances, Ellie, and I understand Jason needs to see what he might be up against over there. Melanie and Curlie need to feel like princesses, at least while they have the chance," he says thoughtfully. "I think we should do it too, my little love button."

"And I want a fairytale wedding in a faraway land; not something we only wish we could have done. We're only going to have one shot at this. I love you Adrian B. Sellers."

"I love you the most, my little ginger snap. We'll work everything out for your special day. I promise you the fairytale wedding of your dreams, a real one."

"It's your special day, too, Adrian. How many people are coming with us? Do you have a head count yet? I think the final number is close to twelve."

Adrian sheepishly hands me a sheet of paper. "Here it is."

With my notebook open, I begin to compare my list with his. "Why is yours longer than mine? I'm sure there were twelve at the last count. Mother, Terre, Dennis, Ginny, and Lindy make five. Melanie, Jason, Curlie, you, me, your Mother, Samuel, his wife Bernie, and Jake makes fourteen. You added Jake?"

"Are you kidding Ellie? There were thirteen people. Jake breaks the superstitious number."

"You're right, but I didn't know you were superstitious, Adrian. When did that happen?"

Laughing, he says, "It was about an hour after I came here! I've seen the shadow pass the front windows, Ellie. You have to admit that it's a little spooky."

"Okay, the new count is fourteen. I can't think of anyone else, can you?"

Adrian flips the sheet over. "Add Levi and a couple of his best people, plus the pilot and co-pilot and that should do it."

"How could I forget Levi? That makes it nineteen. Are you sure, that's the final count? You don't want to go for an even twenty?"

"Nineteen is enough, don't you think? Anyway, Levi thinks that's the only way security can be controlled and I tend to agree. That way, he's with the family when we're away on our honeymoon. He'll be there should anything crazy happen."

"I know Dimmy's paying for a lot of it, so who's coming up with the rest?"

"Ah yes, I knew you would ask about that. Unfortunately, we can't justify it as a legitimate expense through the CIA. I told Levi we'd pay for the rest of it ourselves. Can we go to the racetrack and win what we need to pay for it, sweet cheeks?"

"How much are we going to need, lover boy?"

Adrian grins. "A hundred grand ought to do it, maybe two, lovekins."

"My Dear Mr. Adrian B. Thompson dash Sellers, we can't win that much all at one time. The powers that be at Billingsworth will never let us go there again!"

"Mrs. Ellen Diller Thompson dash Sellers, can't we go to another racetrack? Hey, how about if we go to Meadowland in New Jersey and isn't there one in Kentucky? Here's an idea, there are many racetracks, couldn't we win a bundle at each of them and then go to Billingsworth and win the rest of it? Wada ya say, sweetheart?" Adrian uses his best Bogart impression.

"Levi will never go for that."

"Why don't we ask him?" As Adrian calls Levi, he begins to pace back and forth. Grinning, he says, "Levi says he was about to tap his Special Assignment Fund and would certainly appreciate it if we would pay for it ourselves. It's an unexpected gesture."

Adrian turns to walk away.

"I didn't think he would let us do it. Oh, I get it. There's a catch to it, isn't there? Come on, Mr. CIA man, what's the catch?"

Adrian slowly turns around. "Either Jake or Josh has to go with us. We have to share a room for security reasons. And Josh or Jake sticks with us like glue, or we don't go."

"Is that all? Okay, whatever it takes, I'll go along with it to keep the peace."

"You will? But it means we can't, you know."

"Oh for heaven sake, you've waited this long. But no one comes on our honeymoon except you and me."

Adrian is quiet.

"Tell me the answer to that is no…"

"Ellie, we have to go along with it, because it's part of the security detail Levi worked out. We do this, or we don't go on our honeymoon," Adrian grins.

Adrian and I turn our attention to the racetracks that we will visit over the next several weeks, leaving Jason and Mack in the capable hands of Reed and Glen. To monitor their safety, two members from Alpha and Delta teams will accompany them. Reed mentions that Mack has a good feel for how *Lester* will react under pressure since he's been training with him.

To streamline wedding matters, and to keep Terre from driving me crazy, I've relegated all of *Desert Bliss* (and any part of *Desert Caper*) to Terre. Since she's going to be my matron of honor and wedding planner, she has enlisted the girls to help. They're keeping everything a secret, and even I don't know what my dress looks like, but I can't stop to whine about it.

Mother knocks on the door of my office. "May I interrupt you?"

"Sure. What can I do for you?"

Mother hands me a small box. "I opened it the other day. I forgot to give this to you. You could tuck it into a little purse. It's your something blue. You know, it's that old saying for brides so that she has a happy wedding day."

"Do you mean the thing about something old, something new, something borrowed, and something blue?"

"Yes, that's it. It doesn't say that the thing has to be four items. Your dress is new. I think the item in the box is old, and you can consider it borrowed. Why don't you open it?"

I open the box to stare at its contents. "Mother, where did you get something like this?"

"Ravi gave it to your father for safekeeping when he first came to Chicago. He intended to put it into our safe deposit box at the bank, or maybe he forgot to put it into the vault at CIA Headquarters. He gave it to me for safekeeping. I hid it so good that I forgot where it was until a few days ago. Thank God those awful moving people Lenard sent never found it."

As I hold the large blue stone up to the light, the brilliance is as dazzling as the little secret barely visible at its center. "It is stunning."

As I read the note at the bottom of the box, tears form in my eyes. "I thought I was completely over this kind of emotion!"

"I'm not at all sure we ever do get over the deep emotional things that affect us, sweetheart. I still have dreams about what happened to us as children during the war. Daddy and I never talked about that part of our lives. It must have been painful for him too. I'm sorry Ellie; I don't want to talk about it now. I wanted you to have this, as it rightfully belongs to you."

"It must have been a devastating time for you and Daddy. We all have baggage, Mother. Ravi certainly had some and so did Daddy. Come to think of it I have several matching pieces."

"I had some myself, Ellie."

"How did you cope with it?"

"My issues didn't come out until after you and Terre were born, but I did go for counseling. The doctor's thought it was baby blues. I missed my birth mother and desperately wanted her there with me. I didn't even want to go to France or even travel there. It helped to get those feelings out so we could. Someday you might consider going too, to help you cope with what you have gone through so far."

"I don't think it's the right time for counseling. Who would believe my bizarre story anyway?"

"A professional would not judge you, Ellie. They're supposed to help you find the answers, not turn you into the police."

"Okay, I'll think about it. It's not at the top of my priority list right now."

"The secret of health for both mind and body

is not to mourn for the past,

not to worry about the future...

but to live the present moment wisely and earnestly."

~ Siddhartha Gautama Buddha

Chapter Six

A Trip To Remember

When our *Racetrack Caper* adventures (Levi's code file for this) are over, and behind us, he calls a special meeting to go over the preparations for *Desert Caper/Desert Bliss*, apart from the ones Terre has refused to divulge.

We have explicit instructions about restrictive weight and sizes of the two suitcases and one carry-on case that we're allowed to take with us. The girls are already stressing over not being able to fit everything they want to take into them. How will they possibly survive such a tragedy? Terre has told them not to worry, as there are washers and dryers available at all the hotels we'll be staying at, including the Royal Palace.

Laundry...they have to do laundry! Are you kidding?

After the initial shock and the laundry catastrophe was solved, we moved on to other items as Levi laid out his latest plan.

"On our way over, we'll have several vehicles, three different airports, with a short layover in New York. That's where we'll board Akdemir's private jet. His jet will fly us to Canada, where we'll stay in a hotel for one and a half days. We'll fly out on the same jet that will take us to Stuttgart, Germany."

Mel raises her hand to ask a question, but Adrian shakes his head in her direction, and she lowers it again.

"Please hold your questions until I'm finished explaining. We will remain there for two days, then continue to Saudi Arabia where King Akdemir's security detail will meet us on the tarmac. According to their customs, they will take the men first, with the women after them, to waiting vehicles. The women and girls are required to cover their heads, before disembarking the jet."

"Do we have to do that?" Ginny asks.

Levi continues, "Yes, all the women must do that, including you girls. The trip to the Royal Palace should last approximately one hour. Once we arrive at the Royal Palace, the men will go first, with the women after them. We will then be escorted to our respective guest rooms where we will remain until someone comes to get us for activities. Once the women and girls are beyond the inner Royal Palace walls, you'll be able to remove your head coverings."

"I didn't realize that this was going to be so complicated," Mel says.

"Hold on, it gets better," Levi says. "A schedule of activities will be posted in each guest room, giving the times for all communal meals that will take place in the dining hall. Proper attire is required at all times. No jeans are allowed." Handing each of us a list showing what is acceptable, what is not, he adds, "This includes all meals and outings within the Royal Palace walls. There are no exceptions."

Interrupting, I ask, "Mr. Levi, I have a question. Did Dimmy's people include a map of the Royal Palace?"

"Why would you need one, Ellen? The layout is quite adequate to help guide everyone around the inside. Anyway, it's imperative that, under no circumstances, must anyone go outside the Royal Palace inner walls. And that goes for wandering around the halls without an escort, too."

"What kind of place are we going to?" Dennis asks.

"Mama, why do we have to do this?" Curlie wonders. "I thought this was gonna be fun?"

"Will Akdemir keep us prisoners like he did Ellen?" Mother inquires.

Everyone chimes in with their opinions. It takes a loud whistle from Josh to control the angry mob. The girls wonder how they'll experience the local marketplace and do sightseeing, most especially to a Mosque.

Levi tries to calm everyone's fears. "The Royal Palace is a fortified city within a city. There will be plenty of things to do within the palace walls, people. There's a market that sells local produce along with all the bangles and baubles and objects any girl could want, a theater on-site near the horse arena, a bowling alley, fencing lessons for anyone who wants them, horseback riding, archery--and the list goes on. Unfortunately, the Mosque is strictly off limits, but maybe one of the adults can get a photo for you."

"I wanted to experience that myself, Mr. Levi," Mel says forlornly.

"None of you will be allowed through the town area except when we arrive and depart the Royal Palace. It isn't merely paranoia. I'm sorry to say that some tourists have gone missing. King Akdemir and his people are adamant we adhere to these rules!"

"Is there more, Mr. Levi?" Terre sighs.

"Yes, our luggage will have an inspection at all points of entry, and then delivered to our rooms upon arrival. Homeland Security will confiscate any items not allowed on any domestic or international flight. Should any of us even try to sneak anything into our luggage, the item or items will be removed, and discarded. You'll never see them again."

"Aren't you taking weapons to guard us?" Lindy questions.

"What a tough crowd. The exception to this rule are those firearms that I, Adrian, and our team members will carry. Also, no alcohol can enter the Royal Palace! It's a biggie we must all stick to."

"How long might we be gone, Mr. Levi? We'll need time to plan for the girl's homework," Terre inquires.

"The timetable for our entire trip will have an additional week's extension, because of the added days to go to and from our destination. It means that you'll have to plan for about a month."

"That shouldn't be too difficult," Terre says. "Ellen, remember when we did this when we went overseas with Mother and Daddy?"

"Yes, we learned more that way than from our history books," I say fondly remembering.

Terre adds, "We'll ask each teacher to come up with a set of guidelines for the study of a foreign country to satisfy each grade requirement. We always loved doing that, because it's almost like a scavenger hunt. You'll probably be required to keep a daily journal, collect the currency of the country we're in, and take photographs to share with your class."

"If we can't go out anywhere, how can we take pictures?" Mel wants to know.

Levi steps in to say, "Okay, it might be hard to do that part, once we're in Saudi Arabia, but you can do that everywhere else. We'll figure it out as it happens, perhaps I can bend the rules somewhat. The actual flight plan will be modified continually because Akdemir's security people want to keep our trip under the radar of his enemies. With these many family members traveling to and from the Royal Palace, he doesn't want to take chances."

"Sir," Adrian says interrupting. "How are we going to handle the side trip to Paris?"

"Good question, Adrian. Your trip will begin with one of Akdemir's smaller private jets. It will leave precisely at one p.m. the day *after* the wedding and land in Paris. A limousine will take Ellen, you, and Jake to the *Hotel de Crillon*. Jake will be in another room in your suite."

"Do you speak any French, Ellie?" Adrian asks nonchalantly, "All I know is vera jacket. You know, it's the little song that goes like this; vera jacket, vera jacket, where are you? Where are you?"

Everyone starts to laugh as they throw pillows at him. Then Mother proclaims the correct pronunciation is *Frère Jacques*. I'm now grateful that she took the time to teach Terre and me the little phrases that will get us through our week there.

"I know enough not to order squid for dinner," catching Mother's proud smile.

Dennis starts to tease Adrian. "Why do you have to know French? You probably won't ever leave your hotel room!"

Trying to ignore him, I say, "I'd like to see the Louvre again."

"Isn't that where the Mona Lisa is?" Melanie asks. "I'd like to go to Paris, too…but I don't wanna go with you on your honeymoon!"

"Aw, honey, we'd make room for you."

"No!" Mel says, shaking her head. "Sorry for bringing it up."

Terre adds, "It's a wonder, almost as spectacular as the British Museum, maybe they're both equally as grand."

"And I want to see that show with the cancan girls," Adrian says, smirking. "They still do that, don't they?"

Mother laughs. "You mean the Moulin Rouge?"

"We should go to Versailles, and we can't miss the Eiffel Tower…"

I'm lost in thought when Levi rudely reminds us of possible vulnerability. "You can't stay in your hotel room and pretend to go out?" Everyone in the room starts to laugh. "You're going to present quite a challenge if you want to do all that stuff."

Jason seems left out, sitting quietly while everyone else is talking. Adrian is aware that Jason is the only person who doesn't seem to be enthusiastic about this trip. "Jason? What are you thinking?" he asks.

"I don't know where I fit in all this. What am I supposed to do while everyone else has stuff to do?" Jason says sadly.

Adrian starts to chuckle. "Didn't you get that memo we sent you? Uncle Dimmy is going to keep you so busy you won't have time to notice what the rest of us are doing."

"Honey, he wants to introduce you to several influential people. Then he wants you to start fencing lessons," I add.

"What if I don't want fencing lessons, Mom?" Jason says flatly.

"I believe that Jam-ale is hoping that you'll join his group that rides the Arabian Stallions, right Adrian?"

"Yes," he says. "You'll probably be working so closely with the Big Guy and his merry band of horse people that you won't notice the time pass."

"Oh, sure, he would do that, sorry," Jason says smiling. "I forgot that Jam-ale mentioned that."

I regret the words as they leave my mouth. "You keep forgetting how indispensable you are to Uncle Dimmy, Jason."

"That's because you keep telling me not to get a big head over it, Mother."

Everyone stops to laugh with us.

Adrian's family is expected at any moment. We'll have a chance to spend a little time getting to know each other before our big trip. Adrian mentioned that his Mother, Jeanette, is about Mother's age and he's sure they'll like each other. He's also looking forward to spending time with his older brother Samuel, and his wife, Bernice.

Once everyone is settled in, and our dinner finished, we move to the library where Adrian's Mother chats quietly with mine while Terre and Dennis talk with Sam and Bernie. They fit right in with our boisterous and exuberant crowd.

Sam hilariously regales us with stories of when he and Adrian were growing up. Adrian knew early in life that he wanted to be either a police detective or a firefighter. Then the FBI and the CIA started to fascinate him and the rest, as they say, is history.

When the day comes for our departure, Levi orchestrates his elaborate plan. It's no easy task to round up nineteen people plus their luggage, moving them from one security point to another in a large airport without drawing undue attention.

Once we are in our seats on the jet that will take us to New York, Adrian leans toward me, saying, "We're on our way to our new life together, Ellie May. Are you ready for our great adventure?"

"Yes. I like your family, Adrian. I'm glad they're here with us."

"I am too. You would've liked my father, and he would have liked you, Ellie, I know my family does."

"Daddy would have liked you, too. Where did the name Adrian come from?"

"It came from Adrian Balboa. You know, from the Rocky movies?"

"Wasn't his name Rocky Balboa and his girlfriend's name was Adrian?"

"Yes, but my father wouldn't let my mother name me Rocky," he says chuckling.

"Hum, Rocky Sellers. Mrs. Rocky Thompson-Sellers. It has a certain ring to it, connected to the mob kind of like."

"Aren't you glad she won? Mom figured that with a name like Adrian Benson Sellers, I'd be going places."

"I do like the name Adrian better than Rocky. I don't think Jasper could take two of you."

"Mom thought I'd be fighting with every tormenter that came along if I was named Rocky, so Dad relented."

"Would you have been a fighter if you were named Rocky?"

"You know how silly Sheriff Rocky sounds, don't you? I'm still waiting for Bullwinkle to show up. I'm no fighter, Ellie. I am who I am today because names don't make the person; the person makes the person."

"I love you, Mr. Adrian B. Thompson dash Sellers, the way you are."

"Thanks, I'm kinda fond of you, too." Kissing my hand, he says, "We are going to have a long and incredible life together, my little Ellie May. And I assure you, it won't be dull."

The first leg of our trip is uneventful. After landing in New York, Homeland Security reviewed our passports so there will be a minimum fuss when we transfer to the royal jet. As we board, it appears spacious and comfortable, large enough to accommodate as many as thirty people. It reminds me of the smaller ones Lenard and Gene took me in from Kauai to Virginia.

When will those two wicked clowns leave my memory?

Dimmy has spared no expense when it comes to comfort. The seats are a soft butter-color leather and fully recline. Ginny and Lindy discover the large snack bar, helping themselves while we wander around the interior choosing our seats.

Our flight attendants, who are members of Adrian's special teams called Delta (Bryce) and Alpha (Elizabeth), give us the pitch about doors, lavatories, electronic devices, etc. for the second leg of our journey.

Not long into the flight, the pilot's crackly voice states that we are about to pass over Niagara Falls. At this point, Levi unbuckles his seatbelt and stands up to address us. "May I have your attention? Is everyone ready for our adventure?" With a straight face, he says, "Please take the parachute that is located under your seat and place your arms into the straps. There has been a change in our plans."

Jeanette's eyes go wild with fright as Mother's mouth flies open, which she then covers with a trembling hand! A collective gasp comes from everyone else.

Adrian unbuckles his seatbelt and stands abruptly, saying, "I don't understand, sir. You didn't tell me about this change!"

Jason and Levi begin to laugh.

"Kidding," Levi says, snickering. "Had you going there for a minute, didn't I?"

"Yes you did, sir. Yes, you did!" Adrian says, sitting back down.

"We were all so tense that we lost sight of the essential part of all; we're all together to have some fun!"

We discover that Mr. Levi has a wicked sense of humor!

Our jet lands in Québec, Canada where it comes to rest near a small building where two men are watching us approach. As Steward Bryce opens the door and releases the stairs, Levi waits at the top until they give a pre-assigned code.

Once the men are on board, Levi hands them our passports and customs documents. (For security purposes, our identities are changed) One of the security men asks who's getting married, but Levi declines to say, as protocol (apparently, we have them too) dictates that this information remain unavailable to them.

While the meeting with the security people took place, attendants took our luggage to the vehicles that will take us to our hotel. Once we are there, we inspect our rooms, which consist of two adjoining suites decorated almost like the presidential one I stayed in before flying to Virginia. Each suite has four bedrooms with two queen beds each and a shared living space.

Memories begin to overwhelm me when I see it. I don't have time for this. GET OUT OF MY HEAD! Trying to rid my mind of any reference of that time, I make a conscious effort to squelch it, but it might hit twice as often when we step into the Royal Palace. Both Mother and Adrian are aware of how I might react and try to keep me busy with our Paris plans as a distraction.

We'll spend the next day and a half in this quaint town, do little else other than eat and relax as we must stay together to ease Levi's mind. We spread shiny brochures of Paris across the coffee table. It wasn't easy to narrow down what Adrian and I wanted to do on our honeymoon, but Levi put some restrictions on it to keep Jake from going crazy. We can't reserve or purchase tickets before our trip, in case someone is watching, so Jake will buy them when we arrive.

It seems like a whirlwind tour, but Jake says, "It will be tough to keep you busy and safe all at the same time."

While we examine the brochures, we haggle over what we'll eat (of all things), as the girls implore Levi to allow them to go out, arguing that this will be the better part of their grade.

Levi surprises the girls, by taking them to the old city of Québec to the Battle of the Plains of Abraham. It was a crucial moment in the Seven Year's War. American History books refer to this as the French and Indian War fought from 1756 to 1763.

They don't have the three or so hours to spend looking and walking the beautiful grounds of the park, and Melanie seems sullen until Levi convinces her that lunch and shopping will end the day. While they're out, the adults hang back at the hotel to visit.

Adrian knows that Levi is superior at his job, and enjoys his foray into the field, and remembers how he has missed it! But when Levi returns with the girls that afternoon, he can only roll his eyes and admit he's tired. Perhaps someone else can go with them the next time.

At precisely seven forty-five p.m. the following day, we depart Québec for Stuttgart. We're ushered out of the hotel and into limos and back to the airport for the third leg of our journey. Dimmy's little jet is sitting alone on the tarmac next to the building we left a day ago, and the stairs are down in preparation for our arrival.

The air is crisp and the night sky threatens to unleash early snow. Thoughts of wintertime are suddenly reminding me of Chicago, autumn leaves, and the crunch of ice under my boots. Mother takes me aside, saying that we're about to embrace new memories and to let go of the past.

How did she know what I was thinking?

Our flight attendants go through their usual routine to prepare us for takeoff, once the tower has cleared us to do so. It will be a long flight of almost eight hours in length.

Hours later, our steward awakens us with a hot washcloth. We are coming down in altitude and will be on the ground in less than an hour. Curlie bounces down the aisle and practically jumps into my arms. Although Mother had to tell her to be quiet and go to sleep last night, she's excited and can't wait to see Germany.

"Can I take photos from the window?" Curlie asks.

Levi sees nothing wrong with this, so she readies her camera while the others wake up. Jason seems unusually quiet and reserved. He's understandably apprehensive and questions my decision to visit the place where I was held captive. I sit down next to him to talk.

"I do and don't understand why we're doing this, Mom."

"It's too late now, Jason. We're almost there!"

"Are you doing this for me? Because if you are, I don't want you to relive what you went through," he sighs.

"I've mostly come to terms with it, sweetie. It might bring back some things, but it won't be so bad. Please don't worry about it, but thanks for your concern. It's a happy time for all of us."

"Are you sure? I guess we didn't talk about it much, you being held prisoner and all. I don't want you to have nightmares or anything!"

They have all but disappeared.

"I haven't had nightmares for a long time, Jason."

"Mom, I thought..."

"We are visiting your Uncle Ak-dim-er at the Royal Palace, and you're going to see where your father came from and where he lived. It'll be okay."

"Are you sure?" he asks.

Jason reminds me so much of Ravi when he has that thoughtful expression on his face. It's times like these that I want to hug him, and instead, pat his arm.

"You'll be making a life-altering decision someday, and you need to experience this, Jason. Does that calm your mind a little?"

"Yeah, it does a little, Mom. I don't understand why there is so much drama between us and Uncle Dimmy and his family."

"That's funny. Where there is family, you will have drama, Jason. It doesn't matter where you are. You need to be more excited, honey. We're going to your father's place of birth. Don't you want to see that?"

Hesitating, he says, "I was afraid if I appeared too enthusiastic you would think I already made up my mind. But you're right. I need to see where Dad came from."

"There's nothing wrong with wanting to experience the Arabian side of your heritage. Your father would be very proud of you. Even if he didn't want to share that part of his life with us, he would want you to know about it; eventually, I suppose."

Jason reaches for my hand. "Guess you're right, Mom. I have to be there to know if I want to--whatever Uncle Dimmy wants me to do."

"You're a good person. Your father would also be proud of the way you think, and I am too. I can't influence your decision, you must do that yourself, and if I seem sad at the prospect of you going so far away, it's because, sweetie, it's so far away! We're coming down now; we can talk later, okay?"

Akdemir's jet lands quietly and without preamble. Luckily, Levi speaks fluent German and knows the head of security. German security seems to be a little tighter here, and before we can disembark, all papers will get a thorough once-over.

As the city wakes up, Curlie and the girls try to snap pictures out the window of our moving van. At our hotel, we inspect our spacious suites. It doesn't take long when the girls begin to beseech Levi into allowing them access to the outside to scavenge for homework assignments.

When he asks Melanie to see her list, he starts to laugh, saying the only shopping she'll be doing is in the gift shop of the hotel but doesn't see any harm in a walk around the hotel with an escort.

When Levi shows the girls a brochure of the Hohenzollern Castle, Ginny and Lindy began to shriek so loudly we thought one of them was hurt. As it turns out, they were hoping they could visit a castle, but their hopes seemed dashed when Levi said they could only walk around the outside of the hotel.

Since Levi knows the territory and can speak the language, he will escort them to the castle with the help of Bryce and Jake. Since they will be out for several hours, it gives the remaining adults time to unwind.

We huddle around the dining room table trying to decide what to order for dinner. Levi has a connection to a local restaurant that specializes in authentic food found all over Germany. We'll be able to choose items from an extensive menu that includes some unusual beer. Along with that, we also order *weinersnitzel, schweinsbraten, sauerbraten, kartoffelsalat, spatzel* and *knopfle,* along with *gaisburger marsch.*

When Levi and the girls return, they regale us with stories of what they saw, showing us photos and currency along with the items they purchased in the gift shop at the castle. After the girls settle down, we embark on a culinary trip around Germany. Everything is scrumptious, but it's too much for all of us to eat for one meal, so the rest goes into the refrigerator to enjoy tomorrow.

We've added a delicious cake of six thin layers with chocolate buttercream in-between the layers called *prinzregententorte.* And if we're still in the mood for a sweet snack later, we can dunk the *springerle* cookies in milk or coffee.

Levi says to drink up, because we won't see alcohol again until our return to Germany, except for the honeymooners who are going to Paris, that is.

Did he say no alcohol at the wedding? How did I miss that?

What else am I not going to like? I'm already stressing that I won't fit into my wedding dress, but Terre laughs, saying there's plenty of material to go around, so it doesn't matter! Should I be concerned that she won't let me see this secret wedding dress?

Before we turned in last night, Levi took the adults aside to tell us one more detail. "We won't know the terminus airport or the actual city of our destination. They do this purposely, so we're unaware (should we be captured) by the warring factions!"

An involuntary shudder runs up my spine. "Are you kidding?"

"That's why it was such a nightmare for security, Ellie," Adrian says.

How can I allow my son to be a part of this?

"Where's your big girl pants?" Adrian asks. "Hope you packed them!"

The fourth and final leg of our journey starts promptly at eight a.m. on the second morning of our stay in Stuttgart. We are ushered into our limos and taken to the airport where we board Dimmy's jet that will take us on the six-hour trip to an airport with no name.

Terre and I take seats near the rear while Adrian talks with his family closer to the front. We're deep into a discussion about *Desert Bliss* when I demand to see my dress. Opening her notebook, she hands me a page from a magazine.

"Please tell me you're kidding, Terre!" I'm trying to stifle my surprise. "It's beautiful, but I'm not sure about the color."

Terre seems disappointed. "Ellie, this is a traditional wedding dress. You didn't expect a white one, did you?"

"No! But I didn't expect to wear red either. It looks like heavy material."

Terre frowns. "I don't think it is. Dimmy's people said this is what you need to wear for the wedding ceremony. The King is taking care of everything on his end; food, drink, entertainment. He expects us to follow their traditions to the letter."

"The drink is probably juice and water and since you haven't told me about these traditions, how can I agree to anything? Do you expect Adrian to wear that robe thing they all wear there? Does he know about any of this?"

"We'll go over everything once we get there. Don't worry, Ellie, everything is under control," Terre says smiling.

"I can't wait to hear the rest of it."

"We'll talk about it a day or two before the ceremony," she whispers.

"Why can't we talk about it now, Terre?"

"Shush, I don't want little ears to hear. They don't know everything, because I thought they would tell you and spoil the surprise." Terre is rolling her eyes. "It's supposed to be mysterious and exotic, Ellen."

"What if I don't like the dress, sister dear?"

"Trust me, Ellie, okay? I know you'll love it!" she says, pursing her lips.

"Terre dear, I've heard those words before." Slumping down in the seat, saying, "I don't really like surprises. You of all people should know that."

"I'm your sister, you better trust me!" she says, raising her eyebrows in defiance.

Levi mentions that the girls should turn the flash off on their cameras, just in case.

"In case of what?" Curlie asks.

"Just in case they stop and search us," he says candidly.

"Who would stop and search us?" Mother asks.

When Levi doesn't answer, we take that to mean that he's not about to delve into an explanation and to stop asking questions.

Our ride from the airport through bustling cities is a fascinating journey that includes exotic aromas, striking colorful materials hanging in marketplaces, impressive architecture, and muted sounds. While all the men are in an all-terrain vehicle with dark tinted windows, the women follow with Alpha Team Member Elizabeth. Levi radios to ask that we cover our heads and faces as we near our final destination.

Off in the distance of this desert-like setting, a mountain range comes into view. The stone edifice nestled against it reminds me of National Geographic photographs that accompany articles by world-traveling journalists, and it is both impressive and breathtaking, because of its sheer size.

As we approach, men in sandy-color clothing stand at intervals along the top of the walls where large hinged doors swing slowly open. We pass the outer walls as another wall comes into view, but these walls are not as high. It appears compressed against the mountain where there are more men positioned at intervals along what seems to be a walkway. These men have rifles slung loosely at their shoulders, and an ominous feeling passes through my body.

As if the horse show is given to us alone, two lines of mounted riders who wear blue and silver greet us on Arabian Stallions. They flank the doorway in a path wide enough for our vehicles to pass without touching. Assuming that this is Jam-ale and his army of men, he must be the biggest one at the end near the doors, and the only one to raise his sword to his head in greeting.

Jam-ale motions for our vehicles to follow him and we come to what must be the front of the Royal Palace. Elizabeth explains that these foot-thick doors intricately carved we now pass through will lead into the inner city of the fortress. At the second set of doors, is the entrance to the Royal Palace itself. It's a wonder how they move so easily given their immense size.

Nothing is remotely familiar except for the two men who stand inside the elaborately decorated doors. Jam-ale dismounts, standing next to the first vehicle to welcome the inhabitants, directing them through the doors. When all the men are inside, he walks to our car, opens our door and reaches in to take Mother's hand.

"I don't like their strange tradition," I mutter. Terre reacts by saying that I need to be quiet, we'll talk about things later.

Sheyanna and Tieynza appear to show us to our rooms. As we transverse the hallways on a journey that takes about twenty minutes or so, I try to point out the extraordinary features as we pass. Everyone seems to be as entranced with the elaborate metal grillwork, colorful ceramic tiles, and furniture as I once was.

When we stop at the first door, there is a little wooden plaque with a familiar symbol and my heart skips a beat, and not in a good way. Sheyanna then explains that Jason will occupy that room while he's here. She then begins to tug at my arm to move me along the hallway.

In the days before the wedding ceremony, Terre shares more of *Desert Bliss*, taking me to see the lavishly decorated hall that includes a stage, catwalk, and seating areas for the women. She explains that the men's side of the reception is less decorated, yet still elegant.

"What do you mean by the men's side? Why didn't you tell us about this? Does it mean I can't see Adrian?"

Terre's expression changes, saying, "The groom is allowed to enter the women's side and possibly some of the men, but it will be much later in the evening. I know that look, Ellie. Saudi Ministers will be on hand to restrict access between the two areas. That's how they do it here."

"Let me see your clipboard. I would never have agreed to this." The more I read, the more agitated I become. "I'm going to have a little chat with Dimmy and Adrian. Most of this is out of the question, Terre."

"But I thought, we all thought you wanted a traditional Saudi Wedding! We can't change things now, Ellie! It's too close to the wedding day!" Terre says, throwing her hands up in the air.

"Would you like to place a wager on that, sister? We can and will change this. Why didn't you let me know about these things? Does Adrian, Levi, or Mother know?"

Terre's eyes fill with tears. "Only Mr. Levi knows. We kept it a secret from everyone else. We all thought you wanted a traditional ceremony, Ellie. It is their way of doing things. I thought you knew what it entailed. You said you did research. You're not going to like any of it!"

"I did research on the wedding cake and the ceremony itself. Terre, I doubt Adrian will go along with this either. We'll meet with Dimmy and get this straightened out. I do love the fact that you went to so much trouble, but we need to change it a little. Don't worry; I'm not mad at you."

An hour later, Bryce escorts me to Dimmy's library. When the wooden doors open, overwhelming feelings that I have been here and done that hits for a split second, and I'm once again back as Abdul's prisoner. The lemon scent wafts from the bookshelves, mixing with the musty smell of old books. The only difference is that Jam-ale's menacing face is missing.

Adrian is standing inside the room and reaches for my hand. We haven't seen each other since dinner the other night, as he's busy with the men's activities. Dimmy sits at his enormous desk, and rises, motioning for us to come forward.

"Welcome, my dear Ellen, Mr. Adrian. I hope you are enjoying our peaceful surroundings and excellent amenities." Dimmy is smiling while shaking Adrian's hand. He proceeds to kiss both of my cheeks, motioning for us to sit down near his enormous desk.

"We have a situation, Ak-dim-er. It is not how I envisioned my fairytale wedding."

"You were given the Etiquette of Formal Occasions beforehand, Ellen. It was my understanding that you agreed to it," Dimmy says dryly and without expression.

"My sister, in her infinite wisdom, confiscated the etiquette stuff and didn't share them with us until an hour ago. We are Americans, not Saudi citizens and I insist that we dispense with this ridiculous notion of separate parties!"

"You are in my country, my dearest Ellen. You must observe our customs," he says, offering us bottles of water that are standing like little soldiers on a silver tray near his chair.

Handing Adrian the papers, he begins to read, then starts to laugh, clears his throat, and starts to laugh again. "I didn't know about this either. I agree with Ellen."

"Maybe we should cancel everything. Adrian and I will wed some other time, not like this! To have two separate parties and not even see my new husband for hours is so ludicrous it's funny! I'll admit that I don't know much about your culture or religion, but they are your observances for weddings, not ours. Can we do this somewhere else, so we don't offend anyone, like in the city itself?"

"I do not know what to say to this request," Dimmy says. "Having an event in the city is not allowed."

Adrian is thoughtful for a moment. "Or are you able to pare it down to include the wedding party, you, and Turlock, and his family?"

"We don't need this elaborate party when all we want is a simple ceremony and a nice dinner. We mean no disrespect, it's too much for us," I implore, suddenly nauseated.

After a few minutes, Dimmy says quietly, "I do see what you mean. Let me think about this for a moment, and perhaps we can come up with a solution that serves both of our purposes. Something that is both elegant and lavish and something that is simple. Would you agree to that?"

"Yes," Adrian says. He stands to walk around the cavernous room, touching the books much as I did that first time I was here and I wonder what he's thinking. Dimmy seems amused as Adrian's head bends sideways to inspect the spine of a large book.

"I wanted to give you a traditional wedding, Ellen. When no one objected, I assumed that we would move forward with our plans."

"My sister thought it would be best to keep it a secret and didn't share most of it until a few hours ago. Terre means well, but it's too much for us. We hope you haven't gone to too much trouble."

"My dearest Ellen, it was years before Basim let me know that he was married. He did keep me informed when your family grew, the significant events that you celebrated, and visited as often as he dared. Perhaps I was trying to overcompensate for the fact that I could not join him and his family. We will come to a compromise. It is your wedding, after all."

"Thank you," I say gratefully, feeling a little lightheaded.

Dimmy leans forward, saying, "I invited several dignitaries, and they were looking forward to…all the traditions that accompany the groom's party. They are all so anxious to meet Jason."

"They can still meet Jason. They don't have to wait until the wedding to do that, do they?" Adrian says.

Dimmy is watching Adrian. "No, we can arrange another time for that."

"What kind of traditions am I going to miss, if I might ask?" Adrian says.

"I will try to explain," Dimmy says with a twinkle in his eye. He begins to fill in the missing parts that even Terre knew nothing about, and Adrian cordially declines to wear the traditional Arabic Bisht, asking if he can wear the suit he brought.

Although I agree to wear the dress my sister hid until the day of the wedding, we mostly compromise to allow a short ceremony conducted by Alliance Royal Ministers. The party will include a lavish dinner comprised of only the wedding party and family that came from Virginia, along with Dimmy's immediate family to include Turlock, his wife, and their three daughters. No other guests, friends, family members, or dignitaries will attend, except for Jam-ale—who seems to pop out of the walls when you least expect him.

"There will be no band. There will be no alcohol; however, there will be a delectable wedding cake with a table of delicate pastries. Jason is working on something that involves the Arabian Stallions. One of our traditions will include brandishing of swords with celebratory gunfire."

Adrian seems curious, but concerned. "There's going to be gunfire? And what kind of brandishing of swords do you mean? That might wreak havoc with our security people. What kind of display is it? Does Levi know about this?"

Dimmy's eyes twinkle. "Mr. Adrian, it is simply a small display for the wedding party. It should cause no bother to anyone or your security. Jamaile has men that will use ancient weapons that symbolize our lineage. Your Mr. Levi has already consented."

"I see. Aren't we allowed one bottle of champagne?" Adrian asks.

Dimmy shakes his head slightly. "The Arabian Stallions and their riders will entertain us. Are you agreeable to this, Ellen? Adrian, there is no alcohol in the Royal Palace; you knew that before you came. We will not change that for you. What are your thoughts on the rest of it, Ellen?"

"I see nothing wrong with the rest of it. What do you think about this, sweetheart?"

Adrian absently shakes his head up and down. "That would be alright." Smiling at me, he nods at Dimmy, then mumbles under his breath about the alcohol.

"I'm curious about something. What is the colored liquid that is served at dinner? If it isn't wine, what is it?"

"My dear Ellen, you must be referring to the juice we consume?"

I can't believe this. "Are you saying it isn't wine?"

"No, we are strictly forbidden to have such beverages present. You thought it was wine. We have several different juices made from berries and fruit, I believe, unfermented."

Was it the residual of the drugs that made me think it was wine during that time I spent here? Is he pulling my leg, because it sure tasted like wine!

On the day of the wedding, there is a flurry of activity as the girls bounce in and out of the rooms. I have a slight headache and feel feverish, but mother attributes this to wedding day jitters. Maybe I should drink some cold water, eat a little something; I look a little pale.

Terre appears with the wedding dress, and I'm suddenly overwhelmed. Made of lightweight, silky fabric in a sultry shade of red, it only looks as if it weighs a ton. Embroidery runs down each long sleeve, crisscrosses the high-necked bodice, and around the hemline. It's quite breathtaking!

Mother watches as Terre helps me step into the skirt while I put both arms into the sleeves. As she pulls the dress up, she zips it. It feels snug and slightly claustrophobic to me when she adds the shawl and the top headpiece that completely covers my hair. Sheyanna then attaches a matching veil across the bridge of my nose and proceeds to drape jewelry, covering my forehead, exposing only my eyes.

Any movement of my head brings the tinkle of bells. A memory surfaces and I try to squelch it quickly. "How am I supposed to eat dinner like this?"

Sheyanna ignores me, tugging here, there, and then stands back when she's satisfied. Meanwhile, Mother and Terre have excused themselves to round up the girls and help Tieynza get them ready. They will also be in traditional dress for the evening and I chuckle to think how enveloped they'll be in yards of fabric, have matching little slippers on their feet, and draped in jewelry.

We will keep out of sight to prolong the mystery Terre so wants us to experience. At half past the hour, according to schedule, Jam-ale appears with Bryce and Elizabeth to escort all of us to the ceremonial room where the nuptials will take place.

Jam-ale bows graciously, offering one of his big arms. He's dressed in the blue and silver costume, minus the headpiece to hide his face. In uncharacteristic conversation, he mentions how lovely I look. As we walk the corridors and transverse the stairs, I'm grateful that there will be an end to this ordeal so Adrian and I can finally be alone on our honeymoon (almost alone anyway). I'm also grateful that the soft slipper-shoes have no real heel.

We arrive at a small room adjacent to the ceremonial room where we wait for Elizabeth's signal. Jam-ale explains that it's a waiting room for dignitaries. Royal Ministers often meet here to hold council, sign critical documents, or settle disputes between King Akdemir and his many family members.

Elizabeth's job is to see that everyone follows the seating chart for both the ceremony and wedding dinner. She pokes her head into the small room, tapping her earpiece while Terre tries to rein in Melanie and the girls as they giggle nonstop. When the signal comes that it's time for the mothers to go in, we all assemble in the hallway where Terre, Jam-ale, and I wait behind them.

When Elizabeth opens the double doors, it allows for a quick peek inside the formal room. It's not what I expect. It is a rectangle shape and has no windows. The walls are an exotic wood; the floors are marble, covered with thick Persian carpets.

The vaulted ceiling has a cloud/fantasy/tree motif that flows down to gold color trim, where a rather large crystal chandelier hangs over a small round table. Three upholstered chairs are against the wall facing the doorway along with groups of chairs on either side of the table that form a wide aisle.

Once everyone is in the room and seated, Turlock pokes his head out to signal that it's time to bring me in. Jam-ale takes my arm and follows Terre through the door.

Two Ministers are standing near the table while Adrian, King Dimmy, and Jason are sitting in the three chairs facing us. No music is playing in the background, but Adrian and my Mother both stand when they see us, as it's our custom to stand up when the bride comes down the aisle.

Everyone else follows suit, including Dimmy and Royal Family members, and tears threaten at this genuinely touching gesture. When we reach the table, Adrian grasps my hand as Jam-ale backs away to stand near the door. I didn't realize until this moment that he was giving me away.

The Ministers perform the short ceremony, and we exchange rings. Adrian surprises me when he says, "Life is not measured by the breaths we take, but by the moments that take our breath away. Ellen, looking at you, right now, you take my breath away. I hope and pray that we will feel as we do today, for the rest of our lives. I love you with all my heart, Ellen May Thompson dash Sellers."

"That was truly lovely, Adrian. I didn't prepare anything, but I love you with all my heart. I will cherish this moment, always."

This romantic and loving gesture genuinely moves me. We manage to rub our noses together, as it's not possible to kiss given all the fabric and jewelry dangling in my face. Adrian and I turn to face our guests, and they congratulate us.

The Royal Ministers present us with a document, which Terre, Dennis, Adrian, and I sign on the small table. After the Royal photographer poses the wedding party, taking several photos of both groups and single shots, we're ushered out and down several flights of stairs.

Levi stops us mid-way, leaning in to say, "You done good kid." Adrian throws his head back in laughter, but I can't figure out what it means.

The area becomes instantly familiar the lower we go. It also gets warmer and a bit smelly, like a stable. I'm suddenly back to that last night when Jam-ale and his men took me out of the Royal Palace on our journey into the desert. Given all the doors we had to go through to get into the Royal Palace, I wonder now how they did this without drawing attention to what they were doing. Perhaps we used a secret passageway, maybe more than one.

Clinging to Adrian and stumbling slightly, I become lightheaded, and for a moment a little disoriented.

Adrian grabs my arm. "Are you okay? I can't tell what's going on under all that stuff, but you are lovely, Ellie. Are you feeling okay? How can you see anything?"

"It must be all the excitement. Is it warm in here or is it me?"

"Not really. Did you eat lunch? You know how you get when you skip meals," he asks.

"I got a little dizzy, that's all. Do you think we're going to eat soon? Do you suppose they'll let me take this stuff off my head then?"

"I'm sure they will, Ellie. It's great that Jason's been busy planning something for us."

We are sitting on soft cushions, and from what I can see, it's the Arabian Stallion horse show all over again, except that it's only for the wedding party.

The stallions are magnificent as Jam-ale puts them through their paces. As the horses line up on one side of the arena, two riders meet in the middle. They slide off their horse, and each pulls out a sword. It takes a few seconds to realize that one of them is Jason.

The two men are approximately the same height, except for the mustache and the fact that the other man is stocky compared to Jason. They engage in a pretend sword fight, and the meatier one feigns a fatal wound by falling onto the arena floor. Jason puts his boot on his stomach, raises his sword in the air as we all applaud. The rest of the group surrounds them, and they yell something in Arabic (I think), and then lift Jason high in the air.

The wounded man stands up, and they all mount their horses to march around the arena. On Jam-ale's cue, two lines form as they put their swords in the air, and with tips touching, Jason rides his horse under the swords, coming to the front, where his horse does a curtsey.

Dimmy stands abruptly to applaud. Nodding at Jam-ale, we take this to mean the show's over, and the wedding party dutifully follows the procession up to the dining hall. Although we were in this room last night for dinner, he was not going to dismiss everything and has allowed Terre to transform the large room.

A small stage sits against one wall, with a curtain to hide a three-piece ensemble that plays soft music. Clustered at intervals, balloons in red, blue, and silver rise from chairs as streamers of silver and blue dangle from the glittering chandeliers. The huge table is set with such care and deliberate opulence that it brings tears to my eyes.

It triggers the memory of the first time I stepped foot into this enormous room. Other recollections threaten to obscure my vision when Sheyanna gently takes my hand to lead me to a chair. Someone hands me a glass of juice as she begins to remove the veil and jewelry from the front of the headpiece to expose my face. She then takes me to sit in the chair next to Adrian.

Servers begin to place large platters of food down the long table. The women and girls have pulled their veils aside as they can finally mix with the men during our dinner. Everyone begins to comment on the food; however, it tastes flat to me.

Halfway through dinner, Akdemir proposes a toast, and then others follow. Levi gets a hearty laugh when he mentions that we'll be dropped into Paris to enjoy our honeymoon, then goes on to wish us a long and happy life together.

As the music plays softly in the background, Adrian and I cut our cake. We manage to put a chunk into each other's mouths without a gesture of a smudge. Then a server passes the scrumptious delicate pastries around the table.

It signals that Sheyanna and Tieynza will take the women and girls to a small party arranged for them. The remaining men will move to another part of the palace to pursue a game of billiards if they wish. Royal Ministers and dignitaries have eaten their dinner in another room of the Royal Palace where they await Jason.

Turlock has the distinction of escorting us to our honeymoon suite. I'm not at all sure he understands much English, so we merely smile at him.

When he throws open the door, Adrian exclaims, "Now this is a fairytale wedding suite."

I'm flabbergasted! This lavish and large room, which is located down the hall from where I've been staying is elegantly furnished. Large vases of flowers, placed around the room, give off a heady perfume scent which threatens to make me ill.

As Turlock silently closes the door behind him, Adrian bolts it from the inside. He spots fruit and caviar on a table where something protrudes from a bucket covered with a towel. He pulls it off to reveal a bottle of champagne.

"Look what our illustrious leader has brought us!"

"I thought Mother and I were already staying in the most beautiful of rooms, but this is something else entirely."

With a muffled pop sound, Adrian sets about the business of pouring the champagne into flutes. Handing one of the glasses to me he says, "Come here my little chick-a-dee-dee-dee!"

"I don't think I can drink that, Adrian. I don't feel so good right now."

"Take a little sip," he encourages.

"Help me out of this dress first, will you?"

"It will be my distinct pleasure…where's the zipper?" he asks.

"Oh, I forgot, Sheyanna sewed me into it so you might have to use your teeth."

"Why Mrs. Thompson dash Sellers, I do believe you're making me blush," Adrian chuckles.

"Sorry, sweetheart. It's there somewhere. Please hurry before I die in this thing!"

"Be who you are and say what you feel, because those who mind don't matter and those who matter don't mind."

~ Dr. Seuss

Chapter Seven

Anticipated Turmoil

I wake to a pounding headache, and when I attempt to sit up, it's impossible to stand. Adrian is near me, as the bed moves, his aftershave lingers in the air.

"Ellie, what's wrong with you? You're usually the first one up, and you haven't stirred for the longest time. Are you okay?"

"I don't feel well, Adrian."

"Please don't be sick today, not today!" he pleads.

"I'm sorry, Adrian. I can't travel like this. Can we go tomorrow? My head is pounding."

"I'll get you something. Is it a migraine? Don't you carry stuff for that?"

"Yes. Look in a side pocket of my case." I can't keep my eyes open.

Gentle hands appear with a cold cloth for my forehead. Mother puts a pill in my mouth, and a straw to my lips then says to drink. Sleep is my only salvation from the intense pain that runs along my spine and the pounding headache. I am aware that Adrian or Mother comes into the room every so often to cover me or to get a fresh cloth for my head, but little else. I cannot see the clock, so time seems irrelevant. Someone opens my eyelids, and I feel a prick on the inside of my left arm.

"How are you feeling?" an unfamiliar voice asks. "You are going to be fine, a little rest, and fluids, perhaps. I have started an IV drip. You rest, my dear." Flinching at his touch, as every part of my body hurts, even my teeth.

"I'm hungry. Can I have something to eat?"

"I do not see why not if you can keep it in your stomach. Call me should the symptoms worsen," the faraway voice says to someone else in the room.

Mother puts her face near mine, asking if I want some soup and crackers. I can't move my head, so I whisper yes. Adrian is sitting on the bed and pulls the coverlet up to my neck, but I'm too warm already and whisper to pull it away.

"I'm so sorry, Adrian. I have a terrible headache, my spine hurts, and I can't get up."

"We're all worried about you, Ellie. Dimmy insisted that we call in the Royal Physician. You've been like this for almost three days."

The reality of the timeframe is disturbing. "Paris…we missed our trip to Paris?" Tears form in my eyes, then roll into my hair.

He wipes them away with a gentle hand. "I don't care about that. It makes me crazy that you're sick. The doctor doesn't know what's wrong with you, but he thinks it could be the flu, or a virus. Then he said it could be all the excitement of the wedding, or maybe you're dehydrated."

"It isn't the flu, Adrian. I'm hungry."

"No one else is sick, so what is it then?" he asks.

I must drift off again until Mother and Sheyanna start tugging at my arms, then at my legs. I realize they're trying to pull the sheets off the bed with me still in it. As they walk around the room, they converse as if they're old friends. They stop when they see my eyes are open.

"Here Ellie, Sheyanna made you more of that tea. I think it's helping you," Mother says. "How do you feel today?"

I hesitate to move for fear the headache will return once I stand up. It isn't the same feeling from the drug-induced stupor, and I don't know that it isn't the flu, but I'm sure that it isn't normal.

"I feel much better today. What day is it?"

Mother frowns. "It's Friday. You've missed the better part of this week, sweetheart. Shall I get Adrian for you?"

"Oh, Dear Lord, no, don't get him yet. If I can stand up, I want to take a shower. I have missed my honeymoon. How unfair is that? Why did I have to get sick now?"

Mother shakes her head. "The doctor didn't have an answer. He was the one who came to take care of you when you were here the last time," she says.

"Is everyone else at least having fun? Are the girls okay?"

"No one was allowed in except me, Sheyanna, and Adrian, in case you were contagious. Now that I think of it, didn't this happen to you about ten years ago?"

"It feels like that. There was a bad headache, back pain, and I was hungry."

Mother bundled me into the car and took me to the urgent care center where the doctors couldn't come up with an explanation for what ailed me then, either. No one else contracted anything, and the strange thing is that I gained three pounds during my illness.

"I remember coming to help out. Daddy and Ravi were both out of town." Mother is quiet, and I'm betting she's remembering what Levi told us about both of them working for the CIA and was often out of town together.

"It's water under the bridge, Mother. Don't think about that okay?"

A sluggish feeling persists, but the dizziness and headache are mostly gone. Swinging my legs slowly over the side of the bed, Mother and Sheyanna help me into the bathroom. The hot shower feels good and helps to wash off the days of sleep.

When the family finds out that I'm better, there's a steady stream of people in and out of the room, as all are anxious to tell me what they've been doing while I was ill. Melanie, Curlie, and the girls have almost all of their homework assignments completed. Tieynza (along with a guard) took the girls on many forays into the marketplace. Tieynza even showed them other parts of the Royal Palace rarely seen by outsiders.

The older women shared high tea each day, while the men continued with their activities. They were privy to the intricate workings of the Arabian Stallions, often watching Jason train with them. Jason gained valuable insight and found a basic understanding of what it would be like to live in the Royal Palace should he choose to take on the role of Uncle Dimmy's rightful heir to the throne.

Now that I can sit up and eat, Adrian chooses to remain with me for our meals. Food trays with familiar shiny domes appear at mealtime, as I'm not feeling good enough to transverse the hallways and stairs yet. I chuckle at the idea of having our food delivered and presented to us as if we are royalty. I certainly didn't feel like royalty during my incarceration.

Since it is our last night in the Royal Palace, our host has invited us to a formal event as dignitaries will be present. I'm feeling much better and will be able to walk a longer distance, so I'll attend the gathering. I'm grateful that no one showed up with that ridiculous contraption Jam-ale tried to pass off as a wheelchair when I was here the last time.

The King greets us wearing the traditional Bisht, not unlike what he wore for our wedding ceremony. "I am pleased to see you have recovered from your illness, my dear Ellen. It is good that you can join us for this little celebration," he says graciously.

"Thank you. I can't believe we didn't go to Paris." My cheeks flush in embarrassment.

Adrian is standing by my side. "Don't worry about that; we can see Paris another time."

King Akdemir takes a champagne flute from a tray, presumably filled with juice. "Your family has no doubt told you of their adventures and activities while you were ill? They seem to have enjoyed themselves. Ms. Francesca and Sheyanna especially have been busy taking care of all of you. You may stay on here for as long as you wish."

Remembering that I was extremely rude to Akdemir when he extended a similar invitation before Jam-ale took me back to Kauai, I shove that memory to the back of my mind, saying, "We have imposed upon you long enough, but thank you for the offer. May I ask some questions that have been bothering me since I left the last time?"

The room suddenly goes quiet. As I glance around, Levi appears as if he's frozen in place. Is he afraid I might say something inappropriate? According to his instructions, we're allowed to ask specific questions; however, sticking to subjects about household, furnishings, food, clothing, and drink only. I must stay away from anything that remotely relates to my abduction, Ravi's death, or anything to do with my rescue.

We must also stay away from our subsequent new life brought about by the unmitigated circumstances of a few years ago. Those subjects are strictly taboo.

"Don't worry everyone. I know what questions to ask."

Akdemir raises his eyebrows comically, cocks his head to the side in the exact way his brother used to, and I finally realize why I had those moments where I thought he was Ravi because he did that very same thing. "Yes, my dear Ellen, you may ask your questions."

"Can you explain how your people get meals to us that are piping hot?"

Adrian wishes he had asked that one.

Akdemir lets out a little laugh. "There is a kitchen below that set of rooms that is supervised by Sheyanna. The chef there can prepare meals quickly."

"What I'd like to know is how does the food get to us while it's still hot?"

"I see what you mean. Sheyanna takes it from the kitchen, up the elevator to your floor, and presents it to you, piping hot as you say. Isn't that correct, Sheyanna?"

Sheyanna smiles sweetly and shakes her head up and down. I can't believe what I'm hearing. "Elevator? You mean there's an elevator?"

Akdemir begins to laugh, as is most everyone else in the room. "How else do you think we get around this enormous place, hum?"

"Then why didn't you use...why didn't Jam-ale..." I stop myself before I head over the protocol cliff. "Let me rephrase that. Why was I not aware of this elevator before now?"

"Jamaile said you wished to walk to the library. You didn't mind walking to dinner. We thought you wished to walk for the exercise."

Staring at Levi and then at Jam-ale, they both turn away, because they knew about the elevators. "Elevators? There's more than one of them?"

Adrian now sees how confused I am and starts to recall my notes and the long dissertation about the long walks to and from the various rooms, dining hall, and even to the library. He gently takes my hand, giving it a little squeeze. Bending his head close to my ear, he whispers, "You need to let this go, sweetie."

"My dearest Ellen, there are a series of elevators and walkways to connect each part of the palace. It is built almost inside this mountain.

Your Mr. Levi thought the same thing, and that is why no one used them at first."

"It would have been nice to know they were there in case we wanted to use them."

Adrian steps in to add, "Don't give it another thought, Ak-dim-er, we enjoyed our stay here and wanted to thank you for hosting this crowd and throwing us an incredible wedding, right Ellie?"

"It was my pleasure to have all of you here at the Royal Palace." Moving to a side table, Akdemir picks up a small box, where he turns to place it into my hands. "I believe this belongs to you, Ellen."

Pulling off the lid, I find my old camera. After I purchased a new cellphone, it made this one obsolete, because it takes better pictures than the camera ever did. For many years, I gave it little thought, except that one day, I had hoped the photos I carefully took of the beautiful Island of Kauai would find their way back to me.

"The memory chip has been wiped of any pictures. They were the last taken of Basim. We could not take the chance that they would fall into the wrong hands. We wanted no reference where you are concerned. It was for your safety as well as ours. I am sure you understand."

"No, I honestly don't understand. What harm would the pictures of Kauai have done? Some of those were of plant material and waterfalls. What about the laptop? There was a lot of information on it that had nothing to do with Ravi. It took years to reconstruct some of the files that were on there."

Akdemir frowns. He then proceeds to explain that information on my laptop would have damaged the Royal Family's image. As for the other items, they too have been disposed of, and I resigned myself a long time ago that my possessions were forever gone, and there is finally closure to my abduction, pictures or no pictures.

Turning to Mother, she hands me a small box along with an envelope. "We genuinely appreciate everything you did for us during our time here. You are a generous and thoughtful host, Ak-dim-er. I believe this rightfully belongs to you. Mother had it for safekeeping."

Mother steps forward. "We have all enjoyed your hospitality, and we all sincerely thank you."

"Here, here," the crowd declares in unison as we sip from our glasses.

Handing Akdemir the envelope, he reads the note silently, then pries the lid off as we crowd around him. He gently lifts out the shiny blue glass-like stone about the size of a golf ball. He squeezes it in his hand, and then brings it to his chest, closing his eyes.

"My father gave this to Basim before he left on his first adventure. I am happy that it still exists and is unbroken," he says quietly. "That was so long ago. It symbolizes what our families mean to us, the blue of the sea is the color of our strength. If ever he needed money, Basim could break it and use the diamonds embedded in it to help him return home."

Jason stares at the stone. "Dad showed that to me once, but I thought it was a pretty blue stone. He never said anything about where it came from or what it meant. What does the note say?"

Akdemir hands Jason the note written in his father's handwriting. "Would you read it for me, Jason?"

Jason opens the fragile paper and reads it to himself. With tears in his eyes, he quietly hands the note off to Melanie. "Here, you read it," he whispers.

Melanie reads the note and gazes at me with tears in her eyes. "Dad wrote this! It's Dad's handwriting. Oh my God, it's about you Mom, did you read it?"

"Yes, sweetheart. He loved us so much he…"

Mother says in a quiet voice, "When my husband first gave me the box, he merely asked me to keep it in a safe location. I'm glad Ravi never asked for it. I'm also glad that he didn't have to break it."

"As am I." Akdemir then places the blue stone gently back into the box, handing it to Jam-ale.

"What is something like that worth, if you don't mind me asking?" Levi bluntly asks.

"It is priceless, Mr. Levi. It is meant to be passed from one generation to another if it remains unbroken. I shall hold on to it until Jason is ready to accept it."

"Will somebody please read the note out loud because I wanna hear it!" insists Curlie.

Melanie hands her sister the note, sniffing, "Okay, you do it then." Curlie starts to weep, then asks for a tissue, handing it back to me without saying another word.

"Everyone wants to know what it says, Ellen. May I?" Terre asks. Taking it gently out of my hand, she begins to read.

> *Dear Little Brother,*
>
> *Father said to keep this close and use the contents should it become necessary. He said it will bring luck to those who possess it and indeed, it has as I have fallen in love with the woman who will share my life.*
>
> *I may not always be around to celebrate with you, but know that I left our country behind, not you. If ever you need me, Jamaile will know how to get in touch with me.*
>
> *Be safe and take good care of yourself. My hope is that you find your one true love as I have. Always follow your heart, for this will always and forever be your destiny.*
>
> *Basim*

Terre hands the note back to Mother where she inserts it into the envelope. Akdemir puts a hand on Jason's shoulder, letting it linger there until a server appears to usher the group into the dining hall where we partake in a sumptuous dinner. After consuming tantalizing desserts, the women retire to pack for our return home while the men stay behind to converse with the dignitaries.

It's nearly midnight before Adrian returns; I'm still awake, restless from an overabundance of sleep.

"I can't believe our time here is over. All that planning for the wedding and honeymoon and it's over. I'll make it up to you someday, Adrian, I promise."

Adrian grins his toothy smile at me, and in that instant, I feel that everything is right with the world. Who could want anything more? "That's okay, my sweet, rested, wonderful, shiny new wife. We have the rest of our lives together. Who needs a honeymoon?"

Who indeed? Who needs Paris when we all felt a little like royalty right here?

Levi seems more nervous than usual as his eyes dart from left to right as he nods his head at Jake. All of the men, including the pilot and co-pilot, have said their goodbyes and are in the first vehicle. The women stand near the outer door to say farewell to King Dimmy and his gracious household. The contingency from Virginia then departs for the drive to the airport once Levi and Jake close our vehicles' doors.

As we clear the palace walls, Alpha Team's Elizabeth, who is in the second vehicle with us women and girls, taps her earpiece, saying 'copy that.'

When we approach the airport, both of the vehicles begin to veer away from Dimmy's jet that sits on the tarmac, and I get an odd feeling that something is wrong.

Terre notices and asks, "Shouldn't there be guards near the jet?"

"Shouldn't the stairs be down so we can board it?" Turning to question Elizabeth, "Is everything..." she touches my arm, and I immediately understand that I should not pursue this. We all know the drill; if Levi's team wants to share information with us, they will.

"We have a little change in plans," Elizabeth says finally.

"Oh boy, Levi's not planning on dropping us out of the plane again, is he?" Mother chuckles.

"No, nothing like that. We'll be there in a moment or two, sit tight."

Then Elizabeth calmly explains that Levi decided not to use Akdemir's jet. The engine needs attention, so we're traveling on a commercial plane to Germany; it's that simple.

Does the maniacal man named Fariq have anything to do with this change?

The commercial jet is about the same size as Dimmy's, minus most of the excellent amenities, such as the fully reclining seats and the stocked drink and snack bar. An overly protective (and astute) Levi had it reserved in the event it was needed.

Once we're all onboard and seated, Levi comes to sit in the open seat across the aisle from us to give us the rundown. This change in plan turns out to be a wise decision as someone tried to lure the guards away from Dimmy's jet on the pretext that something was amiss at the Royal Palace.

Levi knew that information was false and instructed Captain Jam-ale to tell the guards to vacate the jet quickly and as nonchalantly as possible. It sounded a little too familiar, but the threat that the plane might explode upon takeoff was not something to take lightly.

Although Dimmy alleges that Fariq has a proclivity for stretching the truth, and is behind many things (some of them true, some of them false), Levi couldn't take the chance that it was not a real threat.

A few hours later, we arrive in Stuttgart and settle into our adjoining set of suites where we again embark upon a culinary journey through the foods of Germany.

"Don't forget to order something in the green family!" Mother refers to the green and leafy vegetables, of course. There wasn't much of it when we blew through here the last time. Then she lies down on her bed to fall fast asleep. We assume she's exhausted from keeping up with all of us.

Then we get into a discussion about what famous people came from Germany, besides Albert Einstein. Curlie's assignment has a particular segment that has to do with music. She proudly tells us that famous composers such as Ludwig van Beethoven, Bach, Mendelssohn, and Handel all came from German towns. Unfortunately, time constraints will prevent visits to their birthplaces.

To pass the time between feedings, Adrian has his laptop open, tapping away at the keyboard. "Did you know that 70% of German highways have no speed limit?"

Sam looks at him in surprise. "Really? I thought the Audubon was the only highway that has no speed limit."

"Nope. Did you know that there are around 300 varieties of bread made here?"

"I think we sampled about twenty of them," Bernie says.

"Did you know that there are over 1,300 breweries, making over 5,000 brands of beer?"

"I had no idea there were that many," Dennis says. "So many beers, so little time to sample them."

"Here's a good one." Adrian begins to laugh. "Did you know that a broken toilet sank a German sub during World War II? Evidently, the toilet malfunctioned."

"Potty-mouth talk, nice one Adrian. I'm going back to the suite for a nap," Jason yawns. "Let me know when it's time to eat again."

Tapping Adrian on the arm to get his attention, saying, "That sounds like an excellent thing to do. I'm still a little deflated from last week, care to join me?"

"Yes, right behind you, my little flower petal." After we close the door, he launches himself onto the bed to sprawl out, kicking his shoes off. "It sure will be good to get home to a familiar routine again," Adrian quips.

"I agree, it feels like it's been three months since we left Ashwood and I lost an entire week out of the middle of it!"

Sitting up, Adrian declares, "I lost a pound or two with all the walking up and down the hallways and byways. I had to punch another hole in my belt." Adrian sees the expression on my face. "Sorry, my love, you don't look at all happy."

"That is wrong; I gained three pounds…while I was sick! I don't know how you do it, Adrian, but it's plain ridiculous! You eat and lose weight, and I don't eat and gain it!"

"There, there, my little chin leaps, not to fret. I will love you if you are thin or fat."

"My dear new husband, its *liebchen* spelled l i e…oh, never mind. I guess I should be glad you didn't call me *lederhosen*. I still can't believe I got sick and we missed our honeymoon."

Adrian pulls me toward him. "I couldn't have gone without you. Don't give it another thought, *Fräulein* T dash Sellers. I have it on good authority that Paris will still be there in case we ever want to visit it in the future."

"Sweetheart, you can't... It's a good thing we don't have to converse with anyone here because you don't know how to speak German."

Adrian raises his eyebrows. "And you do? I was present when you tried to order food the last time. And I do know some German. There are wiener sizzle and speck-in-zee-dust."

Throwing a bed pillow at him, he ducks, as it narrowly misses his head. "By the way, I think it's pronounced *Sprechen Sie Deutch?* It's asked as a question."

"Isn't that why Levi's here with us? He speaks their language, and he's getting us some interesting beer right now. By the way," he says changing the subject, "What do you want for Christmas, Ellie? I was going to buy you something spectacular in Paris."

"I already have everything I want or need. You'll have to surprise me. Maybe Levi will let us do some shopping here."

Adrian raises his eyebrows. "I think Levi has other plans. Haven't you heard?"

"What did the girls talk him into this time?"

"They ganged up on him, and he's taking them to a museum." Adrian plops his suitcase on the bed and starts taking items out of it.

"What's the name of the museum? Maybe we should go with them?"

"I think he said Sta ta Galla…gall something. I can't pronounce it," he says giving up.

Trapped within the recesses of my mind, a memory of Daddy and two men are flashing as if a video is replaying. "I think I remember which one he's thinking about, Adrian. We were supposed to go there…it was when Terre and me…"

Adrian stares at me. "Ellie, you have a funny look on your face. What's going on?"

"If I had known then, what I know now. Oh my God, Adrian, we have to talk with Terre and Dennis, they need to be part of this."

Adrian appears serious. "What kind of revelation have you had?"

"Daddy did a good job of hiding what he did for a living. I thought of something."

"Okay, we were going to tell them everything at some point anyway. I guess this is as good a time as any. Did you ask Francesca if she said anything to them?"

"You know, with one thing or another, I don't remember asking Mother if she told Terre and Dennis anything beyond that those two idiots put us into *'the program'*, and we had to move to Virginia. Terre and Mother communicated with code until Lenard and Gene were out of the picture and you and your CIA folks came to the rescue. Didn't your teams at the CIA inform them of the stuff before they came to live with us?"

"Good question, Ellie. I don't know what they were told."

Taking Adrian by the hand, I lead him into the common living area where fanned brochures are laying on the dining table as the adults mill around it. Motioning to Terre to come into our room, Dennis is right behind her.

"What's all this about?" Terre wants to know, "Is it CIA stuff?"

Taking a deep breath, I exhale saying, "My God, I don't know how to say this, Terre."

"Ellen, say it. I won't be shocked or anything," she says.

"Were you and Dennis debriefed about anything before you came to Ashwood?"

Terre looks surprised. "Do you mean, did Levi tell us about what happened to you and how you got there?"

"Yes, that kind of stuff."

"No, not really. Dennis and I know about parts of it." Terre says.

"Has Mother shared, I don't know…any information about what our father did for a living?"

Terre seems confused, glancing at Dennis, she says, "Didn't Daddy work for a large company? They let him travel the world and sometimes we went with them. No, I don't precisely know what he did. It never occurred to ask questions, why?"

"For a teacher, you don't question many things, do you?" I inquire.

Terre is wary. "I question lots of things, Ellen. What's this all about?"

"Do you remember the time we were here in Stuttgart with Mother and Daddy? I believe the year was 1975. Do you remember what happened when we were here?" Shoving the suitcases out of the way, I sit down on the left side of the bed.

Terre sits down slowly on the right side saying, "Humm, let me think. I was only eight at the time, Ellen. How am I supposed to remember something like that?"

"Give it a try, Terre. It was something significant."

"What significant event happened in 1975?" Terre takes in a deep breath and lets it out slowly. "Was it when the Vietnam War ended?"

"No, we talked about it for about three hours, and Daddy said we couldn't go to the museum because he was waiting for some people to show up. You threw a hissy fit, and he promised you some incredible cream pie or ice cream thing. We kept asking him why, but he said we had to wait."

Terre is chewing on her lower lip. "I do remember throwing a fit about some unbelievable dessert or something, but not what the conversation was about."

"Oh, I know! Didn't Jimmy Hoffa disappear that year!" Dennis offers.

Adrian is searching what history happened around the world in the year 1975. "Let's see here, there's the one about where Franco dies in Spain, OPEC agrees to raise crude oil prices by 10%, and here's something I didn't know, the British Conservative Party chooses their first woman leader, Margaret Thatcher. I thought it was later than that."

"No, Adrian, it's none of those, keep going."

Adrian taps away on his keyboard and starts to throw out some statistics. "How about this one; the US carries out Vietnam Operation Babylift, bringing Vietnamese orphans to the US."

"No, that's not it, Adrian."

"New York City avoids bankruptcy when President Gerald R. Ford signs a $2.3 million loan."

Banker Dennis corrects Adrian by saying, "Don't you mean that it was a $2.3 billion loan?"

"Yeah, you're right, it was billions not millions. Did they ever pay it back?" Adrian questions.

"Come on Adrian, be serious, will you?"

Adrian continues to tap keys. "Here's another one...the Cod War breaks out between Britain and Iceland when Iceland extends its fishing rights to 200 miles. That can't be what you're looking for is it, Ellie?"

"As in the fish cod or the thing baseball players put over their..." Dennis wonders.

"Will you two be serious?" I'm standing next to Adrian, pointing to the one below it.

"I would have gotten it with a little more time," he mumbles.

Dennis asks, "What are you two talking about and what does this have to do with anything? Is it some deep, dark secret that might explain why you and your family might be in the you know what?"

"Funny you should mention that Dennis, but now that you have, it could. An assassination took place. It was King Faisal of Saudi Arabia."

"What does that have to do with our father, Ellie?"

"Give me a second, and I'll try to explain. Did I ever tell you what Ravi did for a living?"

Terre seems exasperated. "We never discussed it, but wasn't he in electronics or something? Can't you come right out and tell us without all this rigmarole? Geeze, Ellie, tell us for crying out loud!"

Adrian and I stare at each other and then he calmly tells them, "Buckle up you two, you're about to hear one hell of a story which, after we're done, you'll have to swear never to divulge it to a living soul."

"Ooooh, this is CIA stuff," Terre says. "Do go on."

Adrian and I proceed to tell them what we know, including the part about how their son Danny inadvertently joined our drama when a rogue arrow flew through their back door and embedded itself into his shoulder, leaving out specific information that might otherwise make them bolt for the door.

Terre then makes the astute observation that it explains so much and sees the connection. Even though she appears unsettled by the information and can't believe what we've been through and sacrificed, she's glad to be a part of it. Now that she and Dennis know, we can discuss things openly; however, we'll refrain from telling the children for now.

"So why didn't Daddy let us go to the museum? Come to think about it, weren't there other times he disappeared?" Terre turns toward Adrian. "What on earth was he into?"

"He was going to meet with the operatives who witnessed the assassination," he says. "Back then, he was working alone and happened to be in Germany when the operatives crossed the border. It was his job to see that they reached safety. As Levi found out, they were not part of the assassination, but they were present. Your father didn't want to worry about you, so he made you stay in the hotel until things blew over."

Terre mutters to herself, "That explains a lot, but why all the secrecy? And oh," she begins recalling, "that time in Italy when Daddy disappeared. Did he really disappear? Was he ever in real danger?"

Adrian stares at her. "Of course, he was in danger; he was the best CIA operative around, ask Levi."

Now it's my turn to question. "How would Levi know, Adrian? Did he train with him? Was he one of the men he was waiting for?"

"Humm I hear some *wenersnitzen* calling my name," Adrian sidesteps my question and moves toward the door at lightning speed.

Terre sees the potential for an argument, saying, "Okay, I think we're done for now. How about we go to that museum and check out their magnificent old paintings?"

"That's an excellent idea! I'll see if Mother and the rest of the adults want to come with us."

When we arrive at the Staatsgalerie Stuttgart, there is an extensive collection of paintings, which the word magnificent cannot adequately describe. Mother gently nudges us to keep going, as there's so much to see. It doesn't take the place of the Louvre, but it does make me feel a little better.

As if in rewind, we leave Stuttgart to fly back to Québec. Since we left Dimmy's jet behind, Levi had to make other arrangements. We're actually on a chartered flight that is very comfortable, has some amenities, and a happy crew. When we arrive, limos provide transportation to our hotel.

It doesn't take long for the girls to begin their bombardment on Levi. Didn't he promise them a cruise down the St. Lawrence Seaway? They have almost completed their assignments, and this is the last one they need. They do not let up until he agrees.

"I'm so tired that I think we'll stay here and take a nap," Terre yawns.

Dennis agrees. "You should go; we'll stay with the others."

"What makes you think we're rearin to go? I'm as tired as you are. We've already been on a cruise down the St. Lawrence Seaway. Terre and I sailed on that ship long ago."

Adrian mutters, "It's settled, us old farts will stay here while the youngins are on their adventure."

"Hey, speak for yourself old man," Sam says, tossing a small pillow at Adrian's head.

"Then why are we so tired?" Adrian throws the pillow back to his brother. "It's probably jet-lag or something."

Sam throws the pillow at Dennis. "It's because we did a lot of stuff while we were gone, don't you remember?"

Dennis starts to laugh, catching himself before he snorts like a pig, as he grabs the pillow. "Oh yeah, you mean…" then stops himself, turning his head toward Adrian, clamping his mouth shut quickly.

Bernice shakes her head, then screws her face in a comical expression. "They don't want us to know what they did, Ellie."

"We made a solemn oath, remember?" Sam says, as Dennis and he throw pillows at each other. "We're all blood-brothers to Gee-man or something, right Jason?"

Jason walks toward the refrigerator. "Don't drag me into this. I was with the horses most of the time. Whatever you guys did, I don't wanna know." Finding something tasty, he says, "Let me know when dinner is. I'm going to my room."

Sam catches the pillow, saying, "Right," drawing out the word.

Dennis snickers as Sam throws the pillow at him again. "What did you ladies do while we were, um, otherwise occupied?"

"You guys are hysterical," Bernie says, picking up another small pillow to push into her husband's face. "None of us want to know what mischief you men were up to because we did some pretty exciting things, too."

A pillow flies over my head. "Did you all have a good time? How about your Mother, Sam? She seems a little quiet as my Mother does."

"You better believe she did. They're both taking a nap. They had a great time with Sheyanna and her girls. They exchanged emails so they can keep in touch," he says, as Dennis throws a pillow to him.

Adrian throws a pillow at Dennis, and I have to duck my head. "How about you, Bernie, did you have a good time?"

"Yes, Ellie, Sammy and I had a great time. We haven't been away much, and this was the perfect time before our kids come home for Christmas. We don't spend near enough time with them. This trip made us realize that."

Dennis playfully tosses the pillow at Terre. "I, for one, have had enough excitement for one year, and I'll be glad to get home to my boring old life."

"Me too." Terre muses, catching the pillow, turning it to stuff into his face. "Now if we can only get the girls to settle down when we get home. My, will they have some tall tales to tell their friends."

Adrian shakes his head. "You do know that they can't say we've been in Saudi, don't you? Security, remember?" Adrian mutters, "Levi will censor their homework assignments, too."

A thought occurs to me. "Does that mean we're not married?"

"Oh, we're married, Ellie, we have that paper to prove it, don't we?"

"Come on, Adrian," Sam says. "We don't even know what city we were in, so how could we tell anyone?"

"Oh, didn't Levi tell you? The CIA conducted a sting operation while we were there and no one can say we were out of the country," Adrian says with a straight face.

Everyone is silent, and then Adrian starts to laugh.

"I'm only kidding…" We all pick up the nearest pillow to throw at him. "Hey…"

I loved this time away, but it'll be good to be home.

Christmas will be here before we know it. It'll get us in the spirit if we all pitch in to decorate. We'll also string garland and lights along the fence near the road and in through the pathways along the horse trails. Wreaths and red bows will once again grace the windows, and it'll be quite a display!

Before our trip to Saudi, we arranged for Mona and Glen to spend two weeks in Florida with their family. As promised, they'll share a suite with their children and grandchildren, having five full days at Disney World; all expenses paid. The only catch is that they have to promise to relax and have some fun while they're gone!

Adrian and Reed will take care of the *Magic of Christmas* this year. It was Reed's brainchild, developed when he first came to Ashwood that includes our Clydesdales, named *Frick*, and *Frack*. It's little more than a glorified hayride along the horse trails, but people seem to enjoy it knowing their donation goes to a good children's charity.

Jason and Mack seem bummed when we suspend training and racing until spring, but Adrian has some ideas for them to mull over. Would they like to take over for Reed, giving him a break? With a new baby on the way, he could use the extra time to get things done for new mommy Jessica, but they flatly turned this down.

Adrian and I have discussed the possibility of sending Jason and Mack to New York State for a ten-week course in foreign language and a sampling of martial arts training. Mack's father was totally against this until Adrian convinced him that he wouldn't have to spend one red cent; we'll pay for everything.

"It's time we start thinking about Jason's future, Ellie. If he intends to live in another country, he needs to be able to communicate with them, too. We did our share of gesturing and pointing at things when we were there in November."

"It can't hurt. It should come in handy when Jason has to…we know he's leaning toward going to Saudi, don't we? It might give him a leg up, especially in understanding what they say. You know, when I was there, the previous time I mean, I kept thinking Dimmy and Jam-ale were talking about me while I was sitting right there. They used to whisper to each other and then smile at me. When I asked them questions, they wouldn't answer them."

"Are you wondering how we'll keep Jason and Mack busy and out of trouble if they don't go on this little trip to New York?" he muses.

"That had crossed my mind."

"I told him that he and Mack would stay in a co-ed building and he jumped at the chance to get away from all of us," Adrian grins. "He asked how soon they could leave."

"Then he's okay with this?"

Adrian takes my face in his hands. "Yes, my little turtle dove, what he doesn't know, is that they'll have a 24/7 security detail. We'll not only know what the boys are up to, but we can also monitor their activities," he says quietly.

"If they find out, won't they think it's a little sneaky, Adrian?"

"My dear Mrs. Thompson dash Sellers, that is what I do for a living, you know. I'll admit that it's a little sneaky, but safety is my middle name," he utters, kissing my nose.

"I thought your middle name is Benson, as in Benson the Butler."

"Come on, Ellie, they've taken the bait, and they're all for it, my little snickerdoodle."

"What kind of security detail are you talking about here? Will they have a code to use as Levi does for our clandestine capers? Will it be the Jason slash Mack Caper?"

"I made it clear that the team will not make contact unless there's a clear threat. If the boys hear the phrase, *it's an electric day*, then something's up, and they better pay attention."

"That's a strange code. Why not give Jason and Mack a simple code, like the ones we use around here? Like *Fire Drill, Houston we have a problem,* or new ones, like *how's your mama,* or how about this; *SOS, code orange,* maybe *something's amiss, Mr. Watson.*"

"We don't use things like that, Ellie."

"Then, how about something simple like *we have a situation.*"

"Thanks, Ellie, but I got this."

My mind begins to go in different directions. "Can you describe what kind of clear threat would make the team blow their cover? Will it be like someone shooting at them or running them down with their vehicle? Will it turn out to be one of their martial arts teachers that turns out not to be their teacher?"

"Mrs. Thompson-Sellers, you need to stop that kind of talk right now. I would never intentionally put those boys into harms' way, especially if I'm not there with them. Do you remember the couple that came to stay here when we went to the Cape? They'll handle it. They'll see to it that everything stays copasetic."

I grab Adrian to pull him into a bear hug. "Humm, they better take exceptional care of them, Mr. CIA man!"

"Okay, okay…I love you, too, now can you let go? They'll teach the boys the basics of the Arabic language, and I'll bet Jason will have it figured out by the first week."

"Yeah, I'll bet he'll have it figured out by the time the plane lands. I know how you bet, Adrian."

"You gave up on me too soon. I would have gotten it if you had spent more time with me. Can we try it again, honey? I promise to listen this time—Please, Oh Mighty Guru of the Racetrack!"

"No Adrian, please don't put me through that again. You're never going to get it, so for the sake of my sanity, give it up!"

"Never…say never, my dear," he says, turning to leave.

"Now see, that would be a good code to use."

Adrian turns around. "Naw, the code's all set Ellie, let it go, will you? Say, if we were to bet, what would you bet? Is it a night on the town with your favorite fella?" He pretends to pull at an invisible mustache.

"The only way you could win a bet with me, Mr. CIA man, is if you cheat."

Adrian sniffs. "You offend me, dear lady. I would never do that. I would find a way to get around it, but I would never cheat!"

"If Josh and Jake are gone for the holidays, who's going to take up the slack in the barn when the boys are gone? Would that be you?"

Cocking his head to the side, saying, "Not to worry, my little butterfly, Josh and Jake will be back before the boys leave."

"Don't you people from the CIA have lives of your own? What if they had families, how could they be away from them so much? Hum, now that I think about it, Daddy and Ravi managed to be around for most of the holidays."

"We do what we have to, Ma'am; it's all in the line of duty. It's the secret code and all that. Look, can we do this later? Levi sent me a text to call him."

Moving out of his way, "I'll give you secret code!"

"Is that a threat lady? Bring it…" Pushing my hand in Adrian's face, he starts to lick it, then grabs my wrist and begins to kiss my hand progressing up my arm until I stop him.

"Later darling…"

Jason and Mack are so agreeable about these college courses that I'm a little suspicious. When I ask Jason if he's all right with this time away from his family, he says it's a trial run. What will happen if he can't stand to be away from us? If he can't take ten weeks away, how will he be able to go out of the country for more than a year or two?

He does have a valid point, and Mack will be with him, so how much trouble can they possibly get into there that he wouldn't get into here? It isn't what worries me. I'm not worried Jason will have a hard time being away, I'm afraid that he'll *like* being away.

Along with learning the fundamentals of the Arabic language, Jason and Mack will also study Jiu-Jitsu and a myriad of martial arts. At the end of week eight, they'll be exhausted, but not as tired as they'll be after week ten, because Adrian included a little surprise.

The boys will leave the first week in January and be back in time for spring training. They'll be on their own, except for the security detail that's being set up. They're anticipating this time away from us as a learning experience.

I'm having trouble coping and have mixed feelings about Jason being away. Mother continually mentions how moody I am. Will I stow away in Jason's duffle bag when he leaves? I'm not a clingy person by nature, but I have reservations about this as the time for their departure gets near.

Do all mothers feel as I do when their children start leaving the nest? Perhaps I'm not like other people who can't wait for their children to leave home so they can have some peace. I don't want them to go away. I happen to like their unique personalities, and there's plenty of space here to accommodate them.

Then I start to worry about what will happen when they all move away. Mother helps me realize the absurdity of this line of thinking. It may not happen; they could all want to stay here. We do live in a small hotel, after all.

And maybe I shouldn't worry about it until I have to.

As we gear up for our third Christmas here at Ashwood Stables, there is a flurry of activity as we wrap presents, bake cookies, and lay in a supply of hot chocolate for those who will come for the *Magic of Christmas*.

As the dollars add up from this venture, Reed faces an unusual dilemma, as he tries to decide which children's charity will benefit the most from it this year.

All the women pitch in to do the cooking and baking as Mona and Glen enjoy their long-anticipated vacation with their family. They are not expected back until the end of January, as we insisted that they stay in Orlando to get well-deserved rest after their family goes home.

Uncle Dimmy sent lavish gifts because he knows we celebrate this, of all holidays, in a major way. Although his gifts are far more elaborate and expensive than they need to be, no one wants to return or exchange them.

As we turn the calendar to the new year, and January eighth approaches, I begin to get emotional as Jason packs his duffle bag. I'm slightly more apprehensive than usual, given all the crazy things that happen to us.

"You got something on your mind, don't you Mom?" Jason asks when I wipe a tear from my face. "Come on, let's have it. You don't want me to go, do you?"

"I want you to go, sweetheart. You should experience a little of life before you..."

"And you only want what's best for me, but you don't know how to say it," he says.

"I do only want what's best for you, Jason. All I want is for you to make good decisions, that's all, sweetie."

Jason tenderly reaches for my arm, and says, "I know what you're anxious about, Mom, but you don't have to worry about us. Mack and I will be fine."

"We don't have to talk about this right now, Jason."

"Yes, we do. We've avoided this for a long time. You're worried that I'll like being away and won't hesitate to go to Saudi, right?"

When I don't say anything, Jason sits on the bed, so his face is right under mine. "Mom, that's a few years off. I haven't made up my mind yet. Sure, it would be amazing to go back to the Royal Palace and be whatever Uncle Dimmy wants me to be, but I'll only be gone ten weeks. We can talk every week. Every Sunday afternoon, okay?"

Hugging Jason tightly, saying, "I thought you were all lost to me once and I couldn't live through that again."

"I wouldn't want to live through that again, either."

"I want you to have this." Handing Jason a wristwatch, it reminds me of the first time I met Adrian. It's a smaller version of the silver and black necklace he gave me that I still wear every day. "It will send a signal when the face is depressed. Use it if you think you need to. The signal goes straight to Levi's group."

"Geeze, Mom, do you honestly think this is necessary? Mack and I'll be fine. What do I need another watch for, anyway? This one looks a little strange," he moans. "It's very unusual."

"Humor me, okay? Use it only if you need to. I'll feel better if you take it."

"I didn't know it would be this hard for you, Mom."

"Part of me wishes you won't go and part of me wishes you do go. I need to let you go. You know how hard it's been these last few years. You are and always will be my only son, and I'm a silly old mom. I love you, Jason. I want you to go out into the world prepared to do whatever is your destiny. You can't learn all you need to here at home. I often wonder what your father would do when these things come up. He's not here, Adrian is, and he thinks that you and Mack will learn something of real value and I tend to agree with him. He's our rock now."

Jason sighs heavily, taking the unusual wristwatch to put into his pocket. "I guess you're right. Adrian told me about some interesting things that might be difficult for Mack and me, so we won't have much time to do anything besides eating and sleeping."

"I'd feel better if you wore the watch, Jason. Do it, please?"

Jason smirks, saying, "Okay. And I also don't mind about the secret security detail."

"You know about that? How did Mack react when you told him?"

"I didn't tell him. I figured that I'd tell him when we were alone. He doesn't question much of anything, but maybe it's time to let him in on why we need it. He's a good friend, Mom and I trust him. He thinks we're all a little strange sometimes, especially when something bizarre happens. Guess he puts it together all by himself. I get the feeling that he might not want to know stuff anyway."

"Me too. Mack does have family drama where he lives. Why don't you tell him what you think he can absorb, but don't tell him anything about how your father died or my abduction. And maybe nothing about how we got here, okay? Certain things need to remain a secret, especially the part about that dimwit Lenard and *the program*. I'm not sure we're supposed to tell anyone else about that."

Jason agrees not to reveal how we came to be in Virginia. He'll tell Mack what happened to our horses, as that seems to be an ongoing threat and he should be aware of it.

About fifteen minutes before we leave to take Jason and Mack to the airport, Reed rushes into the kitchen to say he's driving Miss Daisy, as he lovingly refers to his wife Dr. Jessica, to the hospital. Her water broke! A customarily reserved Reed seems flustered beyond words.

"I got this," Adrian says, kissing my forehead. "Take care of yourselves fellas and stay out of trouble, okay? Think you can get these two to the airport without me, sweetheart? Are you going out like that?"

"Sure, no problem. What's wrong with what I'm wearing?"

It's a quiet ride to the airport as Jason and Mack talk mostly about what they'll do once they get to the campus. When we get near the airport, Jason starts to laugh.

"Please don't get out of the car, Mom. You can drop us off at the departures, okay?"

"Why? We were going to grab a sandwich before you left. I wanted to stay until you had to go through security."

"Mom, you're wearing two different shoes."

"What?" Looking down, sure enough, there's a black loafer on one foot and a white sneaker on the other. I must have been so distracted that I didn't notice. "Okay, there will be no long drawn out farewells." Then I signal to the driver behind me that I want to switch from the short-term parking to the departure lane.

"We can say goodbye from here, okay? I love you, Mom. Pop the trunk, would you?" Jason says getting out of the car.

I watch as Jason and Mack saunter toward the double sliding glass doors that will take them on their adventure. An adventure Adrian and I hope will help them mature, but I can't stop the tears that are forming in my eyes.

Pulling away from the curb, Adrian calls to inform me that they have arrived safely at the hospital and that Reed is with Dr. Jessica. It's only a matter of time before there's good news.

Several hours later, Reed calls. "We have a baby girl! She weighs in at eight pounds two ounces and is twenty-one inches long," Reed gushes excitedly. "Little Amanda Ellen is beautiful, like her mother. And you should see all her hair."

Ah, that was nice of them to partly name the baby after me, then remember that it was Dr. Jess's Grandmother's name.

"Choices made, whether bad or good, follow you forever and affect everyone in their path one way or another."

~ J.E.B. Spredemann, An Unforgivable Secret

Chapter Eight

Choices; Some Good, Some Bad

Jason and Mack cleared security and were waiting to board the short flight to New York, joking about what their freedom was going to mean. Once they were on board, they settled into their seats. Jason reached into the seat pocket under the tray table when he looked up. A man and woman were coming down the aisle, where they took the seats directly behind them.

After a few moments, Jason figured that he had spotted their security detail. He began to listen in to their quiet conversation as the man and woman whispered to each other.

Mack pulled a magazine out of the seat pocket in front of him. "Boy, am I glad that's over, and we're finally on our way."

"Me too, Mack."

"I didn't expect my Dad to go all weepy on me as he did. I did expect my Mom to gush. Think they'll feed us something besides a bag of pretzels? I'm hungry."

"You're always hungry." Jason continued to listen as the couple behind him talked mostly of mundane things, but he was having difficulty as Mack kept interrupting.

"Hey, look at this, Jas," Mack said, opening a folded paper.

Adrian gave them a map of the campus with instructions to contact a person named Ray as soon as they arrived at their dorm. He would help them get a sense of where other buildings are located such as the cafeteria, the library, their language arts classroom, and the gym.

Mack suddenly noticed a man and woman who was glaring at them before they seated themselves near the front of the aircraft. "Wonder who they are?" he said. "Why were they looking at us like that?"

"Who?" Jason asked.

"That couple that sat down up front. The woman's wearing a black covering around her head, like a turban or something. The guy stared at us."

Just as Mack said this, Jason's seat moved as the man sitting behind him must be leaning heavily on his tray table. He then felt the sensation that the man was trying to see between the cracks in the seat. He whispered something to the woman, asking if she knew who the people were.

"It's no one I know, Jimmy. Can you get a fix on them?"

"I'll try," the man replied.

"Let's keep an eye on them when we get to baggage claim," the woman said.

Jason felt the man fumble with the tray table as the steward shut and locked the door in place.

"I hope this doesn't spell trouble," the man said. I'd hate to start off this way."

"It would be a terrible start to a wonderful experience for the boys," the woman answered.

It's a short and uneventful flight. When the attendant opened the door and the passengers began to deplane, Jason and Mack followed the signs to the baggage claim area to wait for their duffle bags to come out of the chute.

Jason was curious about the couple from the front of the plane who were standing off to one side. When he began to stare at them, they averted their eyes quickly. It convinced him that something wasn't quite right about them.

Mack stuck an elbow into Jason's arm. "Hey, that woman who was sitting behind us on the plane is coming toward us."

"How do you know that, Ace?"

"Act natural," he whispered.

When the woman got close to them, she said, "Hello boys, are you going to the University by any chance? It's such *an electric day*, isn't it'?"

Adrian briefed Jason earlier that morning that if the secret detail felt that it was necessary, they would use code to alert them of potential danger. He and Mack would need to go along with whatever the couple asked them to do. Something seemed familiar about this woman, but he couldn't put his finger on why that was.

Jason nodded, saying, "Yes, it's *an electric day*."

"Didn't your parents ever teach you not to talk to strangers? Are you crazy, Jas? Why are you talking to her?" Mack said in a low tone.

"It's okay, Mack." Jason turned to the woman. "Yes, we're going to the University."

"Would you mind if my husband, Jimmy, and I share a taxi with you? By the way, my name is Sharon Lindsay. It will save you a taxi fare if we share a ride."

Jason turned to Mack, "It's okay with me, how about you?"

"Why can't they get their own taxi?" Mack answered impolitely. "What I mean is, why would we share a taxi with total strangers? We don't know these total strangers, Jason!"

He realized that he should have told Mack some things to understand what might be going down now. "Don't be rude, dude, it's okay, Adrian knows these people." Then he lightly smacked Mack on the shoulder.

"Why didn't you say so?" Mack said quietly.

"I am sorry," Mrs. Lindsay said courteously. "I didn't mean to put you out. My husband and I know the city, and we thought that if you're new here, we could accompany you, because we teach foreign language there, you see."

"Sorry, Ma'am, we didn't mean…they might be our teachers, Mack…" Jason said out of the side of his mouth.

Mack clamped his mouth together in a comical way, then began to roll his eyes. "How does Adrian know these people? Is there something I should know that you forgot to tell me, Jas?"

"We are your professors of language, Mack, so the correct term for us is a professor," Mrs. Lindsay purred.

"And we wouldn't mind at all if you and your husband shared a taxi to the University with us, right Mack?" Jason said calmly.

Jimmy Lindsay was circling the other side of the baggage carousel, quietly observing the couple who seemed strangely out of place. The woman had a hand over her mouth, then suddenly moved her head in a jerking motion when the man grabbed her arm. He whispered something to her, and she recoiled, trying to pull away from him.

The man then reached into his pocket to pull out a cellphone with his free hand, putting it to his ear, but didn't say anything. It convinced Jimmy that his hunch was correct in thinking that these are people to avoid. They didn't attempt to pick up their luggage until Jason and Mack reached for their duffle bags.

Mr. Lindsay signaled to his wife, who had retrieved their bags and had joined the boys. After quick introductions, they engaged them in animated conversation on their way out of the airport to flag down a taxi. Sharon showed Jimmy the picture she snapped of the odd couple that she forwarded to the authorities.

Mrs. Lindsay then showed the boys the same picture. "Have either one of you ever seen these people before?"

"They were sitting at the front of the plane. That's all I know," Mack replied.

Jimmy Lindsay's cellphone rang. "Yes sir, I understand, and I'll tell the others." He whispered that he has been instructed not to engage the couple in conversation and they are to avoid contact.

Sharon Lindsay said, "We are going to ignore them, okay? There's our taxi now, come along fellas."

Once they were all in a taxi, it moved away from the curb, and gained speed quickly. Another cab followed close behind, and Jimmy said something to the driver in what was unmistakably a language the boys didn't understand.

"What did you say to him?" Jason asked Mr. Lindsay.

Mack looked confused. "Yeah, what was that, sir? I know it wasn't German or Spanish."

"I asked him to lose the taxi behind us as quickly as he could," Mr. Lindsay answered. "I also asked him to take a detour in case. The taxi driver understood the Arabic words I spoke to him, and he obeyed quickly."

Mack turned toward Mrs. Lindsay, and asked, "They remind me of terrorists. Are they terrorists?"

While Mrs. Lindsay ignored Mack's question, Jason knew there might be more than the couple haven't shared with them. "What else did you say to the taxi driver?"

"That's very astute Jason. I also told him that he'd get an extra hundred-dollar tip if he made it snappy." Mr. Lindsay said, smiling. "You will learn how to speak Arabic soon enough, and then you can be the one to tell taxi drivers to step on it."

"I don't know about that. It sounds like the words are hard to pronounce." Jason was unsure if he would even be able to say good day in Arabic in the time allotted, but more concerned about the people that were following them. "Who are they and what do they want with us?"

Jason was sitting where he could observe the goings on in the rearview mirror. The taxi that was following came to a sudden stop as a shiny black limousine came from behind, where it swerved around it as they passed under a streetlight.

As their taxi kept moving, Mr. Lindsay spoke to the driver again, and several seconds after that, he turned the wheel hard to the right. He steered it down an alley which came out at another intersection. During this time, Mrs. Lindsay tried to direct the conversation to the university and away from their situation.

Mack absently turned his head to observe that there were no vehicles following them, then doubted that they were ever in peril or the people named Jimmy and Sharon Lindsay were who they said they were. Jason noticed Mack's facial expression and assured him they will talk when they got to their dorm room.

The taxi pulled into the university driveway where Mr. Lindsay instructed the driver where to let them all off. Then he explained that there were few students right now because of the break in quarters. The university agreed to a ten-week acceleration course as a favor to them.

Mack remarked about how mild the weather seemed to be as the Lindsay's laughed. "Wait; it's usually the month of February when the brutal snow machines crank up," Jimmy Lindsay said.

Jason fondly remembered the lake snow effect that blanketed the Great Lakes region every winter. "I know what that's like; we used to live near Lake Michigan. My mom used to get so frustrated when the snow plows dumped snow right after we cleaned out the end of our driveway. We got out of more than one day of school those winters."

"I don't miss snow since we moved to Virginia," Mack replied. "We get enough there."

"That's nothing compared to what we used to get! Jason laughed.

Once they were in their dorm room, Mr. Lindsay did a sweep of it with a wand-like instrument.

"What the hell are you doing? That thing looks like Harry Potter's magic wand!" Mack uttered in disbelief.

"Sorry for all the drama," Mr. Lindsay muttered, "but we can't take any chances. I know you're confused right now, Mack. It's a procedure to flush out potential bugs."

Mrs. Lindsay nonchalantly added, "We were supposed to stay mostly in the background and only contact you if necessary. You can go ahead and call Ray now so that he can give you two a tour of the campus."

Then Mr. Lindsay declared, "Whatever Jason tells you, Mack, this is on a need to know basis. He will fill you in if he feels that you're trustworthy."

"Okay, that's it, what the frack is all this about?" Mack sat down heavily on one of the twin beds. "Someone needs to tell me stuff!"

Mr. Lindsay cautioned, "Keep your voice down. Jason, let's take a little walk, shall we? I need to go over a few things with you."

"And I need to have a better explanation than that!" Mack stammered.

Sharon Lindsay grabbed her suitcase handle. "We have to leave now, but we'll see you around campus and most especially every morning for your language classes. Bye for now."

After they left, Mack took the large white envelope off the desk to examine the contents, wondering if he should open it or wait for Jason. He could hear Mr. Lindsay and Jason through the open door, and within minutes, Jason was back.

"Let's hear it, old buddy."

"They're here to keep us safe, Mack. Adrian told me he's worried about our safety. He wanted to make sure we're okay while we're here. An incident happened a while ago before you came to Jasper, and he thought that someone might try to kidnap one of us for ransom, that's all."

Mack harrumphed, and sighed, "So those people are here as our babysitters?"

"No, they're more like bodyguards, Mack."

"Why didn't you say so? All you had to do was tell me. I understand; it's cool, it's not cool, but I understand, sort of."

"We should probably open this." Taking the envelope out of Mack's hands, Jason dumped it out onto the desk. It contained a short welcome letter, I.D. cards for each of them, cafeteria passes, and an unbelievable syllabus for their ten-week language classes and martial arts training.

Mack started to complain about it the moment he saw it. "Are you nuts, Jason? Is this our schedule?"

"Come on Macky; we can do this and still have fun."

"No way, Jas! When will we have time to, I don't know…sleep? Maybe take in a movie or two, meet some girls and when will we have time to eat!"

Jason chuckled at Mack, as he was genuinely glum. "We can do this, my friend. Look on the bright side; we do get Sundays off for good behavior."

Sunday: OFF
Breakfast: [cafeteria] 6:00 - 7:30 a.m.
Monday through Saturday, Language 8:00 a.m. to 11:30;
   Language [Room C, Building K, south campus]
Lunch: [cafeteria] 12:00 noon to 1:00 p.m.
   Martial Arts [Gym] training 1:30 p.m. to 5:00 p.m.
   See schedule below:
Dinner: [cafeteria] 6:00 to 7:00 p.m.
   Study time; weeks 1-8, 8:00 to 10:00 p.m.
Week 1 and 2, *Ju Jitsu*
Week 3 and 4, *Karate*
Week 5 and 6, *Judo*
Week 7 and 8, *Taekwondo*
Week 9 and 10, Fencing; weeks 9 -10:00, 8:00 to 10:00 p.m.
To include the following:
- the ancient art of sword fighting/fencing
- Eskrima
- Arnis
- Kali

A sad Mack sighed heavily, "Inmates get better treatment in prison!"

"Now how would you know that?" Jason laughed at his friend again.

Mack began to moan. "A lucky guess. Can I opt out of this insanity and go home now?"

"What, and leave me here all alone to have all this fun without you? No way, Pal. You're here for the duration, like me."

"Jason, there isn't an ounce of fun written anywhere on here!"

"Mack, my friend, you complain too much. Relax and enjoy the journey."

"What journey is that, Jason? Is it the journey to tiredville or the journey to no sleep and no funville? What is all this stuff anyway? I can't even pronounce half of them!"

Mack and Jason were heading to their afternoon training when Mack's curiosity got the better of him. "I don't want to know your business or anything, but Professor Jimmy and his lovely wife Professor Sharon, plain give me the creeps, Jas. They speak Arabic like they were born there. The bad part is they think we can do that too!"

"Come on, what are you truly complaining about, Macky? What else would we be doing right now, hum? You know my Mother would coerce us into taking people on a glorified hayride into the woods if we were still back in Virginia. At least this gives us something interesting to do for a few weeks."

Mack scratched his head. "I'm not sure that wasn't the better thing to do. Why am I even here, Jas? I'm so tired I can't even think of girls."

"Macky, come on, buddy, and old pal of mine, you're here to support me. Adrian thought you'd like to get away, too. We can't race or train until spring, and I'm sorry for getting you mixed up in our family drama, you already have enough of your own."

"Okay, I don't care what it is as long as we're friends and we can get back to training when we get home. Hey, you were gonna tell me a bunch of stuff. Can you tell me some of that now?"

"I've been trying to come up with how I was going to say it. It's complicated, Mack. But, I promise, that someday soon I'll tell you, not right now, cause I'm too freakin tired."

"So, you admit that you're tired too?" Mack cups his outstretched fingers toward his chest, jutting his chin out, he nods his head as if he's a smug punk. "What kind of complicated Jas? Like cloak and dagger stuff? I can take it! Give it to me…"

Jason chuckled. "Give it a rest, Mack! You wouldn't last five minutes in a ring. Remember when we tried to wrestle in high school? Those guys tore us up. A punk would fell you with one blow to your incredibly simple brain. The Lindsay's are here to keep us safe, and we're supposed to listen to them, end of story."

"I know, you already told me that part. Are these illustrious people with the FBI?" Mack persisted. "No? Then are they with the CIA? They are, aren't they?"

"Adrian went out on a limb for us, and that's their job, so leave it at that, okay?" Jason said.

Mack thought he had things figured out. "If it keeps the ridiculous stuff from happening to us that it does at Ashwood, I guess it's a good thing they're here, but honestly, Jas, can't you give me a hint?"

"I can't tell you everything, Mack, because Adrian only cleared me to tell you certain stuff. If I tell you, then I'd have to kill you." Jason laughed at his friend's expression.

"Oh, come on, Jas! Who exactly am I gonna tell, huh? The cook in the cafeteria? How about if I take the librarian aside and discuss it with her?"

It's the second week of training, and the boys bantered back and forth until they reached the locker room. They changed their clothes and greeted their instructor that they called Sensei.

Sensei taught them to refer to the gym as the dojo, as it was sacred to all martial arts disciplines, and to meditate silently in preparation for each session, bowing to one another out of respect. It helped to clear their minds to concentrate on the art of self-defense.

Adrian told Jason that in the short time they were at the university, after each two-week period, each Master of Martial Arts would equip them with the tools they needed to be able to defend themselves against would-be attackers. The object was for Jason and Mack to take a person down and out should the need arise.

As they practiced against each other, it was evident from the beginning that Mack possessed the more aggressive manner while Jason was more cautious and reserved.

Sensei allowed Jason and Mack several practice sessions and then called in other students to join them. Sensei was observing more closely than usual. Motioning to Jason, he calmly said, "Why do you not knock your opponent out of the circle? That is what you are supposed to do."

"I don't feel like doing this today. I'm a little tired and would like to be excused if that's okay."

Sensei straightened. "The power is not in how you feel, Jason."

"Why would I need power? What kind of power are you talking about, Sensei?"

The instructor glared at Jason, and then responded quietly, "You may not feel like doing this today, but one day you will not have time to think about whether you feel like it or not if your life depends on being prepared. Go stand with your friend Mack."

"Yes, Sensei," Jason bowed slightly, and moved toward Mack.

The instructor conversed with the other students for several moments. Then they bowed to each other, and left the dojo. Sensei moved to the middle of the mat to gather his thoughts, and released the breath he had sucked into his lungs, then waved for Jason to join him in the circle. Jason didn't quite know what to do as Mack pushed him forward.

"Let us try again, Jason. Clear your mind of all thoughts and concentrate."

"Yes, Sensei." Jason respectfully bowed, taking his practiced stance.

Sensei leaned forward, whispered something only Jason could hear. Mack watched as Jason stiffened as his body shuddered slightly. As Sensei motioned with his hands and arms much as you see in a movie, Jason cocked his head to one side. When the instructor moved forward in an attempt to unbalance him, Jason went into an automatic response that surprised even him.

Sensei appeared stunned, as Jason remained standing. He went at him again, trying a slightly different maneuver, but Jason instinctively anticipated this, countering it with another move to block him.

"Excellent, Jason. You have learned your lessons. Now let us see if you can…" In the blink of an eye, Sensei fell to the mat as if a bullet had hit him in the chest. Jason looked down at him and approached his instructor warily.

Sensei's eyes were closed, but Jason knew better than to touch him and instead, he knelt on one knee to examine him from a distance. He glanced at Mack, but he seemed frozen in place. Mack opened his mouth as if to speak, but nothing came out of it. At that instant, Jason's senses went on full alert.

In the next second, the instructor had his hands on Jason's left ankle, pulling to unbalance him. Sensei whispered to Jason, but it took a moment before he fully understood the words.

"Anyone could be your enemy, Jason. I could be your enemy."

"Are you my enemy?" Jason sniffed.

Sensei muttered, "You must always anticipate being prepared, Jason. Anyone could be your potential enemy; you must focus your energy."

Jason was miffed. "I am focused! Why did you do that? Is this part of our training?"

Sensei was watching Jason as he sat quietly observing him. "You must always be aware that there is a threat. Then, and only then can you truly know your destiny."

"What would you know about *my* destiny?" Jason snarled.

Sensei stood abruptly, offering his hand to Jason. "You know what you must do in the future. You have done well today. I am proud of you. Until we meet again, be safe Jason." Bowing slightly, Sensei left the dojo.

"What the hell was all that about, Jas?" Mack asked as they walked toward the locker room.

Jason was shaking his head, muttering, "I'm not entirely sure. We can ask him tomorrow. Did you tell him to call me a *sissy*?"

Mack looked down at the floor and shrugged his shoulders, and said, "I figured you would react to that. Sensei asked me a few days ago if there was a trigger word he could use to rile you up, and then he told me to stay off the mat. No matter what I saw or if you asked for help, I was not to interfere. He was gonna try something."

"Well, it worked. I don't like being called a sissy."

"He said to keep my mouth shut even if you looked like you were in trouble. I didn't wanna yell in case it broke your concentration."

"You know that word drives me crazy, don't you?" Jason was a little rattled. He started to strip out of his outfit, and reached for his jeans.

Mack bent to gather his equipment, stuffing it into his bag. "I think Sensei wanted you to react like when they called Michael J. Fox chicken in those *Back to the Future* movies."

"Yeah, I know. He went ballistic whenever anyone called him chicken," Jason said.

Mack slaps Jason on the back. "Pretty much the same thing you do when you hear that word, okay, I won't say it."

"Mack, why would Sensei use a trigger word on me? Have I missed something?"

"If you missed something, then I sure did too. I don't get any of this, Jas. Let's get something to eat. Aren't you hungry?"

"You're always hungry."

The following Monday, a new instructor called Master Sifu arrived for Chinese Martial Arts. Master Sifu was a rotund, short man who was determined to drum into both Jason and Mack that they would be excellent warriors before their time was up. When they asked about Sensei, Master Sifu snarled that they were not to ask any more questions.

As the disciplines changed, (every two weeks), there was a new instructor along with a new outfit. Mack thought all this was strange, but Jason seemed complacent with it. Like slips of paper in fortune cookies, Jason got a little piece of advice from each of them that he was encouraged to memorize.

During the fourth week of training, Jason got a litany of recommendations from a wise instructor. He also included Mack this time. "Always be on your guard and live your life as if you expect danger. You never know when you will need to defend yourself. Expect a test. You will not know where, you will not know when, but anticipate it, because it will happen."

Weeks five and six brought an instructor who taught them the subtler points of judo. He, too, whispered something to Jason as he was showing him a particularly difficult movement and the light bulb finally went off in Jason's mind. He articulated to Jason to focus on one word—*Basim*. Jason was somewhat stunned when he heard this.

"This is your *silver bullet*, the instructor cautioned. Use it to your advantage. You fight for him, Jason. You avenge his death with this word."

Jason seemed confused by this. "How do you know my father's real name?"

"It is not significant that I know, what is vital is that you know what to do for him and your family. In the future, you can expect this testing should you follow your destiny. It is the most important lesson you must learn."

Jason and the instructor bowed toward each other. "Thank you; I will remember this one above all others." He watched as the instructor left the dojo, knowing he would disappear, replaced by a new teacher who would deliver another smart triad.

"What did this one say to you, Jas? Can you talk about it?"

"No, I don't feel like talking about it right now, Mack."

"Okay, but I'm here when you're ready." When Jason didn't elaborate, Mack allowed his friend to sulk and figured that he would tell him when he was ready to discuss it.

Mack nudged Jason as he picked up a piece of paper that someone shoved under their door. "There's a party in room twelve tonight. We should go, Jas, because that seriously cute girl named Brenda will be there. She told me yesterday that they were having this. She said to bring you, too."

"Isn't she friends with the guy I wiped the mat with yesterday in the dojo? I'm way too tired to think about it right now. Besides, I thought you liked my sister?" Jason threw himself onto his bed, and closed his eyes.

Mack said sadly, "Yeah, I like your sister, but she's not interested in me anymore. She's moved on."

"Really? I'm too tired to do anything else today, my friend. I'm not sure I can even eat dinner. You go; you don't need me as your wingman."

Jason was understandably tired and sore today. The instructor felt it necessary to pair him with another martial arts student who was more advanced. Mack stood by to watch the grueling session, and wanted to jump in to help his friend, but the instructor vehemently asked him not to interfere. Jason seemed to recover to focus his energy, rendering his opponent motionless.

After a hot shower and some food, Jason felt revived enough to accompany Mack to room twelve. Loud music floated from the stairwell when they enter their dorm building. The party started prematurely and was overflowing into the hallway above them. Students were standing around with plastic cups filled with beer that was sloshing over the tops. The floor was wet and sticky in places, so they stepped around the puddles.

Adrian exposed Jason to the trials and tribulations of beer and alcohol when he turned eighteen. The problem occurred when he didn't know when to stop. Adrian was also there to hold his hand and his head telling him to say adios to alcohol in any form if he ever wanted to be a Crown Prince in a distant land. That little experiment taught him a valuable lesson.

Aside from that one time, Jason swore off alcohol for fear Uncle Dimmy would find out. Mack, on the other hand, didn't hesitate to stretch out his hand when someone offered him a cup. He had walked across the room to sample a keg that was set up near an opened window.

Brenda spied Jason near the doorway and pushed up against him in a sensual manner, asking if he needed anything. As she did this, Jason saw Mack wave to him from across the small room as a man with dark hair approached him. At that moment, Brenda reached up to put her hands on Jason's face so that he would focus on her, then detected a commotion out of the corner of his eye when he tried to pull away.

Jason asked Brenda about her boyfriend. She seemed a little disoriented and for a moment, didn't appear as if the question had registered. Then she turned her head toward the opened window and blinked several times.

"He was here," she said slurring her words slightly. "He was here with Macky. He's gone. So where were we, Mr. Studly?" She reached up to pull at Jason's neck to kiss him, but he took her hands away as gently as he could and backed slowly out of the room.

As the fire alarm went off, Jason's cellphone rang. It was a missed call from Mack, but there was no message. As the hallway started filling with students, panic ensued in room twelve. During this time, the lights went out in the stairwell as everyone ran down a back stairway.

Jason instantly sensed that something was wrong. He was wearing the unique wristwatch his Mother gave him and decided to press the face, hoping it would send a signal for help as she had explained that it would do. He then set his cellphone to vibrate and proceeded with caution.

As he worked his way down the dark front stairwell, there was no odor of smoke. It occurred to him that this might be the anticipated test he was supposed to be ready for, or maybe a student pulled the alarm as a prank.

It was eerily quiet at the bottom of the stairwell. As Jason pushed the door open, he was keenly aware of black figures that were lurking in the shadows. Gathering his energy, Jason tried to focus on what might indeed be the test.

A shadow suddenly came at him from the right, and he quickly dispatched a move to knock him aside while another moved into his peripheral vision. If this was a test, he surmised they would come at him all at once, not one at a time as they did in the movies. It continued until the headlights of an approaching car illuminated the area. As the dark figures scattered, an emergency vehicle and fire truck arrived at the building.

A firefighter jumped down from the truck, and ran toward him with an ax in his hands. "Are you okay, son? Which way is the fire?"

"I'm okay," Jason managed to say. "It's near number twelve, upstairs toward the back."

Jimmy Lindsay's voice called to him. "Jason? Are you all right? Is Mack with you?"

"No, he isn't. I don't know where he is. We both went upstairs, and he disappeared. Then someone pulled the fire alarm, and I came outside to look for him."

Mr. Lindsay asked, "Why do you think he's out here?"

"He might have fallen through an open window," Jason answered.

"Let's try to find him, okay?" a concerned Jimmy Lindsay said. "What did your instructors tell you to do in a situation like this?"

"They all said to concentrate and allow my senses to take over." Jason stopped for a moment to listen, gazing at the ground for footprints in the light layer of snow, trying to block out the sounds of sirens. He instinctively moved toward the left side of the building where a faint light shone in a window on the second level. Then he noticed something was moving in the ice-encrusted bushes, realizing it was a person.

"Are you sensing something, Jason?"

"Here, over here!" Jason quietly directed them to the side of the building. Together they pulled Mack out, as he was half into and half out of the woody shrubbery. Jason grabbed Mack's arms, helping him to stand, while Mr. Lindsay sliced through the rope binding his hands together.

"Sorry, but this might hurt a little." Mr. Lindsay then yanked at the tape covering Mack's mouth.

"Ow! Hey, what the hell is going on, Jas?" Mack yelled.

Mr. Lindsay looked around quickly, and said, "Be quiet. Is anything broken, Mack? Do we need to get you to a hospital?"

"No, but there's gonna be a big bruise on my leg," Mack complained.

"Let's get out of here before we wake the neighbors," Mr. Lindsay said.

"One minute I'm enjoying a nice glass of beer and the next someone ties my hands, puts tape over my mouth, and then throws me out a window and down a fire escape!" Mack lamented.

"Hush! Keep your voice down," Mr. Lindsay warned again.

Mack shuddered. "There must have been twenty of them. They grabbed me. I couldn't remember anything our instructors taught us. All I had time to do was press a button on my cellphone. I couldn't even move once they tied my hands! What in the hell is going on, Jas? Where *is* my cellphone? Do you have anything to do with this, Jas?"

"Here it is. Why would you think I had anything to do with this? It might be the *test* we've been waiting for."

Mack seemed confused. "What test are you yapping about?" Jason put the cellphone into his hand. "Thanks. It flew out of my hands when they attacked me."

Jason narrowed his eyes at Mack. "How many times have you been hit on the head, Ace? It's the test one of our instructors said was coming down the pike. Don't you remember anything?"

"Come along, fellas." They helped to steady Mack, steering him toward the front of the building. Mr. Lindsay nodded to his wife, who was waiting in a car near the curb. "We can carry on this conversation somewhere else. I'm sure the neighbors are getting a bit curious, and we don't want to stay for the interrogation, do we?"

Other emergency vehicles had arrived, and people were gathering at the front of the building. The odd thing was, none of the occupants of the party were amongst them.

"It's not your usual kind of student prank, Jimmy. I found these on the ground." Mrs. Lindsay handed him a pair of ninja-type tools. "They are *shinobi* Jimmy; imagine that, ninjas, here on this humble college campus."

"I didn't see them, but I heard one of them say something like they'll be back. It was Korean," Jimmy Lindsay added.

Jason pondered this for a moment. "They did look like ninjas."

Mack was rubbing his head, muttering, "What? How do you even know that? Ninja's, really? Seriously people, are you freakin kidding me? Korean? How many languages do you people know?" Mack seemed to be struggling with the absurdity of the situation. "Has everyone here gone bonkers?"

Sharon Lindsay sidestepped Mack's questions. "Let's go for a ride, shall we? Would anyone like a cup of coffee, I'm buying." She drove in the direction of the local coffee shop near the campus that was open 24/7.

A short-order cook and a tired looking server told them to seat themselves in the nearly empty diner. All at once, Jason realized why Jimmy and Sharon Lindsay were so familiar to him.

"You were the couple that stayed at Ashwood when my family went to the Cape, aren't you?" Sharon Lindsay smiled sweetly, nodding her head. "You were there when we had trouble with…"

"Yes, Jason, but let's stick to our agenda for today," she said, winking at him.

"At the moment, we are your foreign language professors Jimmy and Sharon Lindsay. That's all we have to say about that, okay?" Jimmy watched as Sharon moved to the counter to place an order.

Mack started to mutter, "Are you ever gonna tell me what's going on Jas? You already told me about that horrible stuff like the horse killings. And I don't think those thugs were testing us tonight. They weren't testing me, because they didn't even give me a chance to make a move on them."

Jason shook his head at his friend. "Mack, bad guys don't give you a chance to hit them one at a time; that only happens in movies. If they wanna put you down, they'll do it like gang members."

Mr. Lindsay concurred, "That's right, Jason. Mack, the bad guys, as you so astutely call them, don't care whether you've had training. Their only job is to take you down and out in any way they can. Your instructors want you prepared for that very thing."

"Wait a minute, what bad guys would be after Jason and me?" Mack blankly asked Mr. Lindsay.

"Your instructors wanted your senses to heighten so that you will become more aware of your surroundings. Isn't that right? Jason, what were you thinking when you came out of your building?" he asked.

Jason thought for a moment. "I thought that Mack might be in trouble and I needed to find him right away."

"Did you know someone was waiting for you?" he coaxed.

Jason pondered this question. "Yes, I knew something before I pushed the door open. It felt as if there were people out there and they were moving around in the dark, even though I couldn't see them very clearly."

Mr. Lindsay nodded, asking, "Did you hear anything?"

"No, there was no sound. The only sound was the blaring fire alarm. I didn't stop to think about how many or what I was going to do once I went outside. I told myself to prepare for it."

"Think back, Jason. Did anyone call your name or speak to you in a language other than English?" he asked gently.

Jason closed his eyes to concentrate for several moments, then jerked his head to one side as if he was listening to an invisible rewind of the encounter, and finally said, "Yes. I heard them whispering to each other, and someone called my name. It was all very quiet. I thought it was you at first, then when that didn't make sense, I shoved it out of my mind and started listening again. One of them called me a stupid fool, and another said that I was in jeopardy. That one was in English, and another said my mother is a pig."

Mr. Lindsay raised his eyebrows. "No one spoke in Arabic?"

"Yes, now that you mention it, the third person to speak said something in Arabic. He looked like a madman. He said my father is dead and I soon will be. What does that mean? What would he know about my father?"

"I'd like to know how these people know about your father, Jas?" Mack mumbled, "Didn't you say he was dead?"

Jason nodded his head and remained motionless to quietly contemplate the situation as Sharon Lindsay set a tray on the table. Mr. Lindsay asked Mack to let Jason get through this emotional moment.

After sipping his coffee and consuming a cupcake, Mack whispered, "Oh boy, what have you got me into?"

"I'm sorry, Mack. I'm sorry I got you involved in all this. I don't think it's about me at all…"

Mack stared at his friend. "Then who is it about, hum? It's time you told me, don't you think?"

Jimmy Lindsay excused himself to call Adrian to fill him in on what had transpired, asking that he and Ellen permit the boys to remain until their training was complete. The whole purpose of these self-defense classes and martial arts sessions was to pave the way for the last and most essential training of all called, the *way of the blade*.

Mack seemed bewildered. "Why do we even need that type of training, sir?"

"Mr. Adrian felt that Jason needed to accept it as part of the greater picture," Mrs. Lindsay offered.

"Can't I skip out of it and take a nap?" Mack asked.

"May I remind you, Mack, that the answer to that is; we came together, we train together, and we'll do pretty much everything else together until we go home," Jason said solemnly.

Later that night, Jason confided in Mack, swearing him to never divulge to a living soul what he was about to reveal. Jason recalled the conversation he had with his Mother before he left Ashwood, and her clear instructions about leaving certain things out, as some information was too sensitive to be revealed.

Once Mack agreed that he will never divulge the information, Jason proceeded to tell him most of the incredible story surrounding his family and his potential for becoming a Crown Prince. He gave Mack what he felt was safe, which was more than enough for him to mull over.

At the start of their next training session, Jason and Mack went in search of their new outfits as they waited for their final instructor. As in the past, what they wore seems to change in both structure and color. The first one was a white terry-cloth type material for Jiu Jitsu called a Gi, which was similar to the one worn for Karate, except that the color changed to blue and the outfit was called a Karate Gi. Both tops were held together at the waist by a sash, and changed color the higher the rank. Then the garments switched back to a light white material for Judo and a blue and yellow outfit for Taekwondo.

Mack held up the red Hakama pants and started to snort. "What are we supposed to do with these? There's no shirt, only the pants, and a matching sash. I'm gonna feel a bit self-conscious in this!" He launched into a laughing jag because he suddenly found their whole situation extremely funny.

It was challenging to prepare themselves with the usual meditation to clear their minds, as Jason laugh, too. Once they regained a modicum of control, they each put on what there was of their new outfit and went into the dojo. Two men were on the mat wearing the same pants and sash. It dawned on Jason that he knew who they were. They danced lithely about until they suddenly straightened, standing at attention.

A large man stepped out from behind a door and walked toward them. Jason smiled, as he recognized who would be their Grand Master for the final weeks of training. As in all their other training sessions, Jamaile and Jason bowed to one another. Jamaile surprised Jason as he reached to grab his forearm. He found this an intimate gesture on his part and took it to mean that he had gained acceptance into Jamaile's inner circle.

In an unexpected move, Jamaile's big head touched Jason's, and he whispered something to him in Arabic. Jamaile expressed surprise when Jason returned the greeting.

"You have learned your lessons well, little man," the big man mumbled. "Let us see what else you learned." Jamaile gestured to Mack. "Come, the friend of Jason, you stand with him."

Mack walked to the mat and stood next to Jason, bowed slightly, and said, "Hello, sir, nice to see you again." Mack knew who Jamaile was as he was present at their graduation from high school when King Akdemir and his entourage came to Virginia.

Jamaile threw his head back and laughed. "It is time you girls learned how to fight like warriors. Jason, your friend Mack will fight beside you like a backup man. We have only short time. We start with basic technique, move to harder ones when you master those," Jamaile declared.

Mack and Jason nodded in agreement. What else would they do with the Big Guy hovering over them?

"You train with wood swords until you master the basic skill. Real blades are razor sharp. You will progress from that to protective gear, once you are ready to move forward." Jamaile said soberly.

Jamaile observed the training each day, and gave instructions much as he did in Saudi when Jason trained with him and the Blue and Silver. They would use different sticks and tools until they were ready for actual weapons. As they progressed, real daggers and knives were added until they had a proficient grasp of how they worked.

After Mack and Jason mastered these, Jamaile handed them each a lightsaber, teaching them how to hold the sharp instrument, how to place it safely back into the sheath, all without inflicting wounds to themselves.

At this point, Jamaile was not as sure of Mack's ability with either the sword or foil, but was very satisfied that Jason knew the more delicate aspects of how to use them.

On the tenth and final week of training, His Most Royal Highness, wished to reward Jason for enduring the problematic training Jamaile had overseen. During their last session, Jamaile gave Jason two swords along with matching hand-tooled scabbards that depicted various scenes. Jason's Uncle Dimmy knew that he would achieve great success one day and hoped that these gifts would be appreciated.

The initials JLTO were engraved on a new blade; the initials BAFO were inscribed on an older one. Embellished on each hilt were tiny blue precious stones set in solid silver.

Jamaile also handed Jason a foil with his initials engraved on the thin blade, where he explained that all of the edges were made of the finest steel forged and would serve him well. Mack and Jason also received a dagger, with the warning to keep them close to their bodies, as a good warrior never slept without one.

Receiving these gifts were a humbling experience for the boys, and they mumbled their thanks. It was times like these that Jason wished his father were alive. He knew that the initials BAFO stood for Basim

Abdul Fariq Obagur. It meant that Uncle Dimmy had bestowed not only an honor upon him but also priceless gifts.

At the end of the final two weeks, Jamaile stopped to remind Jason (in Arabic) how additional training would be crucial to his future. Perhaps he should consider which discipline to focus on when he was ready to start training. Jason should use this time between now and when he accepted his Uncle's request at the age of twenty-one, to do that.

Jason figured that it was his parting wisdom.

Mack tried to catch a word or two of the Arabic they spoke, then started stringing together what he understood the big man to say, that Jason was a man of dignity. Even though Jason told him some details about it, Mack's face suddenly registered comprehension.

Jamaile and his men stayed out of sight while they were at the university. Jason and Mack saw them only in the dojo, never in the cafeteria or walking around campus. Jimmy and Sharon Lindsay were instructed to keep their distance while Jamaile and his men were there to train with the boys. They mentioned that he took a significant risk in doing this for the family. Although they arranged to have additional security, they found it was unnecessary, as there were no other ninja-type incidents reported.

Professor's Jimmy and Sharon Lindsay had dismissed their students from their ten-week language sessions. They gave Jason a well-deserved A for his participation and for doing well, while Mack received a C plus. He didn't get the hang of the guttural sound needed for the correct pronunciation of the Arabic language, although he did try.

Mack and Jason said goodbye to the ambiguous college campus in upper New York State and were happy they didn't have to do anything for the next several weeks. As they gathered their duffle bags, they remarked that this had been quite a journey.

Jamaile brought a crate, so they packed up the swords, the foil, and the two daggers. They filled another box with paraphernalia, language books, and their many outfits they used for training, which they sent home via the United States Postal system.

The Lindsay's waited near a taxi at the curb, as Jason and Mack came out of their building. "Ready to go home, boys?" Mr. Lindsay asked.

"Ready! I've been ready since the first week we got here," Mack sighed. "I'll certainly be glad to get home. I didn't know how hard this was gonna be."

Mrs. Lindsay seemed amused. "Do you mean the language part or the martial arts part?"

"Both!" Mack and Jason said together.

Mack started to chuckle. "They were both hard, and I'll be glad to speak English in my own house again. I think we need a vacation from all this nonsense. I actually miss my Dad."

"Yeah, that won't last long once you get back, ole buddy. I'm gonna sleep for a week," Jason moaned. "Maybe two."

Jimmy Lindsay recalled a distant memory. "You think that was bad? You should try living in another country for a year speaking only their language, immersing yourself in their culture, and pretending to be someone else. Now that was hard."

Sharon Lindsay poked at him, and smiled. "You did okay, we both learned something every ten minutes or so when we did that! It was a good experience."

"You two merely experienced the beginning," Mr. Lindsay added.

"What is this the beginning of, sir?" Mack wanted to know.

Mrs. Lindsay raised her eyebrows. "Jason knows what we mean. It will take a lot more work on your part to get where you want to go. Do you know what degree of black belt you want to achieve, Jason, eventually?"

Jason struggled with the many things Jamaile told him. He also said that he trained alongside both his father and Uncle Dimmy while they were growing into men. How could he possibly be as good as his father? "I hadn't thought about how far I wanted to go with that."

"I want to go home to my mattress. And personally, I don't want ever to see another gym or get thrown around in one for a very long time!" Mack stammered.

As the laughter subsided, Jason kept thinking about Jamaile's parting words. He knew this was only a sample of the extensive training that he might need. Uncle Dimmy told him when he was in Saudi last November, that if he wanted the respect of Jamaile's men, he would need to train long and hard for many years.

Jamaile also mentioned that it would take years to master and achieve even the slightest level needed if he were to become his uncle's heir. Only then could he take his rightful place in the Royal Palace. Then he suddenly wondered if he had the fortitude and courage to pull it off.

*"Mediocrity knows nothing higher than itself;
but talent instantly recognizes genius,"*
~ Arthur Conan Doyle, The Valley of Fear

Chapter Nine

A Deserved Recognition

Adrian and I are waiting near the gate to welcome home Jason and Mack. We were able to enter this part of the airport after Adrian flashed his badge. I made sure I wore the same boots this time so that they won't laugh at me. The weather has turned unusually cold, and we're in for an untypically record amount of snow.

"Hey, Jason, we're over here."

Jason and Mack are waving as they come through the doors.

"Hello Mrs. T. Hello Mr. Adrian," Mack says politely.

Completely ignoring Adrian, Jason says, "Hi Mom. Thanks for coming to get us. Did you have to wait long? That storm that came through nearly buried us at the airport in New York. They had to de-ice the plane like two times before they would let us go."

"We got a fair amount of snow here, too. We came early, but then we found out you two were going to be late, so we hung out in the restaurant here. Are you hungry or do you want to go straight home, sweetie?"

Jason chuckles. "We're dead tired, Mom, just take us home. Nice boots, I see they match this time."

"How was it, boys? Did you learn anything interesting?" Adrian asks, leading us all to the baggage claim.

Jason glances at Adrian with a disgusted look, then says, "I don't know if I should even talk to you!"

"Why? Didn't you have any fun?" Adrian is leading us down the escalator.

I suddenly get emotional, reaching for Jason as I used to when he was a child, even though he might not want a hug from me right now. Why does he look so different?

"What kind of fun do you think we were having?" Jason says, shaking his head and rolling his eyes upward, as Mack does the same thing.

"Jason, you had all that time with college girls. All that freedom to do whatever you wanted, with no parental supervision; staying up to all hours, no one to tell you to go to bed."

"It was like friggin boot camp, sir, only without the boots." Mack interjects. "Where were all the girls? There was practically no one else, besides us, at the campus until the last few weeks we were there."

Adrian shakes his head. "Come on fellas; it wasn't as bad as all that."

"They weren't with us! I can tell you that!" Mack says, "Besides, we were too tired to even look for any."

"Where were all the girls?" As we walk toward baggage claim, Jason gives me a quick hug and a kiss on the cheek. "I'll tell you where they were. They were partying with the guys who could stay awake past ten o'clock! I missed you, Mom. Did you know you married a masochist?"

I appreciate that much affection. "But you learned something, didn't you? Was it all a waste of time, then?"

"Mom, yes, we learned something, and yes, we liked being away, but it was very, very tough. We got up at six thirty every morning and got to language class by eight. It was grueling, to say the least."

Adrian tries to stifle a laugh, then mutters under his breath. "That doesn't sound anything like boot camp, son, because boot camp is much harder."

"I'm going to ignore you, Adrian. We did learn something, Mom." Jason leans forward to whisper something in my ear.

I'm surprised and jump back a little. "What did you say to me, Jason?"

He starts to laugh and reaches for his duffle bag. "I told you that I missed you and loved you very much."

"It didn't sound like you missed me. It sounded more like you want to rip my face off and hug me at the same time."

"It's really what I said. Once you understand the basics of the Arabic language, it's easy."

"Speak for yourself, Jas. I didn't get the hang of that language at all, Mrs. T," Mack says.

We are now by the car when Adrian throws the trunk open. "We missed you too, son."

"We did miss you, sweetie, actually more than you will ever know. It looks like you both lost some weight and got taller. Did you?"

"Mom, thanks for missing me, but we talked every Sunday. I wasn't gone that long. What will you do when I'm…?" Jason stops suddenly, opening the car door, getting in without finishing his sentence.

After we drop Mack off at his house, we're on our way to Ashwood when Jason volunteers more information. Although we knew about the altercation at their dorm building, his advancement with each discipline, and his progression with Arabic, he left some details out for Mack's sake. We don't want to push him. It's better to wait until he's ready to share it with us.

Jason sighs heavily. "I've been thinking that you were right for sending us to learn martial arts, Adrian."

Adrian nods his head in surprise. "I was? You mean you aren't mad at me for sending you there?"

"No, it gave me an insight into what discipline I want to pursue. Even Mr. Lindsay doesn't know about an incident. I can't seem to remember his real name, and I forgot to ask him when we left. What was it again?" Jason asks.

Adrian stares into the rear-view mirror to see Jason's serious expression. "His real name is Drew McGuire. Mind telling us what happened?"

"It was the sixth week of training. Mack and I were minding our own business when we walked into the locker room, and three guys started knocking us around."

Adrian cautions me to keep quiet. "What did you and Mack do? You didn't send a signal on that one."

"Mack and I thought it was finally the test one of our instructors told us to be ready for, but they weren't students we recognized. I knew enough to know that they were speaking Arabic. They said some pretty raw stuff, and then one of them decked Mack. He went down pretty hard, and he's still a little sensitive about it, but it's more like he's embarrassed."

Adrian squeezes my hand. I'm trying to keep my mouth shut, when he says, "What did they say to you, Jason?"

Jason stares out the window, then turns to say, "They said pretty much what they said when they took Mack that night at the party. Mr. Lindsay said you knew all about that, but this was different. These guys were more menacing than the ones who confronted me that time."

"What did you do, Jason?" Adrian asks.

"I wanted to take them out, so I concentrated using a combination of techniques both Sensei and Master Sifu taught us. I didn't want to kill anyone, but I sure wanted to hurt someone."

Adrian and I stare at each other (*I mouth the word kill*). I'm alarmed to think Jason and Mack were in potential danger, and he didn't mention this to his security detail.

"Why didn't you press the dial on your watch like you did the first time these goons came at you?" Adrian asks.

"Honestly, there was no time to do that. At first, the guys came at me from all directions, but then I focused my energy, and it was as if I could sense where they were in the room. I know I hurt two of them enough to hear bones crack. Mack came to near the end and helped me. I pulled one of their masks off, and he laughed in my face."

Adrian silently pleads for me to keep quiet. "Then what did you do?"

I feel compelled to ask this question: "They wore masks? And did they have mustaches, too?"

"I decked that guy, and Mack pulled me off. I can still see his bloody face if I shut my eyes. Then we got our stuff and left. The next day there was no sign of anything, the locker room was clean, and nothing was out of place except a dumb note taped to my locker, and no, no mustaches, Mom."

Adrian gently coaxes, "What did the note say, son?"

"I can't remember the exact words, but it said something about being aware, be prepared, we watch you, something like that. Who are they, Adrian, do you know? Are they involved with Uncle Dimmy?"

Adrian shakes his head at me, pursing his lips. "I don't know, Jason."

As upsetting as this is to me, Jason seems pleased with himself. I'm glad he could take care of a threatening situation. I'm also pleased that he's come out the other side of it unhurt. What bothers me is the fact that he feels so little remorse. What have they done to my dear, sweet Jason?

"I've made a decision," Jason says breaking the silence. "I'm going to study pretty much what I did the last few weeks, but I want to go for the tenth-degree black belt. I don't want to be good at it; I want to be the best."

I let out the breath I'm holding while trying to swallow the lump that is forming in my throat. "You came home with a decision, that part is good."

"Do you know where you want to study martial arts?" Adrian asks.

"No, I don't know where yet. I'll figure that out in a few months. Mack won't be coming with me. He said he's had enough adventure for a while and wants to stay here to race for Ashwood. I'm too tired to think about it right now anyway."

As we come to our driveway, I'm relieved that Jason has no more decisions to discuss with us.

"Did the boxes I sent home get here okay?" Jason inquires as he gets out of the car.

Adrian presses his fob and the trunk flies open. "Yup, we put them on the library table. What's in them?"

Jason grabs his duffle bag. "Some stuff Jamaile and Uncle Dimmy gave me, and the outfits they gave us. I'll take care of them later."

Mona is taking pans out of the oven and looks up to say hello to Jason when he comes through the back door where some of the family has gathered.

"Hey everyone, hello Grandma."

Grandmother Francesca hugs Jason as Melanie and Curlie stand to the side, staring at their brother. They have noticed something different about him as we have.

"Hey Mel, hi Curlie, how's it going?"

Melanie and Curlie have their mouths open, not saying anything, and not moving, either.

"What are you two staring at?" Jason bends to pat Rosie on the head as she nuzzles his hand. "Hey girl, how you doing? Yeah, I missed you too. Can we talk later, Mom, I want to go to my room."

"Sure honey, we can talk at dinner. That is if you make it to dinner."

Jason trudges up the back staircase with Rosie close behind him. Mother turns to me while the others continue to stare in amazement, as it's apparent to them that our Jason has changed a great deal while he was away.

"He looks so much like Ravi the first time I met him," Mother says softly. "He doesn't look like the Jason who left here only a few months ago. I know he trained with Jamaile, but he appears completely different now," Mother observes.

"Mom, what happened to him while he was gone? What did they do to him?" Melanie asks. "Jason is handsome! I can't believe I said that about my brother!" Melanie squeals, putting a hand over her mouth.

"Yeah! I agree he's changed. Oh, stop that Mel! Why can't we think our brother's handsome? We always thought Daddy was handsome, didn't we Mama?" Curlie says in response.

Adrian nods, saying, "The main thing is he's matured in ways we never thought he would. His professors, instructors, and even Jam-Jam worked magic, huh Ellie?"

"For once, I'm glad he had something to do with it. Okay girls, did you get your homework done?" Catching Mother's eye, she gently pushes the girls out of the kitchen and up the back stairs.

An astute Adrian takes my hand and leads me into the library. "What's bothering you, Mrs. Thompson dash Sellers? Would you like to talk about it?"

"Adrian, he looks like a young Ravi with that long wavy dark hair and the way he walked toward us at the airport. I nearly fainted when I saw him. I thought Ravi had come back from the dead! He could be mistaken for his father. That could cause a problem down the road, couldn't it?"

Adrian is startled. "I never thought of that angle, Ellie. I can understand how you feel, though. Drew could only report his progress and performance. He couldn't tell us about any physical changes."

"You don't suppose that this changes the playing field, do you?"

Adrian pulls me into a hug. "It's food for thought, but I wouldn't worry about that right now. We should celebrate accomplishments and homecomings. Would you like a glass of wine before dinner?"

"Sure." I'm going to file this tidbit in one of the file drawers in my brain, in the drawer that's marked *to do later*. "What do you suppose is in this crate, Adrian? The box looks like it might contain books."

"I suppose the square one could be the outfits. Not all that stuff could fit into a duffle bag. The long one might contain a rifle or a sword. I wouldn't put it past Dimmy to send something like that home with Jason."

"You think it's a gun?" I walk around the library table, touching the crate. "No, it's probably a sword. Jam-ale and a couple of his men were there for the last few weeks, and I'll bet you it's a sword, maybe more than one. Maybe they gave one to Mack, too."

"I will not take that bet, Ellie, and that's enough speculation. We'll find out at dinner, provided Jason even comes downstairs this evening. I have a better idea where you can put all your energy Mrs. Thompson dash Sellers." Adrian kisses my neck and then moves his hands down to cup my butt.

Pulling away from him, I walk toward the window, looking out to see the lawn as dark patches are starting to appear where the snow has melted. "It's a little too early for that, don't you think?"

"Nothing says there's a time limit on that, my little love dove. Where is your mind, dearest Ellie? Where have you gone?"

"It's the Ravi-Jason resemblance. It threw me for a loop."

"I know what will take your mind off things. Now that Jason and Mack are back and training will start soon, you can concentrate on moi. How about if you teach me how to win at the racetrack? Please? I suck at it if I do it myself!" Adrian says pouting.

I can't help but laugh at him because he indeed sucks at wagering. "I don't know if you'll get it. I don't want to be unkind, but maybe you're not cut out to do it."

"Please my darling Clementine, can't you try it one more time?" Adrian pleads. "Nothing is taking up our attention right now. I'm not going anywhere for the foreseeable future, and we have time to do it."

"Okay, we can start the day after tomorrow, but if you don't get it this time, I'm not wasting any more time on it, period, and end of discussion. Do you agree?"

Adrian thinks he has won me over this time. It's a good trait for the line of work he's in, but not for what he needs to win at the racetrack.

It's a crisp, spring morning as Terre and I take our mugs of steaming coffee to the picnic table outside on the screened porch near the back door. We seem to do our best thinking when the sun is waking everyone else up. After Jason left for training, she decided to take his place, and sadly, he has not returned to join us.

Sipping absently at our coffee, we watch as the sky starts to change colors. "Have I ever told you how much it means to have all of you all here, Terre?"

"Yes, about a bazillion times, Ellie. I do love it here. It's so different from Chicago. The kids have adjusted, and Dennis is comfortable with his job at the bank. We can't think of any place we'd rather be than here with you, Mother, and the rest of the clan."

I start to chuckle. "Are we a clan? I do want to thank you for all those photos you gave us. Lenard-the-Terrible destroyed our albums when he found them in Mother's moving boxes. She only got away with a few of them. With your albums, the kids can make copies and remember their past adventures, at least some of them."

"I'm so glad he didn't come anywhere near us when we moved. When Mother first told me that you were alive, she did a great job of keeping us informed. It was incredibly difficult to talk about your double funerals and the children. Thanks for sending Reed to the hospital with the note, Ellie. That sure was a terrifying time for all of us."

"I'm sorry you had to go through that, Terre. I should have trusted my gut and contacted you anyway!"

"Geeze, Ellen…you and your mystery should go talk to someone. How do you keep it all inside? I would have gone berserk if those things happened to my family. Oh, wait, they did."

"That's funny you should mention that. I think it would make a good movie except Adrian said no one could know all the details. We left out a bunch of stuff so you wouldn't freak out."

"I thought what you and Adrian did tell us was bad enough. I don't want to hear anymore, quite honestly. Things are going pretty smoothly now, and we don't need to rock the boat."

I laugh at her euphemism, "Yeah, we do run a tight ship here, don't we?"

Terre sighs heavily, and then says, "I've been thinking, Ellie, with all of us working and being so busy and all, don't you think we should find someone to help with the meals? With anywhere from ten to fifteen people at any given time for dinner; it would be too much for me, and you know how I love to cook."

"Mona has to be tired with all the baking, and she does rely on Mother to help. Terre, that's an excellent idea and one that is very doable! Let's make that suggestion at dinner tonight."

After an intense, but brief search, (and a thorough background check) our new cook, Nancy, will be starting next week. Mother meticulously copied the previous years' menus into a binder, and it will take months to repeat them.

Henceforth, Mona will be relieved of the bulk of the kitchen cooking duties. She can then concentrate on simple breakfast items and low-calorie desserts, freeing Mother to tackle other things.

"Okay, Adrian, we're going to start at the top and work our way down. Set before you are the tools of the trade for high-stakes wagering."

Papers are stacked on the library table, arranged according to what I want to cover today. Adrian pokes at the materials. "Is this a real course? Am I getting college CEUs for this?"

"No, it's not a college course, Adrian. I don't believe it could ever be taught as a college course. Now, we can start with the terms you're familiar with and add more as we go; you might want to write this down, sweetie."

"You want me to take notes?" Adrian asks in surprise. "And you said it isn't a college course."

"It's a lot of information, and you don't exactly have a photographic memory. We are going to go over the Code of Virginia, the Declaration and Condition sheet, and we can examine the different levels of competition at the racetrack."

Adrian raises his eyebrows and then starts to blink. "Will you quiz me after each session?"

I know he's making a joke out of this.

"I hadn't thought of that, but that's a good idea. So yes, Mr. Smarty-Pants, there will be a short quiz after each session. I mean it Adrian; you need to take notes about how to calculate betting odds and payoffs."

Reaching for a tablet and pen, he begins to write his name at the top of the page. "What's the name of this course, Madam Teacher?"

Squeezing my temples with my fingers, I'm trying to come up with the right words, so I don't squelch Adrian's enthusiasm right away. "First, if you aren't going to take this seriously, you won't learn anything. And second, don't call me madam. It sounds so…"

Adrian starts to snicker, and then says, "Bordelloish?"

"Yeah, that's what it sounds like, exactly. Look, Adrian, I don't think I'm the right person to teach you how to bet. Maybe we should stop right here."

Adrian gets down on his knees to plead. "Sure, you are. I'll behave, you'll be proud of me. Go ahead and teach me, Oh Master of the Betting Ring."

"Have you learned nothing of the harness racing world, darling?"

"Yes, I know that if you don't take care of your racehorse, it won't perform for you," Adrian grins.

Oh boy, this is going to take a while.

"Yikes, Adrian, there's more to it than that!"

Using a large tablet on an easel, going through the basic terms, I wait while Adrian writes each one of them on his paper. Then I move on to how to calculate the betting odds and payoffs. It's probably the most significant aspect of wagering; knowing what horse is racing along with how much to wager.

Halfway through the third day, he declares that he's ready to bet. I don't think he is and try to persuade him otherwise. Then he pesters me until I tell him that we can pretend-bet online. We choose a racetrack that has regular straight bets, and I gently guide him through my process.

"Adrian, you need to study the statistics of who's riding or driving the horse in any given race, or it won't work."

"I'm paying attention, my little daffodil, teach away," he says. "Teach away!"

"We'll be practicing a lot before we go to the racetrack, you know."

On a pad of paper, I write down the name of the horse I choose to win along with the betting odds, hiding it from him. Encouraging Adrian to do the same, when he loses the pretend bets race after race, he reaches over to grab my pad to see my list. He sighs heavily, because I picked the winner repeatedly, winning lots of pretend money.

"I don't get it. I thought I did everything you did, but you won, and I didn't! Maybe I should stick to what I do best and go back to the CIA, Ellie. I'm an obvious failure at this. It goes beyond the word suck!"

"Sweetheart, you know that you can go back to the CIA any time you want. Don't feel so bad, my Daddy couldn't do it either. Jason's the only person I know, besides me, who can do this. It can't be taught as a college course, sweetie. Can we stop now?"

"Okay, Ellie. I acquiesce to you." Adrian whips off a pretend hat, and takes a bow. "By the way, there is trouble in River City."

It makes me chuckle as Mother used to refer to potential trouble as they did in the musical *Music Man*. Adrian segues into saying that there's turmoil in Saudi right now. That could explain why we haven't been able to reach Uncle Dimmy for over two weeks.

"It's happened before. Do you think we should worry? Should we try to call him?"

Adrian smiles in that adorable way of his. "Let's let it ride, shall we?"

"Now you get the terms, Adrian!"

Adrian pulls at an invisible mustache, then grabs my arms to dance with me around the library. "Levi will call us if he thinks we need to worry." In the meantime, he starts to sing a little off-key, "Shall we dance, ta ta ta, shall we sing ta ta ta. That's from the musical *The King and I*, remember?"

"Yes, I do. Funny; you don't look like Yul Brynner. I think the rest of it goes, or perchance when the last little star has left the sky..."

"You don't look like Deborah Kerr either, but lighten up, will you? Shall we dance?"

"Yes, we should dance."

As we resume singing the words a little off-key, we narrowly miss the library table as Adrian's cellphone rings. We know by the ringtone that its Levi.

"Maybe I spoke too soon." He moves away to take the call as I go back to my office.

How did the last three years fly by so quickly? Is it because we weren't paying attention? Is it because nothing out of the ordinary happened here at Ashwood or to our animals? Has our universe finally aligned and we're in the right spot, and there are no black holes to fall through?

Whatever it is, we are all grateful for that.

Ashwood Stables is preparing for one of Uncle Dimmy's infrequent visits. We are celebrating Jason's milestone twenty-first birthday along with Melanie's graduation from high school. The Manor House is abuzz with the frenzy that usually accompanies such a combination of events.

After Jason went off to study martial arts, Mack opted to stay behind to continue training and racing with us. That ten-week course in New York convinced him that he didn't want to pursue Jason's line of training. Unfortunately, his mother passed away two years ago of an undisclosed illness, and he was not about to live with his incredibly critical father.

Mack asked if we would allow him to live with us. His father had no objection as a pretty woman (who thinks he's the most wonderful man on earth) is occupying his time now.

What is that saying about love being blind?

Curlie and Melanie continued to gang up on me occasionally, asking why they couldn't visit Uncle Dimmy during one of their school breaks. They wouldn't mind if one of the CIA Agents went with them. However, my reply was always the same. "You are not going, period and certainly without hesitation, end of discussion!"

Jason spent most of his off time here at Ashwood Stables the entire time he was at college, going only one time to visit Uncle Dimmy, accompanied, of course, by Agents Jake and Josh.

We made several crucial decisions over these last several years. Having Mack here is one of the best decisions we've ever made. I thought that selling the antiques was up at the top of the list, right along with the extensive renovations of all the buildings on the Ashwood property. Except for the dairy barn part, which we had to lay to rest by removing the offending section, the very best part was marrying Adrian.

Our cook, Nancy, is so fantastic that we don't know how we did without her all those years. Even Mona admitted that she had more energy than a 'monkey on a hyena's back.' We didn't know what that meant, but we all got a kick out of it when she said it!

It's strange how time has slipped away as it has. In reflecting on the last few years and what brought us to today, it gives me pause to think what might transpire once Uncle Dimmy is here for his visit.

As I try to put it temporarily out of my mind, cherished memories poke through, especially the times we talked via face-time while Jason was away at school. I knew that he was training for the eventual day when he would say yes to his Uncle Dimmy, choosing to take his place as his rightful heir. I also knew there would be an empty feeling in the pit of my stomach, much as I have right now.

Couple this with the fact that Melanie will also be leaving the nest to attend an out-of-state college in the fall, and it's no wonder I feel as I do. It's when I start to blame Ravi for our odd situation in the first place. I know deep down that I shouldn't, but it surfaces occasionally.

Mother's observations are well-meaning. She doesn't hesitate to expound on it. "It's empty nest syndrome, that's all it is. I had it too when you and Terre went off to live your own lives." Mother and I are in the Morning Room having a late breakfast as everyone has left to go on about their day.

"Does that feeling ever go away?"

"No," she sniffs. "It lessens, but it never completely goes away. It's different when people die, Ellie. You miss them, and you know you can never talk with them. When your family goes off on their own, you want to see them and talk with them as often as possible."

"We did that. Didn't we spend every holiday with you and Daddy? When he died, we included you with everything we did as a family," I say sadly.

Mother smiles at me. "It's different when you don't have someone to share it with, Ellie. My house was very lonely after Daddy died. True, you and the children came to visit and occasionally stayed overnight, but you left to go back to your own home."

"I never knew you felt like this. Why didn't you ever say anything? You could have moved in with Terre or me."

Mother shakes her head, reaching for my hand, she says, "Ellie, that is what a mother does. She raises her children to be good people, instills in them right from wrong, and then sets them free to go out into the world to live their own lives."

"But you were lonely, and Terre and I didn't know how you felt."

"Don't get me wrong, sweetheart. I'm certainly not lonely now. I'm trying to help you cope with Jason's eventual departure. I love it here; all of my family dwells within this house, as they did in Sara Ashwood's time. You know, when I sit in the front parlor by the front windows, there are times that I feel a slight breeze. I know she's here with us. I get the feeling she's happy that we're all here."

"I remember the first day I walked into Sarah's bedroom upstairs. I get that feeling too, Mother. Thanks for your words of wisdom. I know you miss Daddy. I sometimes wish Ravi were here, especially when it comes to situations that I know he would take charge of, he'd know what to do. Adrian wasn't around when the children were small, so we don't share that history. I only want to do my best for them."

"You have done a great job, Ellie. We're all proud of them. They each have their special talent, and you will send them on their way, knowing you taught them what they need to survive. It is what Daddy and I did for you and Terre."

"How will I know if they need more?"

"They will be fine dear; you'll see," Mother replies.

I bend to plant a kiss on the top of Mother's head. She must miss Daddy more than any of us know. When Adrian finds me lost in thought, he attributes it to a type of melancholy, asking if I want to see a professional about it, but so far, I feel that there isn't sufficient reason to do that.

"Where did the years go, Adrian? How could Jason be turning twenty-one already? How can our beautiful Melanie be on her way *to* college? Wasn't she wearing pigtails and riding her bicycle only recently?"

"I know, Ellie, it's hard to believe time flew by like that. I wasn't around when they were little, but the last few years we did enjoy the stuff that led up to this, didn't we? Maybe we were having so much fun that we didn't notice the time pass."

My eyes suddenly fill with tears as he reaches to pull me toward him. "Even Curlie's so preoccupied now that she might as well be on another planet! How did this happen? I blinked my eyes and my family not only grew up, but they're also leaving at the same time."

"Hey, some of us are still here, Ellie. Besides, you knew this day would come. You predicted it."

"Did I?"

"Yes, you did. You knew Jason would choose this path. You encouraged him to study for what he must do. You gave him what many mothers would not be able to; a gentle push to go out into the world and made sure he was trained to do it."

"You had something to do with it too, Adrian. You gave him that first push by sending him to New York with Mack. It was you who did that. Mother is the one who told him to follow his dream."

Adrian hugs me, sniffs my hair, and nuzzles my neck, as I melt into him. "But most of the encouragement came from you."

"It's odd that he doesn't want us to fuss for his birthday or his remarkable achievements. He said something like it was no big deal and dropped the subject like a hot potato when Mel brought it up. She thought they could tag-team their parties."

"There you go again, Ellie, you worry too much. Remember, we did this for better or for worse. We've had a lot more betters than worses, haven't we? What time is his Royal High and Mighty supposed to be here tomorrow?"

"The email said the group would arrive around three in the afternoon. They are going in a roundabout way, much the way we did when we went there for our wedding. It must be for security reasons. I still feel sad about missing that wonderful honeymoon we planned. We haven't been able to get away to do that, with one thing or another."

"Hey, maybe we should plan something like that when Melanie and Jason are both gone. Any place you'd like to go?"

My eyes fill with tears again. "We could go to Italy, maybe the Tuscany Region? Curlie won't even notice we're gone. She has enough Mother Hens around here to keep her out of trouble. How will I stand it, Adrian? I know I'll fall apart and start crying!"

"No, you won't, my sassy little friend. You'll act like the wonderful mother you are and send them on their way with love and a promise to send them cookies from home every other month or so. You won't bake them yourself, of course, but it'll be the thought that counts."

"Thanks, I needed your humor, as ridiculous as it is. It's too bad Dimmy's going to miss Mel's graduation ceremony. Did I say that out loud?"

Adrian chuckles. "Yeah, Melanie was a little dramatic when she found out that he wasn't coming until the day after she graduates."

"She probably wanted him to come, so her friends could drool over him at her party. It's bad enough they do that when Jason's around. Thanks for trying to cheer me up, honey."

"Anytime my little chickadee," he says. "Any time."

A few hours before we leave for Melanie's graduation ceremony, Jason and I are in my office during a rare quiet time. "Will you come back to visit every so often if you go with Uncle Dimmy?"

"I know we haven't talked about it," Jason says quietly. "Do you really wanna talk about it now?"

Ravi's face flashes in front of my eyes when Jason smiles or turns his head a certain way, and it saddens me to think of him. Maybe I'm plain sad today and slightly schmaltzy. "Yes, I guess we haven't talked about it much."

Jason touches the photographs of our horses that are cluttering up one of the bookshelves. "Mom, I don't think we should talk about that today. It's Mel's day, not mine. It might make you sad."

Taking the photo of *Didgeridoo* and me out of his hands, he reaches for the picture of *Truly Yours*. "It certainly is your day, too. You graduated from college. In my book, that's an accomplishment to celebrate, a milestone anyway."

Jason puts the frame back on the shelf and turns to face me. "It's no big deal. I'm not even graduating with my class. Those accelerated courses and my major didn't exactly qualify as graduating in the traditional sense of the word."

"Because you aren't graduating with your class doesn't diminish your achievement, sweetie. Are you fishing for a new car, mister?"

Jason starts to laugh. "No honestly, if I wanted a new car, I can go buy one myself. I know how to wager as you do. It's that I don't feel like celebrating for myself. It's Mel's turn."

"I'm so very proud of you. What's bothering you?"

"I'm not sure. Maybe it's all the stuff that goes on before Uncle Dimmy gets here. We all seem to run around trying to get things ready and…" Jason turns his head to gaze out the window.

How many times have I done that same thing when there was something on my mind? "You want to talk about it, but you don't want to talk about it. Why don't we sit this elephant down on the sofa right now and get it over with?"

Jason turns to face me. "I have pretty much made up my mind, about going, I mean."

"And you figure I'll have a meltdown, is that it?"

Jason sighs. "Mom, I know you're going to worry."

"You bet I'm going to worry. You are my son. I'm allowed to worry about you. You'll be thousands of miles away."

When he shakes his head a little, and smiles, his eyes crinkle in the corners as Ravi's once did. "Let's wait until Uncle Dimmy gets here, okay Mom? I don't want to rain on Mel's parade. But I do want you to know that I love all of you very much and it will be hard for me to leave."

"Thanks for putting Melanie's graduation front and center, sweetie. We have about two hours before we leave for the program. Wear that blue blazer with the khaki pants, okay?" As soon as these words leave my mouth, I regret them.

"Mom, I know how to dress, but thanks; I've missed you telling me anyway." Jason walks out of my office as Adrian walks in.

"My baby boy is all grown up and leaving the nest, and I can't do a damn thing about it!" I whine into his shoulder.

"No, we can't stop time from marching on, Ellie. You will have to trust that he'll be okay."

"That's going to be hard to do. If Ak-dim-er can't guarantee his safety, how will Jason know the dangers, Adrian? We need to discuss that with him."

"We will, Ellie. There's time to do that."

Follow your dreams; follow your heart, a voice whispers in my head. Was this what the original Mrs. Ashwood felt when her children left the house to pursue other interests?

Was that her voice in my head now, or my own?

Mel's graduation comes and goes, and so does Uncle Dimmy's polite, but quick visit. Once he knew that Jason had decided to go back with him, he cut his time short, made the excuse that a catastrophic event occurred within the Royal Palace that only he could rectify. He then filed an amended flight plan.

He isn't fooling me. He left when he found out Jason had made his decision in his favor. We are not disappointed that he went, but we are sad that he took Jason with him.

Jason didn't want us to fuss, opting for a quiet dinner and no going away party. He merely spent time with each of us before he left, me being the last.

I didn't cry and chose to help him pack, hugging him and saying that I look forward to seeing his face once a week via the computer monitor. It was after he left that the tears flowed. Adrian came to hug me, whispering that Jason will be all right. It had been his choice to make, not mine. During Adrian's time with him, he told Jason what to expect when he joins his uncle and what the potential is for trouble.

In spite of everyone's assurances, there is a battle raging in my head, and my heart seems heavy!

In the blink of an eye, two years have evaporated! Where has the time gone? Wasn't it only yesterday that everyone was cheerful about something?

During this time, I have made a concerted effort not to dwell on the fact that Jason isn't here with us. We have all continued with our lives, but sometimes the urge to jump on a plane and drag him home is a bit overwhelming!

It's Monday, our usual day to talk, and I know that Jason will call when he can, but I'm hovering near my computer monitor anyway. The seven-hour time difference is maddening because when we're settling down for the night, Jason is getting up to start his day.

The ideal time to connect for both of us is around ten a.m. (EST). It's when I sequester myself in my office to wait for his call.

Adrian wanders in and sits down on the sofa. "Have you heard from Jason yet?"

Looking at the time at the bottom of my monitor screen, it now reads 11:28. "No, not yet. He said they had a program yesterday, something to do with the horses, but he didn't say what time it was over, and I'm waiting for him to call."

"This type of thing happens occasionally, I'm sure he'll call when he can. You know how things get jammed up."

"We've tried different options when that happens. Sometimes we use our cellphone, or we face-time, but mostly it's the webcam that gives us the most grief."

"Maybe he can't talk to you today." Adrian tries to steer me away from the screen. "Why don't we go for a ride? It might cheer you up."

"Go for a ride? You mean right now while I'm waiting for Jason to call? I don't think so, Adrian."

"Why don't we get in the car and go somewhere for lunch? We haven't done that in a while. Whatta-ya-say, sweetheart?" he says comically slurring his words.

I shake my head at him. "Maybe we can go after he calls."

"Okay, let me know when you're ready to leave."

"He's never missed a call before, Adrian. I have a feeling something's wrong."

"We'd have heard if there was anything wrong, Ellie." Sauntering out of my office and into the library, I can hear him plop down on the sofa near the fireplace as he opens the newspaper.

Glancing out the window at the pasture, our ranch hand, Nathan greets one of our horse boarders. Due to Jason's absence, a call went out to one of Reed's best friends, and he agreed to step in to fill the void left in the barn mucking detail.

Adrian conducted a thorough background check of Nathan Martin, and he now occupies one of the downstairs bedrooms off the kitchen, while Mack lives in the other one. He is a large man, as Reed is, and is as gentle and loving with the horses and people.

Then the problem arose as to who would drive the race bikes for us, as I remain out of commission. It all worked out in the end as my nephew Danny, Terre's and Dennis' son, acknowledged that he was not only ready to settle down here in Virginia with us, but also ready to get to work. No one was more shocked than I was when he asked to join our racing teams.

Glen's assessment of him was sidesplitting. He said he never pegged him for poop detail. Danny is too much like his banker father to do that. Glen also thought Danny wouldn't last all that long and would then hoof it right on over to the bank to work with his father.

Thankfully, he was wrong. Danny fooled us all into thinking he knew nothing about horses. Then admitted he had changed his major, to end up at Ashwood Stables, not at the bank with his father. And with their second child (a boy this time) on the way, it gives Reed time to spend with his growing family.

Adrian and I have slowly distanced ourselves from the barn, as we need to be owners now. He has said on more than one occasion that he likes this role and can we start betting a little at the racetrack? Adrian means me of course; he wants me to pick the winners so he can say he won!

Lester's Best and *Raindrop Dew* have performed admirably, moving steadily up in class and have bestowed new respect upon Ashwood Stables. However, if the goal is to go to the championship, it might be time to think about purchasing two new Standardbred horses. *Lester* and *Raindrop* will be too old to compete in the class they need to achieve this. I had meant to buy a few new ones earlier, but somehow the urge left me.

We are indeed grateful that there have been few bizarre incidents in the last several years either at the racetrack or the Manor House. It's a relief to go to the track now without that threat. We have not let our guard down; however, it isn't as apparent as it once was. Adrian still has his ear to the ground as owners, and other people are still part of the equation. It's always the old boys club down at the racetrack, and we speculate as to whether they will ever accept Ashwood Stables as a worthy opponent.

Do I even care about that?

When we are at the track, I place small bets and watch Adrian lose about what I win, because I refuse to let him see what horse I've put my finger on until after the race. He gets so exasperated when that happens, he often rips up his ticket, sticking his hands in his pockets looking dejected. He complains that I haven't correctly shown him what to do, but his stubbornness is what's getting in his way, not my ability to teach him.

All CIA agents, who once roamed the property and kept vigil during our many crises, are back in Washington (or parts unknown). Adrian maintains his connection with Levi and his old partner, Larry, often driving to Langley to take on small projects. Or, he gets involved with special ops teams he continues to train. They often come here to camp out on our back forty acres. That way, Adrian can retain his CIA status and maintain his license to kill.

Melanie completed her second year of college and is due home for the summer. She will begin her barrage two minutes after she gets here, wanting to go to Saudi to visit Jason. So far, I've refused to consider it, but then Mel will no doubt pull the *'I'm almost twenty years old, Mom'* thing! Then a few days later, she'll start in again with the *'don't you trust me?'* part of the conversation. I cringe every time she does this, but I also know that someday she'll go with or without my permission.

So far, Curlie seems to be less enchanted with her status as a Princess, throwing herself into what most other teenage girls do best, boys. She still practices the piano faithfully two hours a day but spends the better part of her evenings talking on the phone to her girlfriends about…boys.

A loud ping startles me back to the computer monitor as a familiar face fills the screen. Jason's voice seems off today, muffled as if he's talking in a tunnel. "Hey Mom, are you there?"

"Yes, sweetheart, I'm here. You're late today. You look tired, are you getting enough rest?"

Jason begins to laugh. "Yes, Mom, plenty of rest, we're fine here."

My eyes suddenly fill with tears. "Why were you so late today? I almost gave up on you and went out to lunch with Adrian. How was your week, sweetie?"

Adrian hears my voice and comes in my office to wave at Jason. "How are you doing, son?"

"Good. We're all good here." Jason says, waving at the screen, "Nothing to report, except the usual state of the crap."

It reminds me of those frequent calls from Dimmy where he began each call with questions concerning our families. Now I find myself doing the same thing.

"Did you get Grandma's cake and Ms. Mona's cookies we sent you last week?"

Jason smiles. "Yeah, you don't have to send them. We do have a pastry chef here, you know. They must cost a fortune to send over."

"That's like asking the sun not to shine. They do it so you won't be homesick. You think I'm going to tell them not to bake and send you stuff?"

Adrian must be bored with the conversation. "Have a good week, Jason. Don't do anything stupid." He turns to leave, mouthing that he'll be in the library if I need him.

Jason shakes his head. "Thanks, you too Adrian. Getting cookies and cake from home is what makes me homesick, Mom. When I get the package, it makes me sad they went to so much trouble for me."

"That is their role in life, Jason. You can't take that away from them. Grandma sends her love. She would've been here, but there's some crazy thing happening in town this week, and she and Mona are baking up a storm at her house."

Jason smiles proudly. "I understand. By the way, I have some good news. Uncle Dimmy wants me to take charge of the Arabian Stallions. He says that I'm as good as Dad was with them. How about that, Mom?"

"What does that mean, Jason?"

Jason chuckles. "It means that I will take the lead, not Jamaile. He is stepping down to let me handle the stallions. I've been training with the men anyway. One of them had to drop out of the group last week, so they think I can handle this. I must tell you that the blue silk and silver threads remind me of our racing silks. In a way, I traded one color for another."

My eyes fill again, but I can't wipe them away fast enough. "You look like your father, Jason...right down to your smile."

Jason cocks his head to the side. "Mom, please don't cry, every time I call, you cry. I won't call you if you get sad like this."

"If I didn't know better I swear I was talking to him, Jason. When did you grow the mustache? What's happening over there? Adrian said there was trouble near the Royal Palace last week."

Jason shrugs, saying, "We're okay. Jamaile and his men would have handled it anyway. I don't get involved with the army side of things. No one mentioned anything to me about it. And the mustache goes with the Blue and Silver costume, Mom."

Am I prying into foreign affairs?

"Are you sure? You would tell me if something was wrong, wouldn't you?"

"Nothing has happened here that I know of, Mom. I swear to you. Oh, I think I know what you're talking about now. There was a little thing last week, but it settled down right away. It had something to do with Fariq. So that you know, he disappeared again. Life is good here, and there is nothing to worry about, honestly. I would tell you, Mom, if it weren't."

Trying to keep my voice calm and even, I'm having trouble controlling the tears. "You are taking this Fariq thing a little too casually, Jason. You know better than anyone that there's always something to be cautious about, especially where that crazy man is concerned."

"Mom, you have to stop worrying so much. We're fine here, honestly."

"This Fariq character is still out there. I remember having a long conversation with Uncle Dimmy about this several years ago. He didn't make me feel as if this person is anything other than a threat. He might want to harm you and maybe Uncle Dimmy, too, you know that!" I say glumly.

"Mom, I can't hide from him. I must live my life. You taught me to reach for the brass ring, remember?"

I start to laugh at this. "Where did you hear that expression, sweetie? I don't ever remember saying that to you."

Jason tilts his head, shrugging his shoulders again. "Okay, you might not have used those exact words, but you taught me that I have inner strength no one can take away. You said to follow my dream. It is my dream, and I'm following it."

"Did I say that?" I did say that. Jason is changing the subject hoping he can redirect my sadness.

"How is everyone else there? What's happening with Mel and Curlie? Is Mel coming home for the summer? Is she coming over to visit me?"

"Not this summer. She's talking about a new job. Curlie likes boys."

"How are Mack and Danny?"

"Mack and Danny are doing some extra training for an event that's coming up. I wish you were here so you could be a part of it. Can you sneak away for a week or two?"

"Come on Mom, you know I can't do that. I have responsibilities here. As much as I'd like to, I can't leave any time I want to."

"I thought you could. It would be good to see you in person. We all miss you."

"I miss you too. You and the family could come here, you know. What's Curlie up to these days besides boys?"

"Nothing that I know of. She has a new boyfriend this week. His name is Benny, and she spends all her time either talking on the phone to him or talking about him to her friends."

"That's nice, Mom." Jason turns his head as a large hand comes into view, obscuring his face. "Sir, I didn't hear you come in."

"Jason, we must talk. Hello, to you Ma'dame Sell ers," Jam-ale says flatly, flashing his nice white teeth at the screen.

"Hello, Captain, how are you? Are you taking good care of my son as you promised? I will have your head if you don't."

"I am well, Ma'dame. We take great care; you see how fat your son becomes when he does not practice," Jam-ale replies, then moves out of view.

"Hang on a minute, Mom. I'll be right back." Although they speak in Arabic, I can hear them talking in the background. Jason comes back to the screen after a few moments. "I'm not fat, Mom, he's kidding. Must go now; Captain Jamaile needs to speak with me about something. Say hello to everyone for me and give Grandma a kiss. Have a good week and I'll talk with you soon, love you."

"So soon Jason? We haven't talked for very long."

"Go have lunch with Adrian. I'll talk with you next week, probably not Monday, because there's an event Uncle Dimmy told me I need to attend. It's some Alliance Ministry thing, and it can go pretty late, so call me, if you don't hear from me by Wednesday, okay?"

"Love you, sweetheart. I look forward to seeing you next week. Tell Dimmy I said hi. No, wait, make something up that sounds good."

The screen goes blank, which reflects my face when the monitor turns dark. I cannot shake a feeling that something is not right there and I'm suddenly depressed.

Adrian pokes his head into my office. "Are you done? Can we go to lunch now? I'm starving. You look sad, my little daffodil. Come on; it'll cheer you up." He's already heading toward the back door with me in tow.

"I'm worried, Adrian. Jason didn't sound right."

"Ellie, you worry too much, he's fine."

"Yeah, things could be worse, I suppose."

"The best way to cheer yourself up is to cheer somebody else up."

~ Mark Twain

Chapter Ten

Cheer Up

Half-way around the world, as Jason hit the END button and his laptop screen went blank, he turned toward Jamaile. "What else do you need to speak to me about, Captain? Is there something wrong?"

"You must listen carefully," Jamaile said in Arabic. "There is a situation that has arisen. My men and I must be away from the Royal Palace for a short time. I hold you responsible for your Uncle's safety."

Jason was curious. "Okay, but what does that mean, exactly?"

"You are to keep His Royal Highness safe and out of trouble while I am gone. You are to keep yourself out of distress." Jamaile pointed a playful finger at Jason's nose.

Jason laughed at this gesture. "You don't scare me, and that's probably what made my mother so afraid of you. You, pointing that big finger at me, ha, you think I'm scared of you?"

Jamaile smiled and most likely was amused with this teasing, as it probably reminded him of his mother, maybe of his father's time here. "You know nothing, little man. Your mother is a tough woman. She was not afraid of me. That was a surprise. She gave me trouble, this is true. She was not afraid of me."

"Where are you going, sir? You don't ever leave Uncle Akdemir for any reason, so why now?"

"That is a good question, Master Jason. I cannot tell you. You will oversee the men who are here in the palace. They expect you to lead them."

Jason switched from Arabic to English. "Are you serious? What am I going to lead them into, Captain? It sounds like I should be ready for a battle. Should I be ready for a battle?"

Jamaile walked toward the door. "Questions, always questions, like your mother."

"Yeah, you miss her too, huh?" Jason observed.

Jamaile narrowed his eyes at him, and said, "You must always be ready to lead. It matters not what *you* think; you are a warrior. You must be ready as a warrior always. You might forget other things. You must remember that."

Jason switched from English to Arabic, "I am ready, Captain."

"No matter what happens. Do you understand my instructions, Jason? I must have your word that you will care for your Uncle Akdemir and yourself while I am gone." Jamaile waited for him to react, then walked back to put his big face down into Jason's where he felt his hot breath spew, "Or I will have your head, little man!"

Without flinching a muscle, Jason replied, "Yes, you have my word. I will sleep in the king's chamber if I must. Is that what you want me to say?" He knew better than to laugh right now.

"You are smart…alex…what is the right word?" Jamaile seemed to be having a conflict, and looked up at the ceiling as if words were written there.

Jason started to laugh because Jamaile was struggling with the translation from Arabic to English and then back again. He also thought he should help him out. "Are you trying to say smart aleck or smart ass?"

"That is the word I want. You are a smart ass. You are also a smart person, Jason."

"Then don't shake that big finger of yours in my face. It doesn't have any effect on me!"

Jamaile hesitated with his hand on the doorknob when an old man appeared in the hallway. He stepped out of the way to allow him to enter. Following the man with his eyes, he added, "I expect much from you! Keep your dagger close. You do not know when it will be needed."

The old man deposited two towels into Jason's open bag that was sitting on the floor. Standing next to it, he awaited further instructions.

Jason made a little salute toward Jamaile and said, "Okay, Captain, I fully understand and will take care of everyone."

"Go now and be quick. His Highness wishes to speak to you. He waits for you in training area."

Jamaile knew Jason's strengths, unlike the standard training for fencing; he continued to train him in the extreme martial arts that included daggers and knives. He knew that he may have a use for them soon. That is, if they believed the word on the street.

Jason grabbed the long bag, trying to ignore the old man. "Okay, I'm going."

"Do not disappoint me, little man!" Jamaile's serious expression changed, and for a millisecond, he broke into laughter, showing his nice white teeth.

Jason traveled the hallways and stairs easily now, very rarely using the elevators so he could remain physically fit. When he got near the training area, he opened the door to see his uncle solemnly staring at a floor to ceiling mirror.

"I am sorry for keeping you waiting, Uncle. I needed to speak with my Mother. You know how she worries," Jason said in Arabic.

Akdemir replied in English, "Your Mother is well, Jason? Your family is well?"

Jason set his bag on a bench. Unzipping it to pull out his engraved foil and a towel, he answered, "Yes, Uncle, they are all well." Then he remembered that he was supposed to make something up to tell his uncle. "Mother sends her love to you." Jason started to snicker at this, as that couldn't be farther from the truth.

Akdemir switched to Arabic and started to laugh. "No, she does not, Jason. You are a terrible liar. She does not want you here with me. She wants you home with her." Taking up his position, he waited, then switched to speak in French this time, *"En garde, Mon ami."*

"Au contraire, je t'aime, tonton," Jason replied. "She also said, *'tu me manqué terriblemen,'* or something to that effect."

Akdemir's English was impeccable. "I do not believe for one moment that she sends me love. Perhaps good wishes, but certainly not love."

"Sure, she does. She can't wait to see you, you old dog." Jason was moving his feet in a non-fencing pattern, and Akdemir laughed at him.

"You have your father's humor, Jason. I remember quite fondly how Basim used to try to make me laugh. It was all too rare as he had a serious side. I will still best you today, so be ready."

It was a private time for Akdemir and Jason, one that they have both come to enjoy. They didn't take each other seriously and teased back and forth during their practice until the Fencing Master arrived and asked them to stop whatever they were doing to concentrate.

Jason reminded Akdemir of his older brother, Basim. He had told him repeatedly that it was almost as if his brother had come back from the dead. He was eternally grateful that Jason decided to go to Saudi to take up his rightful place as his heir-apparent to the throne.

When their time was up, they were tired from the constant lunging and dancing they did to keep the other at bay. Jason was aware of his uncle's preoccupation with the discord between one of his half-brothers named Fariq and his side of the family, and wanted to offer suggestions, but he didn't know how to bring it up. He also knew that too many questions irritated his Captain. Since he wasn't here, maybe it was a good time to do this.

When the Fencing Master left the room, Jason saw this as an excellent opportunity. "Uncle, I've been talking with Captain Jamaile. He said he and a few men were going away for a few days. He wants me to protect and guard you."

Akdemir let out a hearty laugh. "Do you think you are man enough to do that?"

"Yes, I do. You know I'm good at what I do. I'm man enough."

Akdemir sensed Jason's frustration and tried to anticipate his questions. He feared that prying eyes and ears might hear, he wanted to avoid what Jamaile and his men are up to, and abruptly changed the subject. "I cannot speak about what Jamaile is doing. What we can talk about is that of marriage." He felt that now was the time to bring this up.

Jason expressed surprise. "I didn't know you were considering marriage, Uncle? Who is she? What's her name?"

"No, the marriage is not for me, Jason. It is for you."

Jason speculated about what his mother would say about this. He was aware of certain customs of prearranged marriages, but no one said anything to him about this before he came to the palace. "What are you saying? I'm not ready to get married!"

Akdemir smiled at Jason. "It matters not that you are ready or not. The marriage is between you and the young daughter of one of our Royal Alliance Ministers. He is considering this marriage…"

"You never said anything like this before I came here. I will choose whoever I want to be my wife, Uncle, not you," he blurts. "I'm sorry, I mean no disrespect." Jason tried to control his rising anger.

"Jason, as head of this household, if I deem that marriage is in your best interest and will benefit our household, it will be done. You have little to say about it. Let me put it to you in another way, Jason," Akdemir paused.

"It does not matter what way you put it; I won't go along with it. Marriage is not a casual walk in the park, Uncle. I do not agree with this!" Jason sputtered.

"I see this gets us nowhere. We will speak of this another time. I will see you at dinner." Without saying another word, Akdemir picked up a towel from the bench and walked out, leaving the door to echo as it closed behind him.

How could his uncle be so stubborn? How could he possibly think he would marry someone he doesn't even know? Why did he wait until now to tell him about this? He would not have agreed to it. Yes, Uncle Akdemir was head of the Royal Household, but he had already found someone else.

Jason began to visualize his sweet, sweet Amala, who had come to him one night. She slipped into his room and awakened him, and he reached for her as if they were in a dream. The light from the high narrow windows let in enough light for him to see her beautiful face. Her long flowing hair and the softness of her body made him feel as if they were floating. She refused to tell him her name, so he called her Amala, as it meant hope in Arabic.

Amala was neither one of the girls that come to clean the rooms nor was she at state dinners. She came to him all those months ago, or else she must live somewhere within the Royal Palace itself, as why else could get around so quickly.

He tried to question her about how she could move undetected, but each time she smothered his mouth with hers, then they quickly forgot, and fell asleep. Now that his uncle wanted him to marry a woman he didn't know, he was convinced that when he told Amala what his uncle was planning, she would reveal her real name. Perhaps she could help him convince his uncle that **she** was the one for him.

It would have to wait as Jason must guard and protect his uncle. He opted to sleep in the King's outer room while Captain Jamaile was out of the Royal Palace. Then he decided that he would tell Amala the next time she came to him.

Akdemir seemed unusually sullen. As he attempted to stifle oppressive memories to focus on the present, with Jason so close, it was quite unnerving. He reminded him so much of Basim. If only his brother had not left when he did, things would be so different. Basim would have taken charge after their father died, not him. Basim was the Crown Prince, next in line after their father, and duties would fall to him to assume this enormous responsibility.

Basim certainly had his share of disruptions during his time here. It was caused in part, by jealous half-brothers and sisters who were sired by his father and his numerous wives. Jamaile was ever vigilant and understood that if Fariq was out there, the threat would continue. The Royal Household was aware that Fariq wanted his hands on the fortune he thought was rightfully his and might try to prevent Jason from accepting his role as Crown Prince.

Akdemir's mind wandered to the story the Royal Palace gave out about his brother. Few alive know the truth. To the world, Crown Prince Basim Abdul Fariq Obagur was dead and buried almost thirty years ago. Basim was tortured and beaten and with his subsequent death, the final decree, prohibited any reference to Basim by their father himself, meaning that no one could utter his name within the palace walls.

Basim was so unrecognizable after his beating that even the people who hunted him never suspected that he lived an alternative life. It was their father, King Basim, and the CIA operative (Ellen's father) that came up with the ingenious plan. Ellen's father took Basim out of the country, arranging for an altered appearance, giving him a new identity. Known as the American businessman, Ravenalt T. Andress (Ravi), he came to visit the Royal Palace as often as he dared.

After their father, King Basim died, Akdemir convinced the Council of Alliance Ministers that he held the ancient documents. These documents were supposed to pass from one heir to another, ensuring the right of succession with implicit instructions as to how the leaders would carry out established rules. As in many households where sibling rivalry was rampant, the Royal Palace knew of strife within the family;

however, the Ministers could do little until and unless the need arose to intervene.

Akdemir was next in line after his father died, but did not take the throne, because he secretly hoped his brother would come forward as he was the rightful heir. The brothers both feared that the ancient documents might go missing and it was Basim who came up with the creative idea to hide them under the covers of some books.

After all, Basim could carry them wherever he went, and no one would suspect. Why did Basim leave them behind the last time he was here? Did he mean to leave them for his younger brother? With turmoil brewing, Akdemir had to make a choice, keep the secret spy network in place, or tell the world the truth.

The Alliance Ministers ruled that enough time passed and a King was to be named to unite the warring tribes. They hoped that Fariq would take the hint and stop his foolish quest to gain the throne.

Basim told him the last time he had come to the palace that someday he would have to tell his wife the truth, but the chance must not have materialized. Although dead to his family in Saudi, he was happy. Akdemir was sure he loved his wife Ellen and their three children, and he yearned to be a part of that. When Jamaile discovered that Basim left the books, he almost panicked.

Akdemir pondered that fateful day in May when Ellen first arrived as his guest, and he became morose. Was it fate that intervened when his network of people found Ellen and took her to safety? He recalled how difficult it was to explain the explosion that killed her husband when he didn't understand it himself. It meant that Basim was dead, again. He could no longer see his brother and ask for advice, nor could he be regaled with stories of his family, his life, and his world outside the Royal Palace.

Did Basim know it was only a matter of time before destiny intervened again? Is that why he left the books for his brother?

Ellen seemed to be an unwilling participant trapped in the middle of their drama. She accused him of keeping her a prisoner. Then, after careful consideration, he sent her home with the altered books with the idea that he could retrieve them and incorporate himself into her family. He could then be a part of their family which would give him the only link to a true heir.

Was this coincidence, or fate, that Ellen happened to pick up *Moby Dick* and *For Whom the Bell Tolls* that day in the library? When the opportunity presented itself, the books went home with Ellen. He never dreamt she would pull off the covers! The biggest shock came when he discovered that the ancient documents were not together!

Akdemir knew that Captain Jamaile was privy to inside information during the time of Basim's first death and the shroud his father threw over the story. One day soon, he would have an opportunity to discuss it with him. Therefore, he must wait for the right moment.

Captain Jamaile and a few of his men were gone for about three days this time. Upon their return to the palace, he went directly to Akdemir's library to report what they discovered. Jason was with King Akdemir as their chess game had ended. Jason stood to leave, but his uncle motioned that he remain.

It seemed that there had been little disturbances around the area for the last several months. The local Islamic Religious Police kept most of them quiet, but in the previous few days, something dreadful had happened, and King Akdemir thought it best for Jamaile and his men to handle it themselves.

Fires that were deliberately set at some of the oil wells last year were bad enough, but the growing concern now was about the poisoned water in the city outside the Royal Palace walls. Three people had died within the last two weeks; two were local merchants, and the third was Captain Jamaile's cousin.

This news brought back a suppressed resentment when Jason heard this. A distant memory surfaced of Jason's first Christmas in Virginia. His Mother and Grandmother were distraught over the fact that his cousin, Danny, was waiting for surgery to remove a stray arrow. They kept it quiet, but he overheard his Mother and the new man, talking about it.

The story became convoluted and implausible, as there were no woods near his Aunt Terre's house except for a stand of trees. The huntsman would have had to aim his bow and arrow straight toward the glass to penetrate the back door. The fact that the houses are close together and that no one saw anything led the authorities to believe that it was the work of a stealth marksman. It would have to be by design to have had a trajectory into that door! He vowed then that he would find out who was responsible.

When Adrian came on board, he thought to ask him about what the truth might be, however, as with many things, it slipped his mind. He then overheard Mr. Levi as he explained what happened to his cousin while he passed the library during one of his visits. Jason let his indignation simmer. After one of their bizarre incidents, Jason cornered Adrian to ask him questions, but he was warned not to go snooping into things that he could not change.

Adrian also cautioned him not to get his dander up over things he heard, because he might not have all the facts. His words continued to echo in his head, "Leave it alone for your Mother's sake. Don't go trying to be a hero and avenge your father's death, either. And for God's sake, let the authorities do their job."

Jason recalled how he argued about the facts that remained, but Adrian persuaded him to put his energy elsewhere. Therefore, that is what he did. He was a ready warrior now, trained in most, if not all of the martial arts, a black belt, and 10th degree Dan. He was also as proficient in Arabic, sword fighting, daggers, and fencing (which is mostly recreational), but he could deliver a fatal blow if necessary. And out of necessity, he had perfected a mental technique to help him cope with his homesickness.

Uncle Akdemir sent Captain Jamaile on another secret mission. Jason understood the palace walls had ears, and he must be cautious. They must all be watchful as Jamaile again asked Jason to keep his uncle safe and protected.

A few days later, Jason was with his stallion, *Basim's Pride II*, along with the group that comprised the Blue and Silver Horse Ensemble. When Captain Jamaile strode quickly into the arena, his face reflected that things did not go as planned. As Jamaile approached, the men waited for Jason to give the signal before dismounting. Handing the reins to a man named Deffrah, he walked toward the big man.

"Why are you here, Jason? Where is His Royal Highness?" Jamaile asked in his usual gruff tone of voice, almost hissing.

Jason was startled. "I left him with two of your best men, Captain. He had a meeting in the library. He's fine, I'm sure of it."

"If he is not, I will have your head, little man. The horse training could have waited!" he sputtered. "Go protect and guard him, as I told you to do." Then he turned to walk away.

Jason did not understand his Captain's tone of voice. As the other men moved slowly out of the arena, Jamaile turned back toward him, barking insults in Arabic. Jason could feel his face burn with embarrassment. How dare he do that in front of *his* men? They might lose respect for him now, and he worked so hard to gain it. He left his uncle in the safe hands of two of the top-ranking men they both trust implicitly. What was he supposed to do, follow him around like a puppy dog all day?

After he dismissed the riders in the arena and assigned someone to take care of his horse, Jason walked along the familiar hallways. The only sound was that of his boots as they made a muffled slapping sound on the stone floor. When he neared the elevator that would rise to meet a walkway, he heard voices, and he stopped to listen. When he peered around the corner, there was no one there.

Did he imagine the voices?

Jason was aware of the many secret passageways within the walls, some he had yet to discover. His mind went to the first time he came to the Royal Palace with his family, amazed at the secret compartments in his suite of rooms. It was the same room his mother occupied, and formally his father's before that.

Could their configuration and proximity to the passageways be to confuse the enemy in case of a hostile takeover? If that's the case, why hadn't someone shown him where all the secret passageways were? It would be useful knowledge.

Staring at the stone floor to see if they change in color, Jason looked for hidden panels like the ones in his set of rooms, then pulled out his dagger to inspect the cracks for any markings. He stepped back to see where he was, mentally noting that it was a familiar one. This hallway led to the elevator, but if he turned completely around, the other way dead-ended at a wall.

Jason moved toward that wall and put his hand on it to feel if it was different from the one beside it. It felt warm to the touch, not cold. Out of curiosity, he took a flask of water from his belt and wet his hand. Smearing the water on the warm wall, he observed that the water dried almost instantly. It convinced him that it might be a secret passage. When he tried to locate the button or indentation that would suggest how to open it, he was startled when Jamaile's voice boomed behind him.

The big man was standing near the elevator shaking his enormous head. "What are you doing here?" he demanded. "You should be upstairs with your uncle by now."

"I swear I heard voices, but when I came down the hall, no one was here, Captain."

Jamaile's tone changed from annoyance to concern. "What did the voices say?" he asked.

"I was too far away to hear anything because they were whispering."

Jamaile inquired, "You are sure of this? How many voices did you hear?"

"They were here in this hallway. It was a woman's voice and a man's voice. I'm sure of it. I wanted to see where they went," Jason said abruptly.

Jamaile was either disgusted or still annoyed with him, and replied, "There is nothing here. Come…"

"I thought there might be a secret passage we might not know about, as they disappeared," Jason mumbled. He is like his mother in that respect. He won't back down, no matter how big Jamaile was or how intimidating he became.

"Nothing here, I would know. Come, we must get to the library quickly."

They walked toward the elevator in silence. Jamaile then depressed the almost invisible button with the tip of his dagger, and the wall slid silently open to reveal an empty cubicle that would take them to the enclosed catwalk that would eventually lead to the library.

"I gave you a job to do, and you gave to someone else." Jamaile was using an uncharacteristic tone. "You were to guard your uncle. I find you playing with the horses."

"It's called delegating responsibility, Captain. My Uncle is guarded by two of your favored men, Raheeb and Maheer."

Jamaile nodded his head, and then placed his large hand on Jason's shoulder. "There is much trouble these days. They are good men. You did well to have them guard His Royal Highness. I am…"

Jason knew how difficult it was for the big man to apologize for something and he must be struggling to say the right words. "What kind of trouble did you find, Captain?" Jason shrugged off Jamaile's big hand.

The elevator stopped to reveal a hallway much like the one they came from, with the exception that there was a small, almost invisible marking on the wall.

"His Royal Highness will talk about this if he wants you to know."

They walked toward the opposite wall that appeared solid, but Jason knew from experience that it wasn't. Here Jamaile inserted his dagger again into a small depression and the wall slid silently up to reveal a dark hallway. It was an area approximately five feet wide by ten feet tall which was hidden within the walls of the Royal Palace, and few knew of its existence. A musty, dank odor permeated the walls due to the proximity to the mountain and the stone used to create the tunnel. With little air movement, Jason wanted to gag, but he moved along in front of Jamaile anyway, as they flicked on small flashlights.

The first time Jamaile showed Jason the hidden passageways to get around, he questioned who moved in and out of them. Why would they even need them? Then it crossed his mind that it could be how they took his mother in and out of the palace. What was apparent to him now, was that there must be a maze of hidden passageways, not a few as he once thought.

Jamaile dismissed Raheeb and Maheer as they entered the library. The massive doors closed behind them with a thud. Akdemir was sitting at his large desk talking on the telephone. He saw Jamaile and Jason and motioned for them to sit down. They would wait, pretending not to listen in.

When Akdemir finished, he came from around his desk and sat in one of the wingback chairs that he preferred. "You were training with the stallions today, Jason. Good to have you back, Captain Jamaile. Do you have news? Tell me it is good."

Jamaile was reluctant to speak, but Akdemir motioned to go ahead, and said, "This concerns Jason and everyone else in the Royal Palace."

"Highness, the news is not good. We have discovered that Fariq is directly linked to the poisonings of the water," Jamaile replied impassively.

Akdemir was quiet for a moment. "How do you think we should proceed from here, Captain?"

"You must have guards around the clock from now on, both you and Young Jason."

Jason reacted to this and said, "I can take care of myself, sir. I don't need a guard!"

"It is not a question of whether you want one or not, Jason," Uncle Akdemir said bluntly. "If you had been born here, you would already have a companion to guard you. If Captain Jamaile thinks you need to have one now, then he will choose a suitable guard for you. We will not take any chances."

"Yes, Uncle, I understand."

"Have you discovered who is delivering information to Fariq from inside the Royal Palace walls?" Akdemir directed this question to Jamaile while Jason tried to keep his temper under control. Did they know about Amala?

"We questioned all of the Royal Family, and all of the servers, and there is evidence that it comes from within, Your Highness. We do not know who it is yet."

"Are you certain it comes from within the palace?" Akdemir questioned.

Jason observed Jamaile closely, and figured that he knew more, by the shift of his eyes, but was reluctant to tell the King for fear that if he was wrong, it would invoke a rift between them.

"We have narrowed it down to one of two things. It may be one of Fariq's daughters or one of the other wife's children," the Captain said finally.

"You are unsure of who it is, then?" Akdemir probed.

"We cannot say for sure who it is. We will continue our investigation until we do."

"Thank you for your continued service to this household, Captain Jamaile. Would you take care of that other matter we discussed?"

Akdemir's head nodded ever so slightly. Jason knew that when he did this, he dismissed and then thanked the person. It seemed a bit stiff and looked practiced. Jason knew he wouldn't be able to do this when he took the throne; at least not without bursting into laughter, especially if his sisters were present.

"Yes, Your Royal Highness." Jamaile stood, bowed slightly, and left the room.

"Jason, something is distracting you. Do you have something to say to me?"

Jason was unaware of the amused expression on his face and stiffened when his uncle spoke to him. "No, Uncle, I was merely thinking. I would rather not discuss it right now." Jason's face reddened without his permission, and then he realized that it was the second time today!

Akdemir persisted, saying, "You are embarrassed by something I have said?"

"No, it was something Captain Jamaile did." He tried to change the subject quickly, as he remembered how Jamaile yelled at him in front of his men not twenty minutes ago.

"Let me try to guess. Jamaile yelled at you in front of the men you were teaching today."

"Yes, Uncle, he yelled at me."

Akdemir stood to gather a piece of paper from his desk. "If he did that, there was cause, Jason. Captain Jamaile and I have been together since we were boys. He was with your father before that, and I entrust my life to him."

"I don't wish to speak of it now," Jason said.

"It cannot be that bad," Akdemir coaxed.

"He kept yelling at me in front of my men that I should be guarding you, not training with the horses. I sent Raheeb and Maheer. They are the best men available, and they are trustworthy. We have a show in a few weeks, and the men still need lots of work."

Akdemir smiled. "You consider them *your* men. Captain Jamaile said you should be here with me and you should not have been training with the stallions?"

"Yes, Uncle. You said I would take my father's place. Didn't he consider the men who trained with him as his men?"

Jason saw the twinkle in his uncle's eyes as he started to laugh. "Jamaile does this to all of us, regardless of who we are. That goes for you, me, and your father."

"He embarrassed me, Uncle."

"His main job is to protect us, the Royal Family. You should feel pride he considers you family."

"I wouldn't use that word to describe how I feel, Uncle."

"If he fails, Jason, he knows that his head will roll…literally from his shoulders. The shame brought upon his family would be catastrophic. He is a fourth generation guard to the Royal Family."

"Should I be impressed by that, Uncle?"

"You can be impressed or not be impressed, it is your choice," Uncle Akdemir stated flatly.

"Tell me about my father. Captain Jamaile won't talk about him. I have a lot of questions. You said that you would tell me when I came here."

King Akdemir seemed pensive for several moments. "I do recall that I said that to you. The right opportunity did not present itself. What you want to speak of is delicate. We; the entire Royal Household were prohibited from speaking your father's name after the incident that precipitated his departure. Perhaps it is time for you to know about him. What do you wish to know, Jason?"

"For starters, how old was my father when he started to train with swords and daggers?" Jason asked.

"It is our custom to start training as soon as we can hold a sword or dagger without wounding ourselves. In other words, your father started his training very early. We used wood at first. I'd say he was five or six years old."

"And the stallions? When did he start to train with them? What were his favorite things to do when he lived here? Did the two of you get along?"

"All are good questions, Jason. You are like your mother who also asked many questions. I am uncertain when he first sat in the saddle. Perhaps he was ten or eleven. We were forever doing things together, and we got along amicably."

"What did you do for fun? Did you and my father have many friends?"

"Your father and I had many things to occupy us during our growing up years. If I remember correctly, Jamaile has always been a part of those times. He and his family lived here in the palace with us. His father was my father's trusted First-In-Command. We did practically everything together. We also got into trouble together, as most boys do. I do not recall if there was a favorite thing we did. We thought everything we did was our favorite."

"Can you tell me what he did that was so wrong that he had to leave here? No one has truly told me what happened."

"Jason, in due time, we can talk about that. We must turn our attention to another matter. When we were older, Jamaile, your father, and I used to discuss strategy. Your father and I attended university while Jamaile stayed behind to train with those who knew how to keep the peace and how to contain warring factions. We often discussed delicate matters of state, as his father did for mine. I have decided that you need someone around you always. Captain Jamaile will now introduce his son to you."

"He has a son?" Jason stared at his uncle in disbelief. "Wow, that's hard to believe he would attract…given his demeanor. Is he here in the palace? Why don't I know about him?"

Akdemir began to laugh at Jason's apparent naiveté. Perhaps he should be more careful about what he said. On more than one occasion, he had put his foot into his mouth by not carefully weighing his thoughts. When Uncle Akdemir laughed at him, he knew that it was something he must work on more. The Ministers would consider him a complete idiot. He also knew how the palace gossip chain worked.

"Captain Jamaile's son has been in training since his birth. He will one day take his father's place. He is not part of the Blue and Silver that you train with; however, he is involved in your daily care. He watches you closely. Both he and Jamaile now feel that the time is right for you to bond."

Jason had no *vibes* about anyone watching him, although there were plenty of times where he felt as if someone was following. Then he began to feel resentment and betrayal because he should have noticed it by now. "Why did it take this long for an introduction? Shouldn't this have taken place the moment I stepped foot into the palace? I don't know what to say about this. I was not aware of anyone watching me!"

"His name is Khalifa. It means successor. Khalifa is Captain Jamaile's successor. His job is to guard you for the rest of your life as Jamaile guards and protects me. Would you like to meet him, Jason?"

"If this person is supposed to be my bodyguard, I don't need one, Uncle. As you know, I've been highly trained to take care of myself."

"Yes, you are highly trained. I believe that you know more than me and your father put together when it comes to that; however, Captain Jamaile and I feel very strongly that the circumstances have changed. You will like Khalifa. Our only regret is not introducing him to you sooner."

"Why don't I choose someone from the Blue and Silver? I've gotten to know several that I trust."

"Jason," Akdemir stated, "You do not understand how this works here. He has been trained to guard the Royal Family. You are my heir, and that is his duty. You know him by another name. He is the one who tidies your room, puts your clothes away after Sheyanna brings them to you."

"That is Khalifa? I thought his name was Qysay. Surely you are not serious." Jason stared at his uncle, then burst into laughter.

"I am most serious, Jason. Khalifa also takes care of your gear in the arena. He is in the training room to assist you…"

"But he is old and useless. He's hunched, and he walks with a limp. He's very clumsy. He carries too many towels and bumps into things. He knocks stuff over and has broken more than one thing in my room. I almost spoke with Sheyanna about some items that are missing. That man is such a klutz, how is this possible, Uncle?"

"It is all an act, Jason. He is a young man, as you are. He has trained for many years. Jamaile and I feel that it is time for you to get to know each other. We both think that it is past due and we should have done it sooner."

"Perhaps he is your spy, Uncle. I don't like him very much."

"Hold your tongue, Jason! It is Captain Jamaile's son. He would be offended to hear you say such things against him! He is aware that you think of him that way. Khalifa told his father you spoke your mind in his presence many times."

Jason tried to recall what he might have said to this person named Qysay, then decided that they weren't all immoral. "Don't you see that he carries everything back to his father? What did I say that was so bad?"

Akdemir pressed a small button on the underside of his wing chair. Jason had seen him use this when he wanted to summon someone, or he wanted trays brought in or removed. Jamaile must be waiting on the other side of the door. When it opened, he walked in with a young man.

Khalifa could be Jamaile's twin, except for Jamaile's height, as he was two or three inches taller than his son, but their facial features are remarkably similar, right down to their long dark hair and mustaches. When Jamaile introduced his son, there was a split-second of familiarity in the young man's face. Masterfully executed, his disguises made it nearly impossible for Jason to recall this person.

It was awkward at first as the four of them talked both in Arabic and English. Akdemir was ever the patient host and wanted to make everyone comfortable, steering the conversation to the many people Khalifa had been since Jason arrived, hoping it would ease tension.

A knock brought two servers with trays loaded with silver domes and other clinking objects. As usual, all conversation ceased. The servers proceeded to set the table located near the doors at the back of the large room, leaving when things were in place.

"Shall we break bread together to celebrate this union?" Uncle Akdemir asked.

Without saying a word, the little group moved to the table to eat. The conversation continued, as Akdemir made it clear to Jason what would transpire from now on.

"From this day forward, Khalifa will be within mere feet of you, Jason. He has taken an oath much like his father. He has sworn not only his allegiance to the Royal Household, but he will also lay down his life for you, along with any other member of the Royal Family, should the need arise," Akdemir said. "Do you so state, Khalifa?"

"Yes, your Highness. I so state to be Jason's companion and defender, my life for his."

"I don't know about this, Uncle." Jason, wary of this situation, questioned himself as to how Amala would be able to slip past Khalifa.

Perhaps she would find a way to get around that. He hadn't seen her for several months and was secretly wishing for her to come soon. He had grown very fond of her and their lovemaking. He was also aware of the risk Amala took to come to him.

"You have no choice in the matter. It was settled the day you were born, as you are the rightful heir. Khalifa's sole job is to guard you and be your constant companion and defender. There will be no further discussion of this. It is the way your King says it will be. Do you understand?" Akdemir questioned.

"Yes, Uncle," Jason said quietly.

"Do you so state that you accept Khalifa as your companion, defender, and protector for the rest of your life?"

"I so state that I accept Khalifa as my companion, defender, and protector for the rest of my life."

"Good, that is settled."

After a polite dismissal, Khalifa and Jason walked back to his room, but his thoughts kept wandering. Would he forever be at his uncle's mercy? Or worse, would he feel trapped in the Royal Household, as Uncle Akdemir so lovingly referred to it?

Was this how his Mother felt?

Somehow, the enchantment about being a Crown Prince he once felt, slowly started to ebb. He began to worry about Amala. Unless she came to him, he couldn't ask where she was, and certainly couldn't inquire about her.

It began to affect him until he thought he would lose his mind.

A few weeks later, Jason started to resent his limited existence as most activities outside the Royal Palace were being discouraged. He sensed a growing hostility toward him, as Khalifa questioned his decision when selecting daggers and swords they were about to use for a show. He found this almost intolerable.

"You are not happy with my performance, Your Royal Highness?"

Jason cringed whenever Khalifa addressed him in this manner. "Your performance is acceptable, Khalifa. It has nothing to do with you directly. I'm unhappy with myself is all."

Jason didn't elaborate past that for fear the royal spies would take it back to his uncle. He continued to worry about Amala because she hadn't come to him for a long time. The longer she stayed away, the edgier Jason became. Then he began to mistrust Khalifa, wondering if he could be the reason she was absent.

"May I inquire what you are unhappy about, Your Royal Highness?"

Jason seemed unusually prickly today, and his patience with this line of questioning was getting on his nerves. "Please stop calling me that!" he snarled.

"How do you wish me to address you?" Khalifa inquired.

"Call me Jason. It drives me nuts when you say that! I don't feel like royalty."

"Yes, I agree with you. You do not appear to look like royalty to me either. You are frustrated with the stallions, perhaps?"

Khalifa was standing inside Jason's room, waiting for him to finish getting dressed. It was bad enough that Captain Jamaile called him a little man in front of other people, but Khalifa's condescending tone of voice was slowly driving him crazy. Maybe he was a tad resentful. Why did everything have to be so hush-hush around here?

"I am Jason, plain old Jason," he muttered.

"If I may offer some assistance. Perhaps the sash would look better turned the other way."

"I don't need your help with dressing, Khalifa. Maybe if I was born here, I might feel more like a royal person, but I wasn't, so I don't. Do you understand? Oh, for God's sake, I'm not yelling *at* you. I'm frustrated with things that I have no control over, okay?"

Khalifa must be crafting his words carefully. He knew how to set Jason 'off'. "Have you started to regret your decision to stay here, after the King told you that you had to take a wife?"

"How would you know about that?" Jason questioned. Fidgeting with the unique wristwatch his mother gave him, he put a finger under the band to loosen it, then contemplated the implication of pressing its face.

Khalifa smiled sheepishly, which was what drove Jason to distraction. Although Jason couldn't read his mind, he could read his facial expressions which he had come to know as patronizing.

"I know most things that concern you, Master Jason. The Royal Family has no secrets. There is little you can hide from me," Khalifa said smugly.

"That's priceless, Khalifa. So, you know that my uncle has this all planned? You know that he wants me to marry someone that I didn't choose? It is unbelievable! Now you discuss me as you do state affairs?"

Khalifa raised his eyebrows slightly. "What you do has a bearing on what I do, so yes, we discuss you as we do state affairs, as my father discusses things with the King. We are expected to do the same. It is the way of our people. You do not like this?"

Did they find out about Amala? Khalifa could have followed her that last night and could have confronted her in one of the passageways. That might explain why he hadn't seen her for so long.

"I don't wish to talk to you about my personal life. Are we late for something?" Jason scowled.

"We are to be in the training room to practice. I have your gear. We can go now?"

Since Uncle Akdemir introduced him, Khalifa had not worn the old man disguise, or any other, taking openly to walk with him everywhere he went. Khalifa was the first person he saw every morning and the last one he saw at night. He was present when he came out of the bathroom, and was present to walk with him to dinner. He was always present, and it was getting on Jason's nerves.

They walked in silence toward the hallway and the elevator that would take them to a connecting catwalk, as they headed toward the library, where he knew his uncle was meeting with his fellow countrymen.

Uncle Akdemir had not entirely brought him into those meetings. Was he afraid he would disrupt them as his mother once did? She let Jason read the document she prepared for the CIA, only after she knew he had decided to live in Saudi. As the memories of that reading came back, Jason started to laugh to himself at the thought of his mother wearing a long skirt and a scarf that hid her face, sitting in that big library with those men hurling insults at her.

"I am here should you wish to talk," Khalifa stated, breaking the silence.

Stopping, Jason turned toward him. "If I want to go out past the palace walls, would you go with me and not say anything to anyone?"

"Go out? What do you mean by this term go out?" Khalifa asked. "You mean outside the inner palace walls?"

Jason sighed, thinking how much he would have to explain. "Yes, if I want to go out past the inner palace walls, would you go with me? If I wanted to go to a bar or nightclub, would you come with me? Can we go to another city? I'm getting a little tired of the same old thing here."

Khalifa pondered this for a moment. "That would not be permitted as there is no bar or club here on the Royal Palace grounds. There is no place like this inside or out that we may go. They are expressly forbidden."

"Do you have a life outside of guarding me 24/7?" Jason asked.

Khalifa eyed Jason warily. "The only life I have is that of companion and defender to the rightful heir to the throne. The King would flatly refuse to allow it. We have a current situation. What is it you wish to do that you cannot do here? My life is…to guard you always. Do you not remember your uncle's words?"

"Yes, I remember them because you keep reciting them over and over and over again. I'd like to have a life outside of training with the horses. Don't you want to do stuff with your friends? Do you even have friends?"

Khalifa started to shake his head. "You will not be permitted to do this. My life is not your concern."

"Come on, Khalifa, surely there's something out there beyond those walls that you want to see and do. We can do this together. I'd like to dance, with girls. You do know that I like girls, don't you? I want to dance with some girls."

"NO!" Khalifa roars. "It is strictly not allowed!"

Jason decided right then and there to begin formulating his plan of departure. He would find the hidden passageway or hallway that would remove him from the life he now considered so stifling that he cannot stand it anymore. His Mother didn't yet know how he felt about leaving the Royal Palace, but he was glad he told her about Amala.

Jason's worry began to escalate as weeks turned into months and his concern grew even more for Amala. As his bitterness grew, so did his determination. He would dig his way out using his dagger if need be. Was this how his father felt? Is this why he didn't want this life? Was his Mother right to caution him about his motives in trying to recapture what his father might have run from all those years ago?

It was not what he envisioned for himself. If he had been born here, things might be completely different. If his father were still alive, that too would have changed things.

Then the reality of the magnitude of accepting his uncle's request to be the rightful heir hit him.

Jason no longer felt as if he belonged in Saudi.

After all, he was an outsider.

Jason grabbed his dagger and a small flashlight. He sent Khalifa on a wild goose chase that might take the better part of an hour. It would give him the opportunity to venture out without his prying eyes. He had little chance to explore while being so carefully guarded.

Tiptoeing into the hallway, he located each motion sensor and disabled the cameras that watched him, surmising that this must be how they caught Amala either sneaking into or out of his room. They must have followed her and convinced her never to return.

Jason thought he would lose his mind because he missed her terribly. Since his uncle flatly refused to allow him out past the palace walls, there was little chance of meeting Amala. He mistrusted Khalifa and knew he would take any information directly to his father, or his Uncle Akdemir. It could work to his advantage if he gave Khalifa false information. It would be interesting to see how fast it traveled to his uncle's ear.

He located and disabled cameras along the route to the elevator to hide his activities. Since he had never gone in the opposite direction, he headed that way now. When whispered words floated either from the wall or behind a door, Jason stopped to listen. Unsure in which direction it came from, he went strictly by instinct and found himself near a wall that seemed to glow along the outer edges.

The voices began to fade and so did the glow, as he sensed movement away from him. Using the small flashlight to locate an indentation, Jason put the tip of his dagger into it and stepped to the side, so he remained out of sight. As the wall slid silently up, he noticed the floor tiles, realizing they were slightly darker. He also noticed a symbol embossed on them.

Committing this to memory, he traced the hallway in his mind, gazing at his compass for its direction, watching as the needle deviated while he moved. The pathway didn't go in a straight line as most of the others he had seen. This one had two sharp turns. Hesitating near the end, he listened before searching for the *out* button.

When there was no sound, the door/wall slid soundlessly up to reveal a hallway he hadn't seen or been in previously. Making another mental note of the symbol on the floor, he closed the door quickly when he heard voices coming his way.

Jason moved back along the passageway, relieved when he reached his room ahead of Khalifa. Out of the corner of his eye, there was a sudden movement near his bathroom. Moving slowly toward the door, he reached in to confront his would-be attacker.

Whispered Dreams

A soft voice whispered, "Jason, do not turn light on."

"Amala, where have you been?" Jason was surprised. He spoke to her in English in case there was an undetected bug in the bathroom.

"Be quiet. Someone will hear," Amala said quickly.

Pulling her to him in a firm embrace, he said, "I thought I'd never see you again. Where have you been? I've been so worried about you."

"I came to warn you," Amala cried softly.

"I have missed you so much." Jason touched her hair, then hugged and kissed her face. "Warn me about what? Where have you been?"

Amala was trying to pull away from him. "My father not happy with me."

"Who is your father? Did he find out about us?" Jason was unsure if she was sad or glad at this point, but he had a firm grip on her arms.

"I fall in love with you!" she started to sob.

"I love you too. Who is your father?" Jason demanded. By now Amala was crying so hard she couldn't speak. They may only have mere minutes before Khalifa returned from the errand, but Jason pressed her for more information.

"Listen to me. My uncle told me I have to marry a woman I don't know and I don't...."

Amala stopped her sobbing long enough to take one of his hands, placing it on her stomach. Jason realized the mound beneath her garment meant that she was pregnant.

"I must go, Jason. You will never see me again."

"Who is your father? Why can't we be together?" Jason held her wrist so she couldn't leave.

Amala was now digging her fingernails into his hand. "Let go, Jason. They will kill you if they find me here."

"Who is your father?" Jason demanded again.

"Fariq...my father is Fariq. He will hurt me to find I have shamed him." She switched to Arabic when she couldn't find the right words in English. "I failed to make you tell me where the ancient documents are. I am dead if he finds me here. He will kill you, too."

Jason was stunned by this news but doesn't release his grip on the girl. "We can leave here, together. I don't know where the documents are, Amala. Why does he think I know where they are?"

"He says that if they are not in the King's quarters, they must be with you."

"Does he want the throne that bad?"

"You do not understand. I have failed my father. He will find me. There is no place for me to hide. Please let me go, Jason. There is a chance the baby can live. You must let me go," Amala pleaded. "Let me go so I can seek shelter for our baby."

Jason reluctantly let her go. Minutes later, Khalifa returned to find him sitting on the sofa staring at a blank TV screen.

"Are you unwell? Some of the cameras are not working. My father sent his men to determine why." Khalifa moved to stand in front of Jason when he didn't answer. "She was here. The girl was here!" he sputtered.

"What does it matter to you?" Jason replied, and turned away from him.

"Everything about you, matters to me. That woman is the enemy, you fool! Her father sent her to spy on you, you imbecile. That woman will be punished for what she has done! I must tell my father. He must be informed immediately." Khalifa was beyond angry.

Jason tried to control his emotions. "Let it go, will you?"

"I cannot do this!" he screamed. "There are consequences to your actions. I have put your item in the freezer. Do not send me out to fetch like a dog. You will do without!" He didn't wait for an answer and left the room, slamming the door behind him.

Jason half expected Khalifa to lock the door from the outside. Then he started to worry how Amala could have deceived him the way she did. Did her father send her to spy on him? Was she crying because she was pregnant? Or was she crying because they could never be together?

Was Amala the enemy?

Jason felt powerless. How could he stop the ruthless Fariq from harming Amala? Was his only option to ask the one person that may not understand his situation? Did he trust Khalifa enough to discuss this with him? The way Khalifa talked, he doubted that they would ever understand each other. They had not bonded as Jamaile and Uncle Akdemir thought they would. Could he persuade him to see things his way?

Jason suddenly realized the uncertainty that Amala and his unborn child would face. Without protection against the apparent cruelty of her father, his child wouldn't stand a chance.

His child…his baby.

"Oh my God, what have we done?" he whispered, then lowered his head into his hands. "Oh, Dear Lord, please keep them safe."

Whispered Dreams

On the cusp of being paranoid, Jason took out the small device that Adrian gave him. He used it to sweep the room when he first came to the Royal Palace, as his mother surmised there was a hidden camera somewhere hidden here. When he located it, he disabled it, then pulled all the listening devises from their hiding places, and flushed them all down the toilet.

Jason methodically went about it again and wasn't surprised to find more to replace the ones he destroyed. Was there nowhere to have privacy here?

The next morning, Jason decided to ask Khalifa to sit with him over breakfast. "I need to know if you will help me and that you can be trusted. You swore allegiance to me, remember?" Khalifa was stuffing a forkful of omelet into his mouth as Jason passed a handwritten note to him. "You must promise that only you and I will know about this."

Khalifa stopped eating. If he didn't promise, Jason would go no farther. Observing him for a few moments, he sipped his coffee and waited.

> Say nothing to either your father or my uncle.
> I must have your word that you will keep what I am about to tell you, a secret.

"I will promise nothing," Khalifa said rudely, as he crumpled the note, throwing it on the table. "You do not understand our ways or what you ask. I cannot do this. Royal peoples do not have secrets from one another. I know everything about you. And I don't like you."

Jason calmly said, "Then you leave me no choice. If we have no secrets, that means you and I don't have any either. I will tell your father what I know about you. I know that you are the one who is sneaking around and I know that you whisper bad things about him behind his back."

Khalifa dropped his fork onto his plate. "Do not threaten me, little man! You do not have the right information. I do not whisper behind my father's back. I am loyal to the Royal Household."

Jason was seething. "Don't ever use those words again. I know that you would betray your father in a heartbeat. I understand the language, you moron!"

"You know nothing. I stand tall as my father. I will take his place one day very soon," Khalifa said proudly. "You will hopefully not be here then."

Jason knew two could play this game. "What new lie is this? I heard you say yesterday that your father might meet with an accident. It appears that you covet his job so much that you will do anything to get it. How long have you been planning this, Khalifa?"

"There is no wrong here. It is common knowledge that when a person gets too old to perform his duties, that job is taken away. My father is too old to dance with his sword. Many of the men see this, and we talk about it. If he does not step down on his own, then he will be forced into it. When that happens, I will be waiting to take his place, which will leave you out!"

Jason growled at him. "You have gone too far. You and your oath are useless to me. I'm going to speak with my uncle about you."

Khalifa stood abruptly, putting his hands on the table, he spewed, "Does this have something to do with the woman? I will promise you nothing. Your safety was my concern, and it was my job to guard you! She made a mockery of our security, especially a fool out of me! I will not take that!"

Jason started to laugh. "No one helped you look like a fool, Ace; you did that all by yourself."

"She made a mockery of us! She came sneaking in and meeting with you like that!" Khalifa sniffed.

"You cannot be trusted, you jerk. You lie through your teeth to your father and my uncle. I'll bet they don't know that you and your pals go out into the towns, do they? You know where the secret bars and nightclubs are. You eat and drink alcohol with some of the men until dawn when we're away at horse shows. Do you deny that?"

Khalifa straightened. "You cannot prove any of that. No one will agree with you. The men are loyal to me, not you. They will back me up, not you." Then he sat back down and proceeded to eat.

Jason tried to control his anger, and then realized he was yelling. "Who did you swear allegiance to protect, Khalifa? I don't think it was to my uncle or me. I think you're the real enemy. You're not my friend and companion, and you are certainly not my defender or protector!"

Khalifa spit his food out and stood abruptly. "You have no proof, little man. No one will believe the son of a traitor. I have sworn an oath to protect you and the Royal Household. No one asked me to like this job. My father told me I must do this. The great Captain Jamaile insisted that after a while I would learn to like you, but I do not."

"You called my father a traitor! That's a lie! I don't want your protection. Get out of here. I don't need your help any longer. I'll find someone else who can do the job. You are useless," Jason snarled.

Khalifa smiled smugly. "You cannot do anything without my help. No one will help you. They have all sworn their allegiance to me and me alone."

"I seriously doubt that, pal. Many swear allegiance to your father, but not to you. You're betting with the wrong man, Ace. As far as I'm concerned, you are as useless as your plate. I don't want you anywhere near me from now on. Your services are no longer required. You are no longer my guard and companion, and you're definitely fired from being my defender! Get out of here and don't come anywhere near me!"

"This cannot be done. Once you state you accept, the King will not accept this dismissal. Only unto death will the tie be broken." With those words, Khalifa walked swiftly to the door, opened it, slamming it shut behind him.

Jason lamented the fact that he didn't see this coming. He thought, for sure, Khalifa would grovel at his boots when he threatened to expose him to his father, but he didn't. Should he call his Mother or should he call Adrian? Counting the time difference, he decided that it wasn't the right time to call.

How would he get a message to them now with all the spies lurking in every corner? Should he use his computer to send a message? Perhaps he should try to text Mr. Levi. It isn't a matter of life and death, so pressing down on the watch face is out of the question. Or is it?

When Khalifa said the bond between them would not break until one of them is dead, is it possible that he plans something against him? An hour later, Uncle Akdemir summoned Jason to the library where he found Captain Jamaile, and Khalifa, sitting near the far end of the room where King Akdemir was pacing back and forth.

No one spoke for the longest time. Jamaile was somber, and Khalifa would not look directly at him. His body language indicated that his father had already scolded him. Is the big man more disappointed with Jason or his son?

Uncle Akdemir stopped pacing to sit down on his wing chair to face them. "It is a most unusual situation, Jason. I suppose it is due to you and Khalifa not being children together. You did not grow up to understand the roles you play in the Royal Household."

"I can explain, Uncle," Jason said. He wasn't entirely sure what had transpired between Jamaile and Khalifa, nor did he know what was discussed during the time they had to talk. Did Khalifa mention Amala?

"Yes, you will explain. Jason, this is a grave matter. It has never happened before, but then heirs to the throne have grown up knowing that one day they will be responsible for many things. They grow into their roles. I am afraid you two have not had that advantage." Akdemir stopped again, then turned to face Jason. "Is it true that the woman carries your child?"

Jason said calmly, "I suppose you know all about that, so why would you take the time to ask me?"

"Do not play games with me, Jason. Information has come my way that this woman has been to your room on several occasions. It ostensibly has gone on for a long time. I ask you again, is this correct?"

Jason considered his words carefully. "She never told me who she was. She came to me one night. I'm a male…and she…" Jason stopped talking when Uncle Akdemir put his hand up to gesture that he did not want to hear any more.

"Do you expect me to believe that you did not know who she was, Jason?" Akdemir asked.

Jason sighed heavily. "I hope that you will believe me when I say that I didn't know who she was. I do now, but I swear to you that I didn't know then."

Akdemir was unusually annoyed and swallowed several times before speaking again. "Do you know what the consequences are for that woman being in the Royal Palace without my permission? We will have to inform the Islamic Religious Police about this. There will be dire consequences for your actions, Jason!"

"I see that Khalifa has told you his lies. You haven't heard the whole truth. Have you already held the trial and you've concluded that I'm guilty?" Jason's patience was thinning. "May I speak?"

Akdemir closed his eyes and slowly shook his head. "Your attitude does not help your case, Jason. Yes, you may speak."

"She never told me her name. Honestly, I'm an innocent victim here. Maybe Khalifa knows something about that, why don't we ask him? I'm not the one with the attitude. Khalifa has been spreading lies about you and my family," Jason uttered in his defense.

"He will have his say soon enough. The Ministers will be very cross with you both. It is unfathomable for people who, Jason, she will surely lose her life and the life of the child she carries. You will be lucky to retain yours. The woman is the daughter of my enemy, Jason. That makes her **your** enemy."

"She is a traitor!" Captain Jamaile spit. "She infiltrated and sabotaged our security! She got you in trouble under the guise of love. The woman is a bad person. She needs punishment."

Akdemir nodded in Jamaile's direction, and he stopped talking. "At first we could not understand how the woman could have done this. It occurred to us that she had inside help. Captain Jamaile went in search of answers. He came away with some startling evidence."

Jason didn't understand and asked, "What evidence would that be? The woman you describe is not a bad person. On the contrary, she's sweet and loving. I was teaching her English, and we were getting to know each other. Aside from coming to me, we were happy together. I don't know how she got into the palace, and I certainly didn't know who she was. She wouldn't tell me her name. She was so…I'm innocent! I don't care whose daughter she is, I've done nothing wrong except to love her. She is the one I wish to marry, Uncle."

"We have evidence that there was an ulterior motive on her part, Jason," Akdemir stated. "She lied to you."

Khalifa's lips are a tight line. "I saw her coming out of your room. She ran from me as soon as she saw me. When I caught up with her, she said you knew who she was."

Jason closed his eyes, then roared, "That is a lie, and you know it!"

"Her father did not make her do those things," Khalifa spewed. "She did them out of hatred for you, little man."

"My son does not lie." Jamaile shouted.

Jason added bitterly, "In this case, you two are wrong! Khalifa has deceived you, Captain. He is the one we should be worried about."

"That is enough!" Akdemir steepled his fingers, and closed his eyes to think. "It appears that you may be the victim in this and are blameless, however, the girl is not innocent. It will be up to our laws to pass judgment on her. Until this is settled, you will accompany the stallions to the next show; however, you will not leave your hotel room except for meals and the show itself. You cannot talk with anyone unless it is for the stallions or the show. Khalifa and his men will guard you. You will listen to his advice. Do you understand this, Jason?"

Jamaile stared at Jason without expression while Khalifa turned to smile slyly at him.

"Not really, Uncle, I don't like Khalifa, and yet you say he has to guard me. What if he's working with Fariq and he's the enemy? What if he's the one who is responsible for framing me?"

Jamaile's wrath escalated as he rose from his chair, but Akdemir kept him seated with a motion of his hand. "Jason, I have cautioned you to be careful. Those are strong words," Akdemir uttered. "Jamaile and Khalifa have been a part of the Royal Household for many years. I find these accusations extremely troubling."

"Uncle, what if he sold out to Fariq? Why should I trust him? I only met him a few months ago. He's the one that's been sneaking around all this time. He has both of you fooled. He's the one who deserves punishment, not me."

Akdemir seemed stunned, almost raising his voice, he said, "Why would you say such things, Jason? To my knowledge, no one has ever accused one of the Royal Guards of impropriety. What proof do you have for this?"

"That is not possible," Jamaile boomed. "Khalifa is like me; we guard our royal men with our lives. You and he must work out this business of friendship."

Jason glanced at Khalifa, but he turned his head away, avoiding eye contact. "I will get you proof. All I need is a camera."

"Perhaps we should have introduced Khalifa sooner, but the damage is now irreversible. We must move forward not backward. I will think about this situation. In the meantime, you will both need to get ready for your trip. I want no more incidents from either of you. Do you both understand? You two may go." Akdemir flicked his fingers.

Jason and Khalifa stood, and without saying anything, they left the library. After the doors closed, Jamaile bent close to Akdemir's ear and whispered, "They will never be good friends, Highness."

"I am afraid you are right, old friend. I had hoped for better results. In time, perhaps they will see the wisdom in what we are trying to teach them. There is something different about Jason, not related to Basim. Perhaps it is something that comes from his mother's side of the family."

Jamaile reflected sadly, "It could be what might doom our young heir."

"We shall see, Jamaile. In time, we shall see where this takes him," Akdemir muttered under his breath. "See to it that he comes to no harm, my trusted friend. He is my only hope."

The Arabian Stallions are in a pressurized compartment toward the rear of the aircraft, as were most of the men who were traveling with them for shows. Jason, Khalifa, and a few others were in the few seats near the front.

Jason speculated as to how he would escape. Ever since he and Khalifa went at each other in his uncle's presence, they had avoided all contact. With no apparent opportunity to discuss anything further with his uncle, the conversations remained limited to horse shows only. Since there was no one to rely upon for information about Amala, his uneasiness grew daily about her safety, as did his own.

Minutes before the plane touched down, Jason turned in Khalifa's direction. Khalifa had his head against the headrest with his eyes closed.

"Why don't you like me, Khalifa?" Jason spoke English, as the others wouldn't be able to listen in on their conversation. "What have I done to you that you have it in for me?"

"It is you who does not like me," Khalifa said.

"Is it because you don't think I'm fit to take my uncle's place on the throne?"

"You fired me from my job," Khalifa replied dryly. "Royal guards are never dismissed like that!" The others in the plane were staring at him, most probably wondering what Khalifa was going to do.

"You don't look fired to me, pal, and I don't like you, because you're a liar. You think I don't know what's going on, but I do."

"What lie do you accuse me of saying? You and your father are guilty of the same crime," Khalifa snarled, keeping his eyes closed. "Everyone knows this."

Unbuckling his seatbelt, Jason stood directly in front of Khalifa. "Are these more lies? Does Captain Jamaile know what you do when you're away? You kiss your father's boots when he's present, then when he turns around, you talk about him as if he's worthless. What kind of son does that?"

"You and your father disgraced the Royal Household. You want me to take great care of you!" Khalifa grimaced, then opened his eyes to stare at Jason. "The rightful heir will be on the throne shortly. We do not need you. None of us need you."

Jason took in a deep breath. "So that's what this is all about. You don't think I'm worthy to sit on the throne and take my uncle's place! I don't think your father thinks the same thing?"

"You were not raised to appreciate our lifestyle. You mock it at every turn," Khalifa sneered.

"How do I do that, Khalifa? How do I mock your lifestyle, by living mine the way I want to?"

Khalifa began to laugh. "You westerners think you know everything. You think that living with us gives you knowledge? We do not agree with who is in power. We are going to do something about that."

Jason thought about what his Mother would say as the words echoed in his head. "You have no idea who you're dealing with, pal. Captain Jamaile is loyal to my uncle, and he would lay down his life for him and me. You swore that same oath too, didn't you? But I doubt that you'll do that for me. I don't like you, Khalifa. You can't be trusted."

"You come from western ideals that trample on our beliefs. You do not belong in Saudi or at the Royal Palace. You do belong somewhere far from us. You should go back. No one wants you here." Khalifa was proud of himself, and closed his eyes again. "You are the traitor!"

Khalifa remained tight-lipped, and the realization hit Jason that his suspicions that he was a spy and traitor might have manifested itself. Was he aware that he gave it away? By now, the other men on the plane were aware of the banter but didn't know what to do about it.

Jason was not through, putting his hands on the armrests of Khalifa's seat, he got very close to his face. "So you know, if I ever go missing, I've sent a message to someone I trust that will point the finger directly at you. You will not get away with anything, because *you* are being watched."

"You threaten me? Do you think me a fool?" Khalifa said opening his eyes.

Jason sat down as the plane touched the ground. "No, as a matter of fact, I think you're stupid, Khalifa. Anytime you want to settle this, pal, I'll be waiting for you. Until then, stay out of my way."

Jason was unsure if his little talk would be productive but at least he had the last word. How did his father disgrace the Royal Household? The facts were still murky, especially about how his father came to be in his Grandfather Cali's care.

The only thing he knew for sure was that his father needed sanctuary. Could there be more to this story than anyone suspected? Jason was under the impression it had more to do with him not liking the stringent rules of the Royal Palace. Could it also be the inability to go beyond its walls? Now he wished he had asked different questions before he consented to be his uncle's heir.

Jason knew that no one had his back on this trip, so he slept lightly. Khalifa had turned his men against him with his lies. The conversation overheard yesterday about wanting to remove his father, Jamaile, and putting someone else on the throne left little doubt.

Who amongst them will help Jason now? If he went to Captain Jamaile to tell him what he had uncovered, he may or may not believe him. If he went to his uncle, he may not believe that the son of his most reliable guard, defender, and protector is a traitorous liar. Who in the Royal Palace can he trust?

Jason knew that he must talk to her as soon as he returned.

After the horse show concluded and everything was packed and stowed away in the plane, Jason stuck close to the pilots, as he knew that his life might be in jeopardy. He nearly panicked when his cellphone and laptop went missing, but he didn't dare let on that it bothered him. When they reached the Royal Palace, Jason had a plan in place. The person he sought would help him, and he knew where to find her.

Captain Jamaile was waiting near his room with his big arms crossed over his chest, his feet in a relaxed stance. "The show went well, Jason?" he asked gruffly. "Where have you been, the others have taken to their rooms a while ago?"

"Yes, the show went well, but don't you already know that? Khalifa no doubt sent information back to you already. I took a little detour. What are you doing here?"

Jamaile opened Jason's door, and walked in with him. "I am here to protect you!"

"I don't need your help. As I told Khalifa the other day, I don't need him, either. I can take care of myself."

Jamaile shook his big head, moving swiftly to the door. "If you will not accept Khalifa as your guard, His Royal Highness will do something else." Opening the door, he then closed it quickly behind him. Before Jason could react, there was a loud CLICK.

Jason rushed to the door, and banged on it as hard as he could, but he already knew what the outcome would be. Shaking from rage and resentment, he wondered if this was how his mother felt. How could this be happening to him? How could his uncle possibly think that this was going to keep him safe? How could he contact his family without his laptop or cellphone?

A few hours later, there was a slight knock on his door followed by a loud CLICK. When the door opened, Jamaile stood in the doorway where he asked Jason to come with him to meet with his uncle.

Jason wanted to tell him to go to hell, and then thought better of it. It occurred to him that the big man might not permit access to his uncle should he say anything derogatory. He wanted to confront his uncle face to face to ask why he had done this heinous thing.

Uncle Akdemir waved in their direction when they passed through the doorway into the large dining room. "Come in, Jason, come in. I hope the show went well. Jamaile said it was a success. Why are you so glum? You must be tired after your journey. Do you not feel well?"

"You don't usually ask so many questions, Uncle."

Akdemir oozed politeness, and said, "I am glad to see you, Jason."

Jason's irritation was getting the better of him. "I am well, but what the hell do you think you're doing by locking me in my room?"

Akdemir seemed sad. "Profanity is not allowed, Jason. If you do not want Khalifa to guard you, then we take different steps to keep you safe. Now that Fariq knows about you and the girl, he will seek revenge upon you and possibly other members of the Royal Household."

Jason was aware of using his mother's words and chose them wisely. "I feel like a prisoner. Why is this any different than when my Mother was here?"

Uncle Akdemir's face registered shock. Reaching for a glass filled with a light-yellow liquid, he took a long drink. Are memories of Ellen coming back to haunt him? Were they recollections of that first night she came to dinner? Were they the endless questions she spewed at him? "That was certainly not our intention. We will not lock the door again. Captain, please see to it that no one locks Jason's door."

Jamaile answered politely, "Yes, Your Royal Highness."

"Post two guards outside of it instead."

Jamaile responded without the slightest flinch of his facial muscles, "Yes, Your Highness."

Jason was acutely aware of the servers that filed into the dining room and the potential for one of them to be a spy. Looking at each of them, he tried to guess if he could detect the traitor amongst them. Which one was wearing a disguise tonight? Who wanted to harm the Royal Family? Could someone sneak poison into the food? Did the King have a Beefeater to test it first, as the Kings of England had?

"Jason, you have not touched your food. Is this not to your liking?" Akdemir inquired.

"I'm not hungry, Uncle. I ate at the airport before we got on the plane."

"Then tell me about the show while we eat," Akdemir said.

"We wore the Blue and Silver proudly, Uncle."

Akdemir stopped eating. "There were no mistakes as there was last time?"

Jason was a bit miffed. "We are well-trained, Uncle. Who told you there were mistakes last time?"

"I must be mistaken, Jason, please continue," Akdemir said politely.

Jason watched Jamaile for anomalies in his facial expression. "There was only one mistake that I know of, and it was Khalifa's fault."

Jamaile's dander was up. "Be careful of what you say, little man."

"Oh, I get it. You think you know what went on, but you don't. Maybe I should fill in the blanks for you!" Jason shouted.

"Keep your voice down, Jason," Akdemir said. "We need to remain calm."

"The men were so proud of themselves. While they went out to eat and partied after the show, they left me back at the hotel room. I did not have much fun, Uncle, but Khalifa and his men had a great time."

Jamaile was surprised. "Khalifa and I spoke this afternoon. He said you were going to say this. He would not do this. He gave his report one hour ago. Khalifa did not mention they left the hotel. He said they ate in the restaurant at the hotel."

"That's not entirely true, Captain," Jason replied, trying to control his temper. "He only told you that to satisfy you."

"You knew before you left that you would be confined to your room," Akdemir said, picking up the thread of Jamaile's sentence. "Except for meals and attending to the horse shows."

Jason took in a breath and let it out slowly. "Did Khalifa's report also include that they *locked* me in my room? They bolted the door from the outside. The windows had bars on them, and I couldn't open them because of the nails. They left me to eat and never once asked if I wanted anything. They didn't bother to bring anything back for me, either. There was no phone so that I couldn't order anything. That is the truth, not what Khalifa told you."

"We know of no such thing, Jason." Akdemir was astounded.

Jamaile snarls in disbelief, "Khalifa said none of that; he said you refused everything he offered."

Jason stared at his uncle and then at Captain Jamaile. "That is because your son is a liar."

Akdemir sipped his water. "He came to see me not thirty minutes ago, Jason. He reported that you wished to remain in the hotel room by yourself while they went down to the hotel restaurant."

Jason struggled to remain calm. He knew that this was his chance to set the record straight, but he needed to keep his cool. "He has lied to you, Uncle. You only know what he wants you to know. Khalifa is the traitor, not me. He lied to both of you. No one asked me if I wanted to go to dinner, they left without me, and I could not open my door. There were bars on the windows so I couldn't get out. They have stolen my laptop, and cellphone and I want them back immediately!"

"These are serious accusations, Jason." Akdemir switched to Arabic, instructing Jamaile to find out if this could be true. Khalifa said Jason was the liar. Could Khalifa truly be capable of such treachery and deceit?

Jason started to laugh. "Did you forget that I understand every word you're saying, Uncle? I'm not the liar, Khalifa is. He's played you both for fools. He's the traitor along with several of your men, Captain. I can point them all out to you."

Jamaile thundered, "You know nothing, little man. My son is no liar. He swore his allegiance to the Royal Family and took the same oath as I took. We would both lay down our lives to save yours if we need to!"

"That's a nice little speech, Captain, but your son is collaborating with the enemy, not me. He said that death would be the only thing that unbinds us, and I'm sure he's planning something right now, so he can do that." Jason knew he might have overstepped his bounds when the big man rose from his chair to confront him with his dagger drawn.

"Jamaile!" Akdemir said, raising his voice at the big man. "Let us stop this insanity and return to our dinner. We will discuss this like gentlemen."

Jason felt that it was time to reveal his true feelings. "I've made a great mistake by coming here, Uncle. I wish to return home. It has been made very clear to me by some people that I don't belong here, either in the Royal Palace or on the throne."

Akdemir seemed crushed and stopped eating. Swallowing his food, he took gulps of liquid, trying to compose himself. "And who told you this, Khalifa?"

"Yes, Uncle, it was Khalifa. He said someone was going to replace you soon. There are many who have gone to the enemy's side. They want to depose you and put Fariq on the throne. That's their real intention. I'm not a traitor."

"This is most disturbing. You cannot go back, Jason. You have left your life behind to embrace the new one here with the Royal Household and me."

"I don't wish to stay here any longer. I'll inform my Mother that I'm coming home." Jason pushed himself away from the table.

Akdemir was quite disturbed. "You do not have that choice any longer. We will work our difficulties out, Jason. You will see that in time, everything will be fine."

"I don't think the difficulties can be worked out, Uncle."

Akdemir sighed, "Trust me, Jason. Things will settle down, and you will like it here again."

"When you get to the end of your rope,

tie a knot and hang on."

~ Franklin D. Roosevelt

Chapter Eleven

The Heir is missing

Adrian reads the paper while I click away at the keys on my laptop. It's Wednesday, and I'm in a slight panic, as Jason has not called in over a week. "Ellie, you know how the circuits are."

"He told me that if we don't talk on Monday, to call him on Wednesday if I didn't hear from him by then. I tried calling his cellphone, and it went straight to his voicemail, and then it became impossible to leave another message as it stopped ringing altogether—like it was turned off. And he hasn't responded to any of my texts."

"Maybe he's tied up right now and can't call you," Adrian offers.

"For over a week?" Something must be preventing my son from calling me. "I tried to contact him this morning, and nothing happened! Even Jam-ale isn't responding."

Panic begins to take over, as a portentous feeling that something is wrong keeps popping into and out of my mind like a leftover lousy dream.

"Sometimes the circuits are busy, Ellie. Which is nothing new. And sometimes you get right through. He'll call you when he can; you know that." Adrian glances at his wristwatch. "This is not the first time he hasn't made connections with you, and it probably won't be the last. Maybe there's some malfunction with his equipment."

"No, Adrian, I called Dimmy to ask about Jason, but the person who answered the phone said I had the wrong number. That has never happened before, and then they hung up on me. The next time I got through, I asked for Jam-ale, and was told he was indisposed."

"Do you want me to try?" he asks.

"Let's do it together."

When we call the usual number for the Royal Palace, the person who answers the phone says that His Royal Highness is under the weather and he is unable to take calls right now.

"Then would you please tell Jason that we've been trying to reach him?" Adrian says.

The voice on the other end says that Jason is practicing with the horses and he'll pass the message on to him.

"There, you see? His Royal Painness isn't feeling well and Jason's playing with the horses. Now, don't you feel better?"

"No, I don't feel better! Something is wrong, Adrian. Jason would not go this long past our usual time. He always texts back within a few hours. I'm telling you that there's something very wrong over there, I can feel it!"

"Ellie, please, you're overreacting."

"I am not overreacting, Adrian! Would you please call Levi? Maybe he can send someone over there right away. I have to know Jason is okay."

Adrian moves toward the doorway, "I'll call the Sheriff of Nottingham right now, sweetheart, if it'll make you feel better. We can't go in with guns ablazzing, Ellie, remain calm, okay?"

My agitation is rising to near panic by the time he comes back. While he was gone, I tried to connect with Jason and repeatedly got an empty monitor screen. "Each time I tried to call Jason's cellphone, the same message said that the number was not in service. How can that be possible?"

Adrian's face is grave, and my gut says its bad news. "Ellie," his voice makes me stare at him. "I don't know how to say this…"

"Say it, Adrian!"

Adrian pushed me gently onto the sofa. "I spoke to Levi. He said he received a signal from Jason about two weeks ago."

"What kind of signal? Was it from his watch thingy?"

Adrian says, "I don't know how to say this, but…Jason is missing from the Royal Palace."

"What does that mean, Adrian?"

"We don't know that Jason is *not* alright. Maybe he went for a walk."

Tears start to overflow and run down my face. "Where do they think he is? I told you something was wrong!"

"They don't know. Levi is the one who spoke to Jason. He had reason to believe that someone didn't like him being in the Royal Palace and he felt threatened somehow. He said he wanted to come home, honey."

"He did? Jason wanted to come home? Maybe he's heading home right now. Wait a minute, what do you mean he contacted Levi two weeks ago? If it was something like that, why didn't he get him out of there? I talked to Jason eight days ago, so he hasn't been gone that long. Why didn't he tell us he wanted to come home? Why the hell didn't Dimmy tell us right away?"

Adrian reaches to hug me, saying, "That's because Dimmy has only now found out. The latest news coming out of his camp is that King Akdemir has gone into seclusion until the incident blows over."

"What are you saying? Until what blows over?" I know there's more than Adrian might be able to tell me.

"There's been a kind of coup d'état…and…I don't know how to tell you the rest of it," he says soberly.

"Spill it, Mr. CIA man! Give it to me straight." It becomes increasingly more difficult to be brave and not scream and yell.

Adrian stands, saying, "Let's call the family together so we can discuss this as a group."

"I'm wearing my iron big girl pants, damn it. Tell me right now Adrian!"

Turning his head away, he calmly says, "Can we call the family together, so I don't have to repeat it?"

"What is there to discuss? Jason might be on his way home, or he's missing, and I'm going over there right now, find him, and bring him back home!"

Adrian reaches for the walkie-talkie to alert everyone to the family meeting in the living room in thirty minutes. "You can't do that, Ellie," he mumbles. "Let's wait for everyone."

"No! I don't want to do this, Adrian. You're giving up on him too quickly. If he's on his way home, he needs time to get here."

"The family needs to be informed, Ellie. Please, let's wait."

When everyone assembles, Adrian takes a deep breath, letting it out slowly. "I can't sugarcoat this. They found Turlock, his wife Sheyanna, and their three daughters. They were all found murdered last night. Levi can't tell us much more than that, but he's sending a team over to investigate as we speak. He doesn't know why they were targeted."

"Good God, Adrian. They were such loyal and loving people. Who would do such a thing?" Mother gasps.

"He isn't sure. He isn't even sure they'll allow his group admittance to the Royal Palace, because they don't have any authority to delve into the matter. Unless the Royal Palace or King Akdemir asks for this personally, it's considered foreign policy. We don't usually meddle in those types of things."

"What else did Levi say?" Dennis asks.

"He thinks that Fariq is responsible for this incident. He would stop at nothing to gain access to the throne. He thinks it should be his anyway. Has anyone heard from Jason? Ellen hasn't been able to contact him."

No one in the room has heard from Jason in over two weeks.

Adrian continues, saying, "Jason is missing from the Royal Palace. His laptop and cellphone were in his room, along with his wallet. He didn't take them with him…I'm so sorry, Ellie."

Closing my eyes to stop the tears that are leaking out, I can hear family members ask him questions.

"And what are they doing about this?" Reed asks.

Terre wonders, "Did Levi's team say where they think Jason is now?"

"I'll go over there myself if you need me to, sir!" Mack is upset that there's no action yet.

Danny adds, "I'll go with you. Do you want us to go over there, Uncle Adrian?"

"None of us can do anything right now. We can't show up over there. Levi says we have to wait," he says quietly.

"Ya can't leave the poor boy over there without helpin him!" Glen sputters. "What are ya waitin for?" Mona puts a gentle hand on his arm, telling him to hush.

"We have to wait, Glen. Levi will tell us what we need to do next," Adrian says, hanging his head. "I'm sorry Ellie, that's all we know for now."

Opening my eyes, I try to stand, but sit back down. "I don't feel so good."

Adrian lays me on the sofa as the others remain seated. He continues to tell them that he has seen me do this one other time. It was when we found out that my late husband Ravi and Akdemir were brothers.

"Oh Ellie," Mother says inhaling oddly as her body starts to shudder. I know she's weeping. "Our Jason...our sweet Jason."

"I'll call Melanie and tell her the bad news," Terre says sadly.

Adrian's phone chirps and he leaves the room. He steps back in as Terre puts a cold cloth on my forehead. Adrian then explains what Levi has found out, which has turned out to be mostly nothing except that the Royal Palace was searched and there is no sign of Jason; however, they think he might have made it out of the area, but there is no proof of this.

Opening my eyes to see Mother wipe tears from her face, her jaw is tightly clenched. She reaches for my hand to squeeze it. "Oh Ellie..." she says.

"He's not dead, Mother!"

"But Ellie...they can't find him," she sniffs. "Our Jason..."

"He's not dead, Mother. I would know. And he isn't. HE ISN'T!"

Curlie was sitting on the floor next to the sofa and reaches for my other hand. She starts to rock her body and begins to moan, "Jason can't be dead! He can't be! I don't believe it! He's not, is he Mommy?" Curlie wails, "Mama, MAMA!"

When I open my eyes, the room is dark, but the dizziness is still present. Reaching up to remove the damp cloth from my forehead, I try to sit up slowly. The clock on the mantle reads four o'clock. No one else is in the room with me.

Where did I go for two hours?

I must tell Adrian about the strange dream I had about Jason. His face was as clear as if he was standing right in front of me. He said he was okay, but I couldn't determine where he was.

A sound of doors opening and closing brings me fully conscious as Adrian comes into the room with a woman I don't recognize. When I begin to tell Adrian about my dream, he pats my hand and smiles at me. Then he turns to the woman, and they whisper to one another.

Adrian's face is showing concern. "This is Dr. Laurel Stevens, Ellie. I asked her to come and talk with you."

"Hello, Dr. Stevens. I don't wish to be rude, but what are we going to talk about?"

Dr. Stevens is a pretty woman. She's exquisitely dressed, and there isn't a hair out of place on her light brown head. "May I sit down?" Her voice is soft and pleasant. "You've had quite a shock, Mrs. Thompson-Sellers. I'm a mother too, and as a mother, I know how difficult this might be for you. Would you come to my office in a few days? Adrian said he would bring you."

"I don't understand why you're here."

Adrian glances at Dr. Stevens, and the understanding hits me that she must be a psychiatrist or psychologist.

"You think I need a shrink? Because Jason is missing, is that it?"

"I may be able to help you cope with your situation, Ellen," Dr. Stevens says. "It can be a shock to learn that your son is missing. I understand what you might be going through right now. Quite frankly, the sooner you confront your fears, the easier it will be to move on with your life."

"That's where you're wrong, Dr. Stevens. I know Jason is okay because he spoke to me in a dream. Everyone has the information wrong. You don't know he isn't alive. Where's the proof that he's dead?"

Adrian hands me a glass of water and a little white pill as he and Dr. Stevens talk as if I'm no longer in the room with them. "Give her one every twelve hours or so. She'll be all right in a few days, once the shock wears off. I believe my schedule will allow for a two-hour session next week. Would Thursday at one o'clock work for you?"

"I don't need a shrink, if that's what you are, Dr. Stevens."

You are okay, Jason, I say to myself. Find your way back home. He smiled at me and told me so.

"You don't need to be rude, darling. I called Dr. Stevens because the entire family was worried about you," Adrian says.

"He's out there, somewhere, Adrian, and he needs us. It's only a matter of time before we find him! You can't give up on him so quickly."

"Sure, he is, sweetheart. Why don't you rest now, okay? I'll walk Dr. Stevens to her car. I'll be right back."

No one else seemed to share my view. Dinner was less than pleasant when Curlie shouted at me that I should never have let her brother go so far away. Then Melanie called to say the same thing; only she was extremely livid. She wanted to know what we're doing to find Jason. Mel bellowed into my ear that Adrian should go to Saudi to look for him. We can't sit around and wait for the phone to ring! She wanted answers!

"Melanie is right; we can't sit here waiting for the phone to ring," Terre mumbles.

"What *are* you going to do about Jason, Adrian?" Dennis asks.

Mona starts to sniff as she moves around the table. "Oh the poor darlin boy," she says. "I can't b'lieve he's missin. They'll find him, Miss Ellen, they will. We'll all pray that he's found fast and unharmed."

Everyone at the table chimes in with their opinion. What can we do? They all want to know, and then we all turn toward Adrian to glare at him, hoping against all hope that he has a plan of action.

"Look, everyone, Levi and his team are working on the solution. You have to be patient." Adrian seems a bit irritated. "Honestly, they're doing the best they can with what they have to work with."

I throw my napkin onto the table, as the words come tumbling out of my mouth, "Time is not on our side, Adrian! The longer he remains missing, the harder it will be to find him."

"You don't know that, Ellie. I know how difficult this is for all of you! We all love and miss Jason, but we need to let the authorities do their job. If he is to be found, they will find him."

"What do you mean by *if* he's found, Adrian?" Terre asks.

Glen, his old skeptical self, gently reminds us that, "It ain't in our hands, anyway, now is it Missy?"

And Glen is right. It isn't according to our game plan to let our Jason go like this. It's up to a higher power now. We all bow our heads and clasp our hands together, asking our Good Lord to intervene on Jason's behalf, to keep him safe and out of harms' way, to bring him home quickly.

Please, Dear God, find Jason and make it soon. I don't know how much anxiety I can take.

The next morning, I wake to see my bible open on the dresser. I know Mother has found a passage or two to help me cope with life today. She often found the right ones in the past. I've kept them marked by small strips of colored paper, which are sticking out so they can be referred to when needed.

> **GOD SAVES US FROM OUR BROKENNESS:**
> *The Lord is close to the brokenhearted; he rescues those who are crushed in spirit.* **(Psalm 34:18)**
>
> **GOD BRINGS GOOD OUT OF SORROW:**
> *But true wisdom and power are found in God; counsel and understanding are His. He uncovers mysteries hidden in darkness; He brings light to the deepest gloom.*
> **(Job 12:13, 22)**

Adrian's booming voice echoes up the stairwell as he paces in the hallway downstairs. "I want some answers, and I want them now, Jam-ale!" he says to the person charged with keeping Jason safe. When he sees me, he puts the call on speakerphone, placing his finger across his lips. "What have you found out so far?"

After a slight lag, Jam-ale begins to talk. "You have been told all that we know, Mr. Adrian. We know nothing more. Jason was not in his room when I went to get him for dinner."

"Why would you have to go get him? He knew what time you eat!" Adrian retorts.

"He did not come at the proper time. His Royal Highness asked me to go get him. He was not in his room. He was not anywhere we knew he would be. We have searched the entire Royal Palace. We searched the arena, the stables, everywhere."

Adrian and I exchange glances. "Where do you suppose he might be then?"

"We do not know, Mr. Adrian. He is gone."

"Are his clothes and possessions still in his room?"

"His clothes are all here. He is not here, Mr. Adrian."

Adrian has become impatient. "You said you have his laptop and cellphone. Did you check to see who he called last?"

"These items, his computer, and cellphone were on his desk. The hard drive is missing, and the cellphone has no memory chip."

Adrian starts to blink wildly. "And that doesn't seem odd to you?"

"We have a specialist looking at these. It does seem odd to us. What do you wish done with the items? Do you want them sent to you?"

Adrian sighs heavily, then says, "Have you searched everywhere? Have you talked to everyone?"

"My men and I searched every inch of the Royal Palace, Mr. Adrian. There is no trace of him," Jam-ale answers.

"Why do I get the feeling that there's more to this little story than you're telling me?"

"I tell you everything I know, Mr. Adrian. I know nothing more."

Adrian is now quite infuriated. "I would like to speak with the King if you don't mind."

"That is not possible at this time. His Royal Highness meets with officials and cannot be disturbed."

I can't control my temper any further. "Jam-ale! You will have to disturb him because if you don't get him to this phone right now, I'm getting on the next plane and coming over there!"

"Let me ask if he will speak with you Ma'dame Sell ers."

We wait patiently to hear Dimmy's voice, however, when Jam-ale returns, he says, "The King cannot be disturbed. He asks that you call back tomorrow and he will try to speak with you then. He is most apologetic, Ma'dame."

Screaming at the phone, "ARE YOU KIDDING? THAT'S IT?"

Adrian's hand lands on my arm. "Stop yelling at the man, Ellie. It won't help anything." He then growls at the phone, saying, "Tell the King that we will call him tomorrow, Jam-ale. But he better be able to talk with us at that time."

"What happened to the person who was guarding him 24/7?" I ask. When we hear a click, we assume that he has hung up on us or we've lost the connection. I cannot control my tears as Adrian reaches for me. "That's lovely. It's obvious he's giving us the runaround. Something is going on there, Adrian. Can't you and Levi put a contingency plan together?"

"They're working on it, sweetheart, honest they are," he says.

When Jason first went to Saudi, I resigned myself to the fact that he would be far away, but what made it tolerable was talking via face to face every week. The reality of Jason's absence was terrible enough, but when he went missing, it meant that I could no longer see my son's face. Now that the line of communication no longer exists, I struggle with everyday issues.

Out of frustration, I start throwing things at the wall in my office, which mostly consists of crumpled paper and a few pencils.

It has been nearly two weeks with no word from anyone about my missing son.

"Are you playing basketball with your trash? You missed the wastebasket again. Maybe we should get a dartboard for your wall here." Adrian bends to pick up several balls of paper from the floor next to the sofa. Then he pulls at the pencils I threw at the paneling that stick out at odd angles. "Are these lucky shots?"

"I'm tired of sitting here doing nothing, Adrian. Can't we get some people into the palace to look for Jason? Why won't Dimmy talk to me?"

Throwing the paper in the basket near my desk, he says, "Ellie, we're all upset about this, but we have to go through the proper channels. We have to sit tight."

"Proper channels my foot, Adrian. That man is ignoring me like he did when he held me captive there!"

Adrian sits down on the edge of my desk. "We won't be permitted into their country without written permission. Until Uncle Dimmy does this, we must wait it out, Ellie."

"I'm tired of waiting. I hate this, the not knowing part. I hate it! I know Jason's alive. I simply don't know where he is. You should send the ninja's in there."

Adrian raises his eyebrows. "Ninjas, Ellie, really, are you serious? The CIA doesn't have ninjas. Besides, what do you think a ninja can do that we can't?"

"Ninjas are stealthy, aren't they? If you can't get a bunch of them in, why don't you ask Josh and Jake? Aren't they good with stuff like that? They can go in without anyone seeing them."

"Ellie, my little buttercup, I know this is driving you nuts, but we can't send people in there, it's too risky. Fariq is a shadow that has threatened both Dimmy and Jason. He's probably responsible for what happened to Turlock and his family, although there's no proof yet. Do you really think Levi would risk more lives, until he works this plan to our advantage?"

I mentally try to visualize the maze of the Royal Palace, thinking that it might explain how people got in and out without being detected. "He probably came through one of those secret panels or passageways. I know they were there. It must be the only explanation for how they moved about so quickly. Remember the chef that made meals a floor below us when we were there? That's how they got those trays to us so fast."

Adrian gently corrects, "Ellie, they got the trays to us so fast, because of the elevators."

"That wasn't the only way they traveled, Adrian. I saw some of them go through a stone wall because I followed a server."

Adrian frowns. "They went through a stone wall? That doesn't sound plausible, my little snickerdoodle."

"I know it sounds incredible, but I wanted to ask her something and the next thing I knew, she had disappeared behind a stone wall! Here, I'll try to draw it for you."

"That's okay, Ellie. You don't need to do that. Levi has a sketch of the palace. He's checking on that stuff right now."

"Knowing my son, I'll bet that Jason found more than one secret walkway. I'll also bet that he got out of the palace on his own or he had help."

Adrian begins to roll his eyes. "I know you're a betting woman and would only bet on a sure thing, but we don't know anything yet."

"You don't believe me, do you?"

"Come here and sit down with me. Let's say that you might be right, but how can we prove it if we aren't there?"

Slumping over to the sofa, I sit down slowly. "Precisely, my dear Watson. I think we should get ourselves over there right now."

"Therein lies the problem. We can't do that; we must wait until we hear from Levi. It needs to be done by the book, Ellie, okay? Things are delicate over there right now."

"I don't know how much longer I can wait, Mr. CIA man."

"You'll have to, Ellie. There is no choice in the matter," he says.

"Say, do you think the big guy is telling us the truth? Do you think his men had anything to do with this? What's the name of that person who was guarding him? You know the one I mean, what's his name? It was Kali, Kahala, Kaliflower, or could it be Kick-a-Poo-Joy-Juice."

Adrian chuckles, "I think Kaliflower is closer to it. Why don't we kick this around a little more, shall we, like we used to do?"

"Yeah, for starters, what if Jam-ale got Jason out of the palace because someone threatened him? His men could have taken him out to the desert. He could be in that tent thing they put me in the night before they took me back to Kauai. That's a plausible scenario, isn't it?"

"Why would he take him into the desert? Okay, I see your train of thought. Perhaps he was airlifted out. Maybe that's how you got to the Kauai airport. Was it an oasis?"

"I don't know. It was dark, but there was a huge tent. What if someone paid to take Jason to another city, you know, what are other cities in Saudi? Could we send someone to ask around there, run Jason's photo by the local police? What's the name of their police? Put out an ABP or something."

"You can't go to another country and put out an APB for someone. It isn't done like that, especially there, because they have special people. It's the Islamic Religion Police or something."

Scratching my head, I absently look out the window. "What about Interpol?"

"Are you talking about the band Interpol or the organization Interpol?" Adrian muses.

"No, not the band, you ninny, the organization called Interpol. Can't you collaborate with them or something?"

"What do *you* know about Interpol?" Adrian questions, tapping me on the arm.

"Not much. But you see stories about Interpol in the newspapers all the time, and they're mentioned on the news occasionally. Don't they get involved with terrorists and murders, and stuff like that all over the world? Didn't you study this in CIA school?"

Adrian starts shaking his head. "Yes and no, Ellie. They're as politically neutral as they can be. If I have my facts straight, they're forbidden to get involved with any military, religious, or anything of a racial nature. They focus primarily on public safety, terrorism, humanity, environmental crime, and war crimes. Then there's organized crime, smuggling, human trafficking, money laundering and child pornography. I don't see how we can get them involved."

"There, you said the word humanity. Humanity is human trafficking. What if Jason was sold?"

"Who would Jason be sold to and for what purpose? I don't think so, Ellie. Levi and his group will come up with something, and he'll do his best to find the underlying cause of this. But we have to give him more time."

I'm sad again. "Levi doesn't believe Jason's alive, does he?"

"I can't speak for him, but you might be on to something. I'm going to run this by him. You've been to the desert, and you know Dimmy's giant sidekick better than the rest of us. It's interesting how your mind works, Ellie. You might know what he's capable of."

"Do you think Dimmy's in hiding and Jam-ale is protecting him? Maybe he won't let us talk to him so Fariq can't find and murder him. Wait a minute, do you think Dimmy's dead? Are they stringing us along, or maybe Jam-ale tried to protect Jason too, and he can't tell you anything, because the walls have ears."

"Honestly Ellie, I wish the walls had a mouth. Then they could tell us where Jason is," Adrian sighs.

"Ah, you believe he's alive too! I knew you'd see it my way. I merely can't figure out where he is at the moment."

"Hang on to that, sweetheart," Adrian says, hugging me. "Hang on to that!"

Adrian opens and closes the drawers of his dresser as he is in the process of getting dressed. Curlie has a recital tonight. I must force myself to get up and get dressed. "I'm not sure I can come tonight, Adrian, I don't feel much like being happy."

He has been incredibly patient with me throughout these last few months, but tonight he tries to coax me into getting up. "Come on, Ellie. Curlie needs you tonight. It's her big deal, and she needs her Mommy there."

"I don't feel like it. You'll have to make an excuse. I can't go."

"You'll have to tell her yourself. Come on now Ellie. You have to get up and get going or you'll make us all late."

Adrian knows I need to get out of the house and on with my life even though my heart is breaking. No word about Jason in over two months has made me sullen and moody. He waves to Mother, who waits near the doorway of our bedroom.

"Francesca, can you say something to Ellen so she'll come with us tonight?"

Mother takes my hand, wiggling it, she says, "Ellen, your family needs you. You get up this instant. Come on, I will help you pick out a nice pair of slacks, and you can get your face washed. You are going to that recital if I must drag you there. Jason would want you to go on with your life, sweetheart. It would make him very sad to see you like this."

Mother sees the vacant expression in my eyes turn into comprehension. "Okay, you might be right. Jason would be laughing at me, wouldn't he? He'd say, silly old Mom, get up and get going. Didn't I tell him those same words when he didn't want to get up for school when he was little?"

"I know how hard this is for you, Ellie. We have all been affected by Jason's disappearance." Mother refrains from using the word missing as she tries to move the conversation to the clothes we are now picking out in my closet.

"Why has there been no word?" I say absently.

"Here, this blouse goes with those slacks. Don't you have a jacket that goes with it? Here it is, try this on," she says, pushing the jacket into my hands.

"I know it's hardest on you, Mother. I'm sorry to be like this, but it makes me so exasperated that no one has come up with the solution to it all."

"Our family is like a circle, Ellie. The circle never ends, dear. You see your whole family sad, and there isn't a damn thing you can do about it, but we must go on," Mother says, standing back. "You did it before, and you can do it again."

"I want Adrian to go over there to find him. Why hasn't Levi let him do that?"

"I know you think that no one is doing anything, but Levi won't let him go without more information, honey."

"I don't know what kind of information they need. God knows time keeps ticking away. We have to do something soon."

Adrian sticks his head around the closet door. "Let's go, ladies, time's awaistin! According to my timetable, we should have been there hours ago."

Pushing a hand in Adrian's face to shoo him from the closet, so I can dress in peace, I say, "We're not late, yet. We don't have to be there until four o'clock. I heard Curlie say so this morning. See, I'm paying attention even though it looks as if I'm not."

Along with other gifted students who have displayed exceptional music skills, the school has planned a recital. Our little Curlie has turned into a real beauty. At fifteen, she is delighted that her reddish/blonde hair stayed springy. When other girls her age are struggling with their hair, Curlie allows hers to flow free, pulling it back with no fuss. She's no longer a chubby, little cherub, (Grandma Francesca's description of her), but a full-blown teenager with the disposition of one.

The house phone rings and I wonder if Curlie will answer it, as she went down the front steps an hour ago to practice. "I'm not quite ready, Adrian, can you get that? It might be Terre or Dennis wondering where we are. They left a little while ago with the twins."

The phone stops ringing.

Adrian goes out to lean over the railing in the hallway. "Curlie, are you down there? Did you get the phone?"

We are descending the staircase as Curlie comes out of the living room to tell us about the strange phone call. Adrian tries to move us along as he glances at his wristwatch.

"Man, was that ever a strange call," Curlie says.

"It happens all the time, sweetie. You know those telemarketers; they have no concept of time."

"Mom, I don't think it was one of those," Curlie says flatly, "it was different."

Grandma seems curious. "How was it different, sweetheart?"

"It was more like a whisper. Then there was a lot of static, and I thought a soft voice said something, but I couldn't understand any real words. With telemarketers, there's a silence for a few seconds, but then they start talking fast." Curlie runs back into the living room to get her music sheets, stuffing them into her bag.

Adrian tries to move us along. "Let's go, ladies..."

"Maybe someone's trying to reach us?" I say absently, and then observe the incredulous looks on their faces. "It could be, you know."

Adrian knows what direction this might take. "We need to leave if we're to get Curlie to the recital hall in time for her big debut."

As we go out the back door, the telephone rings again, but Adrian tells us to leave it as the machine will take a message. We have no time to spare now that it took so long for me to get ready.

"I can't leave it, Adrian, what if it's Jason?"

"I'll get the car and meet you at the front door, but Ellie, be quick about it, okay?"

Adrian herds the others toward the garage as I walk toward my office. The phone stops ringing, but the red flashing light means that there's a message waiting. With a shaking hand, I press the PLAY button. A tinny voice begins to echo, which is accompanied by static. It's so faint that I replay it again. It sounded like a whisper, as Curlie said her call did, but there was so much interference that nothing was audible.

Did I honestly think Jason was calling home?

Adrian blows the car horn, so I reluctantly move toward the front door. As I get into the back seat to sit with Mother, he asks, "Who was this important call from?"

"It was like Curlie described; static and then nothing. If it was Jason, that proves he's alive. If it wasn't Jason..." No one utters a word for fear I might go ballistic and start to cry. It is supposed to be a happy occasion, not a sad one. My cellphone rings. It's my sister Terre.

"Where are you?" Terre asks. "I thought you'd be here by now. What's the holdup? This place is filling up fast."

"We are almost there, don't give our seats away."

Terre sighs, "I have been holding the wolves at bay, but I don't know how much longer I can keep your seats. The crowd is getting anxious for some reason."

"Thanks for doing this, Terre. Did you call the home phone just now?"

"No, this is the first call to you today; why?" Terre asks.

"We got two calls, but they were only static. We'll see you shortly." After I end the call with Terre, I turn to ask Adrian a question. "Can we put Levi's equipment on it to trace the call?"

"We can try. Let's do that when we get home, okay?" he says, maneuvering the car toward the high school.

I can't seem to concentrate on Curlie's performance as the phone calls keep haunting my thoughts. What if it *was* Jason calling? Maybe it was Dimmy. Adrian bumps my arm, and says, "Quit thinking, if it's that important, whoever left the message will call back. Put it out of your mind, okay? Curlie needs you tonight."

How does one continue with life as usual when a loved one may never come home?

Mother reminds me as often as she can, that we did it when Daddy died and again when Ravi went. This situation is different, my son is missing, and no one can tell me where he is!

I'm in a snarky mood today. Why can't people mind their own business and leave me alone? Mother keeps reminding me that the baskets of goodies and sympathy cards are our neighbor's way of being, well neighborly. But I'm sick of it! I'm sick of the helpless feeling that comes over me when I think that Jason needs our help.

Where are you, Jason?

Was I wrong to let Jason go to Saudi in the first place? Melanie and Curlie certainly think so, every chance they get. They don't understand that it was his decision, not mine. They blame me anyway because I'm the Mother and I should know better!

When do children accept the responsibility that is distinctly theirs and stop blaming their parents for their mistakes? Have I not taught my children right from wrong? They know the consequences for taking the wrong path. Ravi and I let them make mistakes so they would learn how to deal with them.

Mother reminds me of the poem about a family being a circle, as she thinks this will somehow soothe me. Reading it makes me weep.

> *"A family is like a circle, the connection never ends,*
> *and even if at times it breaks, in time it always mends.*
> *A family is like the stars, somehow they're always there,*
> *families are those who help, who support, and always care.*
> *A family is like a book, the endings never clear,*
> *but through the pages of the book, their love is always near.*
> *A family is many things with endless words that show who they are*
> *and what they do and how they teach you so you know,*
> *but don't be weary if it's broken,*
> *or if through time it's been so worn,*
> *families are like that-they're split up and always torn,*
> *but even if this happens, your family will always be,*
> *they help define just who you are*
> *and will be a part of you eternally."*

Is Jason's disappearance my fault?

His Royal Highness (pain-in-the-ass), King Ak-dim-er, and his oversized bodyguard, both said they would make sure Jason was safe always. Their guarantee only lasted a few years.

Are they liars?

Did Jason do something wrong?

Was he trying to tell me something the last time I spoke with him?

How could I have missed it so thoroughly?

"The Lord is your guardian;
the Lord is your shade at your right hand.
By day the sun cannot harm you, nor the moon by night.
The Lord will guard you all from evil,
will always guard your life.
The Lord will guard your coming and going
both now and forever."
~ Psalm 121 – King James Version

Chapter Twelve

A Family Mourns

King Akdemir was sitting at his desk in the library, facing the wall. When he turned around, his red-rimmed eyes gave his face an odd, puckered appearance. It was the day set aside for distinguished members of his country to pay their respects to Turlock.

They wished to honor Turlock for his bravery and his devotion to the Royal Household. As was their custom, no one mentioned Sheyanna or their daughters. And out of respect for the King, no one mentioned Prince Jason or his sudden disappearance. An eerie silence pervaded the room. The only sound was coming from the overhead fans that were humming distractedly.

"Thank you all for coming today," Akdemir said to his audience. "Turlock..." he choked on his name, and for an instant Jamaile saw how vulnerable his master was. "Turlock was a devoted man to our Royal Household. Turlock will be missed by many people here. I do not know how I will...it will be difficult to replace him. He was unique, and I loved him as a mentor, an uncle, an advisor, and a trusted friend."

The small gathering waited for King Akdemir to continue, but he turned his chair to face the wall again, and lowered his head into his hands. A few seconds later, his shoulders began to move in a jerking manner as emotion began to overtake him.

One by one, the group of men filed out of the room. When it was empty, Jamaile quietly told Akdemir that he was alone.

"May I get you anything, Highness," Jamaile asked.

"No," he said quietly.

"Come, Highness. A threat exists. You need to be safe."

"How, Jamaile? How did Fariq get his hands on our precious ancient documents? How did he convince the Royal Ministers that he should be here instead of me?"

Jamaile knew Akdemir was frustrated with Fariq's latest demands. "Come with me, Highness. You need to be in a safe place now." Taking Akdemir by the arm, he escorted him toward the large wooden doors. "I do not believe Fariq has the right documents, Your Highness."

"How do you know this, Jamaile?" Akdemir studied his First-In-Command. "They were locked in my safe. They are no longer there now as it has been opened. I checked it this morning."

"My men go room to room to search for Fariq and gather information about how he got in and where the documents might be. One of my trusted men took them from one of his spies."

"You have them?" Akdemir said in surprise.

"Yes, Highness," Jamaile answered. "Fariq gave the impression he has them, but this is not true. They are safe. I have them with me. Come, we must move quickly."

"Then it is only a matter of time before the Alliance Ministers find out and have him taken away. That is if they can get in here without harm to themselves. Fariq seems ruthless enough to harm anyone that gets in his way."

Jamaile nodded his head in agreement. Stopping suddenly, he put a big arm out to push King Akdemir against the wall, as he heard what sounded like footfalls coming their way. When he puts a big finger to his lips, Akdemir blinked in understanding.

They are mere steps away from a small room adjacent to the ceremonial room called the waiting room. Jamaile's men have adjusted the surveillance equipment in the ceremonial room to show the table and chairs, while the hallway projected only stone walls.

Taking Akdemir by the arm, he led him into it. Near the main door, Jamaile used his dagger to open a large cupboard. He then pushed the shelves, and they swung open to reveal a dark space. Pulling Akdemir into it as quickly and as quietly as he could, he inserted his dagger into a slot, and the cupboard door closed. He stiffened; moments later, they heard the door of the room open and then slam shut hurriedly.

Commotion was happening out in the hallway as doors opened and closed. Muffled voices could be heard speaking in a language that was neither Arabic or English. As the sounds slowly dissipated down the hallway again, Jamaile looked through a crack to make sure no one was waiting.

Turning toward Akdemir, he shoved him gently aside. The small flashlight he was holding illuminated a depression into which he slipped an oddly shaped key. As the wall slid up, a room was visible. Taking Akdemir by the arm, he pulled him into the room, then touched a button and the wall slid back down.

"How long has this been here, Jamaile?"

"A long time, Highness. It was your brother and your father who knew there would come a time it would be needed."

Akdemir sighed. "And Basim did not think I should know about this?"

"He asked that you be informed when he thought you wanted to know. There was no time until this one. You were never as curious, as Basim was."

Akdemir stared at his most trusted friend and protector. "You mean you forgot to tell me about it."

"Yes, Highness. Basim has not been here for many years. It was out of my mind as other things came up."

Akdemir was curious. "What did Basim have to do with this?"

"We do not have time to talk now, Highness." Jamaile pulled a bundle from beneath his shirt and presented it to Akdemir. "You will see. It is where you will stay, Highness. You will be safe if you remain here. Do not go out and do not let anyone in, not even me. I will give you a password. I truly fear for your life. Follow the instructions."

"These are the documents, Jamaile?"

"They are safest with you here, Highness. Now I must leave you."

Akdemir said in surprise, "Surely you are not leaving me here!"

"I must, Your Highness, consult the map for the location of things. I will come back for you. Talk to no one and do not come out of this safe place, your life is in grave danger."

"Am I to be a prisoner in my own house, Jamaile? Can I not go to the library? Can I not go to the training room? Can I not go to the arena? I cannot go bloody anywhere! How is it that Fariq has taken this away from me, can you answer that?"

"We will seek answers. I must go now, Highness. I will return soon."

Akdemir asked softly, "Was your son a traitor, Jamaile?"

Jamaile's face contorted, and Akdemir knew immediately that something dreadful had transpired. "Yes," the big man blinked. "He has received due punishment, Highness. There is no room for disloyal liars in your domain, no matter who they are."

Akdemir knew what occurred to disloyal members who strayed. "I am sincerely sorrowful for your loss, Jamaile. So much destruction and distress have befallen us."

Jamaile kept Khalifa in line with the caveat that he would one day be First-In-Command, but that status changed when he allowed Prince Jason to fall prey to Fariq. It was his job to keep the heir to the throne safe, and it was his job to see to it that no harm came to him. Jamaile challenged Khalifa about what Jason said in front of King Akdemir. He thought he had convinced his father that Jason was the liar; at least it appeared that he did.

The playing field changed the day Jamaile confronted Khalifa. He now knows that his son traveled a different path, one that he could not possibly return from, and ordered two of his best men to follow him. Jamaile concluded that Jason was telling the truth when his possessions were discovered in his room, sans the memory chip and hard drive removal. Could he have known about the deadly game taking place and was about to warn his uncle?

Jamaile bowed, stretching his arm across his chest in salute, and said, "I am your servant, as always, my life for yours."

Tears filled Akdemir's eyes, but Jamaile moved out of the room quickly, and the door slid silently closed behind him. Faint light illuminated items on a table: an envelope, a small map, a flashlight, and a box with some strange-shaped keys. Akdemir opened the envelope first, blinking at the familiar writing.

Dear Akdemir,

If you are reading this letter, little brother, it means that you are in the secret compartment built by our Father. May I offer a short explanation? During the time that our father was King, he wanted the Royal Palace to be as secure and safe as possible in case of an uprising.

The wealth that the oil brought to our family brought us riches, but it also brought us sorrow. Greed began to filter in like sand in a tent.

First, the place where you are is very safe. No one can get in or out without the right key. You hold all of them except one, and Jamaile (our most trusted and loyal companion, defender, and friend) has it. This place has everything you might need to sustain you for any length of time.

Follow the map, as it will lead you to different rooms, to food, to water, and an abundance of solitude. Many books are waiting for you to turn the pages while you wait. No one will know where you are. When it is safe, Jamaile will come for you. Until he returns, be at peace and do not worry. I am in your heart always.

Your brother, Basim

Wiping his eyes, Akdemir took the map to open it, then began to shake his head in disbelief. The Royal Palace he knew didn't resemble this map, as some passageways and rooms seemed confusing. Why was there an escape route? Was there a chance the Royal Palace could be compromised?

The whole thing was so clever that Akdemir laughed aloud at the absurdity of it all. Then it dawned on him that Jamaile was trying to tell him that Basim must have used this chamber more than a few times.

If only he had known about it, he would have told Jamaile to put Jason in here. Perhaps that is what Jamaile did, but he cannot divulge this out of fear for him.

Akdemir spread the map of the **Safe Chamber** out on the table in the first room, labeled **Anteroom**. Several sofas and soft carpets were here, which gave the room a large feel, but any space above it was devoid of windows.

MAP OF SAFE CHAMBERS

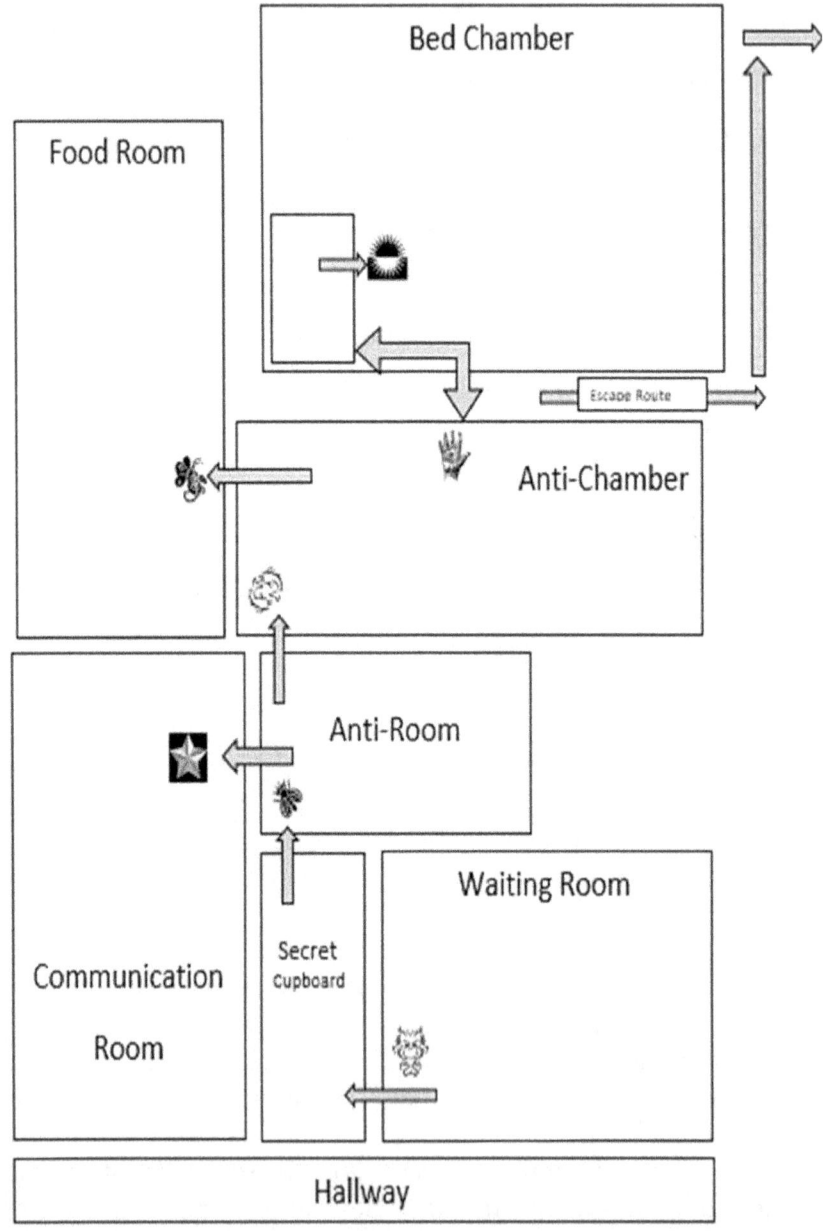

Whispered Dreams

Listening intently for any sound, when Akdemir couldn't detect any, he went back to the map. Other rooms were near a small passageway which interconnected with sliding walls or doors.

Akdemir fingered the keys, and wondered why they were all different. Glancing at the map again, it appeared that some of the rooms went down while others went perpendicular. They all either led to or from the **Anteroom**, except for one. It went directly to the outside via what appeared as a series of tunnels, which was where the escape route would presumably lead out of the palace.

Akdemir speculated how this place came to be here. Did his brother help build things into it? Wishing he had known about it while he was alive, it would have been a great adventure to explore the different levels. But then, this safe place was meant to keep people secreted from the rest of the world, even from him.

If others knew about it, it would not be the safe place it is today.

He located the entrance on the map that would take him to the second room labeled **Food Room**, where a small light winked on to illuminate where the key should go. Matching the key to the diagram on the map, he inserted it gently into the slot. As the door slid silently open, it revealed a table and chairs, a full-sized kitchen, and heavily laden shelves. The oversized refrigerator contained cold drinks, fruits, cheeses, and vegetables.

Moving next to the wall indicated on the map, this would take him to the third room labeled **Anti-Chamber**. It was not below as it appeared, but above it. He found the right key, and a small light again illuminated the key slot. The wall/door opened into a space that suddenly filled with light when he stepped into it. It was empty, which gave the impression that it was a dead end until he stepped forward.

 Putting his hand on the right wall as indicated on the map, a small light illuminated another key slot. This wall/door opened to a contorted staircase which appeared to go upward. At the top of this staircase landing, Akdemir was again perplexed, as all he could see were stone walls. He studied the map, noting with renewed enthusiasm that it led to the **Bed Chamber**. A small light illuminated a key slot, but it was out of reach.

The map showed a strange key that was thicker than all the others. When Akdemir pulled at it, it extended like a pointer, so he tried to insert it from where he was standing, then sucked in a breath as the floor beneath him moved forward.

This wall opened to a large room. Chuckling to himself, Akdemir thought this was similar to what the author described in the Harry Potter books. After he entered the spacious **Bed Chamber**, he located the adjacent closet, which was another room but needed no key for entry.

Sadness suddenly overtook him as he touched garments he knew his brother Basim wore. Perhaps his Father had to use these rooms one or two times during his lifetime.

"Basim! What you must have struggled with to gain your freedom. What have I doomed your son to endure? Jason, be safe, my nephew," he whispered and then began to sob uncontrollably.

When Akdemir recovered from his grief, he continued to investigate each room, reserving the last one, labeled **Escape Route** for another day, recalling Jamaile's warning to stay inside.

Although it felt like a wondrous space, he began to question how long he would have to stay here. How would he survive this dank existence? Had someone thought about that?

Could this be how Ellen felt when he had her locked into Basim's rooms? Her crystal ball would have come in handy right about now. Perhaps he should have looked for that magic carpet, or the Genie in the bottle to grant him three wishes because he certainly felt like a prisoner!

Jamaile let himself into the **Anti-Chamber** with his master key, opening the **Communication Room** next to it. He then surveyed the many monitors and camera hookups to view any activity within the last few hours. The only communication available to anyone inside the **Safe Chamber** was an elaborate system that Basim installed during earlier visits. As it turned out, he knew a substantial amount about electronics and Jamaile smiled when he pressed a button to summon Akdemir.

"This is Jamaile, Your Highness," he whispered. "It is time to rise for the day. I will serve you breakfast in one hour. Use the button on the lamp so you can talk to me."

Akdemir had been awake for some time and had studied his map and information very thoroughly, asking Jamaile for the password. It was an adroit system of words or phrases for each hour of the day and night. He knew that without this password, he would not go to the **Food Room**, even if he recognized Jamaile's voice.

Whispered Dreams

"I will give it to you, Your Highness." Jamaile rummaged in the drawer to find a list of words, moving a big finger up and down to locate the correct code. "The password for today at this hour is **breakfast 0439**."

"Very good, Captain, I will be there presently." Akdemir was relieved that he would have human contact, as it had been almost three days with no word from anyone. He was beginning to think that something had happened to Jamaile and that Fariq had overtaken everything, or worse.

Akdemir, already dressed for the day, consulted his map, placing the right key into the slot to go out of the bed chamber room, moving as quickly as he could in and out of the maze using his set of oddly-shaped keys. He was relieved when the last wall-door opened, and he saw Jamaile's big face smiling at him.

"It is good to see you, my friend. Tell me about any news," he asked.

Akdemir and Jamaile sat down to a simple breakfast that Jamaile fixed from the ingredients he found in the kitchen. The news today was not encouraging. Jamaile and his men confronted several groups that had come into the Royal Palace. They most likely were moving within the secret passageways and had quietly slain some of the servants, disposing of their bodies by throwing them over the stone wall into the marketplace.

"Two Alliance Royal Ministers came the other day to attend a meeting with you that was scheduled. Someone said you are no longer at the palace and they were rudely turned away. They left disgruntled."

"What did you do then, Jamaile?"

"Once I got past the palace walls, I caught up with them to explain our situation. I asked the Ministers to get a message to the Allegiance Council and what higher authority they could muster. I told them as much as I dared. I could not tell them anything else for fear it would compromise your hiding place, Highness."

"Were they receptive to your questions? What did you tell them, Jamaile?" Akdemir asked.

"I told them the Royal Palace is under siege by someone who wishes you harm. It is someone who challenges your line of succession. I told them it is Fariq. I then explained that you have gone on an unexpected holiday to remain safe."

"That was very clever of you. It buys us precious time. When am I supposed to return to the Royal Palace?" Akdemir asked.

"One month from today. No one will look for you for at least that long," Jamaile replied.

"They did not question you as to where I have gone?"

"No, Highness, they were in a hurry to leave. I believe they were uncomfortable seen talking to me."

Akdemir sighed, "What do you intend to do? I cannot stay here that whole time."

Jamaile said, "You must stay here where it is safe. I do not know for how long."

Akdemir dropped his fork on his plate with a loud clunk. "How long will that be? I may go stark raving mad if I have to stay here for very long," he uttered.

"I will show you the other room called the **COMMUNICATION ROOM**. You can see what, and where we are. You can spy on Fariq for me and let me know what he is up to."

Jamaile stood, saying, "Come, I will show you."

Akdemir followed his First-In-Command to the **ANTI-ROOM** where he inserted the funnily shaped key into the lighted slot, and the wall/door moved silently open. Akdemir was stunned by what he saw.

"There are no more keys on the ring. How will I have access to this room?"

Jamaile took the ring of keys and began to insert one key, then another. Each time it opened the wall, it also closed. "It is any of these keys. It was designed by Basim to have quick access. If you must go to the **ESCAPE ROUTE** and out of the palace, these keys will do the same thing, so there is a quick exit."

Akdemir blinked in understanding. "This is clever of Basim. How I wish I had known about this before."

"Your father is the one who had this chamber and all of the rooms built. It was Basim who made it better," Jamaile said proudly. "They were good men. They saw a need of this. Your father used this room during the siege of the nineteen thirties; my father, my mother's husband, was his First-In-Command then. Basim used these rooms maybe twelve or fourteen times through the years."

"Where do you think Jason is now, Jamaile? What have you told Ellen? I know she has called several times. I am worried about him. I do hope he is safe and unharmed."

"I told them only a small amount. Mr. Adrian calls, Ma'dame Ellen calls, and we tell them he is missing. We have no other words. They are outraged they cannot talk with him. They are angry you will not speak to them."

"I know how they feel. I feel as they do, I am also outraged." Akdemir said. "Have you told me everything?"

Jamaile struggled with what he must say next. "Jason left without his computer and cellphone. That leads us to believe he was surprised. All of his clothes, his wallet, everything else is still in his room, untouched."

Akdemir slowly started to comprehend. "Jason said his laptop and cellphone were missing. How could they have been left behind?"

"Jason told us the truth. One of Khalifa's men put them back into his room after he was gone," Jamaile said sadly.

"I see," Akdemir replied quietly. "That explains some things."

"They took them from Jason when they went on the horse trip, as Jason told us they did. We did not understand this at the time. All men who were involved with this misdeed have received punishment according to our laws."

Akdemir shook his head in disbelief. "I cannot believe such treachery within the Royal Household, especially those who were trusted members. These events sadden me, Jamaile. Show me how to use this equipment. I want to know who dares to sneak in and out of here."

After reading the instructions for only a few minutes, the King was a quick study, operating most of the complicated equipment better than Jamaile. He was expertly moving the cameras to scan every crack and crevice where he thought Fariq's men might be lurking.

"I want to catch them and bring them to justice! See there, Jamaile, they are using the passageway to the arena and the one that links the floors to Jason's set of rooms. Get some men there and let me know what you find."

Jamaile moved quickly toward the doorway, giving his salute of honor, uttering a prayer for all to be safe. Akdemir knew that once the wall/door closed behind him, he would have no contact unless Jamaile was near a camera with a microphone. He silently prayed for their safety and thought of Jason.

Was Jason alone?

Was Jason sequestered somewhere safe within the Royal Palace?

Had he been taken out far from here? Or had he made it to another city? Akdemir would not let himself think that Jason was dead. He cannot be dead! He needed him now more than ever.

An irate Fariq was bellowing in Arabic at the woman who was sitting on the floor. She was weeping with her head lowered; her shoulders drooped in defeat. His booming voice was heard as far away as the kitchen below the library, even though the heavy wooden doors were not open.

"You have shamed me, daughter! You have humiliated our family and our household! For that, you will die!"

"Please, father, listen to me," Amala sobbed.

"You were sent into the Royal Palace to gain information. How could you have failed so badly with this? It was the most important thing you had to do in your entire life! You did not get that right. You have failed!" he roared.

The daughter remained silent, knowing she had no defense that would convince her father of her innocence, which was what she did, precisely. She did not do as he had asked, therefore, she was guilty.

Fariq was pacing back and forth near Akdemir's massive desk. When the large doors opened at the end of the room, Fariq halted his insults to look at who dared to interrupt him.

"What is it now?" he rumbled.

A man dressed entirely in black approached cautiously. He was present the other day when the unpredictable leader threw a tantrum, narrowly missing his comrade with a silver teapot. He was expecting a similar reaction with the information he was about to deliver.

"What is it! I don't have all day for this nonsense!"

The man moved as quickly as he dared without running. When he reached his commander, he began to speak, however, after a few seconds, Fariq's demeanor changed from enthusiasm to utter disappointment.

"GET OUT, you fool! You are as bad as the others! GET OUT OF MY SIGHT!"

Fariq put both hands on the desk. He shook his head wildly, then began turning his wrath toward his daughter again. "I need those documents! You were supposed to find out where the documents are! Instead, you come back bearing his child, the enemy's child! I have waited a long time to take what is mine. I will not stop until I have it!" Fariq shouted.

Two men came forward to grab the woman when Fariq nodded his head. She knew better than to say anything and silently let the men take her away. Fariq wasn't watching, turning his attention instead to rummage through the large desk. When he found nothing of interest, he casually began to walk around it, running his finger along the side, stopping at a stack of books to read the titles.

The spacious library was, up until a few days ago, not open to him. He began to laugh to himself to think he had achieved such a great accomplishment. A loud knock suddenly disrupted his thinking.

"What is it now?" he yelled.

A guard opened the door, saying loud enough for Fariq to hear, "You ordered lunch, Your Excellency. It has arrived."

Fariq motioned to the guard that it was acceptable to allow a server into the room. This server was dressed in a white coat and black pants, and appeared as any other in the employ of King Akdemir, except that he was taller than most; his dark hair was tied back with a thin leather strap.

The server set two stacked trays on the table. The top one contained silver domes; the bottom had plates, silverware, and cups. The server proceeded to place the contents strategically around the table as if he had done this for many years. Fariq took no notice of him when another man, a soldier this time, came into the room. He didn't wait until the soldier was close enough to talk, and instead, used the opportunity to scream at him.

"What have you discovered?" he growled.

"We have searched everywhere, sir. None of us can find any members of the Royal Family. We think the King has fled."

Fariq started to pace the room again. "What about the boy? Where *is* he precisely?"

"We do not know, sir. We have asked everyone. No one can tell us. We told you that when we went to his room, he was already gone. He left everything behind. He did not take his wallet or clothes. We did find someone who said he was dead. We questioned him at length. The boy was trying to escape the palace walls and was killed. We do not have proof of this. No one saw his body."

"And the documents, have you at least located the ancient documents?" Fariq thundered.

The nervous soldier stammered, "No, Your Excellency, we have found no such documents. We looked everywhere we thought they might be and found nothing."

"Where is Akdemir? Have you at least found out where he has fled to?" Fariq demanded.

"No, Your Excellency. We have conducted a detailed search. He is nowhere here. No one knows where he might have gone. One of the Ministers said he was on holiday. No one knows where he went."

Jamaile had finished his task and gained critical information. He took the empty trays, hoisted them onto his shoulder, and then stood near the door. The door opened as Fariq shouted for the soldier to get out. After hurling insults at the man, he told him not to return until he had information of good use.

Pleased that Jason might have indeed escaped from the palace alive, Jamaile headed toward the kitchen area to drop off the trays. As he pretended to fill pots, he also continued to listen in on the conversation in the kitchen. Occasionally he interjected things he wanted them to pass on to others, which made it look as if he was a part of the regular kitchen staff.

Some of the staff knew who he was while others did not. He had picked up snippets of information that would be useful, but most of it was complaints against the person who had taken control of the palace. They were not pleased with Fariq's abrupt change in the smooth-running kitchen. They missed King Akdemir, as he was both just and kind, neither traits present in the gruff and demanding person named Fariq.

Captain Jamaile needed to collaborate with his most trusted men and took the steps down toward the arena, being as careful as he could to avoid Fariq's thugs. Accessing a secret cupboard, where he knew the cameras were projecting an image of an empty hallway, he changed out of the server's clothing and into a stable workers attire to blend in.

Stepping into the hallway, Jamaile took another set of stairs that descended near the arena. He encountered two figures in black, who immediately took a defensive stance. Jamaile shook his big head, told them that he was in a hurry and to get out of his way, as he was on a mission from Fariq. In the split-second it took the men to move, Jamaile knocked their heads together, and they fell in a heap at his feet. A member of his trusted team then stepped out of the shadows to dispose of the garbage.

Akdemir was observing this drama as it unfolded from the confines of the **COMMUNICATION ROOM**. When Jamaile's menacing face got close to one of the monitor's cameras, he whispered, "I have information. It is good. I will see you shortly."

Jamaile quickly moved off to consult with his remaining men. Akdemir then switched to another camera to follow him, but something else suddenly caught his eye. On another monitor, he watched in horror as two black figures dragged a woman down a hallway by the arms. Without a scarf to hide her face and dressed in old clothes wrapped around her swollen body, he knew who she was. He would speak to Jamaile about this when he next saw him.

While Jamaile was in the library, he successfully placed bugs on the underside of the table as he set the silverware and plates. They may gain additional information when Fariq sits down with his cronies to discuss their evil deeds. A tiny sensitive microphone will pick up the slightest sound in and around the table area, although it cannot pick up any conversation near the big desk unless someone yells.

Two servers in white coats and black pants entered the library and prepared to serve Fariq and four of his men. They could only listen if Fariq allowed them to stay. Once they had dispatched the hot liquid from the shiny pots, they stepped to the side to wait for further instructions. They had learned first-hand of Fariq's quick temper and his most terrible disposition.

"You may go," Fariq yelled gruffly to the two men. Turning toward the table, grabbing a cup, he said, "We have much to discuss, gentlemen. Let us start with what we know."

The servers left after their dismissal, going back to the kitchen that was directly below the library via the open stairway. After an hour or so, the men returned to the library to clear the table. After finishing their duties in the kitchen, they went toward the open stairway, where they encountered people dressed in black.

One of the men stepped forward to ask the servers to follow him. The remaining figures knew better than to question this, remaining at their positions, as they knew Fariq had a network of secret spies.

The three men went down a series of stairways and passageways that eventually led to the arena. It was where Jamaile had commandeered a small room that he knew would remain well-hidden from prying eyes. He nodded to the man in black, who was one of his army of men in stolen clothing where he remained outside the doorway, to keep guard. Anyone observing this behavior would think that Fariq had conquered the entire palace, instead of only parts of it.

"What have you learned?" he asked the two servers eagerly.

"The kitchen servers spoke of Sheyanna, Turlock, and their daughters," Maheer responded. "Some say they were murdered outright while others say they heard they were all poisoned. They have tried many times, but no one will allow them access to that floor. No one knows if anything is missing."

Raheeb added, "We need more time to talk with them. We could not stay in the library to hear much of anything. Fariq dismissed us when he sat down to eat. They were gone when we went in to clean up."

"You have done well. Go back to the kitchen, listen, and observe. I will contact you soon."

Jamaile would inform Akdemir once he could leave his post, knowing he might have already received the information, via the hidden cameras and the listening devices that he planted.

Akdemir had indeed received the information. He was sitting patiently in front of the monitor screens, smiling, because he knew that the Alliance Ministers would force Fariq to leave the palace. He was confident they would intervene as soon as they had the proper documents. His thoughts drifted once again to his nephew, Jason.

"I hope that you have made it out of the palace. Be safe, my nephew, be safe!"

When Jamaile was satisfied that his trusted men were in place for the evening watch, he quietly went to see Akdemir so that they could discuss the day's events. After gaining entrance to the secret chamber, he was surprised that the conversation went in a different direction.

"Talk to me of Basim, Jamaile. You knew him best. I want to know what you know of him that you have kept from me all these years."

"What do you wish to know, Highness? Have you not heard these stories many times before?"

"I believe that you know more than you have told me, old friend," Akdemir said.

"I know many stories, Highness. Is there a specific one you want to hear?"

Akdemir stared at his First-In-Command. "I want to hear the real reason why Basin left the palace. I think it is time we talked about that. I, like Miss Ellen, have many questions."

"You are asking something that I was sworn never to divulge, by your father, King Basim, Akdemir. I was told never to speak of it again, not even to you--even if you asked." Jamaile eyed Akdemir, wondering how much he could safely tell him without insulting his intelligence or making him angry.

Whispered Dreams

"Since I am a virtual prisoner trapped here and both my father and Basim are dead, there is no one around, Jamaile. I think it is time that you told me all of it. It may have some bearing on what has happened to our young Jason. Ellen told me of the events that keep happening in Virginia. They may, in fact, correlate to one another."

Jamaile relented, "As you wish, Akdemir, it will not be a short story. You might be angry with me after I tell you these things."

"No, Jamaile, I will not be angry with you. You have been a trusted and loyal friend. If you had to withhold this information, then you were only doing your duty. We have all the time in the world right now. I am not squeamish, do not leave anything out."

Jamaile lowered his head to think. "I do not know where to start."

"Start at the beginning. When did you first come to the palace?" Akdemir coaxed.

Jamaile tried to recall his childhood and the events that brought him into the Royal Household. "I was your brother's companion from an early age. I don't ever remember a time when we were not together. My mother was your father's favorite until your mother came along."

"I did not know that, Jamaile. I was under the impression that my father had no previous favorites. What I do know is that your father was my father's First-In-Command, is that not true?"

"Yes, my mother's husband was your father's First-In-Command. That is not the lie."

Akdemir studied Jamaile, then asked, "What lie do you refer to?"

"I will try to explain. My mother and her mother brought me to the Royal Palace when I was very young. She hugged me, said that I would live here from now on. She left. I never saw her again."

"I see," Akdemir said quietly. "Continue."

"I too had questions. No one would answer them. Finally, my grandmother told me the truth when I was eight years old. Again, Akdemir, this was withheld from you for your security, and no malice was ever intended. I was told that from that day forward Prince Basim and I would train alongside each other. I would assume the role of protector and defender much as my father did. He also worked with the stallions and the Blue and Silver."

"That is not the lie, is it, Jamaile?"

"No, Akdemir. My grandmother said that you and I, including Basim, share the same father, not the same mother. We lived in the Royal Palace to be close to the Royal Family until my grandmother died. She took the truth with her."

Akdemir placed a hand on Jamaile's arm when he realized the implications of his words. "Jamaile! You are my brother! Why am I hearing of this now? How could this have been kept from me? Did Basim know?"

"Yes, Basim knew."

"This explains so much," Akdemir said softly.

"We did everything together, as brothers, however, no one called us that. Everyone assumed that the little prince had a playmate. We grew up together, and then you came along. We added you to our training when you were old enough to join us. I was told to protect you both."

Jamaile grew quiet, turning his head to the side as he began to remember long-suppressed memories. He had taken the blame entirely upon himself to protect his charge, Basim. He had no regrets over the incident; however, he wished he had done things differently.

"Basim knew you were our brother yet he deliberately kept this from me. Are you the eldest son, Jamaile?" Akdemir questioned.

"I was born before Basim. He swore me to secrecy when he found out the truth. There are many spies in the Royal Palace. If information got out that my treatment was better than anyone, there would be no end to the scrutiny or the explanations that would take place. Every one of your father's children wanted his favor. I had no aspirations to take up the throne; my place is with the men downstairs, the stallions, and with the Blue and Silver."

"Why did Basim leave the palace, Jamaile? You were there at the time, and you know the real reason. I have figured out that what my father told us about that time has taken a deviation from the truth. I implore you to tell me the truth, as you know it."

Jamaile hesitated, trying to think of how he would answer. "It was not for the reason you think. Basim did not want the role of king. We spoke many times about this issue. He wanted to train with the Blue and Silver Ensemble. He wanted to ride his magnificent stallion called *Basim's Pride*. He wanted to live, as I did, not surrounded by wealth or power."

"I knew that part, Jamaile. We talked about this several times over the years. It was the times he went to London to study that convinced him, didn't it? It was always after he went away and came back that he would renew his quest to see the world. As my father's eldest son, you had every right to be here with us! You could have gone to college with Basim or me in London. You could have been a Crown Prince before me!"

"No, Akdemir, I did not want that. I saw what wealth could do to people. It corrupts them, makes them do stupid things. I chose a simpler life. I wanted to work with the horses and go out when they had a show. I have respect from my men, I guard and protect you. I have everything that I need. I need nothing more."

"What is the real reason Basim left, Jamaile?"

"Our father saw things differently. He demanded that Basim live up to his rightful position. Basim did not want to be a Crown Prince as others did. He always thought you would be a better choice. There were those that wanted Basim removed so they could take his place in the line of succession, after you."

"Why did they want to remove him? He would have made a good leader for our people. He could have stayed to train and still gone out with the Blue and Silver. He didn't have to fake his death to do this."

"No, Akdemir, he would not. King Basim and the Royal Ministers would not allow it. As the eldest son, Prince Basim had no choice in the matter. He was Crown Prince Basim then, next in line to the throne."

"This is a sad and fascinating tale, Jamaile. Tell me more."

"During the third year Basim went to college, he confronted our father. He did not want to return to college. He wanted to remain here to train with me. Then the Ministers and King Basim interfered, insisting that Basim marry one of the Royal Minister's daughters."

"Jamaile, we were about to do that to Jason. Do you think it had anything to do with his disappearance?"

"I do not know, Highness. It may have contributed to this. Basim had found someone to share his bed. Somehow King Basim did not approve of the match. He gave the order to remove the woman. When the news came out that she was with child, Basim went berserk when he discovered what had transpired."

"Basim told me none of this," Akdemir sighed.

"Something went wrong with the birth. I do not recall the woman's name. I respected his privacy and did not ask. Basim only said he loved her and wanted to marry her. He was not going to marry the woman his father told him to marry. We do know the baby boy died."

"There was a child born. History has repeated itself. Jason said he loved this woman named Amala. Is that why Basim left?"

"It is what happened next. Basim was very angry when he found out why the woman was no longer in the Royal Palace. He thought her treatment was extreme. He became sullen and convinced that it somehow caused the death of his child. He wanted to go after her. King

Basim vehemently told him that he was not to look for trouble. He made Basim promise not to leave the palace. Basim went anyway." Jamaile lowered his head, and for a moment, the big man faltered. "If I had gone with him…my one regret…"

"This is hard for you, Jamaile. I am remorseful for having to ask you to recall this. But I must know all of it."

"The woman blamed Basim for the child's death. She came to him not long after and threatened him with a knife. I was nearby. I took it away from her. Her removal from the Royal Palace was swift. I am unsure what happened to her."

"That is a sad story, Jamaile. Why was this kept a secret from me? Why didn't Basim tell me himself? I would have understood."

"When Basim left, it was hard for me. I am glad that you took your father's place. You are a strong leader. Unlike Basim, he would not have done the same as you have for our people."

"You do not think Basim would have made a good King?"

"No, Akdemir. Basim did not have the knowledge or the gift of listening as you have. He did not listen to your father. He went out to look for the woman. Men were waiting for him. They beat and left him to die. When Basim did not come home, a few of us that were close to him went to look for him. Maheer, Raheeb, and I found him lying in a pool of blood, outside the marketplace. We brought his limp body back to the palace. The doctors could do little for him."

"Are you saying that Basim died? This is how they got around that. Go on, old friend."

"King Basim was beside himself with worry. When he consulted with the Ministers, they agreed not to avenge this crime, but to cover it up. It was your father that used this very safe chamber to hide Basim until he had a good plan in place."

"I am grateful this place existed. That was an awful time as I recall. I saw his mangled body and wept over the shroud."

"That was the clever part of our father's plan. Then he sent out the Royal Proclamation that Crown Prince Basim was dead. Photos of his beaten face and broken body went to newspapers."

"Was the intention to trap whoever did this to Basim?"

"Yes, the hope was to flush out the criminals responsible for this deed. When no one stepped forward, and no one admitted to seeing anything, King Basim feared for the Royal Family's lives, not only Basim. He knew that if he could get him to safety, he might live."

"Why did my father not tell me about this? It would have helped to understand it. Perhaps we could have avoided what happened to him later…"

"Fate has a way of intervening, Akdemir. If Basim had recovered and stayed in Saudi, you would have figured out this secret. You might have let it slip. The same people would come after him again. This time they would not stop with Basim, they would most likely come after you and the rest of the Royal Family."

"I'm beginning to understand now," Akdemir shuddered.

"No one here knew that your brother was alive. That is when King Basim devised a plan with Miss Ellen's father to smuggle him out of the country. Her father helped Basim to have surgery for him to live a normal life. It could not be here with us; it would have to be far away for this to work."

"Basim told me parts of this story. When he came back that first time, I remember that you told me someone was here to see me. The shock still haunts me. He looked so different, so very, very different from the brother I knew."

"Your brother took a great risk coming back into the palace to see you. He did not know who he could trust then, besides me. Our father was afraid of the many spies who roam the halls of the Royal Palace. The Ministers are the ones who told the King that Crown Prince Basim would never be a good leader. He was headstrong, did not possess support by the merchant community. He was only marginally popular among general citizenry. When the brutal attack happened, it was a wakeup call. They may have known who his assailants were, however, to keep you safe, your father could not take a chance to expose them."

"I am confused about something, Jamaile. If Basim had part of the ancient documents, were they not supposed to protect him somehow? Why did the Allegiance Council not take possession of them at that time? Why did part of the documents go with Basim? What was the reason they split them up in the first place?"

"It was in case the Royal Palace was in discord with the Ministers or the Allegiance Council itself. There was a time in our history where a King narrowly missed an assassination and another who was not so lucky. King Basim wanted peace; if the Royal Palace were overtaken and not able to defend itself, then the documents would explain the rite of succession. That is why Basim had the ancient documents with him. He and I did not know they were divided."

"It must have been Mr. Peters who decided to remove some of the documents and add the currency. The currency must have been the same thickness as the documents. That was clever. It left me completely out of it, but it was clever nonetheless," Akdemir said thoughtfully.

"Our father was a wise man. The King knew there was a traitor in the palace. He could not take the chance the documents would fall into the wrong hands and gave his blessing for Basim to leave. His wounds eventually healed, but his heart was always here with us. He came back as often as he dared. He told of great adventures and swore that he would find the woman someday to make things right."

"Did he ever find her, Jamaile?"

"I think, in the end, it might have been her that had something to do with Basim's plane exploding. I cannot be certain, but someday we might find that to be true."

Akdemir sat in stunned silence, reflecting on what Jamaile had told him. Then he started to quote something. *"Heaven has no rage like love to hatred turned, nor hell a fury like a woman scorned."*

"That is something you learned at college, Akdemir?"

"Yes. Jamaile, this quote is about love."

"If this woman loved Basim so much, why did she kill him?" Jamaile asked.

"That I do not know. The quote also means that the woman was out for revenge. She might, as you have mentioned, been that elusive operative that was responsible for the explosion. So much loss, Jamaile, so much sorrow has befallen us. It is all so senseless."

"How did this woman have the means to do this?" Jamaile was curious.

"I do not know that, my friend. Jamaile, this could mean that the woman is still out there. It also means that she has not sought resolution for her situation. She could still show up here demanding things. Do you think that she took Jason?"

"No, I think Fariq had something to do with it. You need to rest now. I will return as soon as I am able. Sleep well, Akdemir."

"You loved my brother. I wish I had known about that. We could have done so much more together, you, me, and Basim. There have been many surprises lately, but none as big as the one you have told me. If I was to have another brother, I am proud to have you as one. Sleep well, Jamaile."

"We have more information, Captain," Raheeb reported to Jamaile. "You were correct. The woman who Khalifa found in the passageway leading from Prince Jason's room is the same woman who is with child. We heard her say several times that she loved Prince Jason and told Fariq nothing."

"You are sure of this?" Jamaile questioned.

Maheer answered, "Yes, Captain. We are most sure of this. We narrowly missed detection. We followed Fariq's men to the desert where they left the woman to die. We saw what they did to her. The woman was skeptical of us at first, because she thought Fariq's men had come back to kill her. We convinced her that we were there to help take her to safety."

"You took her to the designated place?" Jamaile asked.

"Yes, she is safe. A good family will watch over her and the child when it is born," Raheeb pronounced. "Fariq's dogs left her with no food, shelter, or water. She would not have lasted long out in the hot sun. No one saw us. We made sure of that."

"We left evidence scattered in the area, and sticking out of the sand that leaves little doubt that she perished," Maheer added.

Jamaile seemed thoughtful, then asked, "Have you continued to question everyone? Were you able to ask this woman about where Prince Jason might be now?"

"No one knows anything about Prince Jason. Someone saw Turlock's wife, Sheyanna, before he went missing. All who would tell us seems to be dead, or they are also missing!" Raheeb replied.

"The woman swore she knows nothing. She said that after she came out of Master Jason's room, she was taken...by Khalifa and immediately straight to her father," Maheer said.

"You have done well, both of you. Go back to your posts in the kitchen. I will contact you shortly." As he dismissed his men, Jamaile wondered if Sheyanna had anything to do with Jason's disappearance. Fariq had maintained that Jason was murdered, yet no body had been found. He could not bring himself to tell Akdemir. Instead, he would try to give him hope, as he continued to think that Jason escaped the palace walls and is alive--somewhere.

Two days later, Jamaile took Maheer and Raheeb, where he stationed them along a passageway, as he went to speak with King Akdemir. After he gave the correct code, Akdemir pressed a button on a panel that had been set up inside the **COMMUNICATION ROOM**.

Once Jamaile was inside, he said, "Greetings, Highness, I have news; it is good for a change."

"I have news for you as well. The microphone you attached to the table in the library has produced valuable information. Tell me about your news first, Jamaile."

"Two trusted guards followed the group who took Fariq's daughter into the desert. After those men left her to die, my men took her to safety. At first, she put up resistance, but my men explained they would take her to a nearby family that would care for her and the child when it was born. She is grateful and knows nothing of where Jason is or where the documents are, so she told Fariq nothing of importance, as we already knew."

"That is excellent news, Jamaile. We will help her any way we can, especially her unborn child. Now I want you to hear what the microphone you placed in the library picked up today."

A rustling noise followed several muffled bangs and clinks. "Maheer and Raheeb were in the room to serve. They said that Fariq is intolerable to the help."

"As I have heard, Jamaile. You will hear voices of mostly small talk of the events that will happen and other nonsense."

Fariq was a volatile and dangerous man who grew up in the shadows of his great half-brothers. It was a well-known fact that he had hated them for a long time.

Akdemir raised a finger, "Listen to this part…"

"I do not care how you do it, but you must find the documents! Then you must find that idiot Akdemir! Those documents are what I need to get him off the throne and out of the country! Tear every inch of this palace apart if you must. Question everyone; servants, those men who ride the horses, EVERYONE!"

"We are doing everything we can, Your Excellency. I do not know how much more we can do."

"Try harder! If we do not find them soon and the boy shows up, I do not know if we can keep it from the Alliance Ministers. They are already asking too many questions! I am running out of options! And patience!"

The recording stopped, so he turned to face Jamaile. "Jason must be alive. If Fariq does not know where he is, then Jason surely escaped, not murdered as we thought."

"It does appear so, Highness," Jamaile speculated.

"I am grateful you were able to retrieve the documents, Jamaile, and bring them to me. Fariq has not discovered the fake ones you planted yet. We will give him a little more time. I suppose that when he does, he will be even angrier. We shall strike back at him then. Were you able to get a message to the Alliance Ministers of our plan?"

"Yes, everything is in place. We wait for your command to proceed."

"Excellent! I am grateful for what you have endured, Jamaile. It has been a terrible ordeal for us all. It started the day Basim left. Both of our families have suffered great loss. My family will forever be in your debt for what you have given up for us."

In an uncharacteristic gesture, Akdemir put his arms around Jamaile to embrace him. For a moment, Jamaile did not know what to do, and then he put his big arms around the King. For several minutes, the two men seemed lost in thought.

"You are my brother as surely as Basim was my brother. Jason is my son as surely as Jason was my brother's son. You have lost yours. For that, I deeply grieve, Jamaile. Our family has caused you a great loss; what we have both lost is incomprehensible."

"I blame you not, Akdemir," Jamaile offered. "Perhaps it was ordained, as your life was from the moment of your birth, as is all of ours."

"You have been a part of the Royal Household for as long as I can remember. Because of this…because of this…" Akdemir falters.

Jamaile knew what he was referring to. "Khalifa knew the consequence of stepping to the wrong side. He became greedy, saw wealth as power. It was a grave mistake. I did not know him as most know their sons. Perhaps this is why he did what he did."

Jamaile went further by saying that Khalifa knew what his fate would be, as every one of his men knows: *to cross the line, is to lose your life*. Khalifa chose wrongly, and he lost. When Jamaile accused him of sleeping with the enemy, it was probably more than he could endure. That was most likely when he hatched the plan that would deceive Jason into false security.

Khalifa assumed that Jason would not figure out that he was the liar and traitor. Although he never admitted doing the deed, he also never imagined that his disposal of Jason would go so wrong. Jamaile would take this secret to his grave if need be, to give Akdemir hope.

"Someone saw Sheyanna coming out of Jason's room the day he went missing," Jamaile stated finally.

"Is this a reliable person? Is there something to this?" Akdemir asked. "That does not seem unusual. Sheyanna often went into his rooms to make sure he had laundered clothes and to stock his shelves."

"What was unusual was she went in with a bundle of clothes and came out without a bundle," Jamaile added. "I will try to get videotapes of that day, but I do not hold out hope as Fariq had most of them destroyed."

"How can I contact Ellen?" Akdemir asked, changing the subject.

"You cannot try this. Calls can be picked up and traced. The thickness of the walls may also prevent such calls. Remain patient and secluded until it is safe to return to your position out in the palace. Then you will be able to make telephone calls."

"I see," he said sadly. "How can I get a message to Ellen?"

Jamaile sees the expression on Akdemir's face. "We wait to send any message until Fariq is gone and the Ministers have sent out a decree that you are safe."

"Yes, Jamaile, I understand what you are saying. I will listen to your guidance. Thank you." Akdemir felt more than a little guilty. Perhaps it was remorse at not being able to control specific events.

"Grief is like a stranger who has come to stay.
~ Carol Staudacher

Chapter Thirteen

The Blue and Silver

"**A**drian, I can't stand it any longer. Why doesn't Levi call you with a plan? It's been so long. Can't he let you go over there and look for Jason?"

"Ellie, they won't let me into their country. How am I supposed to get into the palace without permission? We have been over this at least a hundred times. I can't drop from the sky, now can I?"

"Why not, Adrian? They waltzed in here, didn't they?"

"Sweetheart, you are not rational today, and that was different. Don't you have something exciting to do to keep yourself busy?"

"There is nothing to do, Adrian."

He sighs, and says, "Can't you redo a room or something?"

"All the rooms are redecorated and finished, and there is nothing that needs attention. There is nothing to renovate."

"Maybe we need a little vacation," Adrian offers. "How about we plan that trip to Italy? How about Spain? We could use the time away."

"Hum, how about Paris?"

Adrian narrows his eyes at me, frowning, he says, "Is that so we can be closer to Saudi if we hear any news?"

"I thought that if we both don't have anything to do right now, it would be a good opportunity to go on the honeymoon that I made us miss."

Adrian's cellphone chirps and we both know its Levi by the ringtone. "Gotta take this, honey. How about we pick this up when I'm off the phone, okay?"

"Ask him what his plan is! Tell Levi how nuts this is making me!"

As we both walk toward the kitchen, he continues to walk out the back door where he jumps up on the fence in our secure area in the southern pasture. I pour myself a cup of coffee and wonder what Levi is telling Adrian, hoping that his illustrious team has put together a good plan of action.

I watch Adrian through the window near the sink. He stares blankly in my direction, but he doesn't move from his position on the fence, nodding his head occasionally. Some minutes later, he pockets his cellphone and walks solemnly toward the back door.

"What did your renowned leader have to say? Did he come up with a good plan that involves us going over there to find Jason?"

"He wants us to meet with one of the Alliance Ministers. He feels that now would be a good time to go, but it comes with a catch."

"I've been packing my suitcase in my head for a long time now, Adrian. What's happened? When do we leave? What's the catch?"

"No one said you could come, Ellie. You can't go with us; it's too risky."

"I'll take that risk."

Adrian hugs me. "The only reason I'm even going is the fact that Levi and I have been to the Royal Palace and we know our way around it. I hope you understand, honey."

"I don't. You know your way around the Royal Palace! That's a big laugh. I don't understand why you would go without me. I know my way around that place better than you do, Adrian."

"Levi will not consent to your going." He looks sad, and says, "He's adamant about that."

"You and I both know who got lost when we tried to navigate those hallways and stairs. You need a map, and you know it. You need me, Adrian!"

"No, we really don't need you. We'll have a map. Levi has one from our trip there; besides, the good Captain of the Clams promised to get one that includes the passageways and byways."

"You talked to Jam-ale? What does he say about all this? I was mad at him for a long time, but at least let me talk to one of them!"

"Ellie, I didn't talk to him, Levi did, and no one, not even Levi has talked with King Dimmy. He's in seclusion until this all gets straightened out."

"I can do so much more there than staying here, waiting. It's the waiting that's so hard, and the not knowing anything."

"Someone needs to hold down the fort, and that someone is you," Adrian says kissing my forehead.

"No, that is why Glen, Reed, and Nathan are here. They don't need me, Jason does. I don't know how much more I can stand of this. There's so much territory to cover. There's the humongous desert, and the oil tankers; he could be almost anywhere by now, Adrian. Find him, please find him before I go completely crackers. Everyone is mad at me for even letting him go there."

"You still got it, Ellie, did you say oil tankers?" Adrian cocks his head to think.

"Yes, I said humongous desert, too. Oh, now I know where you might be going with this. How can you survive in the desert without a whole bunch of stuff? Don't you need a tent and maybe some water?"

"That is not the direction I would go, but what if he somehow got on an oil tanker and he's headed home?" Adrian wonders.

Strange thoughts are running through my mind. "What if Jason can't let on who he is because the ninjas are following him?"

"Ellie, I told you they don't use those. Why do you keep going back to ninjas?"

Sighing heavily, I say slowly, "You won't believe me."

"Try me; sometimes your little things turn out to be real, Ellie."

"It's more than sometimes, Adrian. You know how I tell you that things come to me, even in the middle of the day, not only at night?"

"Go on," he says.

"One day, I thought someone was whispering to me. It was a little weird. There was something at the corner of my vision, and it was dressed all in black. Now before you start laughing, it was not one of our resident ghosts."

Adrian turns to leave, "Oh boy, here we go! I've got to get ready."

"Wait, Adrian, our ghosts are friendly, they aren't harmful. Adrian, wait! I got a bad feeling about this black figure, though."

Adrian is not amused and heads up the back stairs. "What did this black figure whisper to you?"

"It was too dark. But two nights ago, I had a whispered dream as I call them. The black figure came floating out of nowhere. One character spoke to me in a foreign language, but I couldn't understand it. Then suddenly the words started making sense. It said to '*come with me,*' and '*your fate has been sealed.*'

"What language was this black figure speaking?"

"I think it was Arabic. No, I take that back, it was Chinese. Now I'm not sure. Anyway, his eyes were mean-like; like a ninja's."

Adrian seems annoyed. "It's your mind playing tricks on you, Ellie. Maybe you're reliving the story Jason told when he was away studying martial arts. That's a possibility, right? It's called projection, I think."

"That was what, maybe five years ago? No, this was different. I knew you wouldn't believe me. Why do I even bother?"

"You bother because you care, Ellie. Come and help me pack."

As Adrian takes his suitcase out of the closet, I'm clinging to him. "I want to come with you. Please don't leave me here. I'll go stark raving crazy with worry."

Adrian gently pushes me aside to pull some items out of his dresser drawer, carefully placing them into his oversized bag. "No, you won't. You're not trained to come on a mission like this. You'll be in the way there. Why don't you try to do some research on your idea of the oil tankers?"

"Is that your way of placating me?"

He tries to humor me, and for a split second, I can see my worry reflected in his eyes. "Yes, it will keep your mind busy, Ellie. If you find something, call me right away, and I'll pass it on to Levi so his team can get on it like a tick on a dog."

"You mean a flea on a dog," I say, correcting him.

He laughs, saying, "Then it is a tick on a stick."

We both laugh, but we also know the gravity of the situation. Time is not on our side. The longer it takes to find Jason, the less chance we might have to see him alive.

"You'll call me as soon as you get there, right? Levi knows how anxious I am for news. I must know you are safe too. I don't know how much more of this I can stand!" My eyes fill and I am once again a sniveling idiot.

"Let me do my job, Ellie. By the way…" A car horn beeps, and I absently glance out the window to see Josh and Jake's jeep. "I made arrangements for special ops to be here while Levi and I are away."

"Why did you do that? Don't you trust me? Do you think I'll do something stupid while you're gone?" The light bulb goes off in my mind. "That's the catch, isn't it?"

He shakes his head, and says, "Levi pulled Josh and Jake from other duties to stay at Ashwood Stables while we're away, and that's all. We don't know what to expect. You'll have them here to help you."

"Help me do what? What are you expecting to happen here, without you?"

Adrian finishes packing and sets his case on the floor. "Didn't you tell me to put my money where my mouth is? Think of this as an exercise in faith, or maybe it's trust."

"You might think it's faith, but trust has nothing to do with it, Adrian, and neither does money."

He reaches out to me, taking my hand and says, "Yes, it does, my darling Clementine. You trust that I'll be alright because Levi will be with me. Think of this as an exercise in faith that we'll find Jason. Or at least find the thread to find him."

"Faith is all I have right now, Adrian. And hope. All I have is faith and hope."

Adrian hugs me tightly. "There you go; you keep on believing we'll find him."

"You better find him, Mr. CIA man, because I'm counting on you." My throat begins to constrict, and I'm about to break down. "You have to promise to call me every few hours or so…" Adrian pulls away from my grip. I realize that this is an unrealistic request. "Okay, call when you can, but you have to call me every day!"

"That I can do, sweet Ellie May, that I can do!"

As family members drift out of the house and barn toward Adrian's blue convertible, Mona shyly hands him a small plastic bag of her delicate little cookies. She tells him not to eat them all at once and then gives him a quick hug.

Mother is next, whispering something in his ear. After he hugs her, he turns to chat with Reed. Glen, Danny, and Mack begin to offer little bits of wisdom. They don't know how difficult this trip might be for him, but they want him to know they'll keep a close watch on Ashwood while he's gone.

As everyone heads back to what they were doing, Josh and Jake talk with Adrian as I stand near the car.

"Thanks for being here, guys. It means a lot. You'll report directly to Langley, so the information gets to Levi and me quickly, and vice versa," Adrian says.

"Levi briefed us on that. Sure wish we could come with you," Jake says.

"I'd like to have you, too, but Miss Ellie might try to sneak away, so keep a close eye on her, won't you?" Adrian says, throwing his bag in the trunk.

"You don't think she'll try to find Jason on her own, do you?" Josh asks.

"Naw," Jake says. "She'd want to be here if he came home."

Jake is watching me, as Adrian talks. "She thinks she can do a better job of finding him than Levi and me! She's a rootin tootin cowgirl who knows how to wield a gun, and if she gets a bee in her bonnet, she'll follow her lead like a bloodhound, so keep an eye on her."

Jake chuckles, "You've been out in the country too long, pal."

"Still here fellas and I'm not a cowgirl, an equestrian, a harness driver maybe, but not a cowgirl!"

Adrian turns toward me, saying, "Just keep an eye on her boys; she can be mighty slippery when she's wet or on a scent. And promise me, Ellie, that you'll tell them where you're going if you leave, okay, sweetie? I don't want to worry about you too!"

"If you let me come with you, you wouldn't have to worry, because I'd be right there with you!"

Adrian gives me a hug and peck on the cheek as he gets into his car. Then he rolls down the window and says, "If anything happens to her, guys, I'll hold you two personally responsible!" As his car moves down the driveway and onto the two-lane road, I'm immediately sad that he's left me here.

Josh touches my arm, and I turn to stare blankly at him. "Miss Ellen, can we go inside now?" he asks.

"Yes, of course. Let's get you settled in."

After taking care of Josh and Jake, I begin my research into oil tankers. What I've found so far is that an oil tanker is a merchant ship. My thoughts switch direction with the words merchant, merchant marine, mercenaries, and men for hire. Then there are the descriptions of the tankers themselves.

Research reveals that there are two basic types of tankers. The crude one transports large quantities of unrefined oil from the oil fields to refineries, while a product tanker transports smaller amounts of oil or petrochemicals *from* refineries to other locations. Then some tankers are classified by size which is either coastal or inland types.

These will determine how they move in and around water inlets, as some of these tankers are massive. Because of their size, they are too large to navigate most inlets and mostly go along the coastline, or they stay out to sea, bringing smaller cargo ships alongside to off-load their product.

Studying the information, much as I do the daily racing forms, something catches my eye. As I type furiously at the keyboard, the thought occurs to me that if I'm able to communicate with these people, perhaps we can broaden our search for Jason.

Selectively sending known information of what Jason might have worn the day he disappeared, I include his description, but don't attach a photo, making sure that I mention a sizeable reward that might lead to finding him.

About thirty minutes later, my email pings that several new messages have arrived. As I scroll through them, it takes a few minutes to decipher them. Some are gibberish, others are partly in English along with foreign words that are difficult to understand.

I press the DELETE button until most of them disappear, however, there is one that looks promising.

After Adrian cleared the tight security in the lobby of the CIA building where he used to work, familiar personnel who had remained from his time there greeted him warmly. They would be part of the investigation into the anomalous file known as the *Jason Thompson-Sellers Affair.* They were also available to lend their expertise for one of their own.

Levi had taken over a large conference room that was set up with a series of computers, listening devices, contraptions, monitors, keyboards, and whatever Jewels asked to be at his disposal. Some agents were sitting at the table near the windows talking with one another as Adrian strolled in. Most turned in his direction to wave as Levi shouted his name.

"I don't mind telling you, Adrian, we don't hold out much hope. We haven't received new information over the last six weeks. We aren't sure Akdemir's alive, much less if the information coming out of their camp is genuine. We've not heard from anyone from the Royal Palace, or from Jamaile for over a week," Levi declared.

"I understand, sir. Are we still on to meet with one of the Ministers?"

"Sorry to be the bearer of bad news, Adrian, but the Alliance Minister we were going to meet with is dead. His body was found around midnight according to the API report. There were no witnesses. Our sources close to the palace think we should cancel our trip there."

"What do I tell Ellen, Levi? If we go, she'll think we are at least trying to find Jason."

"I'm not at all sure we should still go. Under the circumstances, old friend, it doesn't look good," Levi stated flatly.

Adrian looked at his superior with pleading eyes. "If I don't try, Ellen will have my head! And I thought you were in it for the duration, old friend."

Levi blinked in understanding. "You have a point, but if we don't go, we'll still be alive. I don't think it's a good idea, that's all. You know, without being able to talk with either King Akdemir or the big man, it's hard to know what to do at this point."

Adrian thought that it was a good time to play his ace in the hole. "Don't you owe it to Francesca and Ellen? You knew about her Mr. Andress slash Mr. Basim slash Prince thing way before you told them. And let's not forget the little business of Ellen's father being the star of the CIA for all those years. Or the part you left out about you apprenticing with him at one time."

"So, it's blackmail, is it?" Levi sat down on a chair. "You do make a good argument to go."

Adrian nodded, and then said, "You might say that, sir."

"You're right, of course. We've secured some new equipment we'll take with us. But, I'm warning you right now, Adrian, that no one will be put into harms' way unnecessarily, understand?"

"Got it loud and clear, sir." Adrian turned away from Levi to search the faces in the bustling room when he spotted the team's technical wizard. "What did you come up with Jewels? Hope it's a crystal ball because we're gonna need one!"

"Hello, Mr. Adrian, we've been trying to get our information consolidated for you. I'll have it for you in a sec," Jewels said, going back to his knobs and gizmos.

Levi was standing next to Adrian. "We're going to take another team with us too, as a backup. The more people we can get in, the better we can cover our bases."

Adrian's cellphone pinged that a text message had come in. "It's Ellen. She says she's got something, would I call her. Do you think I should call her back right now?"

"I don't have a wife Adrian, but I have it on good authority, that if you ignore her during her crisis, she'll make your life miserable," Levi said smirking.

"For someone who doesn't have a wife, you happen to be pretty darn smart about that stuff." Adrian began to punch numbers on his cellphone, as he walked out of the room. "Hello Ellie, what's up?"

"Adrian, I found something. I received a message from someone who thinks he saw something to do with someone who fits Jason's description. You know how you said to research oil tankers? This guy was on a tanker not too long ago, and he thinks he knows where Jason might be."

"Where did the message originate from, Ellie? Does he want money for this information?" Adrian asked.

"He didn't say where he was, but he did ask what reward I was offering."

"How much does this person want, sweetheart?"

"Umm…the request is for twenty-five thousand US dollars in small bills," Ellen mumbled.

"And did he say he would give you the information as soon as your deposit clears his bank?"

"Yes…but Adrian, I believe him!"

A period of silence ensued until Adrian asked, "How many emails did you put out there before someone replied, Ellie?"

"I sent about a dozen. Two were curious about the reward and didn't have real information, but this is the only one that specifically asked for money. The guy has real information that he thinks he saw Jason."

"That isn't much to go on, Ellie."

"What if Jason is out there on some desert island or something? What if he has no way to communicate with us because his cellphone was back at the palace? What if he asked someone to do it for him? What if this guy is telling the truth?"

"Ellie, I don't believe this guy; the story is a little farfetched."

"Then I'm sorry to have bothered you."

Adrian's cellphone went silent. He walked back into the conference room shaking his head.

"You look a little dejected, Adrian. Trouble in paradise?" Levi asked.

"Ellie has this notion that Jason was on an oil tanker, or might have been, and there's someone asking her for twenty-five thousand dollars. This person might give her some information, but I don't think it means anything. Can we run the oil tanker scenario for her, in case she might be right?"

Levi turned toward Jewels who was fiddling with a sophisticated piece of equipment. "Sure Adrian. Jewels, would you get the team on that oil tanker thing right away? I'm sorry things worked out like this. I would do anything I could if it were my son that went missing."

"Thanks, Levi."

Have I lost my mind altogether? Did I honestly think Adrian would part with twenty-five grand on my say-so? I can't believe I hung up on him. I was so sure about this. Could I be that wrong? Am I so blinded by grief, that I'm now conjuring things out of nothing?

Get a grip, Ellen!

As I glance around my office, there is a small plaque on the bookshelf with the Serenity Prayer. Reaching for it, I begin to say it out loud.

'God, grant me the serenity to accept the things I cannot change, the courage to change the things I can, and wisdom to know the difference.'

Then I start to think of the past and how I used to walk around the paddock when something weighed heavily on my mind. Stepping out of my office, Rosie runs out of the barn to nuzzle my hand. How did she know I was coming outside? Must be the same thing that's making her whine.

"It's okay girl. There's nothing to worry about." Absently patting her head, I gaze up to see fluffy clouds roll slowly past the top of the spire on the Manor House. "Are you looking at the sky, too, Jason? Where are you? Come home right now!"

"Feelin sorry for yourself?" Glen's voice says near me.

"Yes, I guess I am. Did Adrian tell you to spy on me, old man?"

Glen puts a calloused hand on my arm. "It's not like ya to let things get ya down. We all promised Adrian we'd keep an eye on ya and we aim ta do that, Missy. Ya got somethin ya want ta talk about, ya come see me, okay?"

"Thanks, Dad, I'll do that. I came out to get some fresh air. I was thinking of *Didgeridoo*. What a loss that was, huh Glen? He might have made it."

Glen lets out a chuckle. "Made it ta what, Missy, the Grand Canyon, Carnegie Hall maybe?"

"You know what I mean. We might get to the championship yet, someday anyway."

He scratches his chin, then says, "Sure thing Missy, that might happen."

"Maybe not with *Lester* and *Raindrop*, but someday we might have the makings of a horse that can do it."

Glen knows what a long shot that is, but he also knows it's good for me to think of other things besides my missing son. Adrian must have cautioned everyone before he left that I may not be myself. Someone needs to keep a close eye on me. Mother let it slip that they are to notify him immediately should they even suspect anything is amiss.

"I'm here if ya need me."

"Thanks, Glen. I'll let you know."

Returning to my office, I begin a search for the poem that somehow also popped into my head when I was talking with Adrian. It's a poem about the Island of Life. After it finishes printing, I shove it under my desk blotter with the intention of sharing it with him when he comes home.

Another email message is waiting. I half read it thinking what a naïve person I must be when a thought starts to formulate in my muddled brain. Why not keep trying to communicate with someone on the tankers. Eventually, we might hit pay dirt. What could it hurt?

Redefining the parameters to restate my request, I change Jason's name to Lance, do not attach a photo as before, improving and adding different details.

Lance is six foot two inches, weighs approximately 190 to 220 pounds, has dark wavy hair, is a handsome Caucasian male that speaks English, Arabic, and a little French. He has a 1-inch scar on his right thigh and a birthmark near his left armpit in the shape of a carrot. There will be a generous reward should it lead to his whereabouts.

As I continue my research of oil tankers, I get a feel for which ones Jason could have been on or signed onto, when my thoughts start going in different directions. Working back from the time that I think he disappeared, I focus on which oil tankers would have been coming out of the Persian Gulf at the time Jason went missing. If I contacted some of them, would they allow me access to their manifests or crew lists?

When a storm warning begins to flash at the bottom of the screen, another thought starts to surface. Which tankers might head to safe territory during a big storm? Are Levi's teams doing any research like this? Are they going in this direction and haven't found anything yet and moved on? Figuring that there's no harm in pursuing this angle, I forge ahead. Didn't Adrian encourage me to do this to keep myself busy?

I have emailed five oil tankers with websites and contact information. Sending each of them the same message, along with Lance's new description and statistics, hoping that they'll see my urgency and respond quickly.

In the meantime, my research reveals six tankers were in the Persian Gulf either coming into it or out of it around the time of Jason's disappearance. The satellite images of the Gulf are so detailed that it shows these ships docked at various ports. I take a screenshot of this and print it.

On a piece of paper, I start to make notes of the three tankers who were waiting for crude oil to fill their holds. ***Apollo's Universe***, ***Seawise***, and the ***Alhambra***. The ***Hellespont*** was going out, while the ***Giant*** was coming in. That left the sixth one that has no name.

As I try to find out the name of the last tanker, my email pings. It's someone on the ***Seawise*** that is sure he saw Lance three weeks ago. I discard that one after a few minutes as the timeline is all wrong and go back to my research.

Refining my search to include tankers that might have slipped in or out of the Persian Gulf unnoticed, I discover that a mysterious transporter by the name of ***Sea Nymph*** was also in the area, but no one can confirm if it went into the Gulf.

Since there are no satellite images for this ship, it could have gone around Australia and back again many times. Is this the tanker with no name? I'm baffled as to how something of this size could go undetected.

If Levi's team was on it these last few weeks and they haven't turned up anything new, why do I think there's something to find? All I know is that I can't give up, or I will go completely insane! I cannot let Ravi's murder go without a resolution. I also cannot let Jason go…not like this!

Not before exhausting every avenue!

Whispered Dreams

Several thousand miles away, Adrian and Levi were in a nondescript hotel in a city not far from the Royal Palace to wait for word from Jamaile. For obvious reasons, its location was kept secret for fear there would be repercussions should the information fall into the wrong hands.

"I will not plan a memorial for Jason!" Ellen shrieked into the phone. "I will not, do you hear me? He is alive…you haven't found him yet!"

Adrian pocketed his cellphone and sat in silence for several minutes. "Wow, she's never yelled like that at me before."

Levi was pouring himself a drink from a flask he smuggled into the hotel. Then he filled another glass and handed it to Adrian. "Didn't sound like it went well," Levi said after a while. "Shall we chalk this up to a Mother's denial?"

"You heard that?" Adrian exclaimed.

Levi nodded. "This whole hotel heard your wife screaming!"

"I don't know what to say, Levi. Ellen has it in her head that Jason is still alive and keeps complaining that we're not doing all we can to find him."

Levi watched Adrian. "What set her off this time?"

"It must have been the funeral home, the minister, and a head-stone cutter that called within the last two hours to ask if they have Jason's name spelled correctly. Oh, and would she want to compose an obituary for the newspaper?"

"Come to think of it, I would have a hard time with this, too, if I lost my child and all those people called me."

Adrian sighed. "Ellie has these things; call them premonitions or episodes. She's had dreams about Jason and can't place where he is, but she knows he's alive!"

Levi tried to lighten the mood. "Didn't you say she was partly a witch?"

"Are you kidding, certainly not to her face?" Adrian said shaking his head.

"Yeah, that wouldn't be a good idea, would it? Can she at least tell us if he's here in Saudi or the desert, so we don't have to stay here too long?"

Adrian took slow sips from his glass. "No, she can't narrow it down like that."

"How do you think we handled things yesterday?" Levi said, tilting the liquid from his glass into his mouth. "Give me your gut feeling about it."

Adrian drained the contents of his glass, stood up, and crossed the room to stare out the window. "I don't know. Sometimes I think Jamale is waiting for us to do something wrong so he can whack us with his evil looking sword. He could be putting on an act, though."

"I don't think he'd do that, Adrian. He is big and all that, but I don't get the feeling that he would harm you. And I was talking about Fariq, not Jamaile. Are you having trouble concentrating?" Levi took their empty glasses to the makeshift mini-bar to add ice, splashing vodka and orange juice into them.

"Yes. This whole thing is making us all crazy. Ellen won't go to a shrink, and no one can persuade her that Jason is dead."

Levi considered something. "You know, Akdemir may already be dead. We haven't seen or talked with him." Levi handed Adrian his glass and sat down on the sofa.

Adrian gazed at his wristwatch, noting the time difference. "No, if I were a betting man…"

"I've heard how you gamble, Adrian," Levi laughed. "How much money have you won at the racetrack? Yourself, I mean, with no help from Miss Ellen?"

Adrian smirks at his superior. "I'm still learning how to do it! Here's what I think, I bet that Akdemir is alive and living somewhere very close by and Jam-ale doesn't want us to know where that is."

"That could be, but he said that the king was out somewhere on holiday."

"That might be a diversion. Dimmy might even be inside the palace walls like Ellie thinks he is," Adrian added.

"How come she can pinpoint the King's whereabouts and not Jason's?"

"I don't know how it works, Levi. She merely said she could see him somewhere inside something and it reminds her of the Pyramids in Egypt, only she swears it isn't Egypt."

Levi pondered this. "If that palace were shaped a little differently, it could be what she's been talking about."

"Come on, Levi, there are a bazillion passageways and tunnels and all kinds of places to hide in that place. It wouldn't surprise me if we found Jason there, too, except Ellie doesn't think he's at the palace."

Adrian abandoned the window and went back to sit down to drum his fingers on the end of the sofa.

"Where does she think he is?" Levi asked.

"That's just it, Ellie can't give a better description than what I told you. She says it doesn't look like the Royal Palace or Saudi. Look, I can't squelch her enthusiasm, Levi. Faith and hope are all she has of ever seeing Jason again."

Levi sighed. "Tell you what, my good man, we'll hit this thing again in the morning. We've almost exhausted our resources and haven't had any new leads. It might be time to give it up. Jewels has *nada*. They traced all communications, checked all airlines in and out, all trains, boats, both large and small, and any other way out of Saudi and elsewhere, and there is no trace of how Jason would have gotten out of here."

"Have we tried dog sled? Or the underground tunnels that lead to the ocean?"

Levi shook his head. "Are you serious? Underground tunnels, really Adrian?"

Adrian looked thoughtful. "I'm not ready to give up yet, how about camel train…"

"I believe you are out of options, my friend."

Adrian sat ramrod straight. "Wait now, isn't there a camel train that goes east to China to get spices?"

"The spices go in cargo tankers now." Levi opened his eyes and slowly apprehended. "Tankers…oil tankers; didn't we already consider that angle, Adrian?"

"I thought Jewels did a data search on oil tankers and he didn't turn up anything of significance."

"They did, he did. When you told me what Ellen said about paying money for information, I thought we should at least check it out. Kelly and Drew went into the field some time ago, and they reported nothing noteworthy. They did say they wanted to stay in the area as some smuggling issues are plaguing small islands. It's certainly worth another look."

"How could Jason have even gotten onto an oil tanker from where he was?" Adrian speculated. "The Persian Gulf is miles away from the Royal Palace."

Levi took a sip from his glass. "Someone would have had to help him get there."

"After he got there, he would have needed identification. Jam-ale said Jason's wallet was still in his room along with his computer, cellphone, and presumably his passport," Adrian said.

"Jason sent a message about two weeks before he disappeared. He said that a Khalifa person was causing problems. He wanted to come home, Adrian."

"Why didn't you tell me, Levi?"

"Because he said he'd contact us again if we were needed. He never did, so we thought everything was okay."

"I don't think I can tell Ellen this. She'd be serving both of our heads on a silver platter," Adrian mused.

"Then you're gonna like what I have to say even less," Levi replied.

"There's more you haven't told me?"

"You weren't part of our day to day operations then, Adrian."

"But this concerned me and my family!"

"Then hold off your criticism until you've heard it all, okay?"

"Go ahead. I promise I won't kill you yet," Adrian said with a straight face.

Levi drew in a deep breath, letting it out slowly. "May I remind you that nothing I say shall ever leave this room?" Adrian nodded in agreement. "Signals came from Jason's watch that we can't explain. Jewels thought at the time that someone was playing with the face of it and it finally went silent."

"Go on."

"Kelly and Drew went to the location after we pinpointed where the signal originated, but it finally stopped. No one they questioned knew about it and they reasoned it was possible Jason sold it to someone, or he could have lost it. More likely, it was stolen or he was never there in the first place. Jason's wrist was not attached to it anyway."

"Where were the signals coming from, could they determine that? Can't we check it out to satisfy Ellen's curiosity? Okay, my curiosity then."

"It was a little strange, Adrian. We thought we had him, but then the signal began to move all over the Pacific Ocean. After a time, it went dead. A whale could have swallowed it for all we know."

"Pacific Ocean? How could, wow, we should have put a chip in Jason's head like Ellen wanted to do," Adrian said sadly.

"Okay, it wouldn't hurt to try again. Let's run another search on which tankers might have been near the Persian Gulf at the time of

Jason's disappearance, but this time, let's change the parameters to include some other data."

"I think that's what Ellie was working on; a theory about them anyway. She hasn't come up with anything, or she would have called. If you think it will do any good, let's try again. I'm sure Ellie will appreciate that."

Levi and Adrian began to shuffle through the mound of information that was littering the coffee table.

"Have you heard from Kelly and Drew lately?" Adrian asked after a while.

"No, not for some time. Kelly and Drew are resourceful people that know their way around. They might dig something else up that we're working on, but I can't go into detail. It's classified, even for your level. I know that look, Adrian. You want to go back to the Royal Palace, don't you?"

"There has to be a way out of there. Why don't we get in touch with Jam-ale? I have an idea," Adrian pronounced.

Jamaile was not at all pleased that Adrian and Levi insisted on a return to the Royal Palace, as they were in the middle of what he called the final battle to remove Fariq and his men. Fariq discovered the false documents that were planted some time ago and almost had a coronary. The Royal Alliance Ministers then declared Fariq could never assume anything regarding the Royal Palace, as he had defiled the decree.

The authentic ancient documents, written in such a manner as to exclude any/all persons who used force, excess or otherwise, would automatically be bypassed. These persons would be removed bodily, along with any of their followers, where they would stand before a tribunal to receive their punishment by the highest courts available.

After a designated Alliance Minister read the statement to Fariq, his removal happened quickly and quietly. Any remaining followers were apprehended, some merely disappeared. After his disposition, Jamaile took Adrian and Levi along some of the secret corridors that led out of the Royal Palace.

Could this be how Jason might have gone, smuggled out by Turlock perhaps or someone he trusted? Jamaile explained that he and his men found no sign of anything to suggest things were out of place. They conducted a thorough investigation and found no scratches to indicate anyone used a knife to access the exit, and found no chips or dust on the floor to suggest anyone was in the passage at all. All routes exhausted, they lead nowhere.

As the months dragged on, the longer it went with no new information, the more Levi reasoned the investigation should end. But the real reason this was coming to a swift close was that higher authority had said it needed to stop. It was then that Adrian and Levi decided that enough was enough.

With a heavy heart, Levi asked Jamaile to inform His Royal Highness, whom no one had seen for several months, to issue a new status for the missing prince.

The official word from the Royal Palace was that Prince Jason was no longer missing, but presumed dead. If he were alive, he would have contacted his mother long before now.

Since there had been no contact with Jason or new information in the year since his disappearance, Adrian felt that the family could put this all behind them and move on with their lives.

All except Ellen, because she refused to believe Jason was gone.

"Sweetheart…Levi and I are coming home," Adrian exclaimed.

"What?" Ellen tried to control her voice, "You can't give up now! You haven't tried hard enough!"

"We have all come up empty. Levi has exhausted every avenue, we have tried everything, and Jam-ale has no new leads here. I'm sorry, Ellie…we tried. Honestly, sweetheart, we tried."

"You have choices.

A single choice, whatever that choice may be,

you have to live with the consequences it brings.

That's all. A choice."

~ G. Gutierrez

Chapter Fourteen

Whispered Dreams

Trying to keep myself busy and immersed, so I don't have to think about how I feel, I'm at my computer early to do research again. Endless messages are now streaming in that I'll have to decipher. It's evident that there are some very lonely sailors on those very huge tankers.

Some of the email messages are brief, while others are so long I delete them, as they have made up so much stuff it can't be right. Most all of them are from men who have been with the Merchant Marines for a long time.

Then there are those who have only been away from home a short while. Some express sorrow, because they had no idea what they were getting into when they signed on, while others are anxious to get the hell '*off this barge and never get on one again.*' Perhaps, the fact they can't set foot on land for so long is the troubling factor.

Sifting through the emails, one catches my attention. It's from a man who claims that someone drugged him, then severely beat him, and then they put him on a tanker bound for Hong Kong. Wasn't there a movie not too long ago that had this same plot?

The horrible realization hits me. This scenario could have happened to Jason. If it did, he could be almost anywhere by now! The ping of another email brings me back to my monitor screen. It's a message from a woman, and it stands out from all the others. Replying to her along with two others, I again wait for their response. When there is no quick reply, I turn off my computer to sulk.

When Adrian returns home, he mentions that the family seems more sullen than usual. I try to explain that we don't blame him for coming back without Jason, we are, however, not happy with his new status of being presumed dead.

As we go through the motions of everyday life, it becomes apparent that most of us are also going through the various stages of grief. How can any of us get past this, if I can't let it go?

Adrian tries to convince me to talk with Dr. Laurel Stevens, but I don't want to spill my guts to a total stranger.

If I can't cope with my nightmares, then I'll consider it.

Adrian and Mother went ahead and planned a commemorative service for Jason, even though I told them both I would not attend. I can't find the strength to get dressed or even react to this ridiculous situation, because they have decided Jason is never coming home.

"Ellie. Ellie. Ellie, my little sweetheart, it's time to go downstairs. Everyone is waiting for you."

"Go away, Adrian."

"They understood why you didn't want to come to church, but honestly, you need to come down now and at least thank everyone for coming."

Adrian holds my hand and tries to coax me into moving. A black sheath dress is draped across the bed, black pumps are on the floor, but I don't remember putting them there.

"You can thank them for me. I'm not coming down."

"The Minister is here. Francesca and Mona are serving coffee. You missed a lovely service. Ellie, please talk to me."

"I have told you a hundred times, Jason is not dead. We haven't found him yet. I don't want to have this conversation with you. Why did you have a service for someone who isn't dead?"

Ever since Adrian returned from Saudi with Levi, it has been a nonstop bombardment of when to do the memorial service, when will I choose a tombstone, what about a church service, how about the programs, candles, and I found it to be so tedious I couldn't talk.

I have rejected the stories they have told me. I have also refused to get dressed most mornings, keeping to myself, trying to ignore most of the family, who do not side with my way of thinking. Everyone thinks that Jason is dead. The only one who does not get on my case is Mother.

"He's gone, Ellie. We can't bring him back, no matter how hard we try."

"Show me the body, Adrian. If he's dead, then show me his body!"

"I've told you, Ellie…sometimes there is no body. Please don't yell at me. I'm only trying to help you. Come on, honey, I'll help you get dressed. Dimmy is here, and he wants to talk with you."

Trying to digest this news, I become so livid that I want to scream! I know that I must confront the man who not only took my son away; he is most certainly behind what has happened to him. "When did he get here, Adrian? Why didn't you tell me he was here?"

"I did try to tell you, but you told me to go away. I've been trying to talk to you for weeks, and you brushed me off." Adrian looks dejected.

I fight hard not to cry, then realize Adrian is only trying to help. "I'm so sorry to have done that. Help me get dressed and I'll come downstairs. I want to give that bastard, I want to slug him in the face; maybe shoot him where he stands."

"Oh no, Ellie, please. I wouldn't suggest that. Jam-ale's here too. And you know what he's like, overprotective, I would say. Please promise me that you won't cause a scene?"

"I can't reach Jam-ale's ugly face. How about I punch him in the stomach instead? Why would there be a scene Adrian? We entrusted Jason into his safekeeping and they both promised to keep him safe! And now everyone thinks he's dead? Why would there be a scene over that?"

Grabbing the dress off the bed, I head toward the bathroom to get ready for the confrontation I want to have with Dimmy. Suddenly overcome with emotion, the stranger in the mirror gives me pause. She would never allow the outside world to see her sweat, never back down from a fight, and most certainly would pick herself up and dust herself off and start all over again.

As I look in the mirror, the dull eyes that stare back is no longer that person. Am I a broken spirit? Have the events of the last few years finally taken their toll? Scrubbing my face and applying some makeup, I brace myself for what is coming.

Jason would want me to go on, so I must be strong for him. I'm shaking slightly as we slowly descend the stairs. Adrian mentions what sacrifice Jam-ale made for the Royal Household, but it has little effect on me.

As Adrian brings me into the living room, I glance around at family members, our church friends and Minister Smith, Adrian's CIA colleagues, and neighbors who have come to pay their respects. Time seems to stand still. Mother stiffens, and Mona stops serving as Dr. Stevens lowers her cup to the coffee table. Is she here to subdue me if I step over the traditional code of conduct?

Did someone warn the crowd I might do something stupid?

King Dimmy stands near the fireplace. He is in the exact place he was standing the morning of that surprise visit some years ago. The hand wearing the silver and blue stone ring rests on the mantle as he stares into the fireplace. Is it the one he gave Jason, or did he have another one made for himself? Big Jam-ale stands close to him. He gently taps Dimmy's shoulder, and he turns to face me. His face registers sadness.

"My dearest Ellen," he says, moving toward us. Dimmy reaches for my hand, but I can't stand the thought of his touch and back away from him. "You came to talk with me. Thank you. I know that you will never forgive me. I do not know if I can forgive myself for what has happened."

"Jason is not dead!" I turn toward the people in the room and say, "Thank you all for coming, but you all came for nothing." Turning back to Dimmy, I decide that the right time has come to confront him. "You said you would take care of him. You promised me you would take care of him and that no harm would come to him. You promised!" When Dimmy tries to explain, I put my hand up to stop him. "I do not want to hear anything from you. You will listen to me."

As I say this, Jam-ale sucks in a breath and makes that incredible 'tsk' sound I loathe. Out of the corner of my eye, Mother is inching her way through the crowd as Melanie takes her gently by the hand, and then Curlie reaches out to coax their grandmother to sit on the sofa next to them.

Adrian clutches my arm but does not pull me away. "I do not want to hear another word out of you, Dimmy. There is absolutely nothing you can say that will fix this! Unless you can produce my son or tell us where he is, you are not welcome here. Get out of my sight!"

Adrian leans in to whisper, "Ellie, they came out of courtesy for our family. Please stop. You're embarrassing us."

"I'm not finished yet." Ignoring Adrian, I move in front of Jam-ale.

Adrian is concerned about what might come out of my mouth, but he won't let go of my arm. "Please don't yell, not in front of everyone. We can do this out in the hallway or your office if you like, okay?"

"In a minute." I'm craning my neck to look into Jam-ale's face. "You were charged with my son's safety. It was your life for his, remember? What do you have to say for yourself, Jam-ale?"

Without blinking, he unceremoniously bows his head, saying, "My son, Khalifa gave his life for Jason."

"What did you do with him? Did you send him away? Is it somewhere safe where we can't find him? Answer me, damn it!" Adrian begins to yank at my arm, then glances in Dr. Steven's direction, but I stand firm. "What did you do with my son?"

Dimmy's eyes fill, and he puts a hand on Jam-ale's arm, nodding his head slightly. Jam-ale is somber, not his typically gruff self. "I do not know where Prince Jason is, Ma'dame Sell ers, none of us know this."

"May we talk privately, my dear Ellen, perhaps in your office?" Dimmy pleads.

"Good idea!" It's difficult to control my emotions; however, the thought of making a more significant scene seems most appealing right now.

Adrian quickly leads us out, then glances back at our Minister who is at a loss for words. "Sorry about this everyone. Can you carry on without us for a few minutes?"

Stopping in the hallway, unsure of where I want to be right now, Adrian is right behind me. "May I have a drink, Adrian?"

"Sure, Ellen," he says, leaning in to whisper, "Please, give the guy a chance to explain, will you?"

Adrenalin pumping, I say, "Only us, and no one else will be in there! Jam-ale stays out, or it's all done right now!"

Adrian must realize that my Glock is locked into my office and stops suddenly. "Don't pull any funny business, Ellen. It will compound the situation. If they have information…if you do something unthinkable, that chance goes away. Promise me that you won't do anything stupid." Adrian says this rather sternly as Levi, Josh, and Jake step into the hall near the stairway.

"I promise. I left the key upstairs anyway. Don't worry. I'm not going to do anything stupid. How about that drink, darling?"

"My dear Ellen, it will be you and me, no one else," Dimmy speaks quietly.

"Josh and Jake will stay with Jam-ale while I go be with our guests." Adrian nods to his friends and colleagues. "Stay in the library while they talk. Come on Levi. I don't think we'll have any trouble now."

After Josh closes the door, Dimmy sits on the sofa as I pace back and forth in front of the windows. Many cars fill the long driveway, and I suddenly feel sad about the reason they are here. It's quiet for so long that I think Dimmy has left when he startles me.

"I know you blame me, Ellen. I know you were against Jason coming to be with us at the Royal Palace. I did not know this would happen to him. We took every precaution…"

I turn toward him as his head drops into his hands. "Why don't I believe you? You promised me you would keep him safe. You sat right there on that sofa and told me you would keep him safe once he was *inside* the palace!"

"I cannot change what happened. I wish I could, but I cannot." Akdemir lifts his head as tears fall from his eyes.

"If you had done everything, you would know where my son is right now!"

"We did everything possible, Ellen. There were factions we had not thought of, and they were able to enter the palace without…"

"You did everything…factions my eye. You failed, and you can't admit it. What was the point of all that martial arts training, if he couldn't defend himself? Can you tell me that? What was the freaking point?"

Akdemir puts a handkerchief to his face. "We do not know that he did not defend himself. We hoped that he made it past the palace walls. Perhaps there were too many of them, and they overpowered him."

"I'm not buying this for one minute. Do you know that for certain or is that conjecture on your part?"

"We do not know where Jason could have been taken. All indications are that Fariq's men found him and removed him. No one has told us otherwise. You know about Turlock and…"

"How could they have taken him…right under your elaborate security noses? I couldn't have sneezed without your people knowing how many times and at what time I did it!"

Akdemir sniffs, "Ellen you must believe me when I say we did everything we could."

"Have you gone over all of the security tapes thoroughly to see if anything is amiss?"

He replies sadly, "The tapes were destroyed along with the men who viewed them."

"I don't think you looked hard enough. Why didn't you let Adrian and his people come there when you first discovered he was missing?"

Akdemir wipes at his eyes again. "Turlock and his whole family were murdered…Jamaile's son also lost his life…there were countless atrocities perpetrated…"

"I can't believe the drama your family has caused mine. I should have fought harder to keep Jason here with us. You should have been more attentive and kept him safe. He could be anywhere on this earth!"

It could even be Timbuktu, I realize suddenly.

"But he is not, Ellen. The man Jamaile captured said that Jason was taken from the Royal Palace and…" Akdemir chokes on these words, and it takes a few minutes to compose himself. "All indications point to his death…"

My eyes fill with tears, and I start to shake with rage. I will not give him the satisfaction of seeing me cry and 'will' them to stop. When Akdemir stands up, he reaches for me, but I back away from him. He opens his mouth to speak, but I continue to back away.

"My dearest Ellen…"

"You have lost the right ever to address me that way. Don't come near me, you monster! I will never forgive you for what you put my family through. Go away Dimmy, and take your henchman with you!"

"I understand," he says quietly.

"You are not welcome here. I want you to leave right now! We are no longer your family. Get out."

"Thank you for talking with me, Ellen. I shall honor your wishes and will leave immediately. I am…so very…regretful," Akdemir chokes out the words.

"You seem to say that every time we meet. I hope I never see you again. I hope you burn in hell for what you've done! You have brought nothing but misery to my family. I wish you had kept Basim/Ravi a family secret and never involved us in the first place! You are dead to me." I turn my back to him to gaze out the window. Not long after, my office door opens and then closes quickly.

A few minutes later, someone knocks, and when I don't answer, the door opens, then closes again. When I turn around, there is a cup of hot tea, three little cookies, and a folded piece of paper. Tears begin to roll down my face as I start to read the paper on the tray.

THE STAGES OF GRIEF (By Carol Staudacher, Beyond Grief)	Prayer of St. Francis
DENIAL; This is a normal reaction to the immediate loss and must not be confused with a lack of caring. As the impact of the loss is slowly acknowledged, the disbelief will diminish. **BARGANING**; People can become preoccupied about how things could have been done to prevent the loss or how things could have been handled. Remorse or guilt may interfere with the healing process if this stage is not properly resolved. **DEPRESSION**; This is a common stage after it is realized the true extent of the loss. Some signs of depression may include sleep or appetite disturbances, lack of energy and concentration, loneliness, emptiness, isolation, self-pity, as well as crying spells. **ANGER**; This is also a natural reaction if the person feels helpless and powerless. This anger can come from a feeling of abandonment by the person who has died, or be angry with a higher power. **ACCEPTANCE;** This is the last stage of the grieving process. In this stage, the person comes to terms with how they feel and accept the fact that the loss has occurred. Healing can now begin when the loss is integrated into the person's set of life experiences.	Lord, make me an instrument of your peace, Where there is hatred, let me sow love; Where there is injury, pardon; Where there is doubt, faith; Where there is despair, hope; Where there is darkness, light; Where there is sadness, joy. O Divine Master, Grant that I may not so much seek to be consoled, as to console; to be understood, as to understand to be loved, as to love. For it is in giving that we receive. It is in pardoning that we are pardoned, and it is in dying that we are born to Eternal Life. Amen."

Whispered Dreams

Turning to gaze out the window again, *Lester* and *Raindrop* graze lazily in the paddock. *Lester* has his head through the fence, munching on a tall grass weed. A limousine near the garages moves toward the portico where I observe Dimmy and Jam-ale getting into it for what I hope is his final visit.

I don't know how long I stand at the window, but most of the cars have left, and only a few familiar ones remain. It probably means that Jason's wake is over. Everyone will carry on with his or her lives as usual, because, after all, they still have their sons.

Have I lost the battle to keep my sanity? The one that started the day Ravi died, and what's been struggling to the surface ever since? Is there an invisible hand that's holding my head under water? Am I flailing and no one can help me, not even Adrian?

It doesn't seem quite real to me. Could I still be in the drug-induced stupor and will wake up in Chicago? If this is a dream, then I want to wake up right now!

But this is not a dream. It is every mother's nightmare. I wish now that I had thrown something at Dimmy, but what would that have solved? Did I say everything I wanted to? Was I awful to him? Should I apologize for my behavior? What must my family think?

I have decided not to apologize for my actions or words, and I will not let go of my thinking that Jason is still alive. Who am I angrier at right now, is it Ravi, Dimmy, or myself? Why didn't I fight harder to keep Jason here with us? Would he have gone anyway, if I asked him not to?

I open the door and walk toward the library table. The items placed on top of it were not there when I went into my office. Adrian is waiting in one of the chairs near the fireplace and stands when he sees me.

Gently lifting the blue and silver scarf that covers Jason's swords and knives, there is also a pile of folded clothes, boots, and shoes. Fingering Jason's shirt he wore for horse shows, I touch his cellphone and laptop. Also on the table is a costume made from dazzling blue and silver material, which has small silver bells that dangle from the sleeves.

Then everything starts to blur as my heart begins to hurt. Adrian stands beside me, and we hold each other for a long time. "My heart is breaking, Adrian. Jason can't be gone. Jason can't be dead! He had so much to live for, and we wanted so much for him. How could all that training be for nothing?"

"Dimmy and Jam-ale left a while ago. I don't think they'll ever come back here. He's a broken man," Adrian whispers. "He shook my hand

and said to let him know if we ever needed anything, we shouldn't hesitate to ask."

"He should feel bad for what he's caused." I'm trying my best to control my emotions. "And he should feel very guilty over this."

"He takes all blame and responsibility for what happened to Jason. He intimated that he was sorry for much more than that. Jam-ale lost his son over this, too, Ellie. They didn't give me the specifics, but he was Jason's bodyguard. He must have been slain trying to protect him. There is still the possibility that Jason made it out of the palace because there were no other bodies found with Khalifa's."

"That doesn't help. It's easy to say I'm sorry. But it doesn't bring Jason home to us, now does it?"

"No, it doesn't bring him back, but you still have a family who needs you now. Levi and the others are all in the living room waiting for you. Francesca especially is worried about you. Melanie says she'll stay for another few days. Would you like that?"

"I can't talk to any of them yet, Adrian, tell them I'm okay. I need some time alone. Did I do something stupid in front of everyone?"

"No, you said pretty much what I was thinking. I would have said it, but you beat me to it. I would have liked to punch Dimmy for you, but he was genuinely upset. It wouldn't have been professionally of me anyway."

"Thanks, Adrian. Have I neglected you too? If I have, I am very sorry. I'll do better in the future. Jason might be missing, but he's still here in our hearts and always will be."

"That's right, sweetheart. No one can take that away from you."

"How long am I going to feel this sadness, Adrian?"

"No one can predict that, Ellie. Minister Smith mentioned that there's no magic formula for grief. No one knows how long it'll take, but the best advice he can bestow is to love and support you. He knows you have a strong faith and courage."

"That was a nice thing for him to say."

Adrian reaches to pick up a small package. "Dimmy brought you a gift. He thought you'd want to have this."

I push the small package back to Adrian, "I don't want anything more from that man."

"Ellie, he said Jason was going to send it home to you."

"In that case, I'll open it." As I pull the ribbon and paper away, the silver engraved picture frame holds a photo of Jason. He is resplendent in his blue and silver costume; a matching scarf is draped around his shoulders, not across his face. When I start to laugh, Adrian gets concerned.

"What's so funny?"

"Jason has a mustache, and he looks remarkably like Ravi."

Jason sits astride an enormous Arabian Stallion. The engraved plate on the front of the frame reads, *Prince Jason T-Obagur and Champion Basim's Pride II*.

"I suppose the T means Thompson. Jason looks happy here, doesn't he? Maybe he was happy there. Maybe the bad men got to him and Dimmy is telling the truth. Maybe there was nothing he could have done."

"Jason does look happy in the photo," Adrian speculates.

"I haven't been myself lately, so I can't get a good feeling about this. Jason wanted to go, you know." Adrian hugs me again. "I don't think I could have stopped him. He would have gone anyway."

"Ellie, you couldn't have prevented this. Doesn't Carmen have something to do with it?"

"I think the word you're looking for is Karma. Oh, you're trying to cheer me up and make me laugh."

"Yeah, is it working?" he says sweetly.

"Karma has a unique definition. If I have the meaning correct, it means that this is the sum of Jason's actions and the previous states of his existence. It also means that his fate was sealed from the moment of his birth and none of us could have prevented what happened to him."

"Then we can assume that you are going to be okay, Ellie?"

"Maybe, but I can still be crazed about it for a little while longer, can't I?"

Adrian kisses my forehead. "We will always remember Jason, and we will always celebrate his life, Ellie."

"Yes, but can I have a few more days to get over it?"

"Take as long as you need, sweetheart. There is no deadline, remember?"

"Deadline? Really Adrian? You couldn't have used a better word?"

Hanging his head, he says, "Sorry sweetheart, that was thoughtless."

"Ahhhhhh!"

"Ellie. Ellie, wake up."

When I open my eyes, I'm sweating and shaking uncontrollably.

"You were yelling, and you'll wake the entire household up!" Adrian gently shakes me.

"I saw him, Adrian! I saw Jason in my dream. He's okay, but I don't know where he is. He's alive! Why am I soaking wet?"

"Sit there a minute, honey." Adrian begins to rummage through my dresser drawers, throwing me a pair of pajamas. "I'll get you some juice. Be right back."

Adrian goes to the kitchenette down the hall from our room. He returns to see me sitting up with tears running down my face. Handing me a small glass, he says, "Here, drink this."

"Wow! Adrian, my dream was so real. It was like Jason was standing right in front of me telling me he's okay. I'm okay, he kept saying, I'm okay."

"It's a dream, sweetheart. It'll go away. Try to go back to sleep."

Adrian turns off his bedside light and snuggles with me, but I no longer want to sleep. I want to concentrate on my dream so I can memorize all the details. I want to home-in on Jason, because I know he's alive. I don't know where he is. Someone is whispering a dream to me, I can feel it. Is it Jason? Perhaps our house ghosts know how to communicate with him.

"Ellie, I don't exactly doubt what you say, but…"

"I told you what I saw, Adrian. You don't believe me, do you?"

"I want to believe you," Adrian sighs. "We must all remain steadfast and patient."

"Patient? How much more patient can I be? I still want to jump on a plane and go over there myself! You know, retrace his steps, look in places where he'd go, that kind of thing. I seriously doubt that anyone did that. You didn't, did you?"

"I know, sweetheart. I wish I could make this all better. Why don't you go and talk with Dr. Stevens? I think she could help you."

"I'll think about it."

Maybe it's time to do that. Perhaps Dr. Stevens can help me get past the dreams that keep whispering that Jason is out there. Then again, maybe I don't want them to stop. They seem to be my only link to him.

Several days later, I am in Dr. Steven's office when she asks me to get comfortable, saying that I can recline on the sofa, maybe remove my shoes while she offers me a cup of herbal tea, as soft music plays in the background.

"You think I'm delusional, don't you?"

"I don't remember saying that to you, Ellen."

"Then what do you think is wrong with me, Dr. Stevens?"

"Why don't you call me Laurel, it's less formal, don't you think? I believe that I assessed that you're going through a very rough time right now. It helps to talk to someone about how you feel instead of pushing it out of your mind. Nothing gets resolved that way."

I take small sips of my tea, glancing around at the spacious office that has several official-looking framed diplomas on the walls, thinking I should have stayed home. "You and Adrian must have discussed stuff. How am I supposed to ignore the way I feel? I know my son is alive."

"Ellen, I have not discussed you with your husband. The only thing we have talked about is the fact that your son is missing and you might be having a hard time facing the fact that he is gone." She begins to press her lips together as she writes something in her notebook.

"He hasn't told you our back-story? He never mentioned that my first husband met with a terrible accident?"

"Why no, Ellen, he never mentioned that." Laurel looks genuinely surprised at this.

"He never mentioned he's with the CIA? Did he say anything about us being in the Federal Witness Protection Program, anything like that?"

"He did say he is an agent for the CIA, but frankly he never mentioned you were in that program."

"And you know nothing of how we all came to live in Virginia?"

"No, Ellen, we didn't discuss anything remotely related to those things. Look, I know you don't want to be here, but I think I can help you. There is the patient/doctor confidentiality code that I adhere to, but Adrian certainly did not say anything about those things. If he did, we would keep that quiet anyway."

Dr. Laurel's office is neat-as-a-pin. One of her diplomas is from the American Board of Psychiatry and Neurology, Inc.

"So, do you subscribe to the Freudian Theory that all men wish they could snuggle with their mothers?"

"We are not here to discuss my qualifications, Ellen. We are here to discuss how you can overcome what troubles you. It sounds as if you have some repressed emotions. Perhaps in time, we can get to the bottom of it, and you can move on with your life."

"So, nothing I say here today goes out of this room, then?"

"No, it stays right here, Ellen, you have my word on that," she says, smiling sweetly.

"Will you tape record our sessions?"

Dr. Laurel stands, coming around to where I have plopped myself down on her sofa to sit on a chair near me. Talking in a calming voice, she says, "I tape all my sessions. It helps to remember everything we talk about and I can play it back when you aren't here. Then I can make appropriate notes to address with you later. I cannot recall everything Ellen, can you?"

"No, that's why I write everything down myself. I tried to keep a journal for Jason when he left for Saudi, but then he went missing, and it made me cry every time I wrote his name. How much time do we have today?"

"As much as two hours, then we can schedule regular times weekly, at your convenience."

"If Adrian agreed that you could help, then he knows what I'm going to say to you. Buckle up Doctor; it's going to be a bumpy ride."

Dr. Stevens gets quite an earful this first session, stopping me occasionally to ask if I can repeat something. I did tell her right from the beginning that it was going to be an unbelievable story, found only in annals of journals of undercover operations or suspense novels. She is slowly coming to realize that it's the tip of the iceberg.

And I do tend to agree with her assessment that first time I came to talk with her. The more I tell her, the better I feel. It doesn't solve anything, except that it helps me cope, allowing me to work things out so they can be put into perspective. I do feel better mentally.

The dreams, however, have not stopped.

The alarming thing about them is that they are increasing in frequency.

"Life sometimes seems like you're stranded
on a desert island waiting for the ship
to come and rescue you
when no one knows you're missing..."
~ Beth Ann

Chapter Fifteen

The Republic of Vanuatu

The Republic of Vanuatu is an island archipelago that comprised approximately eighty-two small islands. Only sixty-five of them were inhabitable. The islands were composed of volcanic rock and sporadic beaches; some were sand, others were rocky.

It had been home to Melanesians for over 2,500 years, and although its history was somewhat confusing, it hadn't deterred these people from the pride they took in living there. Several schools of thought existed as to when these islands were first discovered, but there was also confusion as to who originally discovered them.

One reliable account was that the Spaniards came in the year 1606. A Portuguese explorer named Pedro Fernandez de Quirós, gained the Pope's blessing to embark on an extensive voyage for the Catholic Church. He arrived on the ship called *Espiritu Santo*, and unfortunately, he mistook the area for Australia. Undaunted, he then laid claim to the archipelago for Spain, proclaimed that it was part of the colonial Spanish East Indies. He then proudly named it *La Austrialia del Espiritu Santo*.

Even though previously discovered for Spain over a hundred and fifty years earlier, an equal number of people attributed the archipelago's discovery to Captain James Cook, as he sailed through this chain in the year 1774. It was Cook who charted and named many of the islands, then called the entire breadth of them the New Hebrides, so named after the islands off the coast of Scotland.

Nearly a century later, a trader by the name of Peter Dillon discovered a large group of trees that grew on the island of Erromango, one of the southernmost in this chain of islands. What he found was Sandalwood, which was a species in the genus *Santalum*, which was considered to be one of the most valuable trees in the world, because of its many and varied products used across the globe.

Today, Sandalwood has more than fifteen different health benefits attributed to its essential oils. Many of these were in medicines, skin and beauty treatments, not to mention the numerous products we now had such as deodorants, soaps, and lotions. Mr. Dillon's discovery began a five-year rush to that area that ended in 1830, after a clash between the indigenous Melanesians and the immigrant Polynesian workers ground everything to a halt.

Sandalwood was already a commodity in other areas such as Australia, Fiji, New Caledonia, and parts of the Samoan Islands. It continued to be a source of interest in this region until the 1860s.

That's when a group of owners (known as planters) decided that more workers were needed. They began to orchestrate a long-term labor trade known as 'blackbirding' which merely meant that they needed more people to work their crops. Blackbirding became a dirty word as it tricked, coerced, or kidnapped people to work as laborers. It was a common practice during the sugar cane years of 1842 to 1904. At the height of this practice, more than one-half of the adult male population of several of the neighboring islands were working abroad and parts thereof.

It was about the same time as missionaries, both Protestant and Roman Catholic, began to arrive at the Vanuatu islands. Since it was conducive to growing cotton, settlers also came to create plantations. When the cotton industry began to collapse, the settlers decided to switch from cotton to growing coffee, cocoa, bananas, and coconuts, which they did successfully. The islands started to swell exponentially with a melting pot from several nationalities, comprised mostly of British and French citizens.

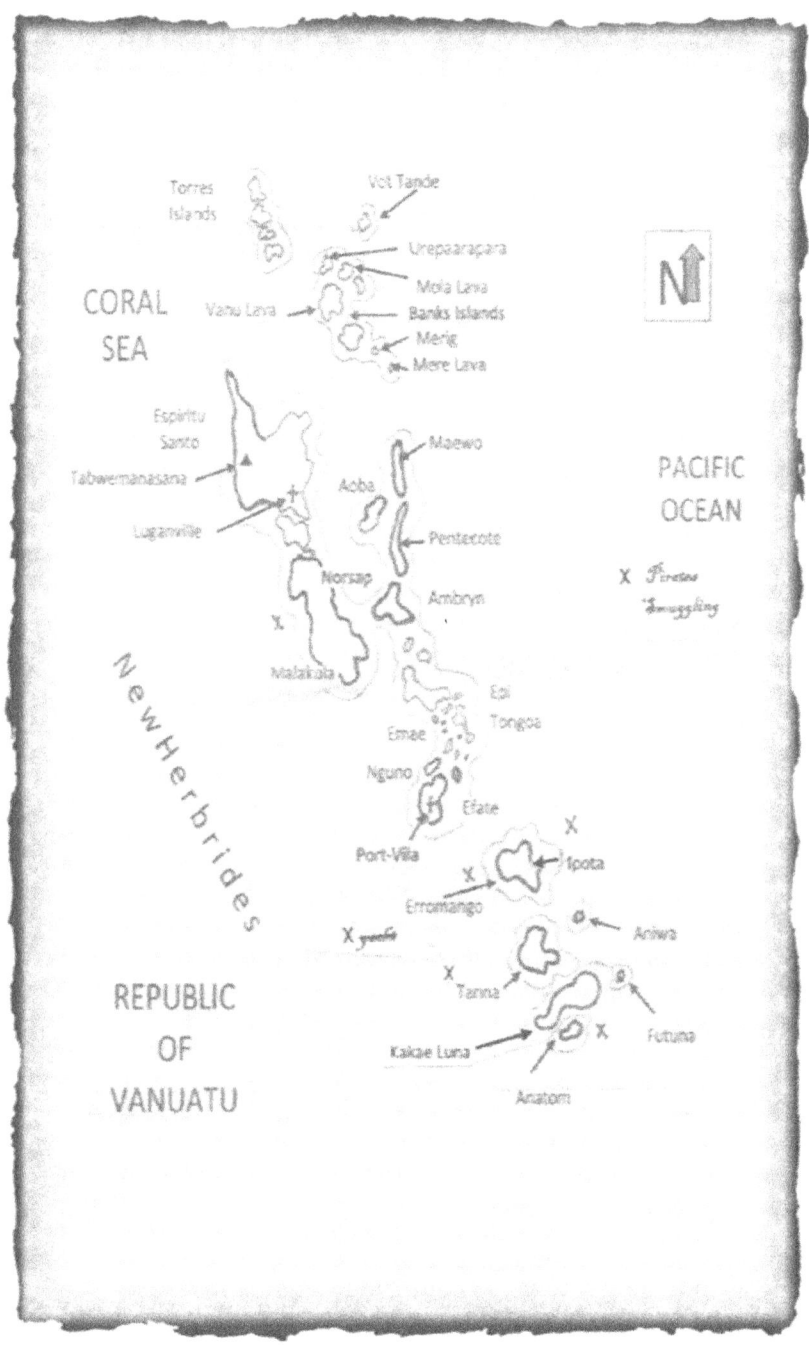

Most every island in the archipelago terrain were different sizes and shapes. Some were open and grew crops, while others consisted mostly of high mountain ranges with rough, craggy textures along the beach areas caused by volcanic boulders rolling down to meet the water.

Ruled for centuries by both Britain and France, the people of New Hebrides grew weary of the rules that were imposed upon them and decided to band together. By 1980, national pride took hold, and the peoples of all the islands declared their independence from Britain and France. It forced both governments to relinquish their grip on the islands, and where the new name of the Republic of Vanuatu was born. Then they promptly adopted a new constitution which was in use today.

Vanuatu was located directly west of Fiji and populated by many cultures, most of which were still Melanesians with a smattering of Polynesian, French and English citizenry, along with a mixture of expatriates from around the world.

The islands were, on occasion, in the direct path of heavy tropical storms. This occurrence would not ordinarily disturb the populace; however, when standard weather models were put together for this area, it was surprising when meteorologists predicted a not-so-typical season. Several weather patterns were calculated that Vanuatu was overdue for a substantial meteorological event.

Some of these models indicated different predictions as diverse as utter devastation, to mild destruction, but no one wanted to acknowledge this at the advent of tourist season. The hope of the many who prayed religiously, was that the weather would cooperate in their favor. As was the case for islands most everywhere that could not supply their own, they needed rainwater for survival, but their wish was that any severe storms would merely blow themselves out to sea.

During the formative years of these islands, as populations ebbed and grew, so did its many languages which now consisted of three official languages. The primary one is Bislama, which was followed by English, and lastly French. However, there were an astounding 113 individual languages listed for Vanuatu.

Because of the massive volcanic boulders that littered the beaches, it made for perfect hiding places for pirates or those who wished to remain out of the limelight. It was a known fact that there had been people lost in and around these islands as there were near the Bermuda Triangle. Incidents of foul-play might go unnoticed as the area to police them was unimaginably vast and difficult to control.

Vanuatu was home to a distinct terrestrial ecoregion known as the Vanuatu rain forests that were considered part of the Australian Eco Zone. This Eco Zone included New Caledonia, the Solomon Islands, New Guinea, Australia, which also included New Zealand. Most of the region was rich in sea life that continuously drew divers, tourists, and anglers, along with a smuggler or two.

The Republic of Vanuatu's claim to fame was the inhabited islands that had miles of pristine beaches. According to the Greater Vanuatu's Office of Real Estate, there was an abundance of affluent people who owned some of the more expensive property that was accessible only by boat. They were also home to some nasty pirates who preyed on those wealthy people from time to time. Some of them occasionally surfaced, such as the poor souls that the local police found washed up on one of the island beaches not too long ago.

Port-Vila was the capital city of the Republic of Vanuatu, the main island of Efate, in Shefa Province and home to the Port-Vila Central Hospital. It was here that a doctor hovered over an unconscious male patient.

A ventilator pushed air into a young man's lungs and his chest rose. This was followed by a wet sounding swoosh as his chest deflated. The doctor pried open his patient's left eyelid, then flashed a small penlight past the pupil. "Sun, can yu hear mi?" the doctor asked.

The doctor then turned to a woman who was standing next to him, asking her questions in a language that sounded slightly like Hawaiian and a lot like Creole.

"His vital signs are stable now, not as erratic as they were when he first came to us. It appears that he is still in a coma."

Shaking her head, she replied, "I hoped he would have opened his eyes by now, but he has not. I will pray that it happens soon."

The doctor gently pried open the young man's right eyelid, still very swollen and purple, directing his penlight across the pupil to see if it would dilate. As the nurse adjusted the solution drip connected to the young man's left hand, the doctor made notes on a chart.

"His temperature was elevated yesterday, but it seems to have stabilized now," Nurse Gor'gena offered, speaking softly.

Dr. Malas turned toward his nurse in attendance. "He looks better today. Your excellent care must be responsible."

"Thank you, Dr. Malas. Do you think he is from one of the other islands around here? My friend Kensi told me that there has been no report of anyone missing. He said no one came forward when it was announced in the newspaper."

"It is difficult to tell right now. There are so many different nationalities within the islands here. Perhaps when the swelling goes down and he begins to speak, we will find out more about him. But, you do know that with this type of head injury, he may not know who he is."

"My prayer is that he wakes up and his family comes to get him. The other two men they found with him were not so lucky. They were without identification, as this young man. It will be difficult for Officer Kensi to identify him without it, but he is good at his job, so I am sure he will find out who they are."

Without further speculation on his patient's prognosis, Dr. Malas slid his pen into his pocket. "Until he comes out of his coma, there is little we can do for him, except to make him comfortable, monitor his pain, and wait."

"I will sit with him this afternoon when my shift is over," Gor'gena said. "I want him to feel that he is not alone and that someone is at least with him."

"He can hear you, even though it appears as if he is sleeping."

Gor'gena's eyes widened. "Then I will sing to him the lullaby of my Mother's people."

"That is a nice idea, Gor'gena," the doctor concluded. "I will see you tomorrow."

Gor'gena smiled as the doctor left the ICU area. "I know you can hear me, young man," she said quietly. "I will stay with you for a little while to keep you company until my shift ends."

Turning to adjust the IV, she then proceeded to straighten the sheets, fiddled with the contraption that was elevating his broken leg, and fidgeted with the young man's arm that was cast to the elbow.

"Sometimes miracles happen, young man, and people wake up and go on about their lives as if nothing happened to them. You rest now and I will be back to sit with you later."

Nurse Gor'gena slipped out of ICU room number eight, and failed to notice a tear that was slowly rolling down the young man's cheek, or that his right hand was beginning to twitch slightly.

According to the paperwork filed by the EM team on the scene, when the ambulance arrived at the beach, there were three bodies. After a

Whispered Dreams

quick assessment, two of those bodies were taken to the morgue, while the third person went directly to surgery via the trauma center.

Also noted in the margin of these notes, was a handwritten message that said that by the time the EM team got to the beach, a crowd had gathered. The EM members were frustrated as few remained to give their accounts by the time Officer Kensi arrived. The EM team then rushed to take the injured man who was still breathing, opting to have another team go back for the remaining two bodies.

The details of this event were sketchy at best. Officer Kensi took detailed notes when he arrived at the scene.

Eyewitness # 1, who was running on the beach that morning, saw a small blue boat out in the ocean as a larger one was pulling away from it.

Eyewitness # 2, who was also running on the beach that morning, mentioned there were no bodies when he went past, however, when he ran back down the beach some twenty minutes later, the three bodies had appeared.

Eyewitness # 3, who turned out to be an old angler, admitted he was the owner of the boat, and it was he who called for the ambulance after he found a young man on the end of his hook.

Eyewitness # 1, asked why the young man's belt was cinched around his legs.

Eyewitness # 2 started to argue with Eyewitness # 3 that he thought he had dragged the bodies to the beach as his clothes were all wet.

Eyewitness #3 rebuked this idea vehemently, and said he was only trying to help. The other two bodies were already on the beach when he dragged the one he snagged out of the water.

None of the eyewitnesses, except for the old man, could understand how the young man did not pass right through the large hole in the old man's net, which apparently, he was still holding. And no one knows how any of these men came to be where they were in the first place, because no one saw how the bodies got on the beach, they apparently washed in with the tide that morning.

Questioned further, the convoluted stories began to sound concocted and difficult to understand, so Kensi dismissed the witnesses with the understanding that they might be called in for further questions should the need arise.

The local police officers were stumped and had no leads about the two dead men. As for the young man, unless he fell out of a passing yacht or dropped from an airplane, they did not know how he got into the water.

When the ambulance technician questioned the old angler, he swore he found him with the clothes he had on his body, albeit within his net. There was no identification whatsoever, no rings, or wristwatch, nor cellphone, nothing.

"Sounds fishy to me," Officer Laput said as he read the report the technician filed. "What do you think about what this old man is saying about this, Kensi?"

Laput was a husky man who had seen the better side of fifty. He was the senior officer of the two who occupied the small police station. He graduated from the Academy of Police Training here in Port-Vila some thirty years ago. He weighed in at a perfunctory 250, had a broad nose, and wore a size thirteen shoe. The local offenders knew better than to mess with him.

"I know of no one who could survive open water like that, unless he was dumped overboard. His clothes were not tattered, so he must not have been in the water for very long. His skin was not bloated or wrinkled as it should have been if he were in the water any length of time," Laput said speculating.

Officer Kensi mused, "If the young man was dropped from the sky, he could have lost his watch and wallet when he hit the water."

Laput shook his head, "But it does not explain the belt thing."

Kensi was a strapping young man who accelerated through the rigors of the same Police Academy, then ended up at the Port Villa station when a vacancy opened. His six foot four inch stature made would-be thugs quake in their boots when he unfolded himself from the police vehicle.

"This is odd, Kensi. The report from the EM team does not mention the old man's name. Didn't you get that when you questioned him?"

"Give me a moment, sir," Kensi said, digging into his pocket for his notebook. "He was eyewitness #3. His name was Abram Cornwall. Isn't it there?"

"Yes, yes, I see it now. Do you think he was telling the truth? Should we trust him?" Laput asked his partner of three years.

Kensi stood next to Laput to look at the photo of the man they were now calling John Doe. "It looks like he was in a fight with a two by four and he lost."

"Can you explain why his belt was wrapped around his legs? Who would do this if it was not pirates?" Laput pondered absently.

"Was it to keep the fish from going up his pants?" Kensi offered. "I do not think so."

"We should talk with your nurse friend to see if John Doe has opened his eyes and maybe he has told her who he is," Laput said matter-of-factly. "Maybe we should go look for ourselves."

"Good idea, sir. I will call Gor'gena to tell her we are coming over to the hospital. But, I don't think he has opened his eyes yet. She would have told me. She has become fond of this young man for some reason."

"Let us head over to the hospital right after lunch," Laput said, reaching for his hat that was dangling from a hook on the coatrack near the door.

Gor'gena was about to insert a needle into John Doe's IV when she mentally noted that most of his bruises were turning blue/yellow versus the black/blue color they were a few weeks ago. She also wondered how old he was and if his girlfriend or wife had put out a missing person's report. She couldn't imagine someone as handsome as this young man was without one or the other. As she daydreamed about who he might be, a man was sneaking up behind her to put his arms around her waist.

He knew better than to put his hands over her eyes.

"Is that you Kensi?" Gor'gena turned around to see the smiling face of her boyfriend. "It is a good thing you waited. I could have hurt you with this needle. What are you doing here? It's the middle of the afternoon."

"So many questions, girl, give a guy a chance to answer, will you? I am here because Laput wants to know if John Doe is awake." Kensi waited for her to finish. "I see that he has not."

Gor'gena shook her head. "The doctor was here. He didn't say this, but I think he should have awoke, by now. Maybe he is not going to. The last CT scan showed some damage to the left side frontal lobe. Even if he does wake up, he might not know who he is or where he came from."

"When the swelling goes down, I will take a photo of him and get his picture out. No one, not even his mother would recognize him the way his face is now."

"If I was his mother, I would be worried. Kensi, he is not a criminal. My feeling is that he is a sweet young man who might have been in the wrong place and got beat up."

"I did not say he was a criminal, Gor'gena. We don't have any evidence to support that. In fact, we have no evidence to support anything at all. None of those bodies had any identification whatsoever. It is difficult to investigate an incident without that kind of stuff."

Gor'gena sighed. "I know, you did not say that he was a suspect in any crime, but the other two you found sure looked like criminals to me. Dr. Malas sent me down to the morgue to check on them to see if we might find out more details about our young man here. The only things I saw were several healed bullet holes, knife marks, and the fatal wounds they sustained. Maybe they were after our young man and things went terribly wrong. You didn't have any luck finding out who they are either, did you?"

"No, we have no other information about those two who were with *this* young man," Kensi said, deep in thought. "You might not refer to him that way. He belongs to someone, you know."

Gor'gena's face changed expression. "Somehow, he reminds me of my brother. He was a sweet man all his life, Kensi, until a car hit him. Do you think that all three of the men fell into the ocean at the same time?"

Kensi remembered the incident that put Gor'gena's brother, Noah out of commission. He was never right after that accident, and ended up in a long-term health facility in Australia.

"Laput and I have no idea about these guys, and we sure do not know what to make of this one. We would sure like to know what he knows."

Kensi could not divulge specific information when a case was open and thought about what the EM report given to the ME stated. According to that report, the two men were left for dead on the beach. Each had gunshot wounds to their torso, shot at close range, the bullets passed right through their midsections, and they bled to death. The folders were then given to forensics to see if they could identify the type of bullets and weapon used.

"Let me know if John Doe wakes up. See you at dinner on Saturday, okay? I will pick you up at six p.m. sharp." Kensi bent slightly to plant a kiss on Gor'gena's forehead.

"Could you pick me up around seven thirty instead, Kensi? That is when the shift changes, and we always talk about our young man here before we go home."

"Sure, I will see you then."

Your young man, Kensi said under his breath, as he walked out of the hospital and back to the police car. He hoped Gor'gena had not attached herself to him too tightly, because he could turn out to be a mobster's son. On the other hand, he could be any one of a combination of jerks they had captured over the years.

Something continuously bothered Kensi, and it wasn't about what happened to the young man as much as whom he might be. Up until a few years ago, drug lords used some of the more remote islands around Vanuatu to misdirect the police. He was still thinking about it when he opened the door on the police car where Laput remained to take a call.

"Say Laput, do you remember that time when someone fell from the sky, but the impact as the body hit the water, that is too gruesome to think about. When was that, do you remember?"

Laput pulled away from the hospital when another call came through. "Okay, dispatch, we're on the way. Are you still thinking about the current John Doe? We already determined that he did not hit the water from any height, or he would be lying in the morgue with the other two dead men. What did you find out from Gor'gena, Kensi?" Laput asked.

"The young man is still badly messed up and has not opened his eyes yet. Gor'gena thinks the doctor has given up on him, but she has not. She still thinks he's going to wake up and talk to her. I have an idea I would like to try out, if you will let me."

"Sure, you have the afternoon. I can field anything that comes up," Laput said. "Drop me off here, I'll walk back. There's a little skirmish at the drug store."

Kensi went straight to his computer as soon as he got back to the police station. He began by starting a search on what might go on around the islands. He wasn't interested so much in fishing, but other things such as luxury yachts that were moored at the marina or wealthy residences that were tucked away at some of the islands.

When that turned up nothing of interest, Kensi redirected his search to the bane of their existence; smugglers and known pirates. Gathered over a long period of time, there was a multitude of information about this subject. Kensi tried to make sense of what he was reading, then quickly got bogged down with it. When he glanced at the clock, he was amazed that it was nearly six o'clock.

Something kept nagging at the back of Kensi's mind, and he had a hard time concentrating on anything for nearly a week. When Saturday night rolled around, he was sitting with Gor'gena at a local restaurant, but he wasn't paying much attention to her, because he was so deep in thought.

Gor'gena observed Kensi's expression as she proceeded to put a forkful of food in her mouth. Chewing for a few seconds, she watched Kensi wrestle with something. "I thought I was stepping out with a date, not a robot!" she said suddenly. "Aren't you going to eat your dinner?"

Kensi gazed at her in surprise. "I am sorry, Gor'gena. My mind is on the John Doe case. Something has made me wonder where I have seen him before."

"You know that young man's identity and you have just now thought of it?"

"No," he said absently pushing his food around on his plate. "I do not know who he is."

Gor'gena was somewhat irritated by this. "Spill the beans, Kensi! I want to know what you are thinking!"

"John Doe seems familiar to me for some reason. I have been trying to place him since I saw him at the hospital yesterday. The swelling has gone down, and his face does not look like it did even a week ago. Without a photo of what he looked like before his accident, it is hard to determine and even harder to do any research."

Gor'gena winced at the thought. "I must tell you, Kensi, that he was so disfigured, that it was hard to see his features when he first came to us. There was so much puffiness that the plastic surgeons had a hard time reconstructing his cheekbones. As it goes down, he will gradually look more normal. His nose was broken and they had to reconstruct that too. He might not look exactly like the same person before his accident. Dr. Malas said he might even have amnesia if he wakes up and he might not be able to speak."

Kensi comprehended the expression on Gor'gena's face. "I need to take his photo and get it into the newspaper again. Someone out there has lost their son, Gor'gena, and I'm sure they would like to know he's alive."

"Why don't we eat and not talk about this right now," Gor'gena replied. "I'd like to leave the hospital behind for a little while at least."

"Okay, but how am I going to ask how your day went? Sorry, that is kind of a dumb question. Would you like to tell me to be quiet now?" Kensi frowns as Gor'gena reached across the table to take his hand gently in hers.

"Kensi, your job is as hard as mine, because we both deal with crumpled and broken people."

"It is, that I cannot get this young man's face out of my mind and I cannot stop thinking about him!"

"Our days fill with good and bad, and that is the way it is for us. We can agree not to talk about either one of our jobs unless we have to, how about that?"

"That sounds like a good plan, Gor'gena."

"That way we can spare each other the hardships that we both know we deal with daily. What do you say?"

"Thank you for understanding. It is a deal then; we will not talk about work unless we have to. Dig in, I promise you will like the dessert tonight!"

In the intervening weeks, the nagging sensation continued to persist as Kensi had the feeling that he knew something, but could not extract it from his brain. Why did the young man seem familiar to him? Where had he seen him before? Was he a professional soccer player? And why were his legs tied with his belt? How did he end up in the ocean? Did he have the misfortune to be with pirates? Was he the son of a wealthy drug lord? Was his photograph in their local paper recently? Did someone make him walk the plank?

"Kensi! Are you still glued to that computer screen?" Laput startled him. "We have a call to handle. You need to come with me on this one. Dispatch said it is an unusual scene."

Kensi complied immediately by saving his information and turning off his computer. "I am not making any progress, sir. I keep thinking that I have missed something, but I do not know what it is."

"Give it time, and it will come back to you. It is a beautiful day today. Look at that horizon out there. Look at that oil tanker, Kensi." Laput was a little more than curious about this. "They do not usually come down this far. I wonder why it is here."

"Maybe it is going to Australia," Kensi said, letting the idea roll around in his mind. "You know, Laput, the young man could have been on an oil tanker."

Laput started to grumble. "On second thought, the oil tanker looks more like a large barge. Don't they do dredging with those? Kensi, it looks odd out there. Oil tankers do not come by here. The water is too shallow. They go much farther north than where we are; or do they go south? Australia, they go south to Australia."

"I am certain that it's an oil tanker, not a barge, Laput, but I think you are right. What is that one doing out there right now?" Kensi's mind began to wander, and he thought he had come up with an idea. "Maybe they're searching for something that fell overboard. Maybe someone pushed that young man off a tanker or barge by an irate captain for not doing his job. Then the captain would not have to pay his wages. Maybe I should start there. I will start with the manifests of the oil tankers that pass by here and get a list of crew members to see if anyone went missing."

Laput smiled and then let out a hearty laugh. "You would make a good detective, Kensi. You ask a lot of intelligent questions." He glanced over to see the expression on his partner's face. "You are not thinking of leaving me to go to detective school, are you? We make a good team, you and me."

"No, the thought never entered my mind. How could I go and leave you after you took me under your wing?"

"Never mind, Kensi. You keep digging because you might ask the right questions and solve our little mystery. We could use some positive publicity after that drug thing last year and what happened to that boat!"

Kensi knew what Laput referred to, and sighed, saying, "Do you suppose it is related to that?"

"They were some rough guys coming at us with a high-speed boat. They had some pretty big guns as I recall." Laput began to shiver with the memory of that chase as it popped into his mind. "I do not know if they are related. We have seen many men do some extraordinary things for money, Kensi."

"This theory does not explain why we found the other two men along the beach at the same time as John Doe." Kensi absently scratched his chin. "I do agree that it is a mystery."

"They may not even be related to our John Doe case, Kensi. There might be things we have not thought of yet that could point to something else that was going on at the same time."

"My gut feeling is that the three of them are linked somehow, but thanks for the go ahead. Gor'gena said John Doe's face might not be normal after he had surgery and that could impede our investigation."

"That might be why there have been no calls about him." Laput shifted the police cruiser into park. As they both got out, he said, "What else does she say about him?"

"She has a theory, Laput. She also thinks no one can recognize him because he looks so different. Some people came last week to take a look, but no one has said that their son or family member was missing. I think they came out of curiosity."

"He belongs to someone," Laput said in his direction." He's part of someone's family."

"But we must try at least, right?"

"Yes, Kensi, we have to try to find his family. We need to do that at least, even if they might not want to have him back."

Laput and Kensi could hear people yelling and screaming from their vehicle. Two men were at the center of a gathering. It might call for evasive action, so Laput grabbed his bullhorn as Kensi pulled out his billy club. No one responded to Laput, so Kensi took out his flare gun, firing it into the air, which brought everything to an abrupt halt.

The Police Academy taught recruits to use flare guns for crowd control; he knew better than to fire his automatic weapon in the air, because, that which went up, must come down somewhere.

When the crowd heard the loud pop of the flare gun, they automatically froze for a millisecond. Then everyone dispersed so quickly, that Kensi was only able to grab hold of the shirttail of a man who had the misfortune of standing too close to him.

Once both officers settled him down, Laput started to tell the man, "You are not in trouble, yet. We only want to ask you some questions about what happened."

"What is your name?" Kensi asked, taking out his notepad and pen.

"Do you have to know that?" Mr. Shirttail said.

"We need it for our records." Laput snarled, "Got something to hide?"

"I don't want any trouble," he said quickly. "My name's Gunnel Links. A young man came to town spreading a story about his father finding a merman. Then he said there are unbelievable, no, there are tremendous riches to be had. No one believed him until he showed us an odd wristwatch."

"What did this wristwatch look like, son?" Laput asked.

"No one ever saw one like this before. The young man pressed down on the middle of the face. It made a strange sound, and a light went on."

"Are you getting all this, Kensi?"

"Yes, sir, every word. Go on Gunnel."

"We were all standing around kind a looking at this thing when this big man, who is a well-known bully, started to demand to see the watch. The young one refused to hand it over. That is when the big one threw the first punch." Gunnel was now shaking his head. "The crowd went nuts and tried to get the big one off the young one. Then you arrived, and they all took off, leaving me here."

"Where is this big bully now? Does he have a name?" Officer Laput asked.

"He left with all the others, but I know who he is," Gunnel sputtered. "He lives in the village, goes by the name of Kimmel, or something like that."

"Can you describe the wristwatch to me?" Officer Kensi asked, flipping pages to a clean sheet.

"Are you able to draw it for us?" Officer Laput added.

"No, I was too far away to see it, but I did see it light up and it did make a humming sound!" His eyes widened with the memory. "From where I stood, it had a regular silver band, but the face of it was a blue color."

"What is the young man's name who had the watch?"

"I only know him as Al - either it's Albert or Alfred," Gunnel said. "There was another young man, older than Albert, who used to come into town occasionally, to try and sell stuff to us, but I have not seen him in a long time."

"Where can we find this Al person?" Kensi asked.

"On one of the outer islands, but I do not know which one," Gunnel added.

"How do you know it is on an outer island?" Laput thundered.

"Because he was bragging that his uncle knows the pirates around there and knows where some of their treasure is buried. Before you ask, I do not know the uncle's name, I only know where he lives, because he mentioned it a few times."

Kensi started to write down the name of the island, then flipped his notebook to a previous page, tapping Laput on the arm. Getting to this man's place of residence would not be easy. The officers would need a boat.

"Not this again," Laput mumbled. "We already have an APB out for this person. What is his name? He was involved with a very messy thing a few years ago. You know the one before the boat thing?"

"I do not remember that. I think it was before my time here, Laput. How far back do your files go? Maybe we can search through those to find out who this person is?"

After they dismissed Gunnel, they got back into the police vehicle. Laput began to wonder about something. "What was he doing there?" he said, "If it is who I think it is, he is a sneaky person, Kensi. I would not put it past him to be involved with this and maybe the dead bodies or even John Doe."

"Do you think he was trying to sell the wristwatch? Was this Al person trying to drum up business for his uncle, maybe?" Kensi asked. "I should try to go there to investigate this further. Should we get a boat and pursue this?"

"You want me to answer that?" Laput said distractedly.

Kensi tried to stifle the chuckle that was threatening to erupt from his throat. "No sir, you do not have to answer that. I know how you feel about boats and water."

"God knows that I do not want to get into a boat and go after that man, but we do have a complaint. We do have to follow up on that." Laput's disgruntled voice meant that he remembered what happened not all that long ago. "I do not like boats, and I do not want to do this. We should have waited for the Harbor Patrol to show up, Kensi. Why did we not wait for them?"

"As I recall, sir, there was no one available then. The regular patrol boats were either busy or in dry dock. I will go instead. I will ask someone to go with me. You can stay here. I will take care of this without you," Kensi volunteered.

The Police Department was entirely devoid of extra funds. They could barely afford the coffee that went into the coffee pot, let alone appropriate boats for wild goose chases, as the Harbor Police were the ones who had always regulated that type of thing. After an anonymous tip came into the police station, the officers were in such a hurry to go after the smugglers reported to be in the vicinity; they agreed that Kensi's fishing boat would never do.

They went to Zucker Marine to politely inquire about temporarily borrowing a boat. As it turned out, Mr. Zucker would no longer allow them the use of any marine equipment, after they created that fiasco last year. It seems that Zucker Marine had a hard year trying to recover and forget that dreadful day when Laput and Kensi 'borrowed' a cigarette boat to pursue what they thought were pirates.

The unfortunate part of this is that they returned to Port-Vila without it! The officers tried to explain what happened to the boat, but Mr. Zucker was so irate he could not speak, and pointed toward the door, shook his head wildly and held his chest.

Mr. Zucker later told his son, Jimy, never to allow the police officers to borrow anything from them again, EVER! It was simply an honest mistake as two boats, moored next to each other, were inadvertently part of an elaborate plan. When the key did not fit into the ignition of the blue boat, they jumped onto the red one thinking Jimy gave them the wrong instructions. Neither Laput nor Kensi knew of this mistake. And apparently, neither did Jimy, until the boat was gone for over an hour. By then, it was too late.

Jimy could not tell his father about this mistake, not before he was about to go away to college, so he kept his mouth shut, letting nature take its course. Unfortunately, it never occurred to Laput or Kensi they were being set up. All hell broke loose when the owner found out that his brand new red cigarette boat was not at the marina, but riddled with bullet holes and sunk in less than twenty feet of water!

Laput mournfully said, "Mr. Zucker will not give you a drink of water after what we did to that boat last year."

"Maybe they have forgiven us, by now."

"Kensi, they have not forgotten, and they have not forgiven us. What makes you so sure he will let you borrow anything?"

"You are right. Maybe we should drop it for now and concentrate on our young man and let the Harbor Police know to keep a lookout for this uncle and his nephew."

"Are you referring to the person named Al or the merman story?" Laput muttered under his breath, "I wonder where that story came from."

"What goes through their minds when they tell such tales?" Kensi said, laughing. "That's a good one. You have to admit."

"I do not know, Kensi. We live in a strange world at times."

Laput dropped Kensi off at the Police Station where he continued his search for oil tankers that might have gone a bit off the mainstream water lines. He discovered several aging tankers were roaming the ocean right now. They did not seem to belong to any one company nor did they have manifests or crew information.

Kensi speculated that other things besides legitimate cargo might be inside their hulls. He wondered how he could find out what they were doing without drawing too much attention.

Was there a connection between the rash of dead men they found on the beaches recently? Could the John Doe that still lies helpless in the hospital have any relationship to all of this?

Kensi thought that he should broaden his search to include owners or corporations. To his amazement, someone had purchased eight ships in a matter of months. Why would anyone need that many vessels and why would someone tie up that much capital? The more he dug, the more he uncovered, and the more he discovered, the more curious he became.

For someone to have that much money meant that they had access to unimaginable funds. Who else, besides wealthy people in business could afford ships like these? Maybe it's the oil people themselves.

Suddenly, Kensi's search shut down, as the information became blocked, nonexistent, or unavailable—then his screen went dark. He reasoned that if someone blocked the data, then someone must be trying to hide something. But who, Kensi asked himself. How could he get around or through this mess to find out?

When Laput returned to the station, Kensi went over what he had learned so far. It hadn't exactly led them to any solid answers; however, it did help them to understand how smuggled drugs might be passing over and around Vanuatu's many islands. Laput told him to keep up the good work and to let him know if anything new developed.

Kensi started with a plan. He made a list of all tankers who were in the vicinity six months to a year ago and then left space for critical information, some he had, others still to be discovered.

Asking himself questions, he came up with a comprehensive list and put it aside to work on another theory. Which tankers might have gone to or around Australia? He had somehow decided that this was an important detail.

When it was time for Kensi's shift to end, he gathered the growing pile of information and shoved it into a box. He figured that he would be thinking of it anyway, so he might as well take it with him.

Over the next several nights, Kensi cut little pieces out of cardboard in the shape of ships to place them on a piece of paper. Then he used a dark marker to draw the current shipping lines, noting such islands that have had drug-related activity and those that concerned the other islands.

It was a slow-going process, as there was so much information. It was no easy task, but Kensi completed this in less than a week. He could only work on it during his off-hours and when there was a lull in activity at the station.

When Laput saw Kensi's display, he was amazed at the thought behind it. "It is good work you have done, Kensi. It might lead to something. It looks like the Game of Sea Battle. By the way, Gor'gena called from the hospital. Our John Doe is now awake." Laput motioned for Kensi to follow him.

"Did he say anything to her?" Kensi asked. "Can he tell her who he is?"

"No, I asked her that already, and she sounded disappointed. She said to come and see him. I will go with you. Nothing is going on here right now."

Name of Oil Tanker	Critical Information
SEAWISE Country of origin	Names/# of crew Manifest/cargo Date coming into area Date going out of area
ALHAMBRA Country of origin	Names/# of crew Manifest/cargo Date coming into area Date going out of area
Hellespont II	Names/# of crew Manifest/cargo Date coming into area Date going out of area
APOLLO'S UNIVERSE	Names/# of crew Manifest/cargo Date coming into area Date going out of area
GIANT	Names/# of crew Manifest/cargo Date coming into area Date going out of area
MONT – scrapped	Oil tanker
Leader of the Universe	Drug related
Hellespont I	Names/# of crew Manifest/cargo Date coming into area Date going out of area
GOOD HOPE	In service/out of service
Tanker with no name	?
Other Boats	Other Information
Private yacht – sunk	
Pirated ships	
barge	

Whispered Dreams

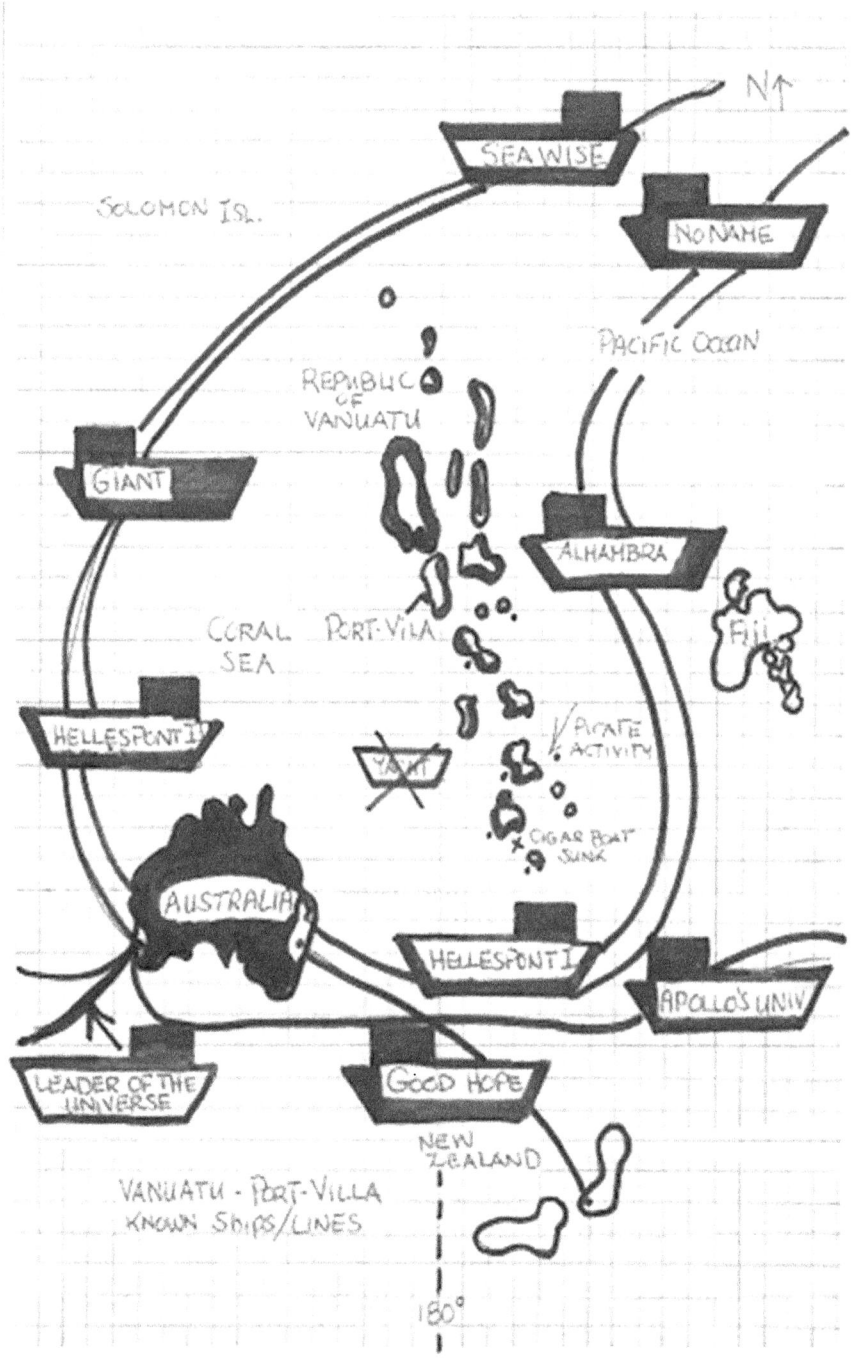

At the hospital reception desk, a plump woman who wore a headset greeted the officers. She knew why they were there and handed them a piece of paper with the number 216 written on it, pointing toward the elevator as she took another call.

When Laput and Kensi got to the second floor, they stopped to view the young man through the glass window of a step-down room within the ICU. John Doe had an expressionless face, neither frightened nor happy. Although his head faced the window, his eyes stared in the direction of the TV mounted on the wall. When Gor'gena saw Kensi, she waved for them to come in.

Gor'gena was standing in front of the young man tapping him on the arm to get his attention. He turned his head slowly toward her as she told him that the officers were there to see him. Laput stepped around her and proceeded to question him.

"Good morning young fella, my name is Officer Laput. What is your name, son?"

The young man blinked a few times, then turned his eyes toward the TV screen, as if he hadn't heard anything. Laput tapped him on the arm and repeated his question.

John Doe did not understand what the words meant. He heard: 'Gud morneng yung fela, mem blong mi Offcer Laput, wanem nem blong yu, sun?"

Gor'gena saw the wild expression on her patient's face and tried to explain why John Doe might not respond. "Officer Laput, he might not understand you. I wanted to warn you that he has not spoken or looked directly at us yet."

"Maybe he does not know our language?" Kensi observed.

"Maybe he is foreign, like we first thought," Gor'gena added.

"Maybe he cannot hear us. Maybe he broke his hearing when he fell overboard. Did the doctor say anything about that?" Laput asked, scratching his head.

"Maybe you two should be quiet. Can you not see that Andru is frightened? He has been through a lot. We will give it time, okay?"

Kensi sat down on the chair near the bed to block the TV so that John Doe had to look at him. He smiled at the young man, and touched his hand gently, then stood up.

"Come out in the hallway so that we can talk," he said, motioning to both Gor'gena and Laput. "Look at us big men in our uniforms, guns at our sides. We look scary to him. No wonder he does not want to talk to us," Kensi said as they leaned against the wall.

"I had not thought of that, Kensi. What does the doctor say?" Laput asked Gor'gena.

"Dr. Malas said that sometimes when people wake up from a coma, they do not know where they are or what happened to them. It is that amnesia thing I told Kensi about."

Laput was curious. "Why does he watch TV like that? Does he respond to you at least?"

"He has had trauma to his brain, and Dr. Malas said it takes time for it to heal." Gor'gena seemed sad at this fact.

"Does he say how long this young man will be like this?" Kensi asked.

"No. No one knows," Gor'gena said, shrugging her shoulders. "It could take years. We do not know the extent of the damage or how much of his brain is injured. Dr. Malas called other doctors to ask what to expect when patients come in and out of comas, and they all agreed that it is out of their hands now. He needs time to heal."

Laput was confused, as he thought that when a person woke up from a coma, they got up and walked out of the hospital or they died and went straight to the morgue.

"It is up to the young man to recover his mental…what was it that Dr. Malas called it?" Gor'gena put a hand to her forehead. "Acuity, he called it mental acuity."

Laput frowned, and then asked, "What exactly does that mean?"

"We can bandage his wounds, and we can fix what breaks, but when it comes to the mind, we have to wait until it heals itself. There is no magic pill for this, Officer Laput!" Gor'gena replied.

Laput got the feeling that Nurse Gor'gena did not like him very much. Perhaps it was his gruff demeanor. "Call us if he has anything to say, okay? Come on Kensi; we have other things to do."

Kensi knew from Gor'gena that people know you care about them when you talk to them, even if they are asleep or in a coma. "I could read to him, and talk to him and maybe in time, he will talk to me," Kensi offered. "I will come by after work and do that."

Gor'gena and Kensi would take turns sitting with the young man they now call Andru. They have named him after the famous Andru from one of the nearby islands who went to the Summer Olympics a few years back.

On the nights that Gor'gena read to Andru, Kensi continued with his search of the tankers and barges and the routes they might have been on during the timeframe of Andru's injury. So far, the information about the eight oil tankers was limited. Someone or something was continually blocking the info or wiped it out as Kensi suspected, but he was not easily defeated and forged ahead.

Weeks went by with little progress, and then months went by and Kensi realized that he had hit a dead end with the tankers and barges, along with the placement of them on his improvised map. Undaunted, he headed to the hospital to visit with Andru who now walked with the aid of a cane. Andru still had not responded to questions, and everyone thought it was because his brain would not process the words.

The photo of John Doe/Andru they distributed brought no response. Laput decided that it must be drug-related. He filed a completed report, then declared that the incident was thoroughly investigated, putting it into the closed file in one of the overflowing drawers behind his desk.

Kensi did not think this was over.

Andru had been transferred to a semi-private room on the third floor now that he no longer needed intensive 24/7 care. When Kensi arrived, he found the door closed and surmised that either a doctor or nurse was with him. He stood across the hall from it to wait. When the door opened, a craggy old man came ambling into the hallway. When he saw Kensi, it startled him somewhat, and he didn't know what to do at first.

"Sir, may I ask what you are doing here?" Kensi asked the man.

The old man nodded his head, mumbled something, then said, "Yes, Officer, I am here to see my nephew."

Kensi was immediately suspicious of this person. "What is your nephew's name?"

"His name is Brian, and his mother is worried about him. I came to see him. He has been missing for quite a while. When will the doctor release him? He would do better at home, with his mother to care for him."

"Yes, I agree that he belongs with his family." Kensi wondered if this man was Andru's Uncle, and wanted to be sure. "Where is your nephew from?"

"Brian comes from the Island of Kakae Luna. You know, it is south of here, past Erromango. He could have told you that himself. Didn't you question him? We have been searching for him for quite some time now," the old man said slowly. "Can I take him home now?"

Kensi eyed the man suspiciously. "Brian, as you call him has not spoken to anyone. The doctor is uncertain when he will regain his memories."

The old man realized that the officer had no clue who he was, and if he could engage him in this ridiculous conversation, the easier it would be to outsmart him. "We are glad that he is alive, but that does explain why he does not seem to know me. Will he be alright?" the old man asked.

Kensi was still skeptical of the old man. "No one knows. He was in terrible shape when he came to the hospital. Do you have a recent picture of Brian? We need to verify your story. What did you say your name is Mr…"

"Forgive my manners," the old man said leaning in to see the nameplate on the big man's chest. "Officer Kensi. I am Rexley Mansale. I am Brian's Uncle Rexley. My brother's wife has been distraught ever since her son went missing. You can understand how anxious she is to see him. His many brothers and sisters are concerned to have him home again."

Rexley began to fumble in his jacket pocket, making sure he didn't pull out his wallet. He then extracted a beat up photo of a young man that remarkably resembled a young Andru.

"This man has darker skin than our patient here, but I suppose it is because he hasn't been out in the sun for a while." Kensi was a little disappointed, but unable to dispute Rexley's claim, so he handed back the photo.

"He does not know me, but I am quite certain that he is my nephew, Brian Mansale," Rexley stated with conviction. "He has been missing for almost a year, and his mother was beside herself with worry until I told her that I found him."

Kensi asked him to wait for a few moments as he slipped into Andru's room. At the sound of his voice, Andru stared in his direction but did little else. He no longer stared straight ahead or to the left to watch the television and turned his head toward voices or loud noise.

Sitting on the bed, Kensi asked Andru if he knew the man who was in his room. Andru did not respond. Kensi asked him how he felt today and again, Andru did not answer. Kensi asked him if the sun was purple, and Andru said nothing. Kensi told him he would be right back.

Mr. Mansale was loitering against the wall, anxiously fidgeting with the loose change in his pocket. "Can I take him home now?"

"Wait here, Mr. Rexley, I will see if the doctor will release Andru to you."

Kensi walked down the hallway to place a call from the nurse's station. The woman behind the desk dialed a number without looking up, then handed him a phone receiver. A moment later, he was talking to Gor'gena.

"There is a man here who claims to be Andru's Uncle." He turned to see Mr. Mansale wave at him. "Gor'gena, this man says Andru's real name is Brian. He said that he and his sister-in-law have been looking for him for nearly a year. Can you come down and talk with us for a few minutes?"

"No Kensi, I am about to start a procedure. I cannot leave now," Gor'gena said. "Can you ask him to wait for about an hour?"

"I will try."

"Dr. Malas wanted to have X-rays taken of Andru's arm and leg."

"Will the doctor release Andru to this man after the X-rays are taken?" Kensi asked.

"There is a chance he might do that, but Andru must continue with his therapy. He needs speech therapy if he is ever to talk again, and physical therapy so that he can walk properly."

"Thank you, Gor'gena. This man seems anxious to take him. He showed me a picture, and it resembles him, even if his face has changed," Kensi winced.

"I will see who can come and talk with you, hold on a moment."

Kensi turned to look down the hallway, but Mr. Mansale was not there. Waiting patiently for Gor'gena to come back on the line, he figured that Mansale went back into Andru's room.

When Gor'gena returned, she said, "The doctor will not give his okay now, Kensi. Andru needs blood work and follow-up rehabilitation for additional therapy sessions before he is released to his uncle's custody."

"Thank you, Gor'gena. That is what I needed to know."

Kensi handed the phone back to the woman behind the desk, politely said thank you, and walked down the hallway to Andru's room. When he pushed the door open, there was no one inside. In fact, there was no evidence that anyone occupied the room at all!

Kensi sighed, mumbled to himself, that he didn't understand why the uncle would not wait for the doctor to release him. Should he let this go and be grateful that someone finally stepped forward after all this time? Why didn't he feel better about this than he did?

What is it that kept nagging at him that he could not seem to recall?

When Kensi returned to the Police Station, he began a search on the man who claimed to be Andru's Uncle Rexley. He was understandably disappointed when the man's photo and address identified him as Rexley Mansale.

Sifting through the police database, Kensi found the name of Brian Mansale and was disappointed that he had been arrested for petty theft. He was from the Island of Kakae Luna, as Rexley said he was and his family owned a business called *The White Sands Resort*. Their website showed a young man carrying towels to a sparkling pool, and it looked remarkably like their Andru.

Why didn't they inquire about him earlier if he had been missing for that long? "Do you know a Rexley Mansale, sir?"

"Mansale…hum…that name sounds familiar," Laput rolled this around on his tongue as his eyes went wide. "Rexley did you say?"

"Rexley Mansale," Kensi repeated.

Laput was stunned as he remembered why the name sounded so familiar to him. "That is the name of the person I have been trying to remember, Kensi. He is the one who got us in trouble with the red boat last year. Why do you ask about this man?"

"Because he was at the hospital and took Andru/Brian with him before I could tell him that the doctor would not give his okay. Why did it take so long for someone to show up for him? Do you recall the photos we sent out of all three men who were on the beach? They went out last year. How can the old man be Andru's uncle?"

"Kensi, it appears that we have been had!" Laput said, slamming his hand down hard on his desk. "Maybe they do not have a way to pay for his injuries, and they took him to skip out on the hospital bills? That is usually what desperate people do when they do not want to pay."

"You might be right about that, he did look scruffy and disheveled," Kensi said.

Laput pondered this for several minutes. "We have to let it go now. Andru is gone home, and the case is closed. You have almost driven yourself crazy working this thing. If the hospital wants to press charges, then we will go after him. Or we can turn this over to the Harbor Police and let them deal with it."

"Something is not right about all this, Laput!" Kensi said.

"You should be glad that Andru, I mean Brian will be reunited with his family, even if his uncle is a liar and a cheat."

"I do not know what it is, but something is not right! What about that watch thing? We never found out what kind it was and what that business about a merman was all about, and maybe we should check into that? They might be related. We might find out that this Rexley character is behind that, too."

"No, Kensi, the case is closed, with a capital C. Let it go now. There may be something in the future that might tie them together, but not now, we have other things to attend to."

Kensi remarked sadly, "Yes sir."

"Put all this stuff away and out of your mind," Laput told him.

"Yes, sir. Do you mind if I take the map home with me? I have room to store it." Kensi started to gather up the map, putting the loose pieces in a plastic evidence bag.

"I see no harm in that. Go ahead. If we need it, you can bring it all back. Someone out there has lost their sons, and it is a shame that they may never know what happened to them."

Laput thought that they had done their jobs as far as it could take them, and they could do no more than that. Then he promptly put this out of his mind to concentrate on the case that had come into the station.

Kensi was glad that Andru's family had found him. The other two victims that were found with him on the beach were not so lucky. Their photos went out along with Andru's many months ago. No one stepped forward to claim their bodies or even called into the station to inquire about them.

It was Kensi's day off, but he struggled with something and had come into the police station to use his computer to satisfy his curiosity. He started searching to see if anyone was trying to find a young man fitting Andru/Brian's description. Then he broadened the spectrum to include international sources and such.

"What have we here?" Kensi said to himself, then went into a flurry of typing as Laput walked into the police station, where he expertly threw his hat onto the coatrack.

"Is it not your day off, Kensi? What are you doing here?" Laput asked.

Kensi looked up at his superior. "Yes sir, it is my day off, but something occurred to me this morning. I wanted to see if I am right."

Laput said distractedly, "I do not know what gets into people, Kensi. Why do they want to harm one another the way they do? Two more men were found on the beach last night, and that is two more people without identification. That makes two more mothers who are never going to see their children alive."

"This may all be related, Laput. Can we run their fingerprints as we did on the last ones? By the way, where are they? The hospital said we had them."

Laput turned solemnly toward Kensi. "Did you look in the right file?"

Kensi stared at Laput. "Yes. Brian's fingerprints were not there, and neither are the two men who came in with him."

"If they are not here, then they were done at the hospital when they took him there. Did you check with them?"

Kensi's mouth fell open slightly. "I checked with them, and they said they thought we did that."

"Oh boy," Laput said in disbelief. "The ME should have the file for the two men we found with Andru. I am sure the technician has them. Why don't you call to ask them?"

Kensi moved quickly to the phone. He already had doubts about this, then rationalized that Andru/Brian's injuries were so severe that there wasn't time to waste. But the reality of it was, they should have done this procedure themselves and not left it to others.

It was easy to coerce Brian into going along with him, especially after he handed him a chocolate candy bar. Rexley Mansale then took his nephew to the Island of Kakae Luna in a small, dilapidated blue boat. As they got closer, he could see his sister-in-law and her family at the boat dock waving to them.

Kalima Mansale was beside herself with joy, because Rexley was bringing her son home today. Her joy quickly turned to sadness when he did not recognize her or acknowledge any of his four siblings.

As the children took Brian to their home, Kalima began to question Rexley. He became evasive and only told her that the accident Brian was involved in knocked all memory of his past from his brain. It is impossible to know the true extent of his suffering until and unless he begins to speak again. (Which Rexley secretly hoped would never be.)

"What do I do with him like this, Rexley? How will I communicate with him?" Kalima asked wildly. "How will he help us do what must be done here at the resort? I tried to hug him, and he moved away from me. He acts like he does not even know who we are!"

"I found him, didn't I? Can you not be happy with that?" Rexley spewed, apparently not wanting to discuss the matter any further.

Kalima persisted, and said, "Since you were the one who lost him in the first place, it was your job to find him. How will he get around on that cane? Why did you take him from the hospital, Rexley? Did the doctor say he could leave? What were you thinking?"

"Do not go digging, Kalima. The police think he is involved with the smugglers as it is. Let him be. Take care of him, and he will come around, you will see."

"What smugglers are you talking about, Rexley? Why was my son involved with them? He is a good boy. He would never do anything like that!" Kalima shouted. "What did you get him involved with?"

"Calm down, Kalima. I said the police *think* he is involved. He said nothing to them the way he is. Can you not see that? No one can question Brian if he cannot speak. We do not want them snooping around here is all." Rexley turned to leave, but Kalima followed him to his little boat.

"If there is nothing to worry about, then the police can come here. If you have nothing to hide, what atrocities would they find, Rex? Are you hiding something here? What did you involve my son in?"

"There is nothing to worry about now. You have your son back, so everything is restored."

Kalima was seething. "Everything is **not** restored. What in God's name has happened to him? You look very guilty, Rex. Tell me what happened! Is it the same thing that happened before?"

"Some other time, Kalima. I must get back now."

Rexley stepped into the small boat and began to unwind the boat line from the dock. He was not concerned with his sister-in-law or his nephew Brian, he was thinking only of himself. He could be in big trouble if the authorities found out that it was he and Brian who were part of the disturbance in which two police officers were chasing a luxury yacht in a red cigarette boat, which unexpectedly was riddled with bullets and sunk last year.

Rexley must also keep quiet about a mysterious man named Mr. Gee and his involvement in the heist that netted a boatload of gold and jewelry. Rexley conveniently used that red boat fiasco as a cover so he and Brian could hide their stash. The sad part in all this is that Brian took the brunt of the blame, not Rexley.

When Mr. Gee figured out what happened, he confronted him and merely took his ire out on Brian. He could not tell his sister-in-law that her son was hurt or dead, she had already lost her husband in one of Rexley's wicked schemes. When Rexley first saw the picture of Brian in the newspaper, the possibility emerged that could vindicate him for his past wrongdoings, taking the necessary steps to plant the seeds of an elaborate scheme. He had to wait and bide his time.

And after a suitable length of time, he figured that if he could slip into the hospital and retrieve Brian without much notice, things would finally go his way.

The newspaper article only stated that a John Doe had no memories of who he was. He sustained a broken leg, an arm, and a multitude of lacerations to his face. Because of the extensive reconstruction of his nose and cheekbones, his family may have to use their imagination to identify him.

Which is what Rexley counted on, but what he did not anticipate is the confrontation in the hallway with the Police Officer named Kensi. Rexley thought about how he would get Brian out of the hospital unnoticed, and when the officer went off to speak with the doctor, the opportunity presented itself.

Could he pull this little caper off quietly and quickly? He smiled to himself to think that he was so clever. The men he took with him waited in the stairwell until he opened it. Then they gathered up Brian's meager belongings, tidied up the room, straightened and tucked in the sheets, and left via the same stairs.

Rexley knew the men would not tell anyone, as he promised them some of his pilfered loot when it was safe to distribute it. He also knew that he could not take the slightest chance that Mr. Gee's men would return and pressure Brian to talk, because, after all, he saw what they did.

Everyone had to remain calm and quiet for this to work.

Rexley built his elaborate plan around the fact that in his present condition, it was unlikely that Brian would ever be the person everyone once knew. He also figured that because his nephew Brian not only had no recall of the heist, he also could not tell anyone about it. The best part was, he couldn't tell anyone where his uncle hid the enormous stash.

Now he could keep all of it for himself.

Half-way around the world, nestled in the sleepy hamlet known as Jasper, Virginia, life continues at a reasonable pace at the farm called Ashwood Stables. The family tragedy that had us all turned inside out has been tucked away in the recesses of my mind, but it has certainly not been forgotten.

Adrian looks up from pressing keys on his laptop. "Going somewhere, sweetie? To see Dr. Stevens perhaps?"

"Why don't you come with me? We can grab some lunch after the appointment?"

"No can do, sweet cheeks. I'm working on a small research project for Levi that needs to be completed by today. Tell her I said hello."

"Will do."

As I drive into town to have my weekly session with Dr. Laurel, my mind keeps wandering to the first time we came into this little town. It was a huge adjustment from our bustling city of Evanston, Illinois, but we quickly got in step with its quaint charm.

I pass the familiar storefronts, the bakery where Mona and Mother take their baked goods each week has a sign in the window that is advertising their latest concoction.

The double-store next to it is Jasper's Antique Emporium. A memory surfaces of how excited Gerald Tillman became when he and his assistants cataloged the antiques and collectibles from Ashwood. I laugh to think that no one would allow him to see the wide-ranging cache hidden inside for so many years until we came along.

Then the memory of Jason's face flashes in front of my eyes. He was so disappointed when we told him we were selling the old Duesenberg he found in the dairy barn. He wanted to keep it and fix it up so he could drive it. We sorely needed the funds back then, and the money the auction and the sale of that car brought us was over the million dollars Gerald thought it would bring.

The bank comes into view, reminding me of Mr. Carl Fancy Yancy Banker where my brother-in-law, Dennis, now resides as CEO and President. We were all astounded when his son, Danny, announced he would take Jason's place as one of our harness race drivers when he came home after graduating from college.

Gladys, the big-haired real-estate woman who accompanied us on a tour of Ashwood that fateful day I was so unceremoniously dumped there, is coming out of her small office. She is waving at me as I pass her.

The town has changed little in the years we've been here. The movie theater still has recently released movies where Jason and his friend Mack often took Melanie and Curlie on a Saturday night.

The drug store still has drugs, the feed store still has livestock feed, but I do not have my son. As I park my car in front of a consignment-clothing store, it takes a few minutes to walk up to Dr. Laurel's second-floor office. Am I starting to resent this? Did I expect more progress toward ending my nightmares?

"Hello, Ellen, please come in. Would you like some tea?" Dr. Laurel says pleasantly, pointing to a comfortable chair, waving to her assistant. "Did you have a good week?"

"It was okay. But I seem to be having trouble coping with reality, today. Everything I look at suddenly reminds me of Jason for some reason."

"Let me turn on the recorder; are you settled?" Laurel is wearing a light blue silk blouse, under a two-piece, dark blue linen suit. Her leather pumps are navy blue. As usual, her hair is neat, and her makeup is fastidiously applied. "You may start when you're ready, Ellen."

"I had an odd dream about Jason last night. Previous dreams have been where I'm looking for him and usually can't find him. Last night, he popped up from behind a big rock and smiled at me. He almost never says anything. He merely stands there smiling."

"Was this dream disturbing to you?" Laurel opens the door to admit her assistant, taking the tea tray from her hands, closing the door with her hip.

"No. That didn't disturb me. But, there is a change in my dreams. All the other dreams I've had of Jason has me waking up thrashing and perspiring."

"So, you didn't lash out at Adrian, then? What else do you remember," she coaxes.

Closing my eyes to recall the dream, I begin by saying, "It was different from previous ones, but I didn't realize it until now. Jason never smiled in my other dreams. I'm always searching for him and don't always find him. When he does show up, or when I try to talk to him, he disappears. But last night was different. When he showed up, he stayed with me, and he smiled. What do you think that means?"

Laurel pours tea while I talk, nodding her head. Handing me a teacup on a saucer, she says, "I believe we have talked about this before. In my professional capacity, it might mean that your subconscious is trying to talk to your conscious mind."

"What exactly does that mean?"

Reaching for a napkin, handing one to me, she says, "Why don't we try something new if you're up to it? We could try hypnosis, starting with past life regression."

"No thanks. None of that mumbo jumbo stuff for me. Besides, what if I told you something Adrian specifically told me not to tell you while I was under hypnosis? We'd both be in big trouble. Do you have a high-level security clearance?"

Laurel laughs slightly, sipping daintily from her teacup. "Perhaps I should explain the process a little more. Past regression is a technique often employed to help people go back to their childhood. It takes you back to your earliest memories. We could start there."

"Why would I want to do that? That isn't the part I can't figure out. It's here and *now* that I'm having trouble with, and my childhood was great!"

Dr. Laurel eyes me cautiously. "Yes, but often when a person goes back, they discover that the root of their current problem stems from something that happened at a previous time. Whatever troubles you often disappear."

"You think by going back in time, it will help me cope with what I'm going through right now? That's ludicrous!"

"You would be surprised what the outcome might be, Ellen," she says quietly. "What do you have to lose by trying it?"

"Nothing, I have nothing to lose by trying it."

For the next half hour, Laurel engages in what she calls '*past childhood regression*' taking me back to my earliest memories. She says I'll wake refreshed and feeling fine, and I should remember everything. After she says to count backward from twenty, the next thing I remember is her snapping her fingers.

"How do you feel Ellen?"

"Fine, but I don't remember a thing. I thought you said I'd remember everything."

Dr. Laurel nods her head. "That's because you fell asleep and didn't say anything. I let you sleep because you must be exhausted. I'll see you again next week, same time. And get some rest, will you? We can try this again."

When I tell Adrian how my appointment went today, all he can do is laugh. He's been saying for quite a while that with all the flaying and thrashing I do in my sleep, it's no wonder I don't take more naps. He also thinks that going back to my childhood seems plausible, although from what I've told him, he doesn't agree that it will solve the current issues, as Dr. Laurel believes.

At dinner that night, the subject of new Standardbred horses is again our topic of discussion.

"Why do ya feel the need ta go and change things when everythin is goin good the way they are, Missy," a cantankerous Glen mumbles.

"Because we need a little change around here, you old grump. I have also decided to tear down the dairy barn that we can no longer fix. We'll get to repairing and renovating the other one attached along the back, to add some new stalls. We are getting a little crowded in there, don't you think?"

Glen mulls this over for a moment. "Humm, yeah, that would help the sit'iation out there. Do I get a new office outta it?"

"Gee, I thought you liked that stinky old office, ole buddy?" Adrian grins. "Then it's settled, Miss Ellen gets back into the swing of things again, decorating-wise, that is."

"Have ya talked with Reed about this? Think he might have an idea or two about it." Glen takes a swig of his sippin whiskey, followed by a large gulp of water.

"No, but I plan to talk to him about some other things. Are you and Mona going to get away to see your children this year? It might be a good opportunity to do it when the barns are all torn up."

"Don't have no plans for that. Ya know how Mona gets when she don't get her bakin in. But, I'll ask her if she wants ta go ta Alec's house."

"You don't need anyone's permission, Glen; take the time, if you need it. You should go and see those kids or have them come here. Lord, between the two places, we have enough room. Dimmy's never coming back, and his rooms are empty."

Adrian chuckles. "Ellie? Perhaps we should plan a little getaway of our own!"

"That's an excellent idea, Adrian. I've been working on that. Can't tell you what it is yet, but when it's all put together, you are going to be quite surprised, at least I hope you are."

Dennis is curious. "Is it something Terre and I would enjoy? Mind if we join you?"

"Dennis, did it ever occur to you that they might want to be alone?" Terre says rolling her eyes upward. "Besides, they never got their honeymoon, remember? You plan your time away without us, Ellen, okay?"

"No problem there…" Adrian grins.

"You don't have to worry about the children, either, honey, I'll take care of them," Mother says. "You should go and have some fun."

After dinner, everyone begins the ritual of removing their dinner plates, etc. as the girls take over their duties in the kitchen. Mother goes up to her sitting room to read as Mona and Glen go off to their Gate House near the entrance to Ashwood.

Nathan has taken over the night duties for the barn and heads there with Danny and Mack to close it up for the night. Reed and Dr. Jessica are cozy in their Carriage House most evenings, opting to spend time there unless there is an occasion to join us.

"Don't forget to do your homework before you get involved with other things, girls," Terre says to her twins Ginny and Lindy, whose turn it is tonight to help Curlie with the dishes.

"That goes for you, too Curlie."

"Yes, Mom…" Curlie mutters at me, crossing her eyes as she pulls on her long plastic gloves to protect her nail polish. As the kitchen door closes, we can hear a string of unintelligible words and laughter as the three of them chitchat.

"It's good to hear them laugh," Terre observes as the adults move toward the library.

"Yeah, laughter is the best medicine. Not those little white pills Dr. Laurel gave me."

"Speaking of that, how is that past-thing going?" Dennis asks.

"You told him, Terre?"

Terre seems defensive. "You didn't tell me not to, Ellie."

"Come on Ellie, we all want to know how it's going," Adrian chortles. "What did you find out about your childhood that you want to share with us? Is it the secret to how you win at the racetrack?"

"You wish, Adrian. The fact is I didn't learn anything when she hypnotized me and asked me to tell her about growing up. There was no revelation, no secrets hidden deep down in the recesses of my subconscious. She concluded that it must go further back and we might explore past-life regression at some point."

"Past life regression," Dennis says. "Past life regression. Does that mean you'll remember you were a famous person?"

"Hey, you could be Cleopatra, and I could be your Mark Antony?" Adrian cocks his head to the side. "Or you could be the jockey that rode Seabiscuit…or you could be…"

"Adrian, please stop."

"We had a great childhood. What could you possibly have an issue with?" Terre asks.

Then Dennis adds, "You could be Helen of Troy and Adrian could be…Adrian could be, darn, what is his name?" Dennis sighs, "I wish I could remember that guy's name."

"You mean Pitt; he played Troy in a movie, didn't he?" Terre asks.

"Will you all stop? We didn't find out anything. I'm no famous person in this life or the last, and I didn't reveal anything deeply embedded in my mind or elsewhere."

Terre's concern turns into understanding. "Are you disappointed about that, Ellie? What happens now?"

"Dr. Laurel finally understands that I'm sad, because of what has happened in the last few years. We had a happy childhood. Terre and I did pretty much what we wanted, didn't we? We traveled, went to college, got married, had children, and lost children."

"Isn't that was what you tried to tell her from day one?" Terre puts her arms around me, and I hug her back. "Does this mean that you don't have to go back to her?"

"No, she wants to try something else. I think it's a technique that helps people deal with grief, loss, and abandonment issues. She thinks that I somehow feel abandoned by Jason, while I'm coping with his loss."

"I never thought of it from that angle," Terre says. "How successful has this technique been?"

"This particular technique is supposed to be better than prescription drugs. The side effects for taking drugs are worse than the actual illness. Anyway, Dr. Laurel thinks that if I can connect spiritually with Jason, it might induce closure."

"You sound skeptical, Ellie," Adrian murmurs. "Is it like a séance? Can we come too? I would like to know some things from my past. Can they predict the future too? Maybe it isn't too late for me to figure out how you win."

"It's not a séance, Adrian; it's a different kind of hypnosis."

"Can we use the Ouija board? Maybe we can contact Daddy. I have a few questions for him," Terre mumbles. "Actually, I have quite a few."

"Focus people, it is not a séance, and we are not going to use a Ouija board, because it probably won't work either, but it might help me sleep better at night."

"You mean you'll stop beating me up? I don't have to buy us twin beds anymore?"

"What on earth goes on in your bedroom," Dennis says suddenly. "Never mind, don't tell me!"

"Let's change the subject, shall we? Terre, do you remember that song about putting one foot in front of the other? I think it was a Christmas special."

"No, can't say as I do," she says.

Dennis laughs, "Can you hum a few bars?"

"Ellie, my dear little twinkle toes; it's about putting your foot in your mouth, and it goes something like this." Singing a little off key, he says, "I got my foot in my mouth; guess I should watch what I say. I got my foot in my mouth; it's probably better that way."

"You made that up!"

"No, I didn't. Someone wrote it, I swear." Adrian retrieves his laptop. Making clicking noises on his keyboard, he finally says, "Here, a man named Chris Tomlin wrote it."

Dennis turns to Terre, "Is it the one about putting your right foot in and your right foot out?"

"You're as bad as Adrian," Terre sniffs. "That's the hokey-pokey."

"Then it's the chicken dance," Dennis insists. "How does that go again?"

"Got it…" Adrian grins. "You're all wrong. It was a Christmas special like Ellie said. *"Put one foot in front of the other, and soon you'll be walking 'cross the floor. You put one foot in front of the other and soon you'll be walking out the door."*

"Who sang it, Adrian?"

Dennis laughs before he can answer, "Mickey Mouse."

"No, you moron, it was Mickey Rooney," Terre says to her husband."

"Oh," everyone says.

"You're feeling better, aren't you darling Ellie?" Adrian says gently. "We've missed you…"

"I hate to admit this, but Dr. Laurel has made me realize that although we might all miss our Jason, we don't have to ignore that he's gone. It doesn't hurt to talk about him. She said that if it makes me feel better, I can pretend to visit with him, don't talk out loud…then everyone will think I'm crackers."

"Everyone thinks you're crackers anyway, sweetheart, but in a good crackers kind of way," Adrian says, grinning. "Wow, I guess she has helped you because you didn't throw anything at me!"

"She also said that if all of you don't think as I do, that's okay too. I can keep thinking what I believe while the rest of you have your own opinions. There, do we all feel better about that?"

No one says anything for a minute or two. Then Adrian pulls me into a bear hug. "We have all missed you. Even if we don't share the same opinion, we get it that you need to keep yours. Jason will always be in our hearts. Maybe someday we'll find out what happened to him, but until then, we're glad you have accepted…or at least let part of it go for now."

I stifle the urge to blurt out that I will never, never give up the idea that we will one day find Jason. That deep down, I know he's alive.

We merely have not found him yet!

Epilogue

As we reflect on our journey through life over the last several years, many events stand out whenever our extended family gathers for holidays, birthdays, awards, and anniversaries.

We make sure to celebrate our milestones with vigor and enthusiasm knowing that it could all change in the blink of an eye. We've pushed the envelope whenever possible—always toward new goals and achievements, as we know what it's like to have that snatched away.

All of us have made that last-ditch effort to overcome obstacles. We are all trying to do better at being more helpful to one another, being grateful for what we have, and not resentful when things don't go our way. It makes each of us a better person.

My family has always given freely with no strings attached, but it's the receiving part we've had difficulty with, especially when the world seems so selfish and self-centered.

Each member of this family has achieved many successes and tested several theories. We've gone to the other side of the world and back and made many choices good and bad, and all while trying to carry on as best we can in the face of adversity.

Most of the family has dealt successfully with their grief and moved on, choosing to pursue other interests. Adrian and I have adopted an unspoken pact where I'm allowed to talk about Jason if I don't go on and on about it. Where once he would have offered unwanted advice and guidance, he now merely listens.

Levi and Adrian continue to stay in touch, but I am no longer part of their conversations. Adrian often goes to Langley for training here and there, but the teams do their training elsewhere, not as they used to do in our back forty acres.

And since we no longer need the CIA's protection, Levi has released all involved, although Josh and Jake show up occasionally to visit, staying in the Guest House.

Levi scaled back his weekly calls to me, and Adrian lets me know about certain things. He probably doesn't want to hear me harangue him about what he's done or not done to further the investigation regarding Jason, and I can't say as I blame him.

For the longest time, I couldn't go into Jason's bedroom. Even after he left for Saudi, it was a constant reminder that he was missing from our lives. He took his most prized possessions with him, except his guitar and drum set. I want his room left undisturbed, as there's still a chance that he'll find his way back home.

When Dimmy brought Jason's items back to us, they were laid out on the library table where they stayed for several days. Then finally, someone took them to the attic as they were a constant reminder that he wasn't here with us.

How much time will it take for my grieving process to end?

I will continue to hope and pray we are not too late…

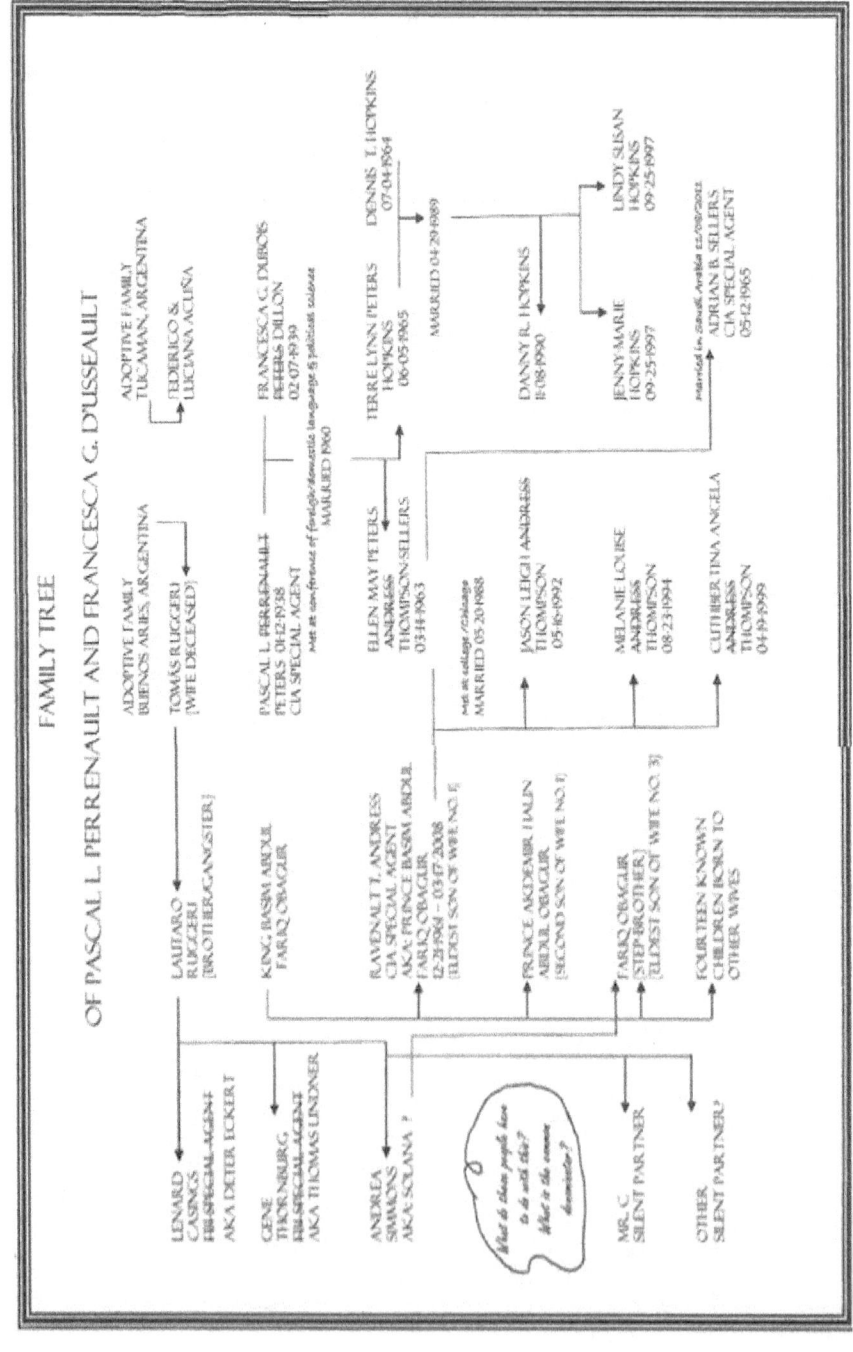

Excerpts from:
Journey of a Thousand Steps,
Book Three,
A Whisper of a Mystery Trilogy

"Man will occasionally stumble over the truth,
But most times he will pick himself up and carry on."
~ Winston Churchill

Chapter One

We Shall Carry On

The day starts as usual, but the dread of what's to come is what honestly terrifies me. Dr. Laurel has chosen today to begin my journey toward confronting my deepest fears. She hopes that the realization that specific events were not preventable will start the healing process. My family has voiced their opinion that I must move beyond this to fully embrace life without my son. It's time to let him go and move on with my life.

Perhaps they're right.

For as long as I can remember, my mother and sister have accused me of being a cockeyed optimist who not only lives in an ivory tower but continuously looks through rose-colored glasses.

Perhaps they are correct in this view.

Have I closed my eyes to pretend that things don't exist to cope with reality? When something unexpected happens to alter the course of your life, how you handle it is what truly matters. Haven't I been treating it okay?

Dr. Laurel insisted that I submit a questionnaire before beginning our new sessions. She mentioned it would help her understand my present anxiety; however, I have anxiety walking into her office because I want to turn around and run the other way.

While filling out the questionnaire, it reminded me about the glass half full/half empty thing. Am I a pessimist with a tendency toward a myopic view of the world? One that my nearsighted views lack tolerance and understanding? Or, am I an optimist, who believes that only good will ultimately prevail over evil?

"Hello Ellen, how are you today? Have a seat in the chair or recline on the sofa, kick your shoes off and make yourself comfortable."

"I'm fine, Dr. Laurel, just looking through my rose-colored glasses today, hoping things will look better. I'll sit over here, thanks. The sofa makes me think you might hook me up to some elaborate mechanism and suck my thoughts out through my ear."

Laurel opens the door and sticks her head around the corner to signal to her assistant. Closing it quietly, she sits down at her desk to press the buttons on her tape recorder. "I haven't heard that expression about glasses for a long while, Ellen. You have a vivid imagination. And the sofa thing only happens in hospitals. Have you been getting enough rest? Any problems there?" she asks, smiling.

"Mother always said I had a wild imagination. I think I'm getting enough rest and dreaming a little too loud for Adrian. Do they hook people up to machines and shock them? Mother keeps reminding me about the rose-colored glasses thing. Does it mean delusional?"

Laurel is a striking woman who wears a blue on blue sweater-set and a black pencil skirt. As usual, her short brown hair frames her oval face, and her makeup is impeccable. "Let's explore that a minute, Ellen. Occasionally the subconscious mind plays out in dreams. Perhaps it helps you to cope with what is stressful to you."

"My dreams are certainly in technicolor, very vivid, along with a lot of action. Now and then, I have the sensation that I'm flying in my dreams. Adrian has to push me over to my side of the bed several times a night. I practically smother him and hit him with my fists. When I wake up, he's sleeping on the sofa pit."

Whispered Dreams

"Dreaming in color is perfectly okay, Ellen," she says, reaching for a pen. "Many people experience their dreams that way. It's the roughness that is worrisome. Are you sure you're getting enough rest? Are you taking that sleeping aid I suggested?"

"I'm getting as much sleep as possible. I do wake up several times a night. Maybe it's all that wrestling in my sleep. Do I look tired to you? And no, I don't need that stuff you prescribed."

Dr. Laurel stops writing to look directly at me. "Let's go back to when you first came to Virginia. We may not have done a thorough job when we talked about it before."

"Are we starting at the beginning? What part did I leave out? If you listened to the CD Adrian gave you, you already know how much I detested those two idiots that passed themselves off as FBI agents. They dumped us at Ashwood and took all our possessions. I still don't understand how they were able to do that."

"Yes, I know all that, nevertheless, when you repeat things, it sometimes helps to resolve issues. It might trigger something that wasn't said before. It's apparent to me that you still harbor resentment toward the FBI agents."

"Wouldn't you if your whole life turned upside down and everything you knew to be right and wonderful in your world suddenly evaporated?"

"Yes, Ellen. I probably would feel as you do. Would you like to talk about that?"

"No. Talking about those idiots only makes me crazy."

"Let's explore something else, then. Any pleasant memories you want to discuss?" Laurel asks gently.

"I told you about the antiques we found in the house, and then Jason found that old car in the barn that was worth a small fortune. I was thinking of that as I was driving here."

"That sounds like a good memory, Ellen. Please expound on that."

"Jason was so pathetic when he found out that we were going to sell it. Then he hounded and pestered me for months until I gave in and bought him a used car. We still have that car. My youngest daughter drives it now. Then we paid off the debts we inherited with the money I made at the racetrack, and we renovated practically every room in our house. What more do we need to talk about?"

Laurel stops to stare at me, then leans forward, saying, "You seem more stressed than usual, Ellen. How can I help you today?"

"Stupid things keep popping into my head and I can't get them to stop! Can you suggest a pill for that?"

Dr. Laurel sighs. "You know it doesn't work like that. Let's talk about how Jason might have felt when he first came to Virginia. Do you think he adjusted to the upheaval that came with moving and leaving all his friends?"

"I think he had an okay time with that. His big shock was finding out that the mother he thought was dead, wasn't. Of all of my children, he was, what I mean to say is that he is the most stable."

Dr. Laurel is thoughtful for a moment. "When a child goes missing, Ellen, the parents might think they're responsible. They typically question why such a thing could happen to their family. They wonder what prompted someone to act maliciously toward them. Do you feel as if you did something to warrant such behavior against Jason?"

Trying to control my sudden anger, I start to laugh instead. "In the case of the missing Jason L. Thompson, age twenty-three, I do not think I'm responsible. I do, however, blame his incredibly insensitive Uncle Dimmy who lives far, far away, in a land I don't ever wish to mention! I would like to point out that it was Jason's father who involved us in that whole mess in the first place. You read the file. Was that part in there?"

"We can't talk about certain things, Ellen, due to the National Security protocols your husband, Adrian, and I discussed. I believe you mentioned in a previous session that you wished you had done more to talk him out of going to that faraway place." Dr. Laurel tilts her head and raises her eyebrows slightly.

If this is my cue to spill my guts, she's in for a surprise. "No. I wish you knew the entire story. I don't blame myself. I'm convinced that Jason would have gone with or without my consent."

Dr. Laurel presses the stop button on her recorder, standing to open the door for her assistant, who is holding a clinking tray. It instantly reminds me of a distant memory. Taking the serving tray, she silently closes the door with her hip. "Would you like a cup of tea, Ellen?"

"Sure."

Is drinking tea supposed to make one feel better? Is it a prerequisite for shrinks to offer this beverage instead of coffee? How about a sugar-high brought about by drinking a soda? On the other hand, why can't she offer me a bottle of water, maybe a scotch and soda?

"Ellen, you look a million miles away," Dr. Laurel says starting the recorder again.

"My mind goes off in different directions, and I can't get it to stop."

Dr. Laurel jots something down on her steno pad, glances up at me, and says, "Shall we get back to why you think Jason's Uncle is responsible for his disappearance?"

"Wow, where do I begin this ridiculous tale of woe? It's so bizarre that I couldn't have made it up."

"Ellen, why don't we let that go for now, and we'll move on to something else? Can you tell me what you've been doing to keep yourself busy?"

"You still think I'm delusional, don't you?"

"I do not believe that was ever my assessment, Ellen. I would never have said that to you. Is that how you feel right now?"

"I wanted you to help me get out of my funk, but all you've done is say I can have some drugs that allow me to have a restful sleep and we keep going back to useless stuff. I don't want to sleep through my dreams, because they're the only connection I have to Jason. Am I the only one who thinks my son is still alive?"

Dr. Laurel tries to steer away from that line of thinking. "Do you have a hobby that would take your mind off everyday things?"

"Do you want me to take up knitting? You think I have a gambling problem, and you're trying to get me to admit it, right?"

"Did I say that I thought you have a gambling problem, Ellen?" she says bluntly. "You seem very jittery today."

"Sorry. I lost my interior design business some years ago, as you know, and it did keep me busy to renovate every room in our house. What I want to do is race again."

"Do you think if you raced again, that you would be happier?" she asks.

"So now you think I'm not happy! You think that's the root of my problem?"

"No, Ellen. All I'm saying is that everyone needs to vent, for many, hobbies help to do that. Some find that punching a bag or taking an exercise class does the trick."

"I don't *need* to race to keep me happy!" Looking directly at her in her perfectly coiffed hair, manicured fingernails, and expertly applied makeup, a snide remark erupts from my lips. "Underneath that persona of professionalism, I'll bet you play competitive bridge."

Dr. Laurel's face slowly transforms into a soft smile. "That is an astute observation, Ellen. Is that how you win so successfully at the racetrack?"

"First, tell me if I'm right! Then maybe I'll share my deepest, darkest secrets with you."

"I'm an avid bridge player with aspirations of gaining enough points to become a Life Master."

"How close are you to that?" I ask, watching her face.

"I'd like to go further, perhaps to either achieve an Emerald or Platinum level," she says.

"How many points do you need to get to that level?"

Dr. Laurel hesitates, leaning forward in her chair, saying, "Are you equating my bridge playing to your horse betting?"

Leaning toward her, I say, "Are you answering my question with a question?"

"Alright Ellen," she says, folding her arms around her notepad. "If it will help to talk about myself, then my goal is to be a Grand Life Master."

"How close are you to reaching your first goal of Life Master? Will it take years, months, or will you get them in your lifetime?"

Dr. Laurel contemplates this for a few seconds. "There are several levels to gain masterpoints. I'm currently at the NABC Master level. Without going into the entire procedure, one must attend sanctioned events to win points. It's rather complicated, so I'll try to keep it brief. I need to accumulate a certain number of black, silver, red, gold, and platinum points to move forward in these events."

"I can tell you're driven to win. How long will it take you to get to the Grand Master stage?"

Dr. Laurel seems pensive, then says, "That would be my ultimate achievement."

"How many points do you need to get to that level?"

"That would most likely take the rest of my life, Ellen. That requires 10,000 points of various events or tournaments. I would have to retire and do that full-time."

"But, you have a goal. I'll bet you won't stop until you reach that goal, am I right? How many points away are you from your first big goal?"

Dr. Laurel picks up her teacup, taking a sip, she looks me straight in the eye. "Alright Ellen, I only need four gold and three platinum points to reach Life Master, but then again it would spur me on for the rest of my life to get to the Grand Life Master status. What I believe you're saying is that everyone should have something to look forward to and you think that bridge is my addiction."

"Bingo! Give the lady a prize! Everyone needs an out, even you. If you think gambling is my addiction, then you don't know me. I only bet on a sure thing and not without doing a lot of serious studying. I do not smoke or drink to excess, and I don't shop until I drop. It's not as if I have to go to the racetrack every day. I only did that when we needed cash, which we don't do anymore. We make money the old-fashioned way. We earn it."

"Let's get back to you, Ellen. You mentioned racing. Didn't you tell me that you gave that up some time ago due to an injury?"

"Yes. I wanted to take Ashwood Stables up in prestige, up in levels as you do for your points, yet, my goal seems almost as elusive as finding my son."

"I don't understand. I thought you had two racers that compete for Ashwood. It sounds to me that they might help you reach that goal even if you aren't doing the actual racing." Dr. Laurel starts thumbing through her notes. "Here it is. Was it winning the Triple Crown of Harness Racing?"

"Yes, I want to win the Triple Crown of Harness Racing. Would you pay someone else to play bridge for you and they earned your masterpoints?"

Her face suddenly registers comprehension. "Ellen, of course, you're right," she sighs. "It takes all the fun out of it if you don't win it yourself."

"You think I need a hobby; something to take my mind off my troubles? Adrian keeps after me to go away on trips. I don't feel like celebrating anything when my heart feels like it's about to explode!"

"Ellen, your heart is heavy with sadness. It's a natural feeling when you lose someone close to you. In your case, you've had more than your share. In time, this feeling will dissipate as we work it out. In the meantime, allow yourself to grieve and carry on as best you can."

"As *we* work it out? Do you have a mouse in your pocket, Doctor? How do you figure this is *we*? How long will this take if *we* are going to do this? Are you going to help me before I grow old, or do I have to figure it out myself?"

Dr. Laurel laughs, "How did you come up with that saying about a mouse?"

"Daddy always said things like that. I had almost forgotten it."

"You are using humor to mask how you feel. It's okay, Ellen. No one knows how long it will take to work things out; each person is different.

Perhaps a year from now you'll look back and say it didn't take as long as you once thought."

"A year is a long time. A lot can go on in a year."

Another year could go by without one word about Jason, and this abruptly annoys me. I don't want to think that Jason is gone forever. In my heart and gut, I know he's out there.

"You don't think Jason is alive and I can't talk about certain things, so what's left to talk about?"

Dr. Laurel glances at her wristwatch, declaring that our time is up for today. When she does this, Jason's unique wristwatch pops into my mind, the one I gave him before he left to study martial arts the first time.

"We can pick this up next week, okay Ellen?" The click of the recorder triggers a sensation, and I turn toward her, and for a split-second, it reminds me of another distant memory.

"Ellen? See you next week?"

"Yes, Dr. Laurel, I'll see you next week."

Are my rose-colored glasses obscuring my vision? Although Mother didn't say it, she probably thinks it's time to throw the glasses away.

In the weeks that follow, I struggle with simple decisions, and can't seem to focus on one thing. During the next few visits with Dr. Laurel, she tries to extrapolate my darkest secrets, then finally concludes that I'm not willing to accept simple facts. The more accurate description is that everyone runs the other way when I mention my ideas about looking for Jason.

After this information comes tumbling out of my mouth, Dr. Laurel ponders this revelation for a few minutes, glances down at her notepad, and then lets out a heavy sigh.

"You seem more stressed than last week, Ellen. I can only help you learn how to cope with what has happened to you. It's quite amazing how you've managed to get through the traumas in your life thus far. You must know that there is no magic formula. It takes time, and your ability to talk things through that will help you over the hurdles."

"You mean it's a wonder I didn't go nuts before now, with the stress, you mean?"

"Interesting how your mind works, Ellen. That's not exactly what I meant."

"Then what did you mean?"

Dr. Laurel sighs again. "I can only lead you to discover how you can help yourself through the steps of therapy. There is no magic pill for grief. Although you may not think so, you are making progress; however, there is irrefutable evidence to suggest that Jason is gone. And there is no way to change this. I can only help you cope with your loss. I'm sorry, Ellen, that's the best I can offer you."

"Do you mind if we end our session now? I don't want to think about this."

"I understand Ellen, will you come back next week?" Dr. Laurel pleads with her eyes. "I think we're making progress."

"Of course, Dr. Laurel, I'll see you next week."

As I drive home, I try to look on the bright side of things; however, there isn't any. Could my optimistic self be changing into a pessimistic one? For the first time in over a year, doubt surfaces.

Could I be wrong in thinking that Jason is alive? Why is there an overwhelming feeling that he's out there waiting for us to find him? And why can't I home in on where he might be? Why didn't we put a chip in his head? But then, Jason vehemently refused to allow Jewel's to put it into his wrist. It could have led us straight to him.

Why, why, oh why didn't we insist upon this?

The words scream silently in my head. No parent intends to have a child abducted. As a precaution, we put a DNA kit together along with fingerprints when Jason, Melanie, and Curlie first enrolled in their new schools here. It's little comfort when these can't help us find him.

Automatically looking into the pasture next to the barn, I maneuver my car past our entrance gate and pull into my spot in the garage under the Carriage House. It seems so long ago. So much has happened since we first came to Virginia. Aside from our missing Jason, we've settled into the house built by Sara Ashwood, and grown comfortable with the new life we have established here.

We have everything we need: family, friends, a steady income, and a gentle whisper from time to time, from one of the resident ghosts that have cohabited peacefully with us. Because of this, we no longer need to go to Billingsworth Racetrack to wager for large sums of money, even though Adrian tries to coerce me into doing so since he doesn't bet effectively.

This undesirable doomsday feeling must go away before it consumes me. Everyone around here, including Dr. Laurel, thinks Jason is dead. I know in the recesses of my mind and heart that he's out there; we merely haven't found him yet!

During our usual nightly banter and commentary around our dinner table, I bring up the possibility that Ashwood Stables might benefit from acquiring a new Standardbred horse. It might be time to explore this idea, but no one offers to help, they simply let me talk about it.

Did Dr. Laurel speak with Adrian? Did she mention that my family needs to appease and agree with me so I won't go off the deep end?

Mother thinks that we should adopt a new motto: 'we shall carry on,' which sounds like a good plan, and in spite of all that we have endured, *we shall carry on.*

BOOKS AND RESOURCES:

Collins GEM English Dictionary, Harper Collins Publishers, New Edition 1998.

2012 Virginia Fact Book This is a statistical guide to the Thoroughbred industry in Virginia, prepared by The Jockey Club. 01 July 2012 http://www.jockeyclub.com/factbook/StateFactBook/Virginia.pdf

The Blue Book of Grammar. Jane Straus. Grammar: 19 July 2014. http://www.grammarbook.com

Kautilya's Arthashastra: Book VI, The Source of Sovereign States. 26 March 2014. Written in the 4th Century, BC. http://www.columbia.edu/itc/mealac/pritchett/oolitlinks/kautilya/books

WORLD WIDE WEB/INTERNET:

Advice to pregnant women: 30 March 2013. Pregnant women should avoid close contact with animals that are giving birth to avoid microorganism contamination. https://www.gov.uk/government/news/advice-to-pregnant-women-to-avoid-close-contact-with-animals-that-are-giving-birth

Arnis: 18 March 2014. Umbrella term for traditional martial arts of the Philippines, improvised weapons to include hand-to-hand combat, joint locks, grappling, and includes weapon-disarming techniques. http://www.en.wikipedia.org/wiki/arnis

Back to the Future: 27 April 2014. Movie distributed by Universal Pictures in 1985, written by Robert Zemeckis and Bob Gale, stars Michael J. Fox whose character, Marty McFly says, "Nobody calls me chicken."

Battle of the Plains of Abraham: 25 April 2014.This battle was a pivotal moment in the Seven Year's War. This is where Levi took the girls during their brief stay in the old City of Quebec. http://www.quebecregion.com

Battleship (game): 04 May 2014. This is the game Officer Laput refers to in the text that Kensi has put together on a grid to study oil tankers. http://www.en.wikipedia.org/wiki/Battleship_(game)

Billingsworth Racetrack: The Thompson family takes their horses to this fictional racetrack.

Billy club: 24 August 2017. This is a wooden club, specifically, a police officer's club, first known use 1885.

https://www.merriam-webster.com/dictionary/billy%20club

Bisht: 03 March 2013. Traditional Arabic men's cloak popular in Arabia and some Arab countries, flowing outer cloak made of soft wool, worn over the *thobe*. http://en.wikipedia.org/wiki/Bisht_(clothing)

Blackbirding: 24 August 2017. This is the coercion of people that is obtained through trickery and kidnapping that takes laborers which first occurred between 1842 and 1904.
http://en.wikipedia.org/wiki/Blackbirding

CIA; Headquarters Virtual Tour. 16 July 2012.
http://www.cia.gov/about-cia/headquarters-tour/virtual-tour-flash/index.html

Coping With Grief: 28 April 2013.
http://www.webmd.com/mental-health/mental-health-coping-with-grief

Code of Virginia: 15 July 2012. Legislative Information System, Title 59.1 Trade and Commerce. Chapter 29—Horse Racing and Pari-Mutuel Wagering, etc. These are the rules sited in the context of this book used to demonstrate violations. http://www.gov.virginia/leg1.state.va.us/cgi-bin/legp504.exe?000+cod+59.1-69

Daily racing form, [Or the daily schedule] this daily listing contains the racing information that includes news, part performance data, and handicapping.

Declaration and Condition sheet: 15 April 2013. A declaration and condition sheet specifies who owns, sponsors, services certain horses and race names, cancellation policies, estimated purse distributions, and how the winnings are divided.
http://www.google.com/#rlz=1C2SKPL_enUS425&sclient=psy-ab&q=declairation+sheet+for+pacers&oq=declairation+sheet

Driving Miss Daisy: 29 April 2014. An American comedy-drama (circa 1989) film distributed by Warner Bros. adapted from the Alfred Uhry play of the same name. Bruce Beresford directed, Morgan Freeman and Jessica Tandy (Miss Daisy).
http://en.wikipedia.org/wiki/Driving_Miss_Daisy

Eng, Richard. Examining Different Levels of Competition at the Racetrack: 24 July 2012.
http://www.dummies.com/hot-to/content/examining-different-levels-of-competition-at-the-racetrack

Eskrima: 18 March 2014. Umbrella term for traditional martial arts of the Philippines, improvised weapons to include hand-to-hand combat, joint locks, grappling, and weapon disarming techniques.
http://www.en.wikipedia.org/wiki/eskrima

Famous Male Athletes from Vanuatu: 16 April 2013. Names of people such as Dr. Malas, Jimy, Kensi, Rexley, and Laput are all fictitious.
http://www.ranker.com/list/famous-male-athletes-from-vanuatu/reference

French Phrases. 25 April 2013.
http://en.wikipedia.org/wiki/List_of_French_words_and_phrases_used_by_English

German words and famous people: 27 April 2014.
http://answers.yahoo.com/questions/German common terms

Gi: 28 April 2013. A lightweight two-piece white garment worn in judo and other martial arts that consists of loose-fitting pants and a jacket, held together with a cloth belt.
https://www.google.com/search?q=what+is+a+gi

Hakama Pants: 07 April 2013. Hakama is a traditional Japanese divided skirt, resembles a wide pair of trousers, and has pleats and a Koshiato, a stiff or padded part in the lower back.
http://www.asianideas.com/liwehapa.html

Harness Racing: 01 July 2012.
http://en.wikipedia.or/wiki/Harness_racing

Harper, Dr. Frederick: Extension Horse Specialist Department of Animal Science, University of Tennessee, Signs of a Healthy Horse: 01 January 2014.
http://www.animalscience.ag.utk.edu/horse/pdf/signsofahealthyhorse

Height & Weight Rations for Males: 17 April 2013.
http://www.livestrong.com/article/356757-height-weight-ratios-for-males

Historical Events Around the World in 1975: 18 April 2014. What events happened in 1975?
- Franco dies in Spain
- OPEC agrees to raise crude oil prices by 10%
- The British Conservative Party chooses its first women leader, Margaret Thatcher

- The Communist forces take Saigon and South Vietnam surrenders unconditionally
- The U.S. carries out Vietnam "Operation Babylift" brought e orphans to the U. S.
- New York City avoids bankruptcy as President Gerald R. Ford signs a $2.3 billion loan
- The Cod war breaks out between Britain and Iceland when Iceland extends its fishing rights to 200 miles
- King Faisal of Saudi Arabia is assassinated; http://www.thepeoplehistory.com/1975.html

Hohenzollern Castle: 19 April 2014.
http://en.wikipedia.org/wiki/Hohenzollern_Castle

Horse Racing Glossary A-Z, Terminology, Jargon, Slang, Vocabulary: 14 July 2012.
http://www.ildado.com.com/horse_racing_glossary.html

How to calculate betting odds and payoffs: 02 July 2012.
http://horseracing.about.com/cs/handicapping/a/aaoddschart.htm

How to say, "Speak the Dutch" in German? 12 March 2013.
http://www.howdoyousay.net/

Islamic Religious Police: 08 January 2014.
http://en.wikipedia.org/wiki/islamic_religious_police

James Bond Movies: 23 April 2014. *Never Say Never* Again is a 1983 spy film based on the James Bond novel *Thunderball* and distributed by Warner Bros. http://en.wikipedia.org/wiki/List_of_James_Bond_films, and http://en.wikipedia.org/wiki/Never_Say_Never_Again

Jasper, Virginia: Fictitious town where the Thompson's live.

Jaws: 28 March 2014. Movie Jaws II, the famous line "Just when you thought it was safe to go back in the water…" Written by Peter Benchley, directed by Steven Spielberg, distributed by Universal Pictures in 1978. http://en.wikipedia.org/wiki/Jaws_(film)

Karategi: 29 April 2013. Similar to a judogi, a looser canvas style cloth to stand up to considerable rigorous application and abuse without restricting mobility, typically, weigh at least 10 oz.
http://en.wikipedia.org/wiki/Karate_gi

Karate, History of, Karate clothing: 10 March 2013. Belt Order, from white to Black Belt 5th Dan. http://en.wikipedia.org/wiki/Karate

Kali: 18 March 2014. Umbrella term for traditional martial arts of the Philippines, improvised weapons to include hand-to-hand combat, joint locks, grappling, and weapon disarming techniques. http://www.en.wikipedia.org/wiki/kali

Languages of Vanuatu: 17 April 2013. http://en.wikipedia.org/wiki/Languages_of_Vanuatu

List of German dishes: 31 March 2013. http://en.wikipedia.org/wiki/List_of_German_dishes

Maps of World: 16 July 2012. Saudi Arabia: Google Maps, http://www.mapsofworld.com/usa/states/virginia/virginia-ap.html

Marriage in Saudi Arabia: 26 March 2013. http://www.nikahnama.com/saudi_arabia/index.html

Names of martial arts instructors: 29 March 2013. Sensei, (Japanese for teacher), and Master Sifu, (Chinese). http://wiki.answers.com/Q/What_is_the_name_for_a_martial_arts_instructor

Ninja: 06 April 2013. Ninja or shinobi was a covert agent or mercenary in feudal Japan, specialized in unorthodox warfare including sabotage, espionage, infiltration, open combat and, assassinations. http://en.wikipedia.org/wiki/Ninja

Oil Tankers: 17 April 2013. Classified by size; inland or coastal tankers of a few thousand metric tons of deadweight [DWT] to mammoth ultra large crude carriers [ULCCs] of 550,000 DWT. http://en.wikipedia.org/wiki/Oil_tanker, and http://www.reuters.com/article/2013/02/26/us-iran-sanctions-tankers

Pain Management: 28 April 2014. Coccydynia Aetiology and treatment. http://www.coccyx.org/treatmen/inflamm.htm

Paris. Tours, Sightseeing, & Things to do in Paris, France: 4 March 2013. http://www.viator.com/Paris/d479-ttd?pref=02&aid=g3308

Persian Gulf: 17 April 2013. http://www.geographicguide.net/asia/middleeast.htm

Racing Secretary. 27 January 2013. http://en.wikipedia.org/wiki/Racing_secretary

Rocky Balboa: 03 January 2014. The films, starting in 1976, chronicles Rocky Balboa's boxing career, grossed more than $ 1 billion US dollars.

Adrian was Rocky's wife in the films.
http://en.wikipedia.org/wiki/Rocky_(film_series)

Rocky and Bullwinkle: 28 April 2014. By Jay Ward Productions, aired from 1959 - 1964, structured as variety show with serialized adventures of Bullwinkle the moose and flying squirrel Rocky. http://en.wikipedia.org/wiki/The_Rocky_and_Bullwinkle_Show

Saudi Arabia: 31 July 2012.
http://en.wikipedia.org/wiki/Saudi_Arabia

Saudi Arabian Wedding Dress: 07 March 2013.
http://www.alibaba.com/showroom/saudi-arabian-wedding-dress.html

Side view of Oil Tanker: 04 May 2014.
http://commons.wikimedia.org/wiki/File:Oil_tanker_(side_view).PNG

Staatsgalerie Stuttgart: (State Museum): 17 April 2014.
http://en.wikipedia.org/wiki/staatsgalerie_stuttgart

Succession to the Saudi Arabian throne: 30 April 2014.
http://en.wikipedia.org/wiki/succession_to_the_Saudi_Arabian_throne

Stuttgart, Germany: 31 March 2013.
https://en.wikipedia.org/wiki/Stuttgart

The enemy of my enemy is my friend: 15 March 2013.
http://en.wikipedia.org/wiki/The_enemy_of_my_enemy_is_my_friend

The Good, the Bad, and the Ugly: 2 April 2014. Italian composer Ennio Morricone wrote theme to the 1960 'Spaghetti Western' movie of the same name, the instrumental piece. The melody sounds like the howl of a coyote. http://en.wikipedia.org/wiki/The_Good_the_bad_and_the_Ugly

The Music Man: 18 April 2013. "Ya got *trouble*, my friend, right here, I say, *trouble* right here in ***River City***."
http://en.wikipedia.org/wiki/The_Music_Man_(1962_film)

The King and I: 14 April 2014. A 1956, 20th Century Fox film, stars Deborah Kerr and Yul Brynner. *Shall We Dance* (written by Oscar Hammerstein II, composed by Richard Rogers).
http://en.wikipedia.org/wiki/The_King_and_I_(1956_film)
http://www.stlyrics.com/lyrics/theKingandI/shallwedance.htm

Time difference calculator: 17 May 2013.
http://www.happyzebra.com/timezones-worldclock/difference-between-Port%20Vila-and-Virginia%20Beach.php

Things to do in the old City of Quebec: 17 April 2014. Excursions on the river, rail cruise, cruise the St. Lawrence River. http://quebecregion.com

TrackMaster Proprietary Ratings Specification, (Harness Racing): 24 July 2012. http://www.trackmaster.com/harness/infor/ratings.htm

U.S. History: 16 April 2014: Operation Desert Storm (Desert Shield, 1990) The United States came to Saudi Arab's aid, deployed over 500,000 American troops to stem an attack by Iraq. January 15 came and went without a response from the Iraqis, the next night, Desert Shield became Desert Storm. http://ushistory.org/us

Vanuatu Bislama Language: 01 May 2013. There are over 113 distinct languages and many more dialects throughout the islands. http://www.tripadvisor.com.au/Travel-g294143-s604/Vanuatu:Important.Phrases.html

Vanuatu, the Republic of Vanuatu; History of: 12 March 2013. Pronounced vah-new-ah-too, an island nation located in the South Pacific Ocean. An archipelago formed by volcanic action, is east of northern Australia and west of Fiji, southeast of the Solomon Islands, near New Guinea. http://en.wikipedia.org/wiki/Vanuatu

Virginia Racing Commission: 15 July 2012. http://www.vrc.virginia.gov/racinglicenses.shtml

White Grass Ocean Resort, Tanna Island: 06 May 2013. Http://www.google.com/#hl=en&rlz=1C2SKPL_enUS425&sclient=psy-ab&q=white+grass+resort +tanna+island&oq=White+Grass+Resort

Wooden Carriage House Garage Doors: 14 March 2013. 10' X 9' Cypress Sectional O/G Carriage House Garage Door. http://www.carriagedoor.com

Women Traveling in Saudi Arabia: 28 March 2013 http://traveltips.usatoday.com/women-traveling-saudi-arabia-43269.html

World Atlas: Vanuatu: 15 May 2013. http://www.worldatlas.com

GLOSSARY and OTHER INFORMATION:

Aloha Greeting: A true welcome to the airport is a fresh flower lei and a warm welcome called "aloha" made from several types of orchids and fragrant flowers. http://www.leigreeting.com/

Arabian Costume: The costume is of upholstery weight velvet, trimmed with hundreds of crystal and cobalt blue stones and exotic silver sequins, tassels are heavily beaded. Many pieces go with this costume; robe, headscarf, hat piece, harem-type pants with a blue shirt; horse has matching neckpiece and saddlecloth; ring to match. They can cost about upwards of $ 1,425. U.S. Dollars, refers to the **Blue and Silver costumes.**

Breeds of horses: North American harness racing is restricted to Standardbred horses. They get their name from "the early years of the Standardbred stud book; that only horses who could pace or trot a mile in a standard time or whose progeny could do so", are the only ones admitted into the book.

A Standardbred horse has shorter legs and a longer body than a Thoroughbred. It has a more easygoing temperament than a Thoroughbred as well, which is more suitable for a horse "whose races involve more strategy and reacceleration than do Thoroughbred races."

Call to the Post: This is the bugle call that is played at horse races (and at dog racetracks) that signals that all mounts (or drivers) should be at the starting gate because the race is about to begin. Once the bugler sounds the tune, there is 5 to 10 minutes before the scheduled start time of the race.

Central Intelligence Agency: (CIA). Other services listed; Office of Intelligence & Analysis, National Clandestine Service: The branch, which is an "elite corps of men and women shaped by diverse ethnic, Educational, and professional backgrounds.

Chief Steward: This is the official that meets with each driver prior to the first race.

CWP: Concealed weapons permit.

Cuthbertina: This is the name given to Curlie, a derivative of the old English word Cuthberta, meaning brilliant, and a feminine form of Cuthbert.

Dojo: This is not a word but a room where you can earn belts through training and become a ninja with the instructions from a Sensei. Japanese word that literally means 'place'.

Enclosure: This is the area where the runners gather for viewing before and after the race.

Frick and Frack: Fricassee and Frackamon are the nicknames of the draft horses that comprise the fictitious team for the 'Magic of Christmas'.

Fräulein: This is a German word, associated with the common use for unmarried women, comparable to Miss in English.

Handicapping: There are many forms and methods of handicapping. Most common types are class, speed, pace, trip, and computer handicapping.

Handicapping 101: These are rules Ellen said her Daddy came up with for her to follow when she first learned how to bet at the racetrack, also found online under *Harness Charts from Harness Eye*. [See specific website under bibliography section].

Hopples: These straps connect the legs on each side of a horse's sides. Horses that pace, are faster and this is important to a better. If the horse breaks stride, the driver will take the horse to the outside until it resumes trotting or pacing again.

Horse Racing Glossary A-Z, Terminology, Jargon, Slang, Vocabulary: This glossary is a complete listing of terms from A to Z of the most often used jargon and includes slang and vocabulary that universally used around the world.

Hypothesis: This is a suggested but unproved explanation of something and based upon assumption rather than fact or reality.

Important Harness Races: 1. The **Hamiltonian** is part of the Triple Crown of Harness Racing for 3-year old trotters. 2. The **Little Brown Jug** is part of the Triple Crown of Harness Racing for 3-year old pacers. 3. The **Breeders Crown** is a series of eight races conducted on one day at different racetracks each year. First run in1984, today's purses, and awards total $13 million. They cover each of the traditional categories of gender, age, and gait (pace or trot).

Kukui Nuts: Dating back to early Polynesians who arrived at the Hawaiian Islands, they brought the kukui trees and nuts with them from south east Asia, cultivated them, and because of their many uses, has spiritual significance of light, hope, and renewal. Made into leis, the nuts come in black, brown, and white.
http://www.leigreeting.com/

Magic of Christmas: This is a fictitious event.

Purse: This may refer to the total amount of money being paid out to the owners of horses racing at a particular track over a given period of time, or to the percentages of a race's total purse that are awarded to each of the highest finishers.

Post position: The position or stall at the starting gate from where the horse starts the race.

Post time: This is the designated time for a race to start.

Race bike: (known as a sulky). The only style allowed in qualifying heats or harness racing. They are lighter in weight and the seat is smaller and harder for a driver to sit on but they are more compact and aerodynamic than the training carts.

Racing Secretary: The Racing Secretary is licensed by the government and is responsible for: the safekeeping and custody of horse papers and ownership documents. Along with forming races, and compiles a list of entries, keeps a complete record of all races, publishes and prints an accurate race program, writes the condition book, provides records for the media, and communicates with the racing commission and/or other government oversight agencies.

Saudi Arabia: The Kingdom of Saudi Arabia has the world's second largest oil reserves that are concentrated largely in the Eastern Province.

Sensei: The definition is that of a teacher or instructor usually of Japanese martial arts (as in karate or judo).

Sifu or Shifu: The definition sifu (Cantonese Chinese) or shifu (Mandarin Chinese) means accomplished teacher who oversees apprentices in certain traditions and philosophies.

Standardbred horses: Horses that can trot or pace a mile in a *standard* time, or whose progeny could do so. They have proportionally shorter legs than a Thoroughbred and longer bodies, a more pleasant disposition and can stand up to the rigors of what is involved with trotting or pacing, more strategy and reacceleration than do Thoroughbred races.

Starting Gate: This motorized hinged gate is mounted on a motor vehicle that moves slowly toward the starting line. The 'wings' of the gate fold up and the vehicle accelerates away from the horses.

POEMS, PRAYERS, QUOTES, SAYINGS, & IMAGES

Architectural house plans found in this book are not real house plans, and therefore, are not to be used for an actual house. They are included to help guide the reader through the spaces.

Beth Ann, Stranded On The Island Of Life. 21 May 2013. (Chapter 15) http://www.poemhunter.com/poem/stranded-on-the-island-of-life

Butterfly Image: M.A. Appleby created the image that appears at the beginning of all chapter. It is included with the copyright of this book, and may not be used in any form, unless given permission by its creator.

Carnegie, Andrew: 22 May 2013. "There is little success where there is little laughter." (Chapter 2) http://www.brainyquote.com/quotes/quotes/a/andrewcarn382305.html

Congreve, William: 21 April 2014. "Heaven has no rage like love to hatred turned, Nor hell as fury like a woman scorned." (Chapter 13) https://www en.wikipedia.org/wiki/William_Congreve

Cooper, Hilary: 03 January 2014. "Life is not measured by the breaths we take, but by the moments that take our breath away." (Chapter 6) https://www.goodreads.com/author/quotes/756179.Hilary_Cooper

Doyle, Arthur Conan: 19 April 2014. The Valley of Fear. "Mediocrity knows nothing higher than itself; but talent instantly recognizes genus." (Chapter 9) http://www.brainyquotes.com/quotes/topics

Dr. Seuss: 08 April 2013. "Be who you are and say what you feel, because those who mind don't matter and those who matter don't mind." (Chapter 7) http://www.quotationpage.com/quotes/Dr._Seuss

Guardian Angel Prayer: 17 May 2013. http://www.catholicsupply.com/existing/prangel.html

Gutierrez, G.: 12 June 2013. "You have choices. A single choice, whatever that choice may be, you have to live with the consequences it brings. That's all. A Choice." (Chapter 14) http://www.mkalty.org/decisions-quotes

Job 12-13, 22: 20 April 2013. "God brings good out of sorrow. But true wisdom and power are found in God; counsel and understanding are His, He uncovers mysteries hidden in darkness; He brings light to the deepest gloom." (Chapter 14)

http://www.biblegateway.com/passage/?search=Job+12%3A13&version=NIV

Maimonides, 19 April 2014, "The risk of a wrong decision is preferable to the terror of indecision." (Chapter 5)
http//www.google.com/search?q=decisions

Niebuhr, Reinhold: The Serenity Prayer. 06 May 2013. "God, grant me the serenity to accept the things I cannot change, the courage to change the things I can, and wisdom to know the difference.'
http://en.wikipedia.org/wiki/Serenity_Prayer

Nelson, Harriet: 20 May 2013. "Forgive all who have offended you, not for them, but for yourself." (Chapter 4)
http://www.brainyquote.com/quotes/quotes/h/harrietnel170845.html

O'Neil, Nicole M., 30 November 2014. Family Friend Poems. "A family is like a circle…" (Chapter 12)
http://www;familyfriendlypoems.com/poem/a-family-is-like-a-circle

Prayer of St. Francis. 25 April 2013. (Chapter 14)
http://en.wikipedia.org/wiki/Prayer_of_Saint_Francis

Psalm 34:18, 20 April 2013. King James Version. God saves us from our brokenness: "The Lord is close to the brokenhearted; he rescues those who are crushed in spirit." (Chapter 12)
http://www.biblegateway.com/passage/?search=Psalm+34%3A18&version=NIV

Psalm 121:5, 05 May 2013. King James Version. "The Lord is your guardian; the Lord is your shade at your right hand. By day the sun cannot harm you, nor the moon by night. The Lord will guard you all from evil, will always guard your life. The Lord will guard your coming and going both now and forever."
http://www.google.com/#rlz=1C2SKPL_enUS425&sclient=psy-ab&q=%E2%80%9CThe+Lord+is+your+guardian

Roosevelt, Franklin D. 08 February 2013. "When you come to the end of your rope, tie a knot and hang on." (Chapter 11)
http://quotationsbook.com/quote/30042

Siddhartha Gautama Buddha, 09 May 2013. "The secret of health for both mind and body is not to mourn for the past, not to worry about the future… but to live the present moment wisely and earnestly." (Chapter 6)
http://www.myelomablogs.org/category/eight-labyrinths-of-caregiving

Spredemann, J.E.B.: An Unforgivable Secret, 19 April 2014. "Choices made, whether bad or good, follow you forever and affect everyone in their path one way or another." (Chapter 8) http//www.google.com/search?q=choices

Staudacher, Carol: Beyond Grief, 16 April 2013. "Grief is like a stranger who has come to stay." (Chapter 13) http://www.awakenment-wellness.com/stages-of-grief.html

Twain, Mark: 03 April 2013. "The best way to cheer yourself up is to try to cheer somebody else up." (Chapter 10) http://www.goodreads.com/quotes/28897-the-best-way-to-cheer-yourself

Waitley, Denis: 19 April 2014. "Learn from the past, set vivid, detailed goals for the future, and live in the only moment of time over which you have any control; now." (Chapter 3) http://www.brainyquote.com/quotes/keywords/detailed.htm

QUOTATIONS ABOUT LIFE:

Dickinson, Emily: 26 March 2013. "To live is so startling it leaves little time for anything else." (Chapter 5)
http://www.goodreads.com/author/quotes/7440.Emily_Dickinson

Frost, Robert: Cluster of Faith, 1962, 26 March 2013. 'Forgive, O Lord, my little jokes on Thee, and I'll forgive Thy great big one on me." http://www.goodreads.com/author/quotes/7715.Robert_Frost

Guillemets, Terri: 26 March 2013. "Life is not always fair. Sometimes you get a splinter even sliding down a rainbow."
http://www.quotegarden.com/gardens.html

Handley, Jack: 26 March 2013. "I hope life isn't a big joke, because I don't' get it." http://www.quotegarden.com/gardens.html

Hare, William Augustus and Julius Charles Hare, *Guesses at Truth, by Two Brothers* 1827. 26 March 2013. "Life is the hyphen between matter and spirit." http://www.quotegarden.com/gardens.html

Purkey, William W.: 20 August 2017. "You've gotta dance like there's nobody watching, Love like you'll never be hurt, Sing like there's nobody listening, And live like it's heaven on earth." (Chapter 1)
https://www.goodreads.com/quotes/10123-you-ve-gotta-dance-like-there-s-nobody-watching-love-like-you

Thoreau, Henry David: 26 March 2013. "The mass of men lead lives of quiet desperation. What is called resignation is confirmed desperation. From the desperate city you go into the desperate country, and have to console yourself with the bravery of minks and muskrats."
http://www.quotegarden.com/gardens.html

Watterson, Bill, Calvin & Hobbes: 26 March 2013. "I say if your knees aren't green by the end of the day, you ought to seriously reexamine your life?" http://www.quotegarden.com/life.html

Read the National Award Winning Non-Fiction
book that started it all:
RAISING DAVID AGAIN ~ ISBN: 978-1-4984-9873-9
*A Guide To Understanding The Uniqueness of Brain Injury
And How Our Faith Sustains Us*

Other books by M.A. Appleby:
A Whisper of a Mystery Trilogy:
The Ancient Whisper, Book 1
~ ISBN: 978-0-6929-2129-6
Whispered Dreams, Book 2
~ ISBN: 978-0-6929-2133-3
Journey of a Thousand Steps,
Book 3 ~ ISBN: 978-0-6929-2134-0

Visit Author's website: www.maappleby.com

www.ingramcontent.com/pod-product-compliance
Lightning Source LLC
LaVergne TN
LVHW052256070426
835507LV00036B/3094